Innovation in SMEs and Micro Firms

T0330981

What is the role of culture in the innovation dynamic of small firms within the context of their territorial environments? How do shared values, beliefs and practices underpin the knowledge production process that leads to innovation? In what way do symbolic aspects of social life shape European SMEs' innovation processes?

This volume gives an extensive insight into the complex links between culture and innovation in one of the key agents of economic life: SMEs and micro firms. The chapters employ different analytical and methodological strategies in regions of Europe to identify dimensions of culture, especially values, norms, skills and institutions, and to scrutinize which specific components of culture are relevant to firm innovation and to the more general dynamics of regional innovation. The original research presented shows how small firms learn, interact, compete and collaborate with other key agents of the innovation system. Taken as a whole, the volume points the way towards a more comprehensive framework for understanding the nature of innovation in SMEs and micro firms.

The chapters in this book were originally published as a special issue of *European Planning Studies*.

Manuel Fernández-Esquinas is a Research Scientist at the Spanish National Research Council (CSIC). His research interests lie in the intersection of the sociology of innovation and science policy. Currently he is serving as President of the Spanish Sociological Federation and Director of the *Spanish Journal of Sociology*.

Madelon van Oostrom is Lecturer and Researcher at Hanze University of Applied Sciences, The Netherlands and Innovation Manager of Tenerife Science & Technology Park, Spain. Her professional and academic interests concern innovation culture, entrepreneurship, institutions and education, and learning of skills and competences for innovation.

Hugo Pinto is a Researcher at the Centre for Social Studies, University of Coimbra, and Professor in the Faculty of Economics, University of Algarve, Portugal. Economist, PhD in Governance and Innovation, his research interests are regional innovation systems, knowledge transfer and smart specialisation in peripheral territories.

Innovation in SMEs and Micro Firms

Culture, Entrepreneurial Dynamics and Regional
Development

Edited by
Manuel Fernández-Esquinas,
Madelon van Oostrom and Hugo Pinto

LONDON AND NEW YORK

First published 2018 by Routledge

2 Park Square, Milton Park, Abingdon, Oxfordshire OX14 4RN
52 Vanderbilt Avenue, New York, NY 10017

Routledge is an imprint of the Taylor & Francis Group, an informa business

First issued in paperback 2020

British Library Cataloguing in Publication Data
A catalogue record for this book is available from the British Library

ISBN 13: 978-1-138-49842-6 (hbk)
ISBN 13: 978-0-367-58968-4 (pbk)

Typeset in Minion Pro
by RefineCatch Limited, Bungay, Suffolk

Publisher's Note
The publisher accepts responsibility for any inconsistencies that may have
arisen during the conversion of this book from journal articles to book chapters,
namely the possible inclusion of journal terminology.

Disclaimer
Every effort has been made to contact copyright holders for their permission to
reprint material in this book. The publishers would be grateful to hear from any
copyright holder who is not here acknowledged and will undertake to rectify
sany errors or omissions in future editions of this book.

Contents

CONTENTS

Citation Information

The chapters in this book were originally published in *European Planning Studies*, volume 25, issue 11 (November 2017). When citing this material, please use the original page numbering for each article, as follows:

Guest Editorial
Key issues on innovation, culture and institutions: implications for SMEs and micro firms
Manuel Fernández-Esquinas, Madelon van Oostrom and Hugo Pinto
European Planning Studies, volume 25, issue 11 (November 2017), pp. 1897–1907

Chapter 1
Culture and innovation in SMEs: the intellectual structure of research for further inquiry
Miguel Gonzalez-Loureiro, Maria José Sousa and Hugo Pinto
European Planning Studies, volume 25, issue 11 (November 2017), pp. 1908–1931

Chapter 2
Exploring the links between culture and innovation in micro firms: cultural dimensions, social mechanisms and outcomes
Madelon van Oostrom and Manuel Fernández-Esquinas
European Planning Studies, volume 25, issue 11 (November 2017), pp. 1932–1953

Chapter 3
The 'Enterprise of Innovation' in hard times: corporate culture and performance in Italian high-tech companies
Francesco Ramella
European Planning Studies, volume 25, issue 11 (November 2017), pp. 1954–1975

Chapter 4
A new approach to business innovation modes: the 'Research, Technology and Human Resource Management (RTH) model' in the ICT sector in Belarus
Natalja Apanasovich, Henar Alcalde-Heras and Mario Davide Parrilli
European Planning Studies, volume 25, issue 11 (November 2017), pp. 1976–2000

Chapter 5
Strengthening SMEs' innovation culture through collaborations with public research organizations. Do all firms benefit equally?
Julia Olmos-Peñuela, Ana García-Granero, Elena Castro-Martínez and Pablo D'Este
European Planning Studies, volume 25, issue 11 (November 2017), pp. 2001–2020

For any permission-related enquiries please visit:
http://www.tandfonline.com/page/help/permissions

Notes on Contributors

Dora Agapito works at the Lincoln Business School, University of Lincoln, UK, as a Senior Lecturer in the tourism and events management team and is an Integrated Researcher at the Research Centre on Spatial and Organizational Dynamics (CIEO).

Eneka Albizu is Professor in the Business Management Department, Faculty of Industrial Relations at the University of the Basque Country (UPV/EHU), Leioa, Spain.

Henar Alcalde-Heras is a Doctor Cum Laude in Business Administration and Quantitative Methods (European Mention) from the Universidad Carlos III of Madrid, Spain. Since 2011 Henar has been a Lecturer of Business Politics in the Department of Strategy at the University of Deusto, Madrid, Spain.

Helena Almeida works at the Faculty of Economy at the University of Algarve, Faro, Portugal, and is an Integrated Researcher at the Research Centre on Spatial and Organizational Dynamics (CIEO).

Natalja Apanasovich holds a PhD in Economics and is Dean of the Graduate School of Business, School of Business and Management of Technology, Belarusian State University, Minsk, Belarus.

Elena Castro-Martínez is Tenured Scientist at the Spanish Council for Scientific Research (CSIC), working at INGENIO, a joint Institute of the Spanish Council for Scientific Research and the Polytechnic University of Valencia, since 2004.

Marisa Cesário is Assistant Professor at the University of Algarve, Faro, Portugal, and an Integrated Researcher at the Research Centre on Spatial and Organizational Dynamics (CIEO). She teaches Microeconomics and Public Economics at the undergraduate level and Industrial Development at Master level.

Howard Davis is based in the Department of Architecture at the University of Oregon, Eugene, USA.

Pablo D'Este is based at the Universitat Politècnica de València, Valencia, Spain.

Sílvia Fernandes is an Integrated Researcher at the Research Centre on Spatial and Organizational Dynamics (CIEO) at the University of Algarve, Faro, Portugal.

Manuel Fernández-Esquinas is a Research Scientist at the Spanish National Research Council (CSIC). Currently he is serving as President of the Spanish Sociological Federation and Director of the *Spanish Journal of Sociology*.

Francesca Froy is based at the Bartlett School of Architecture, University College London, London, UK.

Daniel Gabaldón-Estevan is Associate Professor (part time) at the Department of Sociology and Anthropology, Faculty of Social Sciences, University of Valencia, Spain.

Ana García-Granero currently works at the University of Valencia, Spain. Ana researches Managerial Economics, Business Administration and Organizational Studies.

Francisco García-Rodríguez is Professor in the Department of Business Management and Economic History at the Universidad de La Laguna, Tenerife, Spain.

Esperanza Gil-Soto is Professor in the Department of Business Management and Economic History at the Universidad de La Laguna, Tenerife, Spain.

Miguel Gonzalez-Loureiro is Professor in the Department of Business Management and Marketing at the University of Vigo, Spain.

Desiderio Gutiérrez-Taño is Professor in the Department of Business Management and Economic History at the Universidad de La Laguna, Tenerife, Spain.

Cristina Lavía is based in the Department of Sociology, Faculty of Social and Communication Sciences at the University of the Basque Country (UPV/EHU), Leioa, Spain.

Mikel Olazaran is Senior Lecturer of Sociology at the University of the Basque Country (UPV/EHU), Leioa, Spain.

Julia Olmos-Peñuela is a Researcher at the Institute for Innovation and Knowledge Management (INGENIO), a joint Institute of the Spanish Council for Scientific Research and the Polytechnic University of Valencia, Spain.

Beatriz Otero is based in the Department of Sociology, Faculty of Social and Communication Sciences at the University of the Basque Country (UPV/EHU), Leioa, Spain.

Mario Davide Parrilli is Associate Professor of Regional Economic Development, Coordinator of the PhD in 'Econs and Management' and Programme Leader for the BA in Economics and BA in Finance and Economics at Bournemouth University, UK.

Hugo Pinto is a Researcher at the Centre for Social Studies, University of Coimbra, Portugal and Professor in the Faculty of Economics, University of Algarve, Faro, Portugal.

Francesco Ramella is Professor of Economic Sociology at the University of Torino, Italy, where he is President of the Undergraduate Programme in "Social and Political Sciences" and Director of the International MAPS Programme held at the Collegio Carlo Alberto (Advanced Master in Public Policy and Social Change).

Inés Ruiz-Rosa is Professor in the Department of Economy, Accountant and Financial at the Universidad de La Laguna, Tenerife, Spain.

Maria José Sousa is based at the Universidade Europeia|Laureate International Universities, CIEO, Research Centre for Spatial and Organizational Dynamics at the University of Algarve, Faro, Portugal.

Madelon van Oostrom combines a professional and academic interest for innovation policy and performance. Currently she is Lecturer and Researcher at Hanze University of Applied Sciences, The Netherlands and Innovation Manager of Tenerife Science & Technology Park, Spain.

Josep-Antoni Ybarra is based in the Departament d'Economia Aplicada i Política Econòmica at the Universitat d'Alicant, Alicante, Spain.

Key issues on innovation, culture and institutions: implications for SMEs and micro firms

Manuel Fernández-Esquinas, Madelon van Oostrom and Hugo Pinto

ABSTRACT
This Special Issue is devoted to studying the role of cultural aspects in the innovation dynamics of small firms within the context of their territorial environments. Cultural elements are viewed as strategic assets because of their capacity to enhance small firms' action and to provide opportunities to compete in the knowledge economy. Innovation studies use a variety of approaches and definitions for studying how the symbolic aspects of social reality shape innovation. In this Guest Editorial, our aim is to help clarify this topic of research. Departing from the contributions of this Special Issue, we use analytical definitions of values, norms, cognitive repertoires and institutions as layers of the cultural domain that can be present both in firms and in the surrounding innovation system. We describe important mechanisms related to innovation processes in SMEs and micro firms. The 10 selected articles provide an intellectual map of current research and investigate different angles of cultural dynamics based on cases in Spain, Portugal, Belarus and the U.K. Based on the findings from these articles, we believe that cultural elements can be integrated and recombined by innovation policies as an essential component of local and regional development.

Introduction

Innovation and culture have always been elusive social phenomena. In the case of Small and Medium-Sized Firms (SMEs) and micro firms (usually with fewer than 10 workers), both aspects are difficult to pinpoint. On the one hand, culture covers a complex array of dimensions that range from fundamental values and norms to motivations and perceptions. Culture is also related to the skills, practical knowledge and routines employed in everyday life, including productive behaviour in work places. In SMEs, cultural aspects are not evident because they blend in with the practices and routines of entrepreneurs and owners, and with the surrounding social and economic context. On the other hand, innovation is not easily noticeable in these firms. Few sources provide reliable information about innovation in SMEs. Official innovation surveys frequently exclude smaller firms from their samples and are often not designed to measure specific elements of small firms because they have few formal internal arrangements and systematic procedures to manage knowledge. Evidence of this topic depends on studies carried out across a variety of disciplines, which are usually limited in their territorial and sectorial scope.

Despite these difficulties, innovation culture in firms has begun to attract attention in innovation literature. Some studies consider that culture is important for innovation because values, informal norms and cognitive frameworks shape the capacity to act and to establish links with key external actors (McLean, 2005). This theme is considered significant in the case of SMEs and micro firms because they represent the majority of firms and employment in many places, especially in peripheral environments. Culture and other intangible elements are believed to be even more important in SMEs than in larger firms because they have a more direct impact on their capacities to generate knowledge and to exchange resources with other actors in the environment (Vossen, 1998).

As a result, a variety of studies from management, economic geography, evolutionary economics and sociology, among others, are focusing on different cultural elements of firms and innovation systems (Cooke & Rehfeld, 2011; Dyer, Gregersen, & Christensen, 2011; González de la Fe, Hernández Hernández, & Van Oostrom, 2012; James, 2005; Trippl & Toedtling, 2008). A major challenge is to disentangle the situations in which cultural aspects can be an important source of or a barrier to innovation. The articles in this Special Issue are an example of this endeavour. They explore various angles of the relationship between culture and innovation in different cases and territories, mainly in peripheral environments. Together, they contribute to describe the current state of the art. In this Guest Editorial, we extract common elements that may provide more coherence to this topic. After this introduction, the second section summarizes the main issues about innovation and SMEs. The third section depicts the main analytical elements that are useful for investigating different aspects of culture. In the light of the articles included, analytical concepts are explained, and their implications for SMEs and micro firms are highlighted. In the fourth section, we summarize the contributions of the articles. In the Conclusion section, we provide suggestions for future research.

Small firms and innovation

Perhaps the distinctive characteristic of the innovative processes in SMEs is the low level of formalization. With the exception of firms working on knowledge-intensive processes and R&D (many of them spin-offs and start-ups), in most SMEs, the core knowledge of the firm is seldom codified and is based on experience (Hirsch-Kreinsen, 2008). SMEs have few internal departments and explicit procedures related to innovation. Knowledge management is therefore implicit. Decisions tend to depend on the point of view of the owner and formalized planning is also difficult to implement. Knowledge is transmitted on the job and depends on workers' abilities (Terziovski, 2010). SMEs' possibilities to innovate are also shaped by their capacity to collaborate and 'learn interactively' (Lundvall & Lorenz, 2007) with other agents in the environment, such as clients, providers and training centres.

In comparison with bigger firms, SMEs have disadvantages for innovation, such as lack of financial capital, absence of power to negotiate commercial transactions and difficulties to access distant markets. In contrast, intangible elements can be strategic assets for these firms because they shape the capacity to act – though some can also be barriers. The strength of SMEs frequently lies in the entrepreneur's specialized knowledge and organizational capacities. The values and the skills of the owner and core workers are normally the predominant values and skills of the firm (De Jong & Vermeulen, 2006). SMEs' cognitive frameworks, beliefs, motivations and shared meanings are especially important for defining and developing innovative activities. These circumstances also shape interactions with external agents in the regional context, as well as their strategies for learning and investing in new knowledge. Therefore, cultural traits are considered crucial for adapting to change and for adopting new productive processes.

Some of the influences of cultural elements on SMEs' innovation activities are studied by scholars who focus on the micro level formed by firms and individuals (De Jong & Marsili, 2006). They usually differentiate between factors internal and external to the firm. Internal factors that are important for innovation are the organizational structure of the firm, the business strategy, skills and motivations, beliefs and perceptions (Keizer, Dijkstra, & Halman, 2002). Several studies have shown that the innovation performance of these firms is related to the cultural characteristics of the entrepreneur, especially motivations, flexibility, and adaptation to change and new technologies (Vossen, 1998). Both characteristics are closely dependent on the educational level of the firm's owner or manager (Bougrain & Haudeville, 2002). As for external factors, the main determinants of innovation are found in the capacities to detect and use external knowledge, especially through links with actors that function as knowledge providers (Gray, 2006). Education, training and cultural aspects are also suggested as important determinants of these interactions. Influential components of a symbolic nature include the strategic vision of the entrepreneur, his/her openness to different partnerships and collaborations, and his/her abilities to build fluent relationships with providers and clients based on trust.

Another stream of research focuses on the meso- and macro levels of a territorial milieu. The extensive literature on innovation systems has given importance to the institutions and sociocultural factors that shape SMEs' capacities to innovate in countries and regions (Bluhm & Schmidt, 2008). Some studies pay attention to the interdependence between regional cultures and the trajectories of regional innovation systems (Cooke & Rehfeld, 2011). Others highlight the interactions and mutual influences between the corporate cultures of the innovation systems and regional cultures (Prud'homme van Reine & Dankbaar, 2011). Given that the corporate cultures of larger organizations present in the territory cannot sufficiently explain the innovation dynamics of a region, especially when SMEs are predominant, cultural factors are still a key issue when describing territorial models of innovation.

Despite evidence of the role of intangible elements for firm innovation and endogenous development, there are still important limitations for research. The first involves the links between different levels of analysis. The separation of studies focusing on specific firms versus the institutional aspects of innovation systems does not contribute to systematic observations of interrelations. Cultural and institutional aspects form an integral part of every organized level of social and economic life, from informal groups and firms to corporations and governments. It is important to acknowledge that values, habits and norms, whether informal or formal, can be embedded in all kinds of social situations to any extent.

A second limitation comes from the conceptual fragmentation of this field of study when referring to symbolic elements of social life in organizations and broader societal domains. There is a wide variety of theoretical approaches to institutions, culture, and other symbolic aspects of social life and their role in innovation. Analytical definitions that were established long ago in sociology, social psychology and anthropology are omitted in the field of innovation studies by virtue of disciplinary fragmentation (for instance, classic analytical definitions of cultural layers can be found in MacIver and Page, 1949. An example in the firm domain is Parker, Brown, Child, and Smith (1967)). An important task for investigating the role of cultural elements in SMEs and micro firms is to integrate the theoretical and methodological tools available in different disciplinary domains into innovation studies. What we propose here is a cross-fertilization of approaches. In particular, the articles of this Special Issue serve to situate several observations about cultural and institutional elements within a common conceptual space that is useful for further research.

Unfolding the cultural dynamics of innovation in SMEs and micro firms

In order to observe the role of culture, innovation must be understood as a socially embedded economic action that is shaped by cultural and structural forces (Granovetter, 1985). This perspective assumes that actors are rational, in the sense of pursuing goals through deliberately selected means, but not socially atomized. On the contrary, relationships and symbolic interpretations enter every stage of the process, from the selection of economic goals to the organization and relevant means of achieving them. From this perspective, cultural elements are a set of explanatory mechanisms. Their specific role in innovation is a matter of empirical observation compared to the role of other influential elements identified by specialized research.

Analytical definitions are extremely important for studying the relationship between culture and innovation. Analytical concepts aid the systematic observation of the forces that drive the innovation performance of particular organizations. For that purpose, it is useful to situate the terms in the conceptual space constructed by classic sociological theory. A classical differentiation examines social life according to two dimensions: the social structural domain and the cultural or symbolic domain (Portes, 2010). This implies a differentiation between the notions of social structure and culture. Social structures are formed by the relationships of real persons, and are organized in economic and social hierarchies. Typical elements of a social structure are power, class structures, status hierarchies and organizations (including the economic and physical resources managed by organizations). Culture is formed by the symbolic elements of social life that are crucial for human interaction, mutual understanding and order. Cultural elements are values, norms, cognitive repertoires, roles and institutions. These elements can be interpreted as being arranged in different layers, from the profound aspects of social life that are difficult to observe to the more evident social phenomena.

This separation is purely analytical because in real life both elements are mixed. Nevertheless, the distinction between the symbolic and structural domains (particularly between organizations and institutions) provides an interesting basis for explaining how innovation actually unfolds in the specific settings of SMEs and innovation systems. In the following paragraphs, we outline the basic definitions of cultural elements. We then interpret them as hypothetical mechanisms that mobilize capacities or resources, which affect firms' innovation performance. The specific mechanisms highlighted are present in the articles included in this Special Issue.

Values

Language and values represent the more profound and stable layers of culture. Values are the criteria that people use to assess their daily lives, organize their priorities and choose between alternative courses of action. They are conceptions of the relative desirability of things and act as the motivating force of moral action (Zelizer, 2010). Innovation can be governed by value introjection, which implies that shared values, or the activation of collectively supported values, influence personal goals in order to engage in new ways of doing things. The desirability about openness to change, tolerance of risk and acceptance of novelty may be a basis for innovative behaviour in the context of a firm.

As social action, innovation is framed by interactions and depends on the opinions, approval and social status of others in the same social milieu. Since innovation is associated with change, it may enter into conflict with the realization of other values. Innovative actions in SMEs are constrained by the social acceptance of key actors in the innovation process, mainly clients, providers and business partners. The realization of innovations in the broader context of an innovation system is mediated by these actors' understandings of the desirability and feasibility of certain behaviours. In this sense, the pre-eminence of values prone to innovation in networks of firms and workers of a given environment functions as a competitive asset.

Norms

If values are related to desired and expected behaviour, norms are more related to constraints (Portes, 2010). Norms embody concrete directions for action in specific situations. The importance of norms for innovation is reflected, in practice, in the level of sanctions and rewards attached to behaviours that have implications for innovation. Economic action is linked to behaviours that have a normative character. For instance, norms that oppose change and adaptation to fundamental aspects of economic life are detrimental to innovation. Conversely, other norms related to business ethics and loyalty in economic transactions provide the necessary stability to develop partnerships for productive processes that foster innovation.

Moreover, given the fact that culture is not homogeneous, the business norms of some social groups are not shared in the surrounding social milieu. Services or products are not readily available because of normative or value restrictions for production and exchange. In this circumstance, some firms find a niche of competitive advantage. For instance, ethnic entrepreneurs often innovate by virtue of doing business with social groups that are structurally separated for religious or ethnic reasons. Entrepreneurs with a different normative background are able to fill a 'structural hole' (Burt, 1992) by acting as intermediaries and recombining resources that are otherwise separated by a social fracture.

Cognitive repertoires and skills

Another very important aspect of culture is the cognitive repertoire of skills and routines associated with activities needed for the enactment of values and norms in a specific productive process. Cognitive frameworks and scripts are considered determinants of individual and social action in any kind of organization and also in firms (DiMaggio, 1997). These cognitive elements are an integral part of innovation inside the firm, and also in the tissue of SMEs and micro firms of any regional environment. The capacity of doing is shaped by socialization both in the craftsmanship and the formalized aspects of an economic activity. Acculturation processes are also important in order to understand the meanings and attributes of specific activities (Lindh de Montoya, 2000). Therefore, certain capacities to act within SMEs are especially dependent on socialization and acculturation within the family, the educational system and on-the-job training. Hence, for SMEs and micro firms, the combination of skills transmitted by personal inter-action in work settings and the vocational education system are closely linked to successful innovation dynamics.

Roles

Roles are generally described as the set of behaviours prescribed for occupants of particular social positions. They are related to norms because norms do not occur in a social vacuum, but appear organized and are attributed to specific actors, at least when those actors occupy a visible social position. Individuals as role occupants are subject to constraints and incentives. The extensive research about roles has seldom been considered by inno-vation studies, although it can be a useful analytic tool. Roles and associated social dynamics can be of interest for linking the symbolic world of culture to the social and economic structures of innovation systems. In particular, a role set associated with an entrepreneur's position is especially influential on innovation in his/her firm. For instance, the existence of role congruence regarding standards of quality, prices and ethical codes to be fulfilled by the entrepreneur, in accordance with the expectations of clients, providers or business partners, facilitates the development of competitive productive lines. Conver-sely, the existence of a role strain in an entrepreneur, when normative expectations are contradictory, is detrimental to achieving coherent results, for instance, when economic benefits are not in line with the quality expected.

Institutions

Institutions are the more visible aspect of symbolic social life. Roles, though not exactly the same as institutions, are an integral part of them. Institutions are the symbolic blueprints of organizations. They comprise the set of written or informal rules governing the relation-ships between role occupants within and between different organizations. People usually develop activities and obtain advantages in organizations formed by groups of roles, associated values, norms and skills, together with economic resources, power and net-works disposed in a hierarchical manner (Portes & Nava, 2017).

This restricted definition of institutions is useful for examining explanatory mechan-isms related to culture and innovation in firms. First, the complex arrangements of values, norms, roles and skills inside the firm are what enable an organizational engine to make products and services with a certain degree of competitive advantage. Second, outside the firm, the social structure of an innovation system is formed by a complex set of organizations (different kinds of firms, knowledge providers, such as universities and technology centres, innovation agencies, business angels, incubators and so on), governed and oriented by policies, institutions and other layers of symbolic aspects (Fernández-Esquinas, 2012). The existence of such organizations, and their cultural and institutional blueprints, determines SMEs' possibilities to cooperate with other firms and to establish relationships with knowledge providers essential for innovation.

Studying the specific influence of cultural aspects on SMEs and micro firms requires an analysis of the different components of culture inside the firm and the relationship with the institutional environment. A key task is to observe the extent to which cultural elements specified above are determinants of innovation, in comparison with other 'hard' aspects of the social structure, including the productive sector, firm size, organizational structure, availability of financial capital or the social networks between people and with other firms.

The articles in this special issue

The first two articles provide a useful analytical map for understanding this field of research. The article by González-Loureiro, Sousa and Pinto, 'Culture and innovation in SMEs: the intellectual structure of research for further inquiry', provides a general overview of the field with a structured approach that analyses the articles found in ISI-WoS and Scopus databases about the topic of the Special Issue. Content analysis and HOMALS statistical procedures are used to characterize the content of the main analytical approaches. The authors suggest that future research should emphasize dynamic perspectives of culture by using mixed approaches from a variety of social sciences.

The article by Van Oostrom and Fernández-Esquinas, 'Exploring the links between culture and innovation in micro firms', is conceived as a conceptual tool for exploring the dimension of culture, especially values, and for observing the specific social mechanisms that shape innovation dynamics in micro firms and the diversity of open innovation strategies. The outcomes of the study present a plurality of cultures of innovation and highlight the importance of firms' knowledge base in the configuration of different innovation behaviours. The empirical findings contribute to existing discussions about homogeneity versus plurality of culture, and about universality and specificity. The results suggest that the debate on open innovation strategies could benefit from an operational framework of culture as presented in the article.

A second group of articles cover innovation dynamics of firms close to research and technology. In 'The enterprise of innovation in hard times', Ramella studies corporate cultures and performance in Italian high-tech companies. Based on a sample of firms with EU patents, the article explores the 'socio-cognitive' and 'socio-normative' dimensions that guide internal relations between employees and external relations with other actors. The article finds that collaborative company cultures influence successful innovation strategies. Analytically, the notion of corporate culture used in this article represents a bridge between structure and agency and provides a useful explanation for social change in firms.

In the article, 'A new approach to business innovation modes: the "RTH model" in the ICT sector in Belarus', Apanasovich, Alcalde-Heras and Parrilli analyse the modes of innovation adopted by SMEs. Inspired by contributions on 'STI and DUI innovation modes', they present a new framework based on empirically grounded 'innovation profiles' and 'business innovation modes' – the RTH model (Research, Technology and HRM). Using a sample of ICT firms operating in a technology-follower country (Belarus), the study emphasizes that the degree of product innovation seems particularly sensitive to the Technology and HRM drivers. This result suggests the need to differentiate between policies dedicated to research from those dedicated to technology, especially in transition countries.

The article by Olmos-Peñuela et al., 'Strengthening SMEs' innovation culture through collaborations with public research organizations', focuses on the role of public research organizations (PROs) on SMEs' innovation activities. In particular, they observe the extent to which firms' innovation culture is reinforced by collaboration with PROs. The article is based on a survey of firms that have collaborated with the CSIC, the largest PRO in Spain. The authors built a specific proxy of innovation culture related to the role of new ideas, worker collaboration and decentralized decision-making. The results of their analysis show how collaboration with PROs encourages innovation behaviours among employees and the emergence of new ideas that challenge the organizational situation of firms.

A third group of articles focuses on important innovation processes for SMEs in territorial milieus. Gabaldón-Esteban and Ybarra's article, 'Innovative culture in district innovation systems of European ceramics SMEs', uses the concept of industrial districts to study the role of community and culture in specialized industrial environments. The authors focus on the ceramic tile sector in Sassuolo (Italy) and Castellón (Spain). They adopt the notion of 'district innovation systems' to observe the cognitive frames and tacit knowledge present in the surrounding environment, together with the actors' linkages, systemic functions and failures. The results provide a useful framework to identify symbolic elements of production and possible application to different sectors.

The article by García Rodríguez et al., 'Entrepreneurial process in peripheral regions', focuses on the entrepreneurial potential for regions' innovation performance and examines cultural specificities and the role of motivation. The results of the quantitative survey of university students in the Canary Islands indicate that motivation influences entrepreneurial intention directly and indirectly through individuals' attitudes to entrepreneurship. The findings have important consequences for entrepreneurial education and policies in terms of the attention that should be paid to motivation rather than to attempts to change individual attitudes.

The article by Albizu et al., 'Making visible the role of vocational education and training in firm innovation: evidence from Spanish SMEs', studies the role of vocational education training (VET) in industrial firms. A survey of a large sample of Spanish SMEs is used to observe the presence and profile of workers with VET qualifications. The involvement of these workers in innovation activities and the specific variables that shape their participation are studied in detail. The article shows the importance of the VET system in the formation of cognitive frameworks and skills that are essential for innovation, especially in low-tech sectors. It also identifies how cultural elements internal to firms determine the level of these workers' involvement in innovation.

The article by Froy, 'Pragmatic urbanism: London Railway arches and Small-Scale enterprise', explores an urban perspective on the small-scale businesses set up in the railway arches of London through recent industrialization history. The findings of this article highlight the importance of the architectural characteristics of railway arches in generating cultures of innovation between micro firms and SMEs through the circulation of people and ideas. The results also highlight the policy implications of urban design, since railway arches and other residual spaces are more flexible and adaptable to new business. The integration of small-sized manufacturers, artisans and retailers into other commercial spaces within urban districts would also reduce industrial gentrification by maintaining the cultural ties of SMEs with local neighbourhoods.

The article by Cesario et al., 'The use of design as a strategic tool for innovation: an analysis for different firms' networking behaviours?', contributes to the understanding of the use of design for innovation purposes. The article employs the Community Innovation Survey (2012) database in Portugal to understand the association between different external linkages and the use of design in the firms' innovation process. The authors find that the access of firms to different information sources, such as public customers, consultants or conference participants, is positively connected to the strategic use of design. Moreover, the development of informal channels with these actors is also associated with better design performances.

Conclusion

The contributions of this Special Issue give an extensive insight into the dynamic and complex relation between culture and innovation in one of the key agents of European economic life: SMEs and micro firms. The articles present valuable contributions that facilitate a theoretical and empirical understanding of the social and cultural mechanisms that influence innovation performance. Lessons and recommendations for policy are identified and suggested. Future research questions concerning the generation and management of cultural elements emerge throughout this Special Issue, in addition to important limitations and challenges for research.

A significant implication for innovation policies is that some aspects of culture can be managed in order to foster positive innovation dynamics. The relation between culture and firm innovation is not just one-way. Different articles have shown how culture is a heterogeneous and changing domain. Therefore, cultural elements can be shaped and integrated into firms' strategies, as well as into regional and local innovation policies. In terms of the implications for future research, an important challenge is to employ analytical and methodological strategies to identify different dimensions of culture (especially values, norms, skills and institutions) and to scrutinize which specific components of culture are relevant to firm innovation and to the more general dynamics of innovation systems, in comparison with other important components of the social and economic structure relating to size, sector, finance, economic influence, networks and organizational arrangements.

Disclosure statement

No potential conflict of interest was reported by the authors.

References

Bluhm, K., & Schmidt, R. (2008). Why should the varieties literature grant smaller firms more attention? An introduction. In K. Bluhm & R. Schmidt (Eds.), *Change in SMEs* (pp. 1–14). London: Palgrave Macmillan UK.

Bougrain, F., & Haudeville, B. (2002). Innovation, collaboration and SMEs internal research capacities. *Research Policy*, *31*(5), 735–747. doi:10.1016/S0048-7333(01)00144-5

Burt, R. S. (1992). *Structural holes: The social structure of competition*. Cambridge, MA: Harvard University Press.

Cooke, P., & Rehfeld, D. (2011). Path dependence and new paths in regional evolution: In search of the role of culture. *European Planning Studies*, *19*(11), 1909–1929. doi:10.1080/09654313.2011. 618685

De Jong, J. P. J., & Marsili, O. (2006). The fruit flies of innovations: A taxonomy of innovative small firms. *Research Policy*, *35*(2), 213–229. doi:10.1016/j.respol.2005.09.007

De Jong, J. P. J., & Vermeulen, P. (2006). Determinants of product innovation in small firms: A comparison across industries. *International Small Business Journal*, *24*, 587–609. doi:10.1177/0266242606069268

DiMaggio, P. (1997). Culture and cognition. *Annual Review of Sociology*, *23*, 263–287. doi:10.1146/annurev.soc.23.1.263

Dyer, J., Gregersen, H., & Christensen, C. (2011). *The innovator's DNA: Mastering the five skills of disruptive innovators*. Cambridge, MA: Harvard Business Press.

Fernández-Esquinas, M. (2012). Hacia un programa de investigación en sociología de la innovación. *Arbor. Revista de Pensamiento, Ciencia y Cultura*, *188*(753), 5–18. doi:10.3989/arbor.2012.753n1001

González de la Fe, T., Hernández Hernández, N., & Van Oostrom, M. (2012). Innovación, cultura y tamaño: la microempresa en una región ultraperiférica. *Arbor. Revista de Pensamiento, Ciencia y Cultura*, *188*(753), 113–134. doi:10.3989/arbor.2012.753n1008

Granovetter, M. (1985). Economic action and social structure: The problem of embeddedness. *American Journal of Sociology*, *91*(3), 481–510. doi:10.1086/228311

Gray, C. (2006). Absorptive capacity, knowledge management and innovation in entrepreneurial small firms. *International Journal of Entrepreneurial Behavior & Research*, *12*(6), 345–360. doi:10.1108/13552550610710144

Hirsch-Kreinsen, H. (2008). Innovation strategies of non-research-intensive SMEs. In K. Bluhm & R. Schmidt (Eds.), *Change in SMEs: Towards a new European capitalism?* (pp. 171–184). London: Palgrave Macmillan UK.

James, A. (2005). Demystifying the role of culture in innovative regional economies. *Regional Studies*, *39*(9), 1197–1216. doi:10.1080/00343400500389968

Keizer, J. A., Dijkstra, L., & Halman, J. I. M. (2002). Explaining innovative efforts of SMEs. An exploratory survey among SMEs in the mechanical and electrical engineering sector in the Netherlands. *Technology in Society*, *22*, 1–13. doi:10.1016/S0166-4972(00)00091-2

Lindh de Montoya, M. (2000). Entrepreneurship and culture: The case of Freddy, the strawberry man. In R. Swedberg (Ed.), *Entrepreneurship. The social science view* (pp. 332–355). New York: Oxford University Press.

Lundvall, B. A., & Lorenz, E. (2007, October 30–November 1). *Modes of innovation and knowledge taxonomies in the learning economy*. Paper presented at the CAS workshop on Innovation in Firms, Oslo.

MacIver, R. H., & Page, C. H. (1949). *Sociology*. New York: Rinehart.

McLean, L. D. (2005). Organizational culture's influence on creativity and innovation: A review of the literature and implications for human resource development. *Advances in Developing Human Resources*, *7*(2), 226–246. doi:10.1177/1523422305274528

Parker, S. R., Brown, R. K., Child, J., & Smith, M. A. (1967). *The sociology of industry*. London: Unwin Hyman Ltd. (fifth impression in 2005 by Routledge).

Portes, A. (2010). *Economic sociology: A systematic inquiry*. Princeton: Princeton University Press.

Portes, A., & Nava, J. C. (2017). Institutions and national development: A comparative study. *Revista Española de Sociología*, *26*(1), 9–31. doi:10.22325/fes/res.2016.1

Prud'homme van Reine, P., & Dankbaar, B. (2011). A virtuous circle? Co-evolution of regional and corporate cultures. *European Planning Studies*, *19*(11), 1865–1883. doi:10.1080/09654313.2011. 618684

Terziovski, M. (2010). Innovation-based differentiators of high performing small to medium enterprises (SMEs): A resource-based view. *Strategic Management Journal*, *31*(8), 892–902. doi:10.1002/smj.841

Trippl, M., & Toedtling, F. (2008, June 17–20). *Regional innovation cultures.* Paper presented at the 25th celebration conference DRUID on entrepreneurship and innovation – organizations, institutions, systems and regions, Copenhagen.

Vossen, R. W. (1998). Relative strengths and weaknesses of small firms in innovation. *International Small Business Journal, 16*(3), 88–94. doi:10.1177/0266242698163005

Zelizer, V. (2010). *Economic lives: How culture shapes the economy.* Princeton: Princeton University Press.

Culture and innovation in SMEs: the intellectual structure of research for further inquiry

Miguel Gonzalez-Loureiro ⓘ, Maria José Sousa ⓘ and Hugo Pinto ⓘ

ABSTRACT

Regional and organizational cultures are commonly considered key enablers to innovation dynamics in organizations, in particular to small and medium enterprises (SMEs). Although this intersection is a crucial topic of research, studies addressing this issue remain limited in number and scope in the case of SMEs. In this article, a systematic literature review of that intersection is presented by gathering articles from ISI-WoS and Scopus databases. It combines a qualitative approach (content analysis) and a statistical procedure (HOMALS) to analyse the information from 1947 articles found. As a result, the contribution is twofold: a map of the intellectual structure of research and a codebook of descriptors. The study helps identify relevant gaps for future research, specifically the need for mixed approaches from a variety of social sciences with a particular focus on regional science. Future research should shift from a static to a dynamic perspective of culture in groups, organizations and territories. In the case of SMEs, this can be labelled as transformational culture: the study of how organizational and regional cultures may co-evolve along with the changes in the environment by seizing on the SMEs' flexibility and flattened organizational structure.

1. Introduction

Culture and innovation in the regional arena have become two important research fields of increasing interest during recent decades (Büschgens, Bausch, & Balkin, 2013; Dobni, 2008). Culture is a social construct that refers to the values and beliefs shared by a group of individuals (Schein, 1984), which is the notion of culture used throughout this article. On the other hand, innovation plays a key role in today's competition (Damanpour, 1991) and regions (Asheim, Moodysson, & Tödtling, 2011a). In fact, there is strong evidence in the literature suggesting that innovation and culture are extremely interrelated and that organizational and regional culture both have a relevant impact on innovation performance (e.g. Büschgens et al., 2013).

ⓑ Supplemental data for this article can be accessed here: http://dx.doi.org/10.1080/09654313.2017.1290052

Both issues are even more relevant for small- and medium-sized enterprises (SMEs) at the regional level, since managers and owners are quite often the same group and they are particularly embedded in the region (Cooke, Uranga, & Etxebarria, 1997). Being more limited in size and having available resources more than do larger firms (Freel, 2000), hitting the right objective on the first try when innovating is especially crucial for SMEs. According to Eurostat data, the more than 21 million SMEs in the European Union represented up to 99% of business, generated 3.6 trillion Euros in value added and employed 88.8 million people across the EU28 in 2013. Thus, SMEs are a particular focus of interest for scholars studying innovation and culture.

In light of this large tradition of research, the time has come to conduct a systematic literature review that maps the intellectual structure of research at the intersection of culture and innovation, with a particular focus on SMEs. The goal is to present the state-of-the-art of this intersection in order to guide scholars' future inquiry. The critical question is whether the extant traditions have been permeable enough to provide a common framework to study the role of culture and innovation in the case of SMEs. To do so, this article analyses the content of 1947 articles found in Scopus and ISI-WoS databases dealing with that intersection. A computer-aided procedure extracted and classified a set of descriptors that are mapped by means of a multiple correspondence analysis.

This review's contributions are twofold. On the one hand, the intellectual structure of descriptors (codebook) will help scholars to further explore the topics in the regional arena. On the other hand, the article provides a stepwise method that eases the reproducibility for future comparisons and restricts the bias naturally introduced by the researcher conducting these reviews manually. This design is similar to some recent reviews (see Dabic, González-Loureiro, & Furrer, 2014; González-Loureiro, Dabic, & Kiessling, 2015; López-Duarte, González-Loureiro, Vidal-Suárez, & González-Díaz, 2016).

The article is organized as follows. The next section presents a brief discussion of the notions and connections of regional cultures, organizational culture and innovation. Next, we detail the method for the systematic literature review. After that, some descriptive results and trends are introduced, as well as the map, i.e. the intellectual structure of research. After discussing the research gaps relative to SMEs, the article ends by suggesting research avenues for bridging them.

2. Background and main theoretical approaches to culture and innovation

2.1. Background of culture and innovation

Culture is commonly defined in terms of a set of values, beliefs and assumptions that define how the firm develops its business, and is an integral source for maintaining a firm's competitive edge (Barney, 1986). Organizational culture is commonly referred to as the values, beliefs and underlying assumptions shared by organizational members (Büschgens et al., 2013). Widening the scope, a certain region and, as a consequence, the organizations located there can exhibit several cultures, i.e. different groups may have different cultures such as workers, middle-line managers and board of directors/ owners, or there can be a dominant culture in a region coexisting with some others. On a sociological level, the usual layers of culture range from the most visible ones – artefacts and the espoused beliefs and values – to the underlying assumptions, which are quite often taken-for-granted beliefs and unconscious in nature (Schein, 1984, 1986). In summary, culture, be it regional, national or organizational in scope, is a social construct that influences and is influenced by the context (Denison, 1996).

A critical problem arises around a workable definition of innovation culture at any level of analysis – the region and the organization – since both of the former notions are multidimensional. Dobni (2008) analysed up to 86 constructs of innovation, while Büschgens et al. (2013) found up to 40 different values that are related to an innovative culture. If brought together, conceptualizations of innovation culture vary depending on the researcher's focus, ranging from characteristics of a supportive culture (Chandler, Keller, & Lyon, 2000) to the culture that fosters innovation or 'culture for innovation' (Frohman, 1998). The nuances lie in whether innovation is an outcome of a managerial process that includes a certain culture in an organization or a region ('culture for innovation') or whether innovation is an antecedent of a certain culture ('culture of innovation'). Or to put it differently, a critical question is to what extent the issue revolves around the self-endogeneity of context and culture: the context is created by interaction but the context determines the interaction (Denison, 1996). In such cases, a first remaining question is, which geographical level of context is optimal to foster the culture of innovation for the case of SMEs. Another issue is then to what extent research has included multi-level models of analysis when it comes to innovation culture and the geographical scope.

Before answering these questions with the review, first we should introduce the main theoretical approaches followed by researchers of this intersection.

2.2. Main theoretical approaches to culture and innovation

The earliest articles included the organizational climate tradition (Forehand, 1963; Singer, 1969). Later on, articles broadened their perspective towards both culture and climate, and in particular, towards how culture encourages and fosters innovation by means of creating a positive ambiance for creativity and knowledge diffusion (e.g. Cosmas & Sheth, 1980). By the early 2000s, research focused on an upper level of analysis, namely the systems of innovation at regional and national levels, rooted in a systemic and social approach to inter-organizational networks and the impact of culture on those relations (e.g. Lechner & Dowling, 2003). A complimentary approach by that time was the quest of whether there is an optimal culture for innovation and how cross-cultural management may foster creativity that leads to improved rates of innovation. Büschgens et al. (2013) found that there is not an optimal cultural configuration for innovative purposes in their meta-analytic review, although the CVF offered a classification of culture with promising but not conclusive results. Previously, Shane (1992) had found that individualistic and non-hierarchical societies are more inventive than other societies in studying the per capita number of invention patents in 33 countries. This issue remains one the biggest questions about this intersection, with an additional need to study cross-cultural sets.

Nine main theoretical approaches were detected from a wide variety of viewpoints (see Table 1), namely sociology (e.g. Ajzen's theory of planned behaviour), regional science (e.g. regional/national systems of innovation) and strategic management (e.g. resource and knowledge-based views of the firm).

Table 1. Main theoretical approaches detected in the intersection of culture and innovation.

Framework	Key references	Focus, level of analysis and main statements
Theory of planned behaviour	Ajzen (1991)	• Individual (psychology) • Behaviourist • Intentions precede behaviour • Three attitudinal antecedents: attitudes toward the act, subjective social norms, and perceived feasibility
Competing values framework-CVF	Quinn and Rohrbaugh (1983) and Quinn and Spreitzer (1991)	• Organization • Organizational behaviour • Three dimensions of organizational values: internal vs. external perspective; flexibility vs. control; means (preferred processes) and ends (preferred outcomes) • Four types of organizational culture traits: group, developmental, hierarchical and rational
Social network theory	Granovetter (1973), Nahapiet and Ghoshal (1998) and Adler and Kwon (2002)	• Sociology • Interaction between nodes (individuals, groups, organizations, territories) by means of ties (social network) • The weakest tie in the network (closeness) is the place through which new knowledge is available for the entire network. Relevance of gatekeepers, network density and centrality in the network. Social capital is a crucial construct
Hofstede's cultural distance	Hofstede (1980, 1994), Kogut and Singh (1988) and Schwartz (1992)	• Sociology • Group's performance • Cultural distance dimensions: power distance; individualism vs. collectivism; femininity vs. masculinity; uncertainty avoidance; long-term vs. short-term orientation; indulgence; restraint; monumentalism; self-effacement • Kogut & Singh's index • Cross-cultural studies and acculturation (dominant vs. non-dominant cultures). Bipolar structure: openness to change vs. conservation; self-transcendence vs. self-enhancement
Schein's framework of organizational culture	Schein (1986)	• Organizational development and behaviour • Organizational culture • Three concentric layers of culture depending on visibility: artefacts; espoused beliefs and values; underlying assumptions. Several cultures may be present in an organization. Alignment between implicit and explicit layers and between them and the organization's goals determines the robustness of the organizational culture. Subsequent studies showed that a strong culture is not always associated with high performance (see review of Büschgens et al., 2013)
Innovation systems	Lundvall (1992) and Freeman (1995)	• Systemic approach • Public actors of national, regional, sectoral and socio-technical systems of innovation • Systems are made of actors and relationships • Institutional architectures create a variety of innovation profiles • Institutions tend to replicate by means of social legitimation in an isomorphic way from system to system. The focus is usually put on institutions belonging to the innovation system such as universities, research centres and the like
Open innovation	Chesbrough (2003) and Etzkowitz and Leydesdorff (2000)	• Systemic approach • Cooperation between firms when innovating • Firms that cooperate when innovating tend to decrease the time needed to achieve an innovation. Organizational culture dimensions such as openness

(Continued)

Table 1. Continued.

Framework	Key references	Focus, level of analysis and main statements
RBV and KBV	Barney (1991), Cohen and Levinthal (1990) and Grant (1996)	to external knowledge or cooperation are antecedents of Open Innovators • Strategic management • Organization • VRIN/O principle governs how the organization achieves a sustained competitive advantage thanks to an idiosyncratic combination of resources and capabilities (R&C). That principle states that the R&C involved must be Valuable, Rare, Imperfectly Imitable or Inimitable, and Non-substitutable plus the Organization must be in a position as to appropriate the rents derived. Knowledge was later identified as the key element among the firm's R&Cs and due to its intangibility is harder to be appropriated hence firms can sustain the knowledge-based advantages easier than other stemming from tangible elements. Culture and innovation are part of the elements and strategic orientation available for a firm to achieve and maintain a sustained competitive edge

Source: own draft from cited authors.

Ajzen's (1991) theory of planned behaviour states that intentions precede behaviour and identifies three attitudinal antecedents of intentions, namely attitude towards the act (to innovate in our context), the subjective social norms (normative beliefs) that affect the individual's perception of 'acceptable' or 'optimal' norms of conduct, and the perceived feasibility based on the individual's perceived control, which is partly rooted in Bandura's (1986) perceived self-efficacy. The culture of innovation is a set of capabilities plus a set of positive attitudes towards the behaviour, which, in the case of SMEs, is influenced by the regional system of innovation (Fernandez-Jardon, González-Loureiro, & Pita-Castelo, 2016).

The competing values framework developed by Quinn and colleagues (Quinn & Rohrbaugh, 1983; Quinn & Spreitzer, 1991) has been extensively used. Quinn and Rohrbaugh (1983) identified three value dimensions. In the first axis, they confronted the internal versus external perspective, while the second dimension classifies culture traits between flexibility versus control. The third dimension includes means (preferred processes) and ends (preferred outcomes) of the model. Accordingly, four types of organizational culture traits were identified by the authors, namely group, developmental, hierarchical and rational.

The social network paradigm was also identified among the theoretical approaches. Largely rooted in sociology, it has been adopted by legions of scholars in the business management field (Borgatti & Foster, 2003; Chauvet, Chollet, Soda, & Huault, 2011). Not only is network an approach but also a methodology, i.e. an analytical tool for studying relationships between actors. In their review, Chauvet et al. (2011) state that a network can be defined as a set of actors (nodes) connected by a set of ties, with the nodes being individuals, groups, organizations or any similar aggregation of individuals. A branch of this approach includes notions such as 'social capital' (Borgatti & Foster, 2003), where Burt's studies are some of the most cited, especially because of the notion of a structural hole, a gap between two agents with complementary resources or information. When the two are connected through a third agent – a mediator – the gap is eliminated, creating important advantages for this third party. Burt (2004) is the example and theoretical explanation of how creativity is driven by network structures and the hole (gap) between different networks. Granovetter's (1973) strength of weak ties is also an essential part of this network paradigm, which is relevant for the culture of innovation at the regional level because the weakest tie in the network (in terms of closeness) is the key source for new knowledge that fuels innovation. This approach has also been adopted by scholars in the strategic management subfield essentially under the form of social capital (notably Adler & Kwon, 2002; Nahapiet & Ghoshal, 1998) that may lead organizations to achieve a competitive edge by managing the social network to understand and meet the social needs with innovative products.

Under the approach labelled as Hofstede, several and interrelated frameworks are grouped. Essentially, they deal with features of culture that help distinguish between cultural configurations. Hofstede's framework (1980, 1994) was originally conceived to study the impact of cultural distance on the group's performance, mainly in international business contexts. Features of cultural distance can be drawn from the analysis of pairs of cultural dimensions, namely power distance, individualism versus collectivism, masculinity versus femininity, uncertainty avoidance, long-term versus short-term orientation, indulgence, restraint, monumentalism and self-effacement. Subsequent adaptations were made by Kogut and Singh (1988), who tried to obtain an index by integrating those cultural dimensions when applied to national culture differences. Schwartz (1992) delved deeper into cross-cultural studies in the quest of a universal structure of values. He identified a set of dynamic relations among values that are relevant to motivate the human group, summarized in bi-polar dimensions – namely openness to change versus conservation, and self-transcendence versus self-enhancement.

Schein's (1986) layers of culture is another relevant approach. It consists of three concentric layers depending on the visibility of the cultural features by the observer. A vast majority of research usually focuses attention on the most visible ones, namely artefacts, espoused beliefs and values. Schein (1986) claimed that several cultures may exist in an organization depending on the group analysed: the managerial culture, the group culture – derived from physical proximity – and worker culture based on shared hierarchical experiences among the workforce. Yet he stated that a strong organizational culture arises when the implicit and the explicit assumptions are in harmony and well-aligned. Consequently, the process of building an organizational culture that fosters innovation strongly depends on the alignment between the hidden and the most visible layers with the organization's or region's goal.

The innovation systems approach is commonly associated with a broader perspective and is usually linked to national and regional development (Cooke & Rehfeld, 2011; Freeman, 1995; Lundvall, 1992). The systemic perspective of innovation underlines that systems are made of different actors, their linkages and specific institutional architectures in the search for particular objectives connected with innovation dynamics in a specific socio-technical landscape (Geels, 2004). The underlying argument is that institutions are considered as an artefact and express the unit of analysis, be this a culture, an organizational form or an idea that tends to persist, expand and replicate by means of social legitimacy. This depends upon the level of acceptance of the social group. This implies that if a certain culture is found to outperform any other in the SMEs' process of innovation, then it will be replicated in close regions and then worldwide following the same original pattern.

Chesbrough's (2003) open innovation paradigm was also identified among the descriptors. As opposed to the traditional way of undertaking the process of innovation, it posits that firms will benefit from collaborating in that process. Strongly rooted in the triple helix model of Etzkowitz and Leydesdorff (2000), it puts the focus on the firms instead of the other agents, namely universities and public administration. This is very relevant for the SMEs since they have limited resources and capabilities to devote to innovation. Therefore, the cultural dimension here should be applied to the multiple levels of agents in the region and the alignment of their culture in order to avoid tensions. This approach is also related to regional, national and sectoral systems of innovation.

Finally, we identified two intertwined approaches from the strategic management field, namely the resource-based and the knowledge-based views of the firm (RBV and KBV, respectively). Barney (1991) claimed that the firm is a bundle of resources and capabilities that are to be combined to build a sustained competitive advantage. Innovation-based capabilities are a source of competitive advantage, and are usually framed within the evolving research on KBV in terms of knowledge absorption (Cohen & Levinthal, 1990). The nuance between RBV and KBV is that the latter is focused on knowledge-based resources (Grant, 1996), with particular attention to how knowledge is managed through the named practices for knowledge management (acquisition, diffusion, learning, etc.). This discourse relates to culture and innovation in two ways. First, culture is part of the intangible elements of the firm and the region, included in the organization's structural capital (i.e. the value created by organizational procedures and routines) and relational capital (i.e. the value created while relating). Second, innovation and culture may be relevant sources of competitive advantages that enable the organizations and regions to develop their distinctive core competencies relative to competitors and other areas. These arguments are particularly relevant for SMEs when innovating, since they have to combine the different types of tangible and intangible resources effectively and efficiently to obtain a distinctive configuration that make each SME competitively different from any other (González-Loureiro & Figueroa-Dorrego, 2012).

All in all, these approaches should address the main dilemmas between the two levels of culture when it comes to innovation, namely the regional and the organizational cultures. In addition, other levels should also be incorporated into the academic conversations, especially those at lower levels trying to explain the micro-foundations of the innovation culture in SMEs. Those tensions are explained below.

2.3. Key dilemmas when it comes to culture and innovation at the regional level

Today there is agreement among scholars about the importance of innovation for the economic success of countries, regions and firms since it generates new possibilities for development, renewal and resilience (Cooke, Parrilli, & Curbelo, 2012). Regional economies are dependent on territorially embedded factors that shape the innovation-based competitiveness of regions (Asheim, Smith, & Oughton, 2011b). These factors are a result of the unique knowledge and cognitive assets anchored in collective learning processes, characterized by path dependence and patterns in the industrial fabric at a regional level.

Innovation does not happen in a 'vacuum', but in a specific social context characterized by specific actors, their linkages and institutions. Particular macro- and meso-approaches such as the social systems of innovation and production (Amable, 2000), the business systems (Fernandez-Jardon et al., 2016) or the regional systems of innovation (Freeman, 1995; Lundvall, 1992) underline the role of the institutional architectures and complementarities in the creation of institutional advantages to economic actors that catalyse their competitiveness. Differences in regional and national cultures have a direct and indirect impact on innovation performance (Efrat, 2014).

There is growing agreement that different regional cultures play a vital role in facilitating innovation in SMEs but differences remain largely unexplored and unexplained (James, 2005). Location is neither static nor given, but simultaneously is a result and the area for social interaction (Cooke & Rehfeld, 2011). Several territorialized models of innovation such as the regional innovation systems (Cooke et al., 1997), the innovative 'milieu' (Camagni, 2005) or the agglomeration of firms (Asheim, 1996) underline the relevance of the shared values and beliefs as the critical building block of innovation and knowledge networks and to structure innovative communities. The identity of the place is an influential factor in terms of social interaction, as well as for the economy and regional planning. Social capital is a territorialized aspect as actors concentrate their social interactions in a certain location (Rutten, Westlund, & Boekema, 2010). This is particularly relevant for SMEs since they tend to be more embedded in the local territory where they were born, and regional systems of innovation create the specific context for these firms to innovate. Accordingly, participation in innovation depends on several circumstances such as the absorptive capacity of the regional innovative actors – specifically of SMEs (Albors-Garrigos & Hidalgo, 2012) – and the implementation of cooperative practices of open innovation among actors (Chesbrough, 2003; Dahlander & Gann, 2010). Demand and interaction are also interrelated with regional cluster dynamics, the chain values undertaken in the location and the global life cycles of economic activities (Asheim, 1996; Ebbekink & Lagendijk, 2013). It then follows that there is a need to dig deeper in these multi-level relations between global and local forces.

Another issue is how SMEs can seize on regional knowledge by learning. The dominant learning modes are essential to regional innovation since they facilitate the knowledge production and exchange dynamics (Jensen, Johnson, Lorenz, & Lundvall, 2007). Research and policy are paying more attention to models that go beyond a simple science–technology–innovation perspective. The process view of doing–using–interacting is to be incorporated as an explicit dimension to planning and hybrid expansions like the territorial embeddedness innovation underline the centrality of considering the specific elements of the territory in the learning modes (Nunes & Lopes, 2015). Recent innovation policies, such as those inspired in smart specialization, directly point to the existing and latent potential competencies and to the process of entrepreneurial discovery that can benefit from the clarification of the role of 'culture' in innovation (Foray, 2014). In the case of SMEs, this implies that more effort should be made to increase the link between regional and global actors that offer valuable, specialized knowledge that exceeds the regional scope. It entails the dilemma of whether regional policies should foster attracting large multinationals or creating new, specialized SMEs following a niche strategy. A tacit component of knowledge is easily shared with proximity, which often goes beyond a simple geographical understanding, but commonly regards an organized feature structured around the importance of a common culture (Boschma, 2005; Torre & Rallet, 2005), i.e. the shared values and beliefs of young entrepreneurs at a regional level.

At this level, Schein's (1986) layers of culture relate directly to 'regional culture'. At the micro-level, the connections between innovation and organizational culture show crucial consequences for planning. Innovative companies tend to present a strong culture for innovation although the specific combination of cultural features may differ between innovative firms (Büschgens et al., 2013). Schein's different layers of organizational culture mediate the innovation support and the firm performance. The valorization of aspects such as success, openness and flexibility, internal communication, competence and professionalism, inter-functional cooperation responsibility, appreciation and risk-taking has impacts on innovation (Hogan & Coote, 2014). Leadership positively influences the climate for innovation (Sarros, Cooper, & Santora, 2008). Organizational learning cultures have a strong positive direct impact effect on innovation and innovative culture (Škerlavaj, Song, & Lee, 2010). Therefore, there can be multiple interactions between the regional level with upper and lower levels of analysis.

Regional culture has an impact on organizational cultures in the core of how the SMEs will behave and relate with other regional actors, shaping the governance and management processes within the region. Cooke and Rehfeld (2011) used different cultural frames (ethnic, landscape, political, labour and business) to analyse how regional culture informs organizational cultures of firms and vice versa. This process of multi-level interaction – between the region and the firm – is crucial for change and evolution. This interaction between the regional culture and organizational culture is characterized by different types of dilemmas (Van Reine & Dankbaar, 2011), as Table 2 summarizes.

Under some conditions, corporate cultures and regional cultures may create virtuous or vicious cycles. Van Reine and Dankbaar (2011), in their comparison of seven European regions, found five different types of patterns: (a) productive interaction (corporate and regional cultures reinforce each other improving competitiveness); (b) limited productive interaction (to specific sectors or areas); (c) negative interaction (tension leads to a

Table 2. Dilemmas between the regional culture and organizational cultures.

Dilemma	Tensions and synergies between
Internationalization vs. Regional identity	The cultural influences from outside and the regional culture, involving the local 'buzz' and the global 'pipelines'
Competition vs. cooperation	Profit orientation through market mechanisms and interaction based in coordination outside market exchange
Closed innovation vs. Open innovation	Protection and active management of intellectual property rights and joint innovation based in collaboration of different types of actors
Building large firms vs. Creating new firms	Creating solid and larger firms or high risk fast-growing start-ups and spin-offs
Technology push vs. Market pull	Innovation based in a R&D linear model or with the understanding of demand from potential users
Entrepreneurial vs. Technical skills	Development of human capital with entrepreneurial education or focus in specific technical training
Hard factors vs Soft factors	Develop the business climate (infrastructure, resources – an attractive region to work) or people climate (green, safe, and vibrant social environment – an attractive region to live)
Shareholder value vs. Stakeholder orientation	Short-term profitability or contributing to the longer-term development
Authority vs. Participation	Strong hierarchical leadership or involvement of a broad range of voices

Source: Inspired in Van Reine and Dankbaar (2011).

negative impact on competitiveness, resulting in negative dynamics); (d) lopsided development (both cultures align at one extreme position neglecting other poles); and (e) disconnected interaction (limited influence of regional culture and corporate culture and vice versa). The term 'culture' can be a coin with two faces. Frequently, it is used in a positive sense, implying virtuous and life-enhancing qualities. Culture can be a positive force, structuring the benefits, for example, from agglomeration economies. However, the other side of coin entails oppression and discrimination from the dominant regional culture – a kind of way to ensure self-reproduction avoiding innovation and institutional change, creating negative consequences in terms of lock-in and path dependence.

Culture needs to overcome its traditional 'dustbin' category in regional innovation, explaining all the dimensions that one cannot explain explicitly. It requires an important effort from regional studies and planning for the clarification and delimitation of the intellectual structure of the intersection between innovation and culture.

3. Methods for the review

The intellectual structure of a research field has been defined as 'a set of salient attributes of the knowledge base that can provide an organized and holistic understanding of the chosen scientific domain' (Shafique, 2013, p. 63). Accordingly, the intellectual structure must contain the 'whats' (descriptors) and the 'hows' (methods) placed in the context.

In literature reviews, content analysis has helped leverage the richness of content while maintaining the accuracy of results (Duriau, Reger, & Pfarrer, 2007). In this type of review, reproducibility is critical in social sciences since we are trying to conceptualize and theorize about the others' perception by rationalizing the existing body of knowledge. As explained below, we have used a method and a statistical technique to yield a map, both of which are reproducible in subsequent periods.

3.1. Search criteria

We decided to collect articles only instead of other scientific contributions, because this type of outcome has succeeded in the proof of pairs review. The content in itself is our focus and not the authors.

The same search strategy was conducted with two of the most reputed databases, namely the Social Science Citation Index-SSCI provided by Thomson-Reuters and Scopus provided by Elsevier. A search strategy was defined as well as some rules for the inclusion and exclusion of articles. The search was unrestricted to any field but to the broader domain of social sciences, which includes business management, regional science, sociology and psychology among others.

The search looked for articles dealing with both lexemes 'innovat*' and 'cultur*'. Accordingly, different forms were included such as innovativeness, innovation, cultural issues, organizational culture, organizational climate, innovation culture, regional/national culture and the like.

We found 1947 scientific articles at the date of extraction (early May 2015), once duplicate registers were deleted. We also did not restrict either the period of analysis or the language of the article. These articles were published between 1963 and the first quarter of 2015.

3.2. Codebook of descriptors

We used Wordstat software for content analysis to extract and analyse each article's title, abstract and keywords. Meaningless expressions were excluded while the rest were retained and grouped thematically in 44 descriptors (see appendix, Supplementary data). The themes are: (a) frameworks, (b) focal unit of analysis, (c) methods, (d) culture features and levels, and (e) influential variables. The descriptors emerged from the analysis and were not determined 'ex-ante'. Our role was just to identify and classify them into common themes as shown below.

A problem may arise in the identification of frameworks since Büschgens et al. (2013) found more than 40 different cultural values that are related to innovation in their review. Thus, the list of theoretical frameworks may be endless. Scholars are requested to investigate the knowledge frontier by testing original hypothesis. Nevertheless, we usually adhere to a certain framework while introducing some variations. This is why we retained separately those that achieved a minimum threshold of as low as 0.5% of the total articles (nine or more articles). We merged thematically where it was appropriate, due to the low number of cases, such as the case of Hofstede, Kogut and Singh, and Schwartz frameworks dealing with national culture differences.

The main theoretical approaches (a) are commented on in the background section. The group of focal unit of analysis (b) comprises two different types of objects. The first typology includes varieties of organizations analysed, ranging from SMEs to large firms and multinationals. The second one contains the level of culture studied, ranging from the lower levels of individual, group and organizational culture to the upper macro levels, namely regional and national culture. In terms of methods (c), we classified articles in quantitative and qualitative, if mentioned explicitly in any of the fields analysed (title, abstract and keywords). If an article was susceptible to have used both methods, then it was double coded.

For the sake of enriching the results, we separately coded some cultural and innovation related features in the block (d). To name just a few, the block of culture included issues such as acculturation, behaviour or cross-cultural, while the block of innovation comprised issues such as ambidexterity, creativity and innovativeness in the case of innovation. In a different block (e), we included topics related to influential variables and processes that play a role in the study of innovation culture. Among others, they are the context, the process of managing the human resource-HRM, learning or strategy. We included here the type of innovation (e.g. product, process) since each process and result are different and require a different type of setting.

As a limitation of our method, we should mention that we searched in the key fields of an article, namely title, abstract and keywords. This is why some other cultural frameworks and variables may have been excluded. Yet authors usually highlight the most relevant of the studies in the key fields analysed, which implies that the excluded issues have attracted only a marginal amount of interest.

3.3. The HOMALS

Homogeneity analysis by alternating least squares – HOMALS analyses the pattern of co-occurrence in the matrix formed by cases (in this study refers to the articles) and variables (the descriptors). Its main result is a low-dimensional map that synthesizes the relative proximity between descriptors. Descriptors with a low marginal frequency of joint appearance will appear distant in the map and closer in the opposite case. This statistical method helps reduce the researcher's bias when presenting the results of a systematic literature review and eases the reproducibility and reliability in subsequent periods. In content analysis, reliability regards the degree to which a coding process is reproducible by different coders yielding the same results (Krippendorff, 2004).

Following the methods reported by Hoffman and Franke (1986) and Hoffman and De Leeuw (1992), a matrix was built. The rows are articles/cases and the columns are descriptors/variables. A one is computed in the matrix if any of the descriptor's content is found in the article's title, abstract and keyword, and zero otherwise.

After that, the HOMALS was performed on this matrix in SPSS software (v. 20). In order to measure the goodness of fit, a loss function is introduced, which is to be minimized (Gifi, 1990). In SPSS, the HOMALS algorithm is conducted with least-squares loss functions. HOMALS falls in the optimal scaling approach, which is rooted in the Fisher (1941) and Guttman (1941) solution to assign numerical values to categories.

The dimensions obtained by this analysis are listed, directly related to the amount of variance explained (i.e. the first dimension explains more than the second one, and so forth). Accordingly, the first dimensions comprise a greater proportion of shared information than the last ones. The first two dimensions are usually the targeted solution, which are linear combinations of the original variables (descriptors). Inertia will report on the share of variance explained. According to De Leeuw and Mair (2009), total inertia is equal to the Pearson chi-square statistic for independence of the Table F with degrees of freedom equal to $(n-1)(m-1)$, where n = total number of rows, and m = total number of columns. In computational terms, total inertia is obtained as the weighted sum of squared distances of the rows' profile to the average profile. According to De Leeuw and Mair (2009), a threshold could be the solution of first i dimensions whose sum of inertias exceeds 50% of the total inertia in the model.

4. Results and discussion

4.1. Trends on culture and innovation

In order to ease the interpretation of the map, the share of descriptors over the full period is first analysed (1963–2015) and then the timeframe is split into two sub-periods. The rationale for the cut-off year was the general crisis of which results were visible in 2008. It can be expected that the new context has an impact on the research topicality. Accordingly, the first sub-period was set to 1963–2007 (44 years) and the second was 2008–2015 (7 years). The uneven timeframe of each sub-period does not affect the relative results introduced in the next tables, since the variation between sub-periods was computed in terms of relative share for each sub-total. For the sake of brevity, we can only comment on some of the main trends.

Table 3 summarizes the key figures of three referential themes of descriptors, namely (a) frameworks, (b) focal unit of analysis and (c) methods. Hofstede's (24%) and Schein's (15%) frameworks have been the most frequently used by scholars.

Table 3. Key figures of (a) frameworks, (b) focal unit of analysis and (c) methods (listed alphabetically by group).

Category	DESCRIPTORS(*)	Total % (N = 1947)	% on n		Variation from P1 to P2
			P1: 1963–2007 (n = 751)	P2:2008–2015 (n = 1,196)	
(a) Frameworks	AJZEN TPB	1.8%	0.9%	2.3%	**151.2%**
	CVF	**11.8%**	**9.9%**	**13.0%**	**32.4%**
	HOFSTEDE	**24.4%**	22.6%	25.5%	12.7%
	INSTITUTIONAL TH	0.7%	0.3%	0.9%	**245.4%**
	KBV	8.3%	5.6%	9.9%	77.9%
	NETWORK TH	1.6%	1.3%	1.8%	31.9%
	OPEN INNOVATION	1.6%	0.1%	2.5%	**1783.8%**
	RBV	7.7%	5.9%	8.9%	51.3%
	SCHEIN	15.6%	**13.8%**	**16.6%**	20.2%
(b) Focal unit of analysis	FAMILY FIRM	0.9%	0.3%	1.3%	**370.9%**
	GROUP	8.2%	7.6%	8.6%	**13.5%**
	(INDIVIDUAL	9.9%	8.7%	10.6%	**22.7%**
	INV	0.3%	0.3%	0.3%	**25.6%**
	JV/IJV	1.9%	2.5%	1.5%	−40.5%
	LARGE FIRM	1.5%	1.6%	1.5%	−5.8%
	MANAGER	9.0%	13.0%	6.4%	**−50.7%**
	MNE	3.7%	3.2%	4.0%	25.6%
	NATIONAL CULTURE	8.6%	7.1%	9.5%	**35.1%**
	ORGANIZATIONAL CULTURE	**33.9%**	**35.8%**	**32.7%**	−8.7%
	REGIONAL CULTURE	7.9%	6.5%	8.8%	**34.6%**
	SBU (strategic business unit)	1.3%	1.7%	1.0%	**−42.0%**
	SMEs	5.0%	3.1%	6.3%	**104.8%**
(c) methods	(c) QUALITATIVE	19.4%	16.4%	21.3%	30.2%
	(c) QUANTITATIVE	**30.9%**	**22.6%**	**36.0%**	**59.2%**

*Appendix 1 contains further information about the content of each descriptor included in tables.
Emphasized in bold are the most relevant figures.

Some emerging approaches arise such as the Open Innovation Paradigm, the institutional theory and Ajzen's theory of planned behaviour. All of them have reached a very low share in the full period; so they can be considered as emerging approaches.

The Hofstede approach has grown in interest less than Schein's framework. Both of them, along with the CVF, are the three main approaches. On the other hand, perspectives from strategic management have grown steadily to reach a joint total share of 16% in the full period (8.3% KBV, 7.7% RBV, with growth rates ranging from +77% to 51%, respectively). The network theory seems not to have attracted a relevant portion of the scholars' interest in this intersection, which is an issue that should be discussed for inclusion in the research agenda. The interest in SMEs is one of the fastest growing in the second sub-period (+104%), up to achieving a total share of 5% of the articles.

In terms of methods, quantitative approaches have been preferred over qualitative ones, although we should mention that the papers were not all empirical in nature nor have all of the authors explicitly mentioned their methods in the title, abstract or keywords. This is a limitation of our method, which encourages us to recommend that editors and authors equally include some type of descriptors relative to methods for the sake of future bibliometric analyses and search strategies.

Table 4 shows the trends in the thematic blocks of (d) culture features and levels, and (e) influential variables and processes. Leadership is a relevant characteristic of managers that has been included in an increasing share of articles. As has happened in the case of the

Table 4. Key figures of (d) culture features and levels and (e) influential variables and processes (listed alphabetically by group).

			% on n		
Category	DESCRIPTORS	Total % (N = 1,947)	P1: 1963–2007 (n = 751)	P2: 2008–2015 (n = 1,196)	Variation from P1 to P2
(d) culture features & levels	ACCULTURATION	1.9%	1.6%	2.1%	**30.8%**
	AMBIDEXTERITY	1.1%	0.8%	1.3%	**57.0%**
	ATTITUDE	2.2%	2.3%	2.1%	−7.7%
	BEHAVIOUR	**9.6%**	**9.7%**	**9.5%**	−1.9%
	CLIMATE	**10.0%**	**10.3%**	**9.8%**	−4.6%
	CREATIVITY	2.9%	2.4%	3.3%	**36.1%**
	CROSS_CULTURAL	5.3%	5.3%	5.3%	−1.1%
	DIVERSITY	1.2%	0.5%	1.6%	**198.3%**
	INNOVATIVENESS	2.4%	1.6%	2.9%	**83.1%**
	LEADERSHIP	6.2%	4.1%	7.5%	**82.3%**
(e) influential variables and processes	ADOPTION	4.2%	4.1%	4.3%	3.3%
	CHANGE	7.5%	8.4%	6.9%	−17.3%
	CONTEXT	**32.3%**	**30.8%**	**33.2%**	7.9%
	ENTREPRENEURSHIP	8.2%	6.4%	9.3%	45.2%
	HRM	**11.3%**	**13.4%**	**9.9%**	−26.0%
	INTERACTION	**18.4%**	**19.3%**	**17.8%**	−7.8%
	LEARNING	7.9%	8.1%	7.7%	−5.3%
	PERFORMANCE	**16.0%**	**11.1%**	**19.1%**	73.2%
	STRATEGY	**19.7%**	**17.7%**	**21.0%**	18.5%
	TYPE_OF_INNOVATION	**13.6%**	**12.8%**	**14.0%**	9.9%

Emphasized in bold are the most relevant figures.

focal unit of analysis, the shift toward the international context of virtually every type of venture seems to have had an impact on the increasing interest in diversity and acculturation, as this is the process that happens when a dominant culture interacts with other cultures in the same context. Scholars have increasingly studied national (+35%) and regional (+34%) levels of culture, although organizational culture attracted more interest (33.9% of share) in comparison with the two other settings over the full period.

Cross-cultural studies have seen a decline in interest. If analysed altogether, there is a need for more cross-cultural studies in different contexts by studying the acculturative process in particular from the lens of SMEs. Sociologically, a point of departure is the two-by-two matrix of acculturation developed by Berry (2005) and the findings of the research on cultural adjustment at work when speaking of expatriates (e.g. Black, Mendenhall, & Oddou, 1991). These two research streams are still marginal in the study of SMEs in light of the review conducted by González-Loureiro et al. (2015), who suggested that adjustment at work and family acculturation are two faces of the same coin. In a more recent review in the field of national culture and international strategic alliances, López-Duarte et al. (2016) also found the need to broaden the focus to include regional perspectives in longitudinal studies, i.e. the interest should now be the co-evolution of culture, context (including regional and national levels) and the lower levels (organization, groups and individuals).

Context, strategy and spaces for interaction govern the research in terms of influential variables and processes (see Table 4). In fact, some authors have found that creativity and innovation are determined by several organizational features such as the binomial strategy-structure and supportive mechanisms (e.g. Martins & Terblanche, 2003). According to Denison (1996), the context influences and shapes the culture, and the culture is created by interaction. The triad 'context–strategy–spaces for interaction' has become central to this research. Strategy and performance has increased relevantly during the last sub-period, which is in line with the increasing interest of scholars in strategic management approaches such as RBV and KBV. Thus, it appears that the recent crisis has motivated a shift in the study of culture and innovation towards a strategic viewpoint.

4.2. Mapping the intellectual structure of research

After the analysis of trends, we introduce a map of the intellectual structure of research (Figure 1). The inertia of the first dimension represents the 36% of total variance while the second dimension represents 34%, which in total exceeds the minimum threshold of 50%. Following the suggestions of Hoffman and Franke (1986) and the examples of González-Loureiro et al. (2015) and López-Duarte et al. (2016), the poles of each dimension should be labelled according to the more extreme and the most frequent descriptors that agglutinate some others. In addition, we conducted a hierarchical cluster analysis of cases on the coordinates saved for each descriptor. The Ward method was used, which implied a Euclidean distance for clustering cases. The dendogram suggested that the solution of four clusters was optimal, as depicted in Figure 1.

On the rightmost side, the descriptors attracting the highest hits were strategy (19%) and type of innovation (13%), while KBV and RBV (8% and 7%) have been the main theoretical approaches. Descriptors relate to innovation and strategy, as for instance, the open innovation paradigm, the ambidexterity of explorative and exploitative capabilities and the network theory. The unit of analysis has been essentially SMEs, as well as large

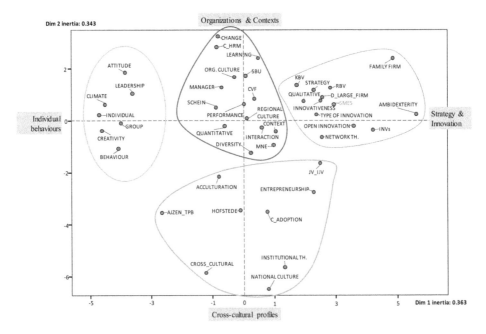

Figure 1. The intellectual structure of research on the intersection of innovation and culture (1963–2015).

firms and INVs to a lesser extent. Consequently, we propose to label this pole as 'strategy and innovation'.

On the opposite side of dimension 1, the key attractants have been climate (10%), individual (9%), behaviour (9%) and group (8%). The other descriptors are leadership, creativity and attitude. If jointly analysed, they refer to how individuals behave in a group and deal with critical issues that form the culture and innovation viewpoints: climate, leadership and creativity. Accordingly, we suggest label this pole, 'individual behaviours'.

At the top of the map, the main attractants are organizational culture (33%), HRM (11%) and manager (9%). The other descriptors relate to change and learning while Schein and CVF have been the most frequent approaches. The central units of analysis have been the organization and the strategic business units (SBUs) with a focus on the performance. It seems, therefore, that the main topics relate to the organization itself and, if we consider the other descriptors included in this cluster of cases, then the context and the interaction in that context are also included. We therefore label this pole as 'organizations and contexts'.

On the bottom, the cloud of descriptors appears more disperse. The key attractants are national culture (8%) in the lowermost of the map and Hofstede (24%). The surrounding descriptors are related to the comparison of cultures internationally speaking. Cross-cultural, adoption or acculturation are some examples, along with Ajzen's theory of planned behaviour and entrepreneurship. Accordingly, the label suggested for this pole is 'cross-cultural profiles'.

4.3. Discussion of results: key gaps for further research

Our ultimate goal was to find research gaps in the intersection of innovation and culture in the particular case of SMEs. To do so, the map should be interpreted in light of the extant dilemmas when it comes to regional and organizational culture, as described in the background section.

The first group of dilemmas has to do with the levels of analysis and the global, international context where innovation occurs. They are internationalization versus regional identity, competition versus cooperation, closed versus open innovation and building large firms versus creating new firms. From regional science, much emphasis has been put on the regional identity shaped by the extant actors in the system, from both the triple-helix approach (Etzkowitz & Leydesdorff, 2000) and the systems of innovation (Lundvall, 1992; Freeman, 1995). However, the issue of internationalization and how large corporations and multinationals can be best involved in the regional setting is still underrepresented in the particular case of SMEs. This international approach is represented by the pole 'cross-cultural profiles', which is quite distant from the dot 'SMEs'. While it is well known that national culture plays the role of moderator between corporate innovation culture and innovation outcomes (e.g. Unger, Rank, & Gemünden, 2014), such relationships deserve further attention from scholars. This is particularly relevant in a moment and context when SMEs tend to go international in order to survive (Puig, González-Loureiro, & Ghauri, 2014), and the relational issues still do not have a relevant impact on the growth of innovative SMEs (González-Loureiro & Figueroa-Dorrego, 2012). This implies increasing needs for the SME to handle different cultural settings while innovating in the international context.

Since the individual group in SMEs is notably smaller when compared to larger counterparts, scholars should devote attention to individual behaviour in small groups. Comparative studies between ventures of different sizes are also an opportunity for future research. In this research avenue, we have found that some approaches are missing such as the Upper Echelons Theory (Hambrick & Mason, 1984), which has been included in strategic management approaches to this intersection (e.g. Elron, 1998). According to that theory, executives' experiences and values have a major influence on how they interpret the situations they face so that perception affects their choices. This influence is even stronger in the case of SMEs since the top management team is smaller. In the particular case of family firms, the manager is influenced by the other family members' perceptions. Accordingly, further research should test to what extent the upper echelons' perspective determines the culture and climate for innovating in SMEs, which lastly has an influence on the cultural configuration of the innovative organization.

By extension, this approach will help alleviate the tensions between competition and cooperation under the open innovation paradigm. To do so, more multi-level studies seem also to be required, as, for instance, the two-level analysis of Dabrowska and Savits-kaya (2014), which included the group and the organization levels. The levels refer to different units of analysis. Since SMEs tend to collaborate in networks of firms, the levels are even more complex than in the case of large ventures. They relate to groups of individuals, groups of ventures, regional and national cultures and their intersection in the international markets. Among the key cultural elements, the manager's degree of openness is to be incorporated, along with regional, national and international related variables. How the regional setting and, in particular, the extant SMEs can benefit from the inclusion of large corporations and multinationals in the open innovation paradigm is also a future avenue for research. Among the manager's cultural features in the case of SMEs, leadership should also be included further in light of the distance of the pole labelled 'individual behaviours'. This will help address the tensions in the dilemma between authority and participation in these firms and between shareholder value versus stakeholder orientation. The key idea is that the regional innovation setting should help resolve the local problems by innovating, while remaining profitable is a must for survival. A relevant concern for SMEs relates to operational efficiency in the short-term when innovating. Hyland and Beckett (2005) showed that there is a trade-off between innovative culture and operational efficiency. While the latter would foster imitation by means of exploitative capabilities, the former would require creativity and explorative capabilities. This becomes crucial for SMEs in light of their limited resources and capabilities, which deserve further empirical tests and theory-driven explanations of how best to deal with such a trade-off.

Another group of tensions is related to the circular notion that context is defined by the interaction, but context also conditions the interaction. This notion revolves around the dilemmas between technology push versus market pull, entrepreneurial versus technical skills, and hard versus soft factors within the regional context. This gap is represented by the distance between 'change', which is included in the pole 'organizations and con-texts', and 'SMEs'. The underlying question is how this research intersection deals with the apparently unchanged culture at both regional and organizational levels. From the meta-analytic review of Büschgens et al. (2013), one can infer that culture remains the same over time. This assumption may not hold from the strategic management perspective as organizations co-evolve with the environment and adapt their strategy and behaviour accordingly (Lewin & Volberda, 1999). Van Reine and Dankbaar (2011), in their comparative study of seven regions, showed that corporate and regional cultures co-evolve and that sometimes the interaction between both cultures results in a virtuous circle. An advancing research line relates to the idea of transformational leadership to 'transformational culture'. Transformational leadership in this context deals with how the leader adapts his/her style according to the capabilities of the group in order to build an organizational climate that fosters innovation (Sarros et al., 2008). Environmental changes affect SMEs more than in larger firms. Therefore, how culture co-evolves in SMEs should be investigated, as well as in the regional setting according to changes in the environment. Culture should not be a fixed characteristic over time. Thus, frameworks should include the variable 'time' in what can be labelled as 'transformational culture': how the unit of analysis shifts its culture depending upon the surrounding context and the internal characteristics of the group in order to perform the best. The SMEs will benefit from an adequate balance between soft and hard factors within the regional context. This regional culture will attract an appropriate balance of entrepreneurial and technical skills in its labour market. Meanwhile, the inclusion of large firms and multinationals in the research agenda will help create the required context in order to evolve towards a virtuous spiral of increasing innovative culture within the regional setting. The critical issue is how to appropriately incorporate methods that account for this two-way relationship between context and interaction in the context.

5. Concluding remarks for a research agenda

This research aimed to review extant research on the intersection of culture and innovation and map its intellectual structure in order to find research avenues in the particular case of SMEs. This type of firms accounts for virtually a 99% of the economic fabric in developed economies, and their current competition requires them to innovate if they are to survive and succeed in the globalized and knowledge-based economy.

To do so, this systematic literature review has analysed the content of research of 1947 scientific articles, which has provided some trends and a map of the intellectual structure of research to date. As a result, some research gaps have been found that have led to a proposal of research avenues in critical issues for SMEs willing to succeed in the implementation of an innovation culture in the regional setting. These gaps relate to the particular characteristics of these organizations and their inherent limitation of resources and capabilities. The research avenues are threefold: more multi-level studies (individual, group, SMEs, sub-cultures, regions and nations), the co-evolution of the SMEs in the regional context and cross-cultural research in the innovation culture of SMEs and regions.

The article's contribution has been twofold: the codebook of descriptors, and the map of the intellectual structure that will serve as a roadmap for further inquiry. Some gaps may have remained hidden in the map for the sake of brevity; so the map should encourage scholars to find new gaps for this topic.

Some critical issues have arisen. First, there is no optimal cultural configuration. In the case of SMEs, which are usually more flattened-shaped in terms of structural levels, managers should seize on the organization's flexibility to achieving the congruence between the cultural setting, its strategy and the context. This argument follows the industrial organization paradigm of fit between environment–strategy–structure. The organization is embedded in the regional, social context where it operates. Competition is currently observed at an international level. If the context changes, then the organization must revise its strategy, structure and cultural setting accordingly. The organizational culture is formed by the dominant regional culture as well. So culture, as a supporting part of the strategy implementation, can be different between SMEs operating in the same regional context, and it depends on the SME strategic response to the environmental challenges. Therefore, scholars are suggested to include the critical issue of the two-way relationship between context and interaction within that context.

Second, the literature has usually considered culture as an immovable feature of the organization and the region or, at least, it has remained unchanged for a long time. It takes time to develop this feature at the organizational level and it takes much more time at the regional level. However, context is created by interaction and interaction also determines the context, which will finally shape the organizational culture. Since the context is continuously changing, then culture should also co-evolve accordingly. This is a relevant research avenue in the current global competition for SMEs since it is very likely that smaller firms can adapt and shift more quickly than large counterparts. This particular research avenue will lead to the concept of transformational culture.

Third, SMEs are usually embedded in networks that are increasingly international in scope. Therefore, managing SMEs in cross-cultural environments is becoming a major requisite for firms. Moreover, according to the evolving research in the theory of internationalization (Johanson & Vahlne, 2009), firms must face the liabilities of outsidership during their first international entries. That outsidership refers to the existing networks of international business and trade. Innovative SMEs are very likely to go international shortly after succeeding in their innovation and to make the most of a niche strategy (Hagen, Zucchella, Cerchiello, & De Giovanni, 2012). Therefore, the binomial innovation-internationalization deserves further cross-cultural research in the case of SMEs, since the cultural orientation of the outgoing innovative SME may clash with the host region.

All in all, the intersection of culture and innovation in SMEs has to face relevant challenges from the soft perspective to manage organizations and regions from the viewpoint of individuals. This kind of 'humanizing' management can be better addressed by combining approaches from regional science, with managerial, sociological and psychological discourses. Moreover, upper levels of analysis relative to the territory – e.g. systems of innovation – should incorporate the individual agent as well and the small group perspective to capture the multi-level interactions that are sometimes absent in regional studies and planning.

Disclosure statement

No potential conflict of interest was reported by the authors.

Funding

This article was supported by national funds provided by FCT – Foundation for Science and Technology (Portugal) through the project UID/SOC/04020/2013. Hugo Pinto also acknowledges the financial support from FCT (SFRH/BPD/84038/2012) funded by POCH and co-financed by the European Social Fund and national funds from the Ministry of Science, Technology and Higher Education.

ORCID

Miguel Gonzalez-Loureiro ⓘ http://orcid.org/0000-0002-4299-1995
Maria José Sousa ⓘ http://orcid.org/0000-0001-8633-4199
Hugo Pinto ⓘ http://orcid.org/0000-0002-8497-4798

References

Adler, P. S., & Kwon, S. W. (2002). Social capital: Prospects for a new concept. *Academy of Management Review, 27*(1), 17–40. doi:10.5465/AMR.2002.5922314

Aguinis, H., Pierce, C. A., Bosco, F. A., & Muslin, I. S. (2009). First decade of organizational research methods: Trends in design, measurement, and data-analysis topics. *Organizational Research Methods, 12*(1), 69–112. doi:10.1177/1094428108322641

Ajzen, I. (1991). Theory of planned behaviour. *Organizational Behavior and Human Decision Processes, 50*(2), 179–211. doi:10.1016/0749-5978(91)90020-T

Albors-Garrigos, J., & Hidalgo, A. (2012). The role of a firm's absorptive capacity and the technology transfer process in clusters: How effective are technology centres in low-tech clusters? *Entrepreneurship & Regional Development: An International Journal, 24*(7-8), 37–41. doi:10.1080/08985626.2012.710256

Amable, B. (2000). Institutional complementarity and diversity of social systems of innovation and production. *Review of International Political Economy, 7*(4), 645–687. doi:10.1080/096922900750034572

Asheim, B. (1996). Industrial districts as 'learning regions': A condition for prosperity. *European Planning Studies, 4*(4), 379–400. doi:10.1080/09654319608720354

Asheim, B. T., Moodysson, J., & Tödtling, F. (2011). Constructing regional advantage: Towards state-of-the-art regional innovation system policies in Europe? *European Planning Studies, 19*(7), 1133–1139. doi:10.1080/09654313.2011.573127

Asheim, B., Smith, H., & Oughton, C. (2011). Regional innovation systems: Theory, empirics and policy. *Regional Studies, 45*(7), 875–891. doi:10.1080/00343404.2011.596701

Bandura, A. (1986). *The social foundations of thought and action.* Englewood Cliffs, NJ: Prentice-Hall.

Barney, J. B. (1986). Organizational culture: Can it be a source of sustained competitive advantage? *Academy of Management Review, 11*(3), 656–665. doi:10.5465/AMR.1986.4306261

Barney, J. B. (1991). Firm resources and sustained competitive advantage. *Journal of Management, 17*(1), 99–120. doi:10.1177/014920639101700108

Berry, J. W. (2005). Acculturation: Living successfully in two cultures. *International Journal of Intercultural Relations, 29*(6), 697–712. doi:10.1016/j.ijintrel.2005.07.013

Black, J. S., Mendenhall, M., & Oddou, G. (1991). Toward a comprehensive model of international adjustment: An integration of multiple theoretical perspectives. *Academy of Management Review, 16*(2), 291–317.

Borgatti, S. P., & Foster, P. C. (2003). The network paradigm in organizational research: A review and typology. *Journal of Management, 29*(6), 991–1013. doi:10.1016/S0149-2063(03)00087-4

Boschma, R. (2005). Proximity and innovation: A critical assessment. *Regional Studies, 39*(1), 61–74. doi:10.1080/0034340052000320887

Burt, R. S. (2004). Structural holes and good ideas. *American Journal of Sociology, 110*(2), 349–399. doi:10.1086/421787

Büschgens, T., Bausch, A., & Balkin, D. B. (2013). Organizational culture and innovation: A meta-analytic review. *Journal of Product Innovation Management, 30*(4), 763–781. doi:10.1111/jpim.12021

Camagni, R. P. (2005). The concept of innovative milieu and its relevance for public policies in European lagging regions. *Papers in Regional Science, 74*(4), 317–340. doi:10.1111/j.1435-5597. 1995.tb00644.x

Chandler, G. N., Keller, C., & Lyon, D. W. (2000). Unraveling the determinants and consequences of an innovation-supportive organizational culture. *Entrepreneurship Theory and Practice, 25*(1), 59–76.

Chauvet, V., Chollet, B., Soda, G., & Huault, I. (2011). The contribution of network research to managerial culture and practice. *European Management Journal, 29*(5), 321–334. doi:10.1016/ j.emj.2011.06.005

Chesbrough, H. (2003). The logic of open innovation: Managing intellectual property. *California Management Review, 45*(3), 33–58. doi:10.2307/41166175

Cohen, W. M., & Levinthal, D. A. (1990). Absorptive capacity: A new perspective on learning and innovation. *Administrative Science Quarterly, 35*(1), 128–152. doi:10.2307/2393553

Cooke, P., Parrilli, M. D., & Curbelo, J. L. (orgs.). (2012). *Innovation, global change and territorial resilience*. Cheltenham: Edward Elgar Publishing.

Cooke, P., & Rehfeld, D. (2011). Path dependence and new paths in regional evolution: In search of the role of culture. *European Planning Studies, 19*(11), 1909–1929. doi:10.1080/09654313.2011. 618685

Cooke, P., Uranga, M. G., & Etxebarria, G. (1997). Regional innovation systems: Institutional and organisational dimensions. *Research Policy, 26*(4), 475–491. doi:10.1016/S0048-7333(97)00025-5

Cosmas, S. C., & Sheth, J. N. (1980). Identification of opinion leaders across cultures: An assessment for use in the diffusion of innovations and ideas. *Journal of International Business Studies, 11*(1), 66–72. doi:10.1057/palgrave.jibs.8490597

Dabic, M., González-Loureiro, M., & Furrer, O. (2014). Research on the strategy of multinational enterprises: key approaches and new avenues. *BRQ Business Research Quarterly, 17*(2), 129–148. doi:10.1016/j.brq.2013.09.001

Dabrowska, J., & Savitskaya, I. (2014). When culture matters: Exploring the open innovation paradigm. *International Journal of Business Innovation and Research, 8*(1), 94–118. doi:10.1504/ IJBIR.2014.058048

Dahlander, L., & Gann, D. M. (2010). How open is innovation? *Research Policy, 39*(6), 699–709. doi:10.1016/j.respol.2010.01.013

Damanpour, F. (1991). Organizational innovation: A meta-analysis of effects of determinants and moderators. *Academy of Management Journal, 34*(3), 555–590. doi:10.2307/256406

De Leeuw, J., & Mair, P. (2009). Simple and canonical correspondence analysis using the R package anacor. *Journal of Statistical Software, 31*(5), 1–18. doi:10.18637/jss.v031.i05

Denison, D. R. (1996). What is the difference between organizational culture and organizational climate? A native's point of view on a decade of paradigm wars. *Academy of Management Review, 21*(3), 619–654. doi:10.5465/amr.1996.9702100310

Dobni, C. B. (2008). Measuring innovation culture in organizations: The development of a generalized innovation culture construct using exploratory factor analysis. *European Journal of Innovation Management, 11*(4), 539–559. doi:10.1108/14601060810911156

Duriau, V. J., Reger, R. K., & Pfarrer, M. D. (2007). A content analysis of the content analysis literature in organization studies - Research themes, data sources, and methodological refinements. *Organizational Research Methods, 10*(1), 5–34. doi:10.1177/1094428106289252

Ebbekink, M., & Lagendijk, A. (2013). What's next in researching cluster policy: Place-based governance for effective cluster policy. *European Planning Studies, 21*(5), 735–753. doi:10.1080/ 09654313.2013.734460

Efrat, K. (2014). The direct and indirect impact of culture on innovation. *Technovation, 34*(1), 12– 20. doi:10.1016/j.technovation.2013.08.003

Elron, E. (1998). Top management teams within multinational corporations: Effects of cultural heterogeneity. *The Leadership Quarterly, 8*(4), 393–412. doi:10.1016/S1048-9843(97)90021-7

Etzkowitz, H., & Leydesdorff, L. (2000). The dynamics of innovation: From National Systems and 'Mode 2' to a Triple Helix of university–industry–government relations. *Research Policy, 29*(2), 109–123. doi:10.1016/S0048-7333(99)00055-4

Fernandez-Jardon, C. M., González-Loureiro, M., & Pita-Castelo, J. (2016). Orientación cultural a la innovación en empresas: un enfoque sociológico en el Sistema de Innovación de Galicia. *Revista Internacional de Sociología, 74*(2), e035–18. doi:10.3989/ris.2016.74.2.035

Fisher, R. A. (1941). The precision of discriminant functions. *The Annals of Eugenics, 10*(1), 422–429. doi:10.1111/j.1469-1809.1940.tb02264.x

Foray, D. (2014). From smart specialisation to smart specialisation policy. *European Journal of Innovation Management, 17*(4), 492–507. doi:10.1108/EJIM-09-2014-0096

Forehand, G. A. (1963). Assessments of innovative behavior: Partial criteria for the assessment of executive performance. *Journal of Applied Psychology, 47*(3), 206–213. doi:10.1037/h0049211

Freel, M. S. (2000). Barriers to product innovation in small manufacturing firms. *International Small Business Journal, 18*(2), 60–80. doi:10.1177/0266242600182003

Freeman, C. (1995). The 'national system of innovation' in historical perspective. *Cambridge Journal of Economics, 19*(1), 5–24.

Frohman, A. L. (1998). Building a culture for innovation. *Research Technology Management, 41*(2), 9–13.

Geels, F. W. (2004). From sectoral systems of innovation to socio-technical systems: Insights about dynamics and change from sociology and institutional theory. *Research Policy, 33*(6), 897–920. doi:10.1016/j.respol.2004.01.015

Gifi, A. (1990). *Nonlinear multivariate analysis.* Chichester: Wiley.

González-Loureiro, M., Dabic, M., & Kiessling, T. (2015). Acculturation and overseas assignments: A review and research agenda. *International Journal of Intercultural Relations, 49*, 239–250. doi:10.1016/j.ijintrel.2015.05.003

González-Loureiro, M., & Figueroa-Dorrego, P. (2012). Intellectual capital and system of innovation: What really matters at innovative SMEs. *Intangible Capital, 8*(2), 239–274. doi:10.3926/ic.273

Granovetter, M. S. (1973). The strength of weak ties. *American Journal of Sociology, 78*(6), 1360–1380. doi:10.1086/225469

Grant, R. M. (1996). Toward a knowledge-based theory of the firm. *Strategic Management Journal, 17*(S2), 109–122. doi:10.1002/smj.4250171110

Guttman, L. (1941). The quantification of a class of attributes: A theory and a method of scale construction. In P. Horst (Ed.), *The prediction of personal adjustment* (pp. 319–348). New York, NY: Social Science.

Hagen, B., Zucchella, A., Cerchiello, P., & De Giovanni, N. (2012). International strategy and performance – Clustering strategic types of SMEs. *International Business Review, 21*(3), 369–382. doi:10.1016/j.ibusrev.2011.04.002

Hambrick, D. C., & Mason, P. A. (1984). Upper echelons: The organization as a reflection of its top managers. *Academy of Management Review, 9*(2), 193–206. doi:10.5465/AMR.1984.4277628

Hoffman, D. L., & De Leeuw, J. (1992). Interpreting multiple correspondence analysis as a multidimensional scaling method. *Marketing Letters, 3*(3), 259–272. doi:10.1007/BF00994134

Hoffman, D. L., & Franke, G. R. (1986). Correspondence analysis: Graphical representation of categorical data in marketing research. *Journal of Marketing Research, 23*(3), 213–227. doi:10.2307/3151480

Hofstede, G. (1980). *Culture's consequences: International differences in work-related values.* Beverly Hills, CA: Sage.

Hofstede, G. (1994). The business of international business is culture. *International Business Review, 3*(1), 1–14. doi:10.1016/0969-5931(94)90011-6

Hogan, S. J., & Coote, L. V. (2014). Organizational culture, innovation, and performance: A test of Schein's model. *Journal of Business Research, 67*(8), 1609–1621. doi:10.1016/j.jbusres.2013.09.007

Hyland, P., & Beckett, R. (2005). Engendering an innovative culture and maintaining operational balance. *Journal of Small Business and Enterprise Development, 12*(3), 336–352. doi:10.1108/14626000510612268

James, A. (2005). Demystifying the role of culture in innovative regional economies. *Regional Studies, 39*(9), 1197–1216. doi:10.1080/00343400500389968

Jensen, M. B., Johnson, B., Lorenz, E., & Lundvall, B. Å. (2007). Forms of knowledge and modes of innovation. *Research Policy*, *36*(5), 680–693. doi:10.1016/j.respol.2007.01.006

Johanson, J., & Vahlne, J. E. (2009). The Uppsala internationalization process model revisited: From liability of foreignness to liability of outsidership. *Journal of International Business Studies*, *40*(9), 1411–1431. doi:10.1057/jibs.2009.24

Kogut, B., & Singh, H. (1988). The effect of national culture on the choice of entry mode. *Journal of International Business Studies*, *19*(3), 411–432. doi:10.1057/palgrave.jibs.8490394

Krippendorff, K. (2004). Reliability in content analysis. *Human Communication Research*, *30*(3), 411–433.

Lechner, C., & Dowling, M. (2003). Firm networks: External relationships as sources for the growth and competitiveness of entrepreneurial firms. *Entrepreneurship & Regional Development*, *15*(1), 1–26. doi:10.1080/08985620210159220

Lewin, A. Y., & Volberda, H. W. (1999). Prolegomena on coevolution: A framework for research on strategy and new organizational forms. *Organization science*, *10*(5), 519–534. doi:10.1287/orsc.10.5.519

López-Duarte, C., González-Loureiro, M., Vidal-Suárez, M. M., & González-Díaz, B. (2016). International strategic alliances and national culture: Mapping the field and developing a research agenda. *Journal of World Business*, *51*(4), 511–524. doi:10.1016/j.jwb.2016.05.001

Lundvall, B. (1992). *National systems of innovation: Towards a theory of innovation and interactive learning*. London: Pinter Publishers.

Martins, E. C., & Terblanche, F. (2003). Building organisational culture that stimulates creativity and innovation. *European Journal of Innovation Management*, *6*(1), 64–74. doi:10.1108/14601060310456337

Nahapiet, J., & Ghoshal, S. (1998). Social capital, intellectual capital, and the organizational advantage. *Academy of Management Review*, *23*(2), 242–266. doi:10.5465/AMR.1998.533225

Nunes, S., & Lopes, R. (2015). Firm performance, innovation modes and territorial embeddedness. *European Planning Studies*, *23*(9), 1796–1826. doi:10.1080/09654313.2015.1021666

Puig, F., González-Loureiro, M., & Ghauri, P. N. (2014). Internationalisation for survival: The case of new ventures. *Management International Review*, *54*(5), 653–673. doi:10.1007/s11575-014-0209-4

Quinn, R. E., & Rohrbaugh, J. (1983). A spatial model of effectiveness criteria: Towards a competing values approach to organizational analysis. *Management Science*, *29*(3), 363–77. doi:10.1287/mnsc.29.3.363

Quinn, R. E., & Spreitzer, G. M. (1991). The psychometrics of the competing values culture instrument and an analysis of the impact of organizational culture on quality of life. In R. W. Woodman and W. A. Pasmore (Eds.), *Research in organizational change and development*, (Vol. 5, pp. 115–142). Greenwich, CT: JAI Press.

Rutten, R., Westlund, H., & Boekema, F. (2010). The spatial dimension of social capital. *European Planning Studies*, *18*(6), 863–871. doi:10.1080/09654311003701381

Sarros, J. C., Cooper, B. K., & Santora, J. C. (2008). Building a climate for innovation through transformational leadership and organizational culture. *Journal of Leadership & Organizational Studies*, *15*(2), 145–158. doi:10.1177/1548051808324100

Schein, E. H. (1984). Coming to a new awareness of organizational culture. *Sloan Management Review*, *25*(2), 3–16.

Schein, E. H. (1986). *Organizational culture and leadership*. San Francisco: Jossey-Bass.

Schwartz, S. H. (1992). Universals in the content and structure of values: Theoretical advances and empirical tests in 20 countries. *Advances in Experimental Social Psychology*, *25*(1), 1–65. doi:10.1016/S0065-2601(08)60281-6

Shafique, M. (2013). Thinking inside the box? Intellectual structure of the knowledge base of innovation research (1988–2008). *Strategic Management Journal*, *34*(1), 62–93. doi:10.1002/smj.2002

Shane, S. A. (1992). Why do some societies invent more than others? *Journal of Business Venturing*, *7*(1), 29–46. doi:10.1016/0883-9026(92)90033-N

Singer, H. A. (1969). The impact of human resources on business: Environment must foster sense of personal worth. *Business Horizons*, *12*(2), 53–58. doi:10.1016/0007-6813(69)90127-X

Škerlavaj, M., Song, J. H., & Lee, Y. (2010). Organizational learning culture, innovative culture and innovations in South Korean firms. *Expert Systems with Applications, 37*(9), 6390–6403. doi:10.1016/j.eswa.2010.02.080

Torre, A., & Rallet, A. (2005). Proximity and localization. *Regional Studies, 39*(1), 47–59. doi:10.1080/0034340052000320842

Unger, B. N., Rank, J., & Gemünden, H. G. (2014). Corporate innovation culture and dimensions of project portfolio success: The moderating role of national culture. *Project Management Journal, 45*(6), 38–57. doi:10.1002/pmj.21458

Van Reine, P., & Dankbaar, B. (2011). A virtuous circle? co-evolution of regional and corporate cultures. *European Planning Studies, 19*(11), 1865–1883. doi:10.1080/09654313.2011.618684

Exploring the links between culture and innovation in micro firms: cultural dimensions, social mechanisms and outcomes

Madelon van Oostrom ⓘ and Manuel Fernández-Esquinas

ABSTRACT

This article analyses the role of cultural components in the innovation processes of micro firms. The article develops an analytical and operational approach to the notion of culture of innovation departing from conceptual contributions from cultural and economic sociology. This framework is used in a study of micro firms in the Canary Islands (Spain). A survey, a group of open-ended interviews and in-depth case studies have been used to identify and explain the social and cultural mechanisms that make up the culture of innovation of small firms and shape their open innovation strategies. The results highlight the importance of firms' knowledge base in the configuration of different innovation behaviours. The findings also help to explore the relationship between homogeneous and pluralistic conceptions of the culture of innovation.

1. Introduction

This article explores the innovation processes in small and medium-sized firms (SMEs) and micro firms in regional innovation systems. Its main goal is to analyse the social and cultural mechanisms through which these firms carry out innovation in the disadvantaged environments of the so-called peripheral regions. Innovation dynamics of firms and underlying knowledge production processes are considered of crucial importance for regional development. However, the capacities to undertake innovation are very context-dependent on both the characteristics of the firms and the configuration of the regional environment, especially by actors and institutions that shape innovation (Edquist, 2005). An important barrier to innovation is related to the profile of firms present in a region. Firm innovation is shaped by productive specialization, internal structure and capacities of firms, and by their external links. Specialized research has widely evidenced that innovation is connected to high-tech sectors, to firms with specialized units and trained personnel able to absorb knowledge, and to firms with fluent relationships with suppliers, clients and knowledge providers (Cohen & Levinthal, 1990; van der Panne, van Beers, & Kleinknecht, 2003). These traits are closely associated with bigger firms. With the exception of the specific profile of small science and technology firms (mainly start-ups and spin-offs), seldom are they found in firms located in most regions (Tether, Mina, Consoli, & Gagliaardi, 2005), especially in peripheral regions characterized by a lack of industrial agglomeration and an overwhelming presence of very small or micro firms. As a result, these firms are beyond the scope of innovation studies (Freel, 2005)

Some important frameworks have started paying attention to sources of innovation in the network of diversified firms of peripheral regions, including SMEs and micro firms not directly linked to R&D. The innovation system approach, especially at the regional level (Cooke, Gomez Uranga, & Etxebarria, 1997), is perhaps one of the more pioneering endeavours focusing on the complex array of elements that help to identify endogenous sources of innovation in the configuration of local firms and other relevant actors in the system. Other complementary frameworks consider firms' potential from a micro-level perspective, such as the open innovation approach, and pay special attention to their capacities and strategies for exchanging and using sources of knowledge available in the environment (Chesbrough, 2012).

What these frameworks have in common is the growing importance attributed to institutional dimensions, such as laws, policies and regulations, capacities and education. Increasingly, they have been paying special attention to cultural dimensions. Regional innovation studies are considering that culture is important for firm innovation, because values, informal norms and cognitive frameworks shape the capacity to act and to establish links with key external actors for innovation (Asheim & Isaksen, 2002; James, 2005; Trippl & Toedtling, 2008). The influence of cultural dimensions on innovation performance has also gained interest in organizational and management theories (Jaruzelski, Loehr, & Holman, 2011). In the case of SMEs, there has also been a reaction to the mainstream innovation literature that ignores the so-called 'softer' sociocultural elements, sometimes considering them as a 'residual' explanation of innovation capacities and performance (James, 2005).

However, there are some important gaps in the innovation literature regarding the role of cultural dimensions, especially in micro firms. In general, there is a lack of conceptual precision when referring to cultural factors. They are often treated as a part of the complex 'institutional thickness' (Amin & Thrift, 1995), while the observation of institutional mechanisms goes unnoticed. A conceptual problem also arises for empirical research because of the blurred meanings assigned to frequently used concepts, such as the different kinds of institutional components referring to norms, values and cognitive frameworks, and their relationship with other important explanatory mechanisms, such as social capital and innovation networks (Pilon & DeBresson, 2003). These mechanisms are especially influential in micro firms because the strategies, relationships and performance of these firms are directly mediated by the cultural traits of the owner and core workers.

In this article, we observe the innovation dynamics of micro firms informed by a cross-fertilization of different analytical approaches that pay attention to the influential role of culture. Theoretical contributions from economic and cultural sociology are employed as a useful complement to innovation studies, together with insights from the regional innovation system approach and open innovation frameworks. For this purpose, we present empirical findings on innovation dynamics in the Canary Islands (Spain). This is an outermost region characterized by a service economy and low innovation performance that can be considered a representative example of a peripheral region where the innovative dynamics of micro firms are an essential component of the regional innovation system. The conceptual exercise is used to inform empirical research based mainly on qualitative interviews and case studies that help to explain the richness and complexity of innovation dynamics in micro firms.

The article is structured as follows: after the introduction, Section 2 reviews the key conceptual frameworks and provides some conceptual clarifications. Section 3 establishes an operational definition of the culture of innovation and its main dimensions. Section 4 describes case study methodology and design. Section 5 discusses the main results. Finally, some implications of interest to policymakers and managers are summarized in the conclusions.

2. Background

2.1. Culture and innovation in SMEs: issues and gaps in current literature

Innovation is generally understood as an interactive process of value creation and problem solving based on both tacit (experiences, ideas and skills) and explicit or codified (technology) knowledge. It refers, on the one hand, to new or improved products, services, processes and methods, some of which are driven by technology and, on the other, to change in organizational procedures. When examining innovation, it is helpful to distinguish explanations at different levels of analysis. For the purpose of this article, it is useful to look at the systemic approach that explains innovation at the meso level of an innovation system and the open innovation approach that studies how firms innovate mainly at the micro level. Both share important consensus about the nature of innovation (in opposition to the linear model that perceives innovation as an orderly outcome of earlier research and development processes) and the interactive and social understanding of innovation processes (Bessant & Tidd, 2007; Drucker, 2014; Edquist, 2005; Fagerberg & Verspagen, 2009; Lundvall & Borrás, 1997; Manley, 2003).

The innovation system approach, whether national (Nelson & Winter, 1982), regional (Asheim & Isaksen, 2002; Cooke et al., 1997), local (Fernández-Esquinas & Pinto, 2014) or sectorial (Malerba, 2005), regards innovation as the outcome of a systematic process in order to explain the generation and use of the technology available in a certain environment. Innovation is considered as a dynamic and social process based on interactive learning processes between the system's key agents and their interactions: knowledge producers (universities and educational establishments), knowledge transfer regulators (governmental agencies), interface organizations (knowledge transfer and innovation centres), and knowledge exploiters and diffusers (firms). Institutions, such as laws and norms, are considered crucial elements since 'they shape (and are shaped by) the actions of the organizations and the relations between them' (Edquist, 2001, p. 3). Innovation systems are thus conceived as the set of organizations and institutions that generate and shape innovation through both collaborative and competitive interactions.

Moreover, open innovation perspectives pay special attention to both the strategies and capacities to exchange information as a key source of firm innovation (Chesbrough, 2012). The value of incorporating information from outside the firm has been highlighted by earlier business innovation literature with notions such as absorptive capacity or permeability that stress the ability to transform external information into internal value

(Cohen & Levinthal, 1990). In addition to contributions associated with open innovation, such as open business models and open innovation for service development (Chesbrough, 2012), other authors highlight the importance of user and consumer feedback (von Hippel, 2005) for firms' innovation performance.

The assumptions of these approaches are especially important for peripheral regions. Peripheral regions are afflicted by various structural problems, for example, lack of capabilities, poor support infrastructure, lack of critical mass and difficult access to markets and technological knowledge (Fernández-Esquinas, Pinto, Yruela, & Pereira, 2016; Trippl & Toedtling, 2008). Peripheral regions are also shaped by specific social, economic and political mechanisms that determine their current situation in the knowledge economy. In these regions, interactions and capacities to access external sources of knowledge and other resources are crucial for SMEs and micro firms, which compose the largest portion of all businesses. Intangible elements, such as cultural values and cognitive repertoires, can also be an important explanatory factor for innovation dynamics. The main reason, as we will explain below, is that these elements are especially influential in the innovation process of these firms.

Although the above approaches acknowledge the social and interactive nature of innovation, they seldom encompass cultural analysis or introduce elements that facilitate the comprehension of cultural aspects. They recognize the influence of institutions, social capital, norms, values, abilities and attitudes, yet there is currently no comprehensive definition of the culture of innovation as a basic and operative element of institutional analysis in innovation studies. One of the reasons may be attributed to the separation of theoretical domains into different strands of social sciences. Innovation studies barely examine innovation through the analytical lens of other streams of research that focus specifically on institutional components. Moreover, institutional approaches that pay attention to culture have not considered firm innovation processes as strategic research sites; hence the need for a deeper understanding of the cultural elements that foster innovation capacity and performance.

2.2. Some conceptual problems and clarifications

The social nature of innovation situates culture in an important position from which to explain innovation processes. Economic activities can be shaped by shared beliefs, perceptions, attitudes and abilities held by the majority of a social group and put in practice through interaction, and interpersonal and social negotiation (Sackmann, 1997; Zelizer, 2010). In particular, the cognitive base that refers to complex rule-like structures can be influential for firm innovation, because these structures constitute strategic resources (DiMaggio, 1997).

A sociological use of the term 'institution' as a system of social rules helps clarify the role of cultural elements in innovation, since cultural aspects are commonly understood as parts of the institutional domain. The sociological lens complements the systemic approach that highlights the more formal and visible aspects of an innovation system, and, as such, contributes to expand the set of observations relating to the institutional components (Casper & Van Waarden, 2005). It involves the study of the beliefs and values of the key actors involved in innovation, together with norms and cognitive skills, integrated with other influential factors that shape innovation.

To that end, the work of Portes (2013) is especially useful for conceptual clarification. The observation of complex social phenomena not easily apprehensible at surface level reveals an important differentiation between *meta-theoretical principles* (the distinctive cognitive lens through which a particular field sees social phenomena and privilege areas or reality), *explanatory mechanisms* (a set of ideas about the functioning of social reality used as 'tool kits' to understand and clarify concrete events) and *strategic sites of enquiry* (locations for research, where observations of social dynamics are present and arguments can be tested). This conceptual differentiation is especially useful when analysing innovation processes.

In the case of innovation in SMEs and micro firms, a meta-theoretical principle shared by innovation studies is to consider all economic actions as embedded in systems of social relations that cannot be restricted to the individual interests of actors (Granovetter, 1985); a cognitive lens which is essentially different from the meta-theoretical principle stated by the utilitarian approach prevailing in mainstream economics. Second, cultural elements are considered to be a group of explanatory mechanisms that may shape innovation processes. They require detailed empirical observation, combined with other explanatory mechanisms usually assumed to be important for innovation, such as the role of social capital or the relationship with knowledge providers. And third, SMEs and micro firms provide a strategic research site for observing this explanatory mechanism, because they contain social and economic characteristics that make the functioning of the cultural elements especially relevant to the explanation of innovation dynamics.

Another key differentiation, also from Portes (2013), is bound up with the meaning attributed to the notion of 'institutions' and their relationship with culture. Portes departs from the classical analytical differentiation in mainstream sociological theory which states that social life can be examined according to two dimensions: the social structural domain (formed of real persons organized in economic and social hierarchies of some kind) and the cultural domain (formed by the symbolic elements of social life crucial for human interaction, mutual understanding and order). This separation is purely analytical, because in real life humans only exist in physical reality. However, it does aid observation of the motivations behind individuals' actions and the consequences of those actions; it also aids distinction between layers of social structure and culture.

Both dimensions are composed of diverse elements that can be analytically defined: from surface phenomena easily perceivable in everyday life to the most profound elements in the constitution of society. In particular, the social structure refers to the position of individuals in society, distributed in hierarchies according to their access to scarce resources, enabled by social relations and individuals' social capital. The most visible outcome of a social structure is a group of organizations present in a given area of activity. Values, norms, roles, cognitive repertoires, roles and institutions form the cultural structure. Values represent a more profound level, are sometimes expressed in norms and are enacted through individual roles. The most tangible outcomes of the cultural structure are institutions, a concept restricted to the symbolic part of organizations and defined as sets of rules that govern and shape the relations between role occupants in organizations (Portes, 2013). Institutions emerge when people manage to bring cognitive and normative elements into practice. Institutions are supported by shared systems of rules and behaviour patterns that limit the ability of actors to act and privilege certain groups endowed with influence and legitimacy (DiMaggio & Powell, 1983). In sum, this scheme helps to analytically identify a sphere of values, cognitive frameworks and accumulated knowledge (culture), and a sphere of interests and social positions, supported by different amounts of resources and power (social structure).

Conceived in this way, a social and a cultural structure of an innovation system can be suggested (Fernández-Esquinas, 2012). The social structure is defined in terms of the group of organizations intervening in knowledge production and utilization, and their interactions or networks of relationships. From this perspective, the social network of any key actor in the system, such as the firm, is conditioned by unequal access to resources (codified knowledge, financial capital, relationships, etc.). The cultural structure is formed by values, skills, norms and institutions, and provides the symbolic base that arranges social interactions. It contains a toolkit of elements that may function as assets: expert knowledge, behaviour, roles, manners, skills, etc. These cultural elements are also identified in cultural sociology as cultural capital or repertoires (Bourdieu, 1986; Swidler, 1986; Zelizer, 2010).

Social capital arises at the intersection of these domains, as it relates both to social networks and their facilitating access to certain resources, and to the value of trust associated with consolidated social relationships. Weak ties between actors with few interactions, built with just enough trust to transmit non-redundant information, are considered essential for innovation, whereas strong ties between actors with densely embedded interactions are supposed to involve conformity and risk avoidance (Granovetter, 1973; Ruef, 2002). These are fundamental elements of the concept of culture of innovation that will be discussed in the analysis. But first, the next section describes the main operational dimensions for observing innovation dynamics in SMEs.

3. Towards an integrative framework for studying the links between culture and innovation

3.1. The complexity of cultural analysis and its implication for innovation studies

The study of culture has been a complex endeavour for social sciences. The origins of cultural research lie in anthropology and sociology, and it has traditionally been analysed from two perspectives, each with its own epistemic and methodological lens: the *etic* and *emic* approaches. A key issue of the discussion is the way in which culture is best studied: through the methodological lens that privileges the insider (*emic*) or the outsider (*etic*). Anthropologists mostly employ *emic* perspectives and ethnographic tools. The *etic* perspective is more common for social psychologists and management scholars, who often approach culture through external evaluation processes. Quantitative research methods are common in this approach, although many organizational scholars also rely on qualitative methods and context-specific observations.

The complexity of cultural analysis is also present in the study of innovation. Innovation has a paradoxical nature because of the combination of dynamism and social change, and the stability needed to produce a valuable outcome. This dual nature is related to *etic* and *emic* approaches and leads to different visions about the analytical tools for studying homogeneity or heterogeneity. Some authors focus on aspects of culture that remain relatively stable, because shared beliefs and values are sustained by the fundamental assumptions that provide order to society. Their methodologies tend to capture a rather homogeneous view of culture, which is common in comparative cross-cultural research that usually employs statistical surveys (Hofstede, 1980; Schwartz, 1994). Cross-cultural research that follows an *etic* approach typically investigates different responses to similar situations and problems in different countries (or organizations), finding different cultural traits in different social domains that help establish hierarchies of human values on a general scale.

The other conception of culture recognizes a greater diversity and internal incoherence between the individuals and groups that share cultures or subcultures (DiMaggio, 1997). This perspective involves a more heterogeneous vision that aligns with the *emic* approach. It conceives culture as the collective construction of social reality through cognitive processes that give meaning to social situations in which individuals negotiate the meanings attributed to actions (Sackmann, 1997). Multiplicity implies more complexity in the empirical observation and understanding of culture. The methodologies of this perspective tend to stress specificity in contrast to universality. They also imply a context-related nature of culture when individuals simultaneously belong to different social groups and assume different roles.

The cultural aspects of innovation can thus be examined at multiple levels of analysis: individuals (groups or aggregates), organizations, organizational fields (innovation systems, sectors or clusters), regions or countries. Actors may belong to a multiplicity of cultural communities (Sackmann, 1997) with different cultural identities. They participate in innovation processes at an individual or group level when they co-create, consume and diffuse innovations, but also in a wider social context as members of work teams, professional communities or organizations. In consequence, in order to study the influence of certain cultural aspects on innovation, it becomes necessary to examine the dominating culture in each of them, especially where innovation has major implications.

3.2. Definition of the culture of innovation: universality or specificity?

We depart from a cognitive perspective of culture. From a methodological point of view, however, it is useful to combine it with the strategy of *etic* approaches by considering a series of parameters that reflect diversified factors regarding innovation. This helps to explain the different responses of actors to common situations, for instance, in firms. It is useful to observe a general set of aspects of culture when considering key components that shape diversity. In this respect, we follow some authors (Jucevicius, 2010) who argue in favour of the idea of a plurality of cultures of innovation, since innovative environments can be highly specific in each particular cultural context, due to growing global complexity.

Different combinations of dimensions associated with culture and their influence on innovation should be considered. The culture of innovation is defined as the set of shared beliefs, values, attitudes and abilities that favour innovation processes. These are considered altogether as toolkits (Swidler, 1986) or repertoires that combine learning with cooperation (Jucevicius, 2007). From this viewpoint, there is not only one specific culture of innovation, but different types of cultures that may shape innovation in different contexts. A culture of innovation can be understood as the combination of a set of symbolic elements related to learning, in order to respond to the changing nature of 'creative destruction', and another set related to cooperation, which responds to the more stable nature of patterns of interaction between actors that have evolved over a period of time and are usually based on mutual trust (Jucevicius, 2007).

This interpretation of cultural elements is important for SMEs and micro firms. Because they are small, they seldom have internal departments. They have few written rules, codified protocols or organizational procedures. Their strength lies in the owner's personal characteristics, such as flexibility and motivation (Vossen, 1998). More often than not, owners are also leaders and the main workers of the firm (Benito Hernández, Platero Jaime, & Rodríguez Duarte, 2012). Their cognitive frameworks, values, beliefs and shared meaning are especially important for defining and developing innovative activities. In consequence, the behaviour of a small business is closely connected to that of its owner or manager (Bosma, van Praag, Thurik, & de Wit, 2004). These circumstances also shape interactions with external agents in the regional context, as well as strategies for learning and investing in new knowledge. The main assumption is that these traits are crucial for adapting to change and for adopting new productive processes.

3.3. Key dimension of the culture of innovation

In order to identify both the general and specific elements that differentiate the culture of innovation, we developed an analytic exercise – summarized in Table 1 – based on an extensive review of the literature.[1] Six main dimensions have been identified as the leading cultural determinants of innovation. Understood as core values and associated skills and practices (Portes, 2013), they are interpreted as hypothetical mechanisms that mobilize capacities or resources which may affect the innovation performance of the firm. Column 1 summarizes the main mechanisms for each dimension. Columns 4 and 5 include the associated values and skills. The rationale for each dimension is as follows:

Dimension 1: Openness to change and novelty. This set of values and skills is expected to help people and organizations adapt to new, uncertain situations that are potentially conflictive. It also facilitates absorption of external information. Associated values are curiosity and interest in experimenting new things with skills, as well as adaptability, flexibility and mobility.

Dimension 2: Willingness to cooperate and share information and knowledge. It refers to the effects of collaboration and exchange of internal and external knowledge on the process of creating new combinations of knowledge. The collaborative relationships between actors inside and outside the firm help to enhance the firm's absorptive capacity. Trust is an important associated value necessary for the creation of social capital. It implies autonomy and recognition in collaborating parties.

Dimension 3: Tolerance of diversity and critical, creative thinking. This set of values is expected to facilitate problem solving through creative processes. Educational, economic, generational, ethnic and gender differences may contribute to problem solving with more creative, divergent and critical outcomes, through different points of view. Associated values such as originality, freedom and imagination may facilitate openness to different views and the acceptance of conflictive points of view.

Dimension 4: Lifelong and collective learning mindset. Emphasis on lifelong learning is expected to enable knowledge absorption and transfer as a continuous process of adaptation to change. Organizational learning processes rely on curiosity and willingness to learn with skills such as learning capacity and open communication.

Table 1. Cultural dimensions of innovation.

Dimensions	Rationale	Homogeneous perspective of innovation culture — Main question: What?	Pluralistic perspective of innovation culture — Main question: How? What kind of?	Values	Skills (repertoire)	References
1. Openness to change and novelty	Openness to change and novelty aids adaptation to new, potentially uncertain and conflictive situations, as well as absorption of external information	To what extent is change embraced? To what extent is attention being paid to novelty?	How is change faced? Are changes accepted easily? Which changes are accepted and which are not?	Curiosity; innocence; love for adventure	Adaptability; flexibility and mobility	Chesbrough (2003); Godin (2008)
2. Willingness to cooperate and share information and/or knowledge	Willingness to cooperate and share information and knowledge internally or externally originates innovation processes through co-creation or crowdsourcing	To what extent is information absorbed? What are the levels of trust? To what extent does cooperation exist?	How are cooperation experiences defined? How are incentives or obstacles identified?	Trust; freedom; peer recognition; sustainability; reputation; openness	Knowledge absorption; ability to cooperate; communication skills; sociability; social capital	Cohen and Levinthal, (1990); Gray, (2006); Himanen, (2001); Werker, Ooms, and Caniëls, (2014)
3. Tolerance of diversity and critical, creative thinking	Tolerance of diversity and critical, creative thinking facilitates problem solving through creative processes such as design thinking	To what extent is diversity appreciated? To what extent is creativity boosted and are critics being accepted?	What kind of diversity prevails? How are critics being managed? How are creative processes boosted?	Freedom; will; originality; ingenuity; inspiration; imagination	Critical complex thinking; creative capital; associative thinking; acceptance of conflict; analytical problem-solving skills	Dyer, Gregersen, and Christensen (2011); Ferrary and Granovetter (2009); Florida (2005)
4. Lifelong and collective learning mindset	Emphasis on lifelong learning enables knowledge absorption and transfer as a continuous process of adaptation to change	To what extent is lifelong learning rewarded?	What kind of knowledge prevails? How is lifelong learning stimulated? How are learning processes managed?	Curiosity; will; flexibility; dedication; motivation;	Learning skills; self-organization; time management; cultural capital	Argote and Ingram, (2000); Himanen (2001)
5. Risk acceptance and tolerance of failure	Risk acceptance and tolerance of failure facilitate experimentation and learning processes and increase the chance of future success	To what extent are risks and failures tolerated?	¿What kind of risk is tolerated? How is failure dealt with?	Tolerance; curiosity	Resilience; ability to take calculated risks; flexibility; experimentation; learning capacity	Hofstede (2011); Jucevicius (2009); Marcati, Guido, and Peluso, (2008); Tellis, Prabhu, and Chandy, (2009)
6. Entrepreneurial spirit	Entrepreneurial spirit, based on a drive for achievement, vision and passion, supplies the necessary resources to start new projects	To what extent is individual initiative rewarded or sanctioned?	What kind of responses are given to individual or collective initiatives? How are they rewarded?	Passion; eagerness for achievement; future vision; perseverance	Leadership; self-confidence; ability to mobilize commitment; negotiation skills; self-organization	Acs (2006); Drucker (2014); Hussler (2004)

Dimension 5: Risk acceptance and tolerance of failure. This set of values and skills may facilitate experimentation and learning processes and increase the chance of future success. Societies with low uncertainty aversion are considered more innovative. Accordingly, firms that are able to learn from their failures may be more tolerant, deal better with uncertainties and develop skills about self-consciousness.

Dimension 6: Entrepreneurial spirit. Values of entrepreneurial spirit, based on orientation to achievement, self-motivation and persistence, are considered a mechanism to supply the resources needed to start new projects. Associated values and skills, also present in entrepreneurs, are the ability to undertake complex tasks involving different people and resources, because they are usually required to start a new business.

Not all six dimensions are necessarily present in all innovative firms. We assume that specific combinations of values and skills may deliver distinctive cultures of innovation. Columns 3 and 4 in Table 1 reflect the perspectives for the understanding of culture that are useful for empirical analysis. Both singular culture (*etic*) and plural cultures (*emic*) perspectives are considered (Jucevicius, 2010). The common research questions from both perspectives are specified for each dimension. When observing these dimensions, we can adopt an etic approach from a mainly external point of view (the main research questions are concerned with 'What', as stated in the corresponding column) or choose an emic perspective that pursues a more insider understanding of the cultural importance (the main questions are concerned with 'How' the cultural traits relate to innovation).

In our research, we consider each of the six dimensions in order to guide our observations and to explain the social and cultural mechanisms that make up the specific cultures of innovation of small firms. Also, we address the open innovation strategies that micro firms develop, according to their cognitive expertise and skills, and the relation with the prevailing cultural assets of their corporate cultures.

4. Methodology

4.1. Data sources

The methodological design follows a triangulation strategy that combines a survey of micro firms with qualitative interviews and case studies of selected firms. Each source is considered useful for observing relevant issues of the innovation process. The purpose of the representative survey is to depict the situation of micro firms in the Canary Islands[2] in relation to innovation. In particular, the survey is used to identify potential innovators and to observe the innovation dynamics of the firms in terms of their capacities, interactions and beliefs. The open-ended interviews to owners of firms with an innovative profile have been used to observe the main characteristics of innovation processes, and also to identify dynamics, according to the role of cultural values. The purpose of the three case studies is to observe the detailed mechanisms of their innovation processes. The case studies are considered typical forms of innovation shaped by cultural elements.

4.2. Survey

This survey was part of a broader study on innovation dynamics of micro firms (1–9 employees) in the Canary Islands. The framework for the population of firms was the

Table 2. Relationship between firms' innovativeness and cultural traits.

	Cultural influences on innovative behaviour		New product or service development in the last 3 years
Beliefs and opinions about innovation	Do you think that the lack of qualified human resources is a burden for innovation?	Yes	27.10%
		No	20.10%
	Do you think that the lack of time is a burden for innovation?	Yes	27.10%
		No	20.30%
	Do you think that collaboration with research groups boosts innovation?	Yes	26.90%
		No	19.60%

Note: The percentages shown in table 2 correspond to answers of firms with an active innovation profile (25.6% of the sample).

registry of firms of the regional government (official statistics do not collect data on micro firms). However, firms with fewer than 10 employees represent 95% of all firms in the region. A sample of 450 firms was designed and distributed according to strata composed by the business sector and the island location of the firm. Fieldwork was based on computer-assisted telephone interviews. The final sample resulted in a total of 434 firms (error of 4.6% for a 95% confidence level)[3].

The findings of the survey help to identify the innovative profiles of micro firms. Only 25.6% of the sample (111 micro firms) has an active innovation profile; 56.2% can be considered as non-innovative firms, and 18.7% of firms have a profile of modest innovators.[4] These results show the low innovation rate of micro firms in the region. The main determinants of the innovative profile are firms' human and social capital, their ability to absorb external knowledge, their values relating to innovation and the existence of stable interactions between companies, researchers and governments (González de la Fe, Hernández Hernández, & Van Oostrom, 2012).

Regarding the relationship between firms' innovativeness and cultural traits, the outcome of the survey pinpointed a certain cultural influence. Table 2 shows that the lack of qualified human resources and time is appreciated to a greater extent by firms that have developed new products or services in the last three years than those who did not. Also, collaboration with research groups is considered important for innovation by a much larger portion of innovative firms (27%) than by those who did not innovate (20%). Some of these items can therefore be considered as proxies of the culture of innovation, since they represent cultural components of firms' innovativeness. However, we view them only as an explorative indicator for a possible cultural influence on firms' innovativeness, since the correlation is weak.

4.3. Interviews

The survey was used to identify knowledge intensive firms. Nine micro firms were selected from those with an active innovation profile[5] and approached in order to explore social and cultural innovation dynamics. The selection was oriented by the well-known taxonomy of Asheim and Coenen (2005), which focuses on the knowledge bases of productive processes: analytical, synthetic and symbolic knowledge bases. This classification helps to establish distinct strategic research sites in order to observe social mechanisms. Open-ended interviews were conducted in order to examine similarities and differences in innovation processes, to study open innovation strategies and to observe entrepreneurs' perceptions and opinions.

Table 3. Characteristics of the case studies.

Case studies/ main features	Case 1	Case 1	Case 3
Knowledge base	Analytic	Synthetic	Symbolic
Sector	Biotechnology	Engineering ICT	Videogames
Founding year	2010	1997	2011
Main activity	Development of microbiological molecules and vaccines for allergic and asthma pharmaceutics	Consultancy and technological development of communication and satellite systems	Development of casual videogames for mobile phones and commercial gaming apps
Employees	8	9	8
International activity	Strong presence in the UK and the U.S. through formal collaboration with university laboratories	Inserted in collaborative networks on the mainland (Spain) and with a commercial officer in London	Inserted in virtual communities (forums) on Internet; strong presence and visibility on social networks
Clients and market	International pharmacy industry	Local and national market for consultancy; national and international market (Central and South America) for satellite technology development	International virtual platforms such as App Store and Google Play for videogames; local and national clients for commercial gaming apps
Profile of the entrepreneur(s)	The three founding partners have PhDs and worked in the international pharmaceutical industry before creating their firm	The founding director is a high profile engineer actively involved in clusters and professional associations	The founding entrepreneur is a self-made and self-instructed artist who was employed in an international animation study before start up
Main knowledge providers	Internal knowledge production	Universities, clients and other firms	Users' community and peers in online forums

4.4. Case studies

The nine micro firms were further screened according to a set of qualitative criteria: (1) whether the firm was a reference in its sector in the region,[6] (2) whether the firm had successful revenues and innovative products on the market and (3) whether the firm had been promoted by entrepreneurs with earlier business experience and possible failures. Three firms were selected for in-depth case studies. Although the three firms share a combination of different knowledge bases, each case is considered as a typical representative form of synthetic, analytic and symbolic knowledge: a biotechnology firm (analytic), an engineering telecommunication firm (synthetic) and a videogames company (symbolic).[7] The characteristics of the three firms are included in Table 2.

The case studies consisted of interviews with the managing owner or entrepreneur of the firms, a review of documentary evidence (brochures, webpages, firms' presence online and in specialized press) and external interviews with regional experts on innovation familiar with these firms (experts on innovation agencies and technology transfer offices). The interviews were semi-structured in order to obtain insights into specific mechanisms regarding the six dimensions in Table 1. The various interview rounds were designed according to the history of the firm and focused on any of the successful innovation endeavours. After coding and content analysis, the results were interpreted according to the main dimensions of the culture of innovation, in terms of homogeneity or specificity of cultural traits (Table 3).

5. Results and discussion

5.1. Social and cultural mechanisms for innovation and the firm's knowledge base

The case studies show different aspects of the six dimensions of the culture of innovation in analytical, synthetic and symbolic knowledge-based firms. First, the findings evidence that some of the dimensions are present in all firms: 'openness to novelty' (dimension 1), 'acceptance of diversity' (dimension 3) and 'entrepreneurial spirit' (dimension 6). This suggests the presence of traits common to a culture of innovation. Second, the other dimensions show a variety of differences that lead to context-specific cultures of innovation. Specifically, the outcome regarding the plurality of innovation culture is reflected in the different presence of 'willingness to cooperate and share knowledge' (dimension 2); 'lifelong and collective learning mindset' (dimension 4) and 'risk tolerance' (dimension 5), as analysed below in each of the three case studies.

5.1.1. Case study 1: Analytical knowledge-based firm

The outcome of this case study shows that the firm develops an internally oriented culture of innovation with strong normative and formal features. Innovation processes lean on codified and universal expert knowledge, which is highly structured, documented and controlled, in close connection with scientific research procedures. For any important innovation, a significant investment in resources and time is required. This results in long-term product development (up to 10 years). The resulting innovation is considered expensive and of high value to the company. Accordingly, changes to business strategies are limited. The high cost of investment explains the firm's interest in protecting innovation by all possible means: intellectual property rights (IPR), confidentiality agreements, patenting, etc.

'Willingness to cooperate and share knowledge' (dimension 2) in this case is rather scarce. When it occurs, it follows strict protocols and non-disclosure agreements with third parties. 'Lifelong and collective learning mind' (dimension 4) is highly present, although it is very specialized and restricted internally to the firm's team members. As for 'risk tolerance' (dimension 5), this type of firm cannot afford to risk any possible leak of valuable information, due to high costs and the long-term development of the new product. The following comment clearly reflects this situation:

> We have very specialised knowledge and we know that nobody works with techniques like ours in our field, and we want to keep it that way. We cannot afford for any information, however unimportant it may seem, to leave the company. (CEO biotechnology firm)

Consequently, collaborative relationships are formal, selective and regulated. Outsourcing to companies is preferred over collaboration. Outsourcing is carried out for non-sensitive tasks, usually different from the core business, or for strategic market issues such as international protection of IPR, which is crucial for small technology-based enterprises (Hossain, 2015). These cases reflect a common situation in biotechnology firms, for which incentives to associate with companies of the same sector are scarce (García Carpintero, Albert-Martínez, Granadino, & Plaza, 2014). Therefore, intellectual capital and patenting of valuable knowledge are far more important than social capital.

As for human capital, different profiles, albeit in the same field of specialization, are complementary for this firm. The organizational structure is hierarchical, with vertical relationships between the project manager and the rest of the team. Learning processes are somewhat individual and in line with the features of innovation processes: structured, documented and controlled. High specialization raises the barriers for learning, which depends on expertise. Proximity to other partners and knowledge providers does not play an important role. Interactive learning is not so important in this case, because an important part of the knowledge base is accessible through global scientific networks and publications.

5.1.2. Case study 2: Synthetic knowledge-based firm

In this engineering firm, the culture of innovation, unlike the first case, is oriented towards external networks and collaboration. Innovation processes are both structured and open, depending on cooperative interactions with business and technological partners. Adjustment to change tends to depend on product development. The terms for product development are between two and three years. Sensitive intellectual and industrial property is protected, but information and common expertise is shared in relevant professional communities. This is useful for obtaining new knowledge but also for reputation and recognition from peers (Himanen, 2001).

'Willingness to cooperate and share knowledge' (dimension 2) for this kind of firm is not only necessary for innovation processes, but also for access to global markets in order to obtain sufficient credibility with bigger international stakeholders. 'Lifelong and collective learning mindset' (dimension 4) is based on coded and tacit knowledge and learning processes that transcend the firm's boundaries. Accordingly, 'risk tolerance' (dimension 5) is less calculated than in the first case. The firm is mostly concerned about core developments, which are protected with formal collaboration agreements and IPR, alongside open relations with external networks. Social networks and collaboration are based on trust and mutual benefit in order to gain credibility and critical mass in global markets. The following statement reflects this situation:

> For a small company, entering global markets (without the correct partners) is not reliable, even with the right experience and competitive technologies, simply because it lacks financial muscle and critical mass to dedicate to the conquest of new markets. (CEO high-tech telecom firm)

The human capital of the firm comprises heterogeneous profiles. The firm frequently incorporates external collaborators from other firms in its projects. Both coded and tacit knowledge are exchanged through interactive learning processes between internal and external team members. Multiple interactions give rise to new shared routines, as a result of learning through practice and use. Therefore, the firm, together with partners, develops a culture of innovation that supports interactive learning with other firms, scientific staff at research centres and clients. The work of this firm is more dependent on the specific context, and proximity gains importance because of the need to access expert partners and collaborators. In sum, for this firm, social capital is as important as intellectual capital.

5.1.3. Case study 3: Symbolic knowledge-based firm

This videogames firm tends to develop a community-driven culture of innovation. User experience (UX) and interactive open collaborative processes are vital for new product development, which takes a few months to be market-ready. Knowledge and development are shared in open-access forums, which allows the community to grow and expand by creatively recombining existing knowledge, sometimes following hacker ethics (Himanen, 2001). Intellectual property rights are not important. Instead, creativity, co-creation and context-specific learning through trial and error are preeminent.

'Willingness to cooperate and share knowledge' (dimension 2) is therefore very important. It allows firms to access and reuse existing knowledge for their new product developments. For this reason, 'longlife and collective learning mindset' (dimension 4) is easily assumed by team members who socialize in open professional communities. 'Risk tolerance' (dimension 5) is especially present because of the benefits of co-creation with users and wider creative communities through knowledge sharing in open environments.

Interactions are very important for peer-learning processes in open virtual professional communities. For this firm, social and creative capital are the main assets. Product development team profiles are very diverse and include designers, artists, developers, marketers, etc. The organizational structure is horizontal and based on distributed team leadership (Spillane, 2012), whose unity and motivation is considered a key aspect. The following comment reflects the collaborating and collective culture of the firm:

> Here the process of creativity is a group dynamic. Everything is done as a team. From the first moment, music, art, everything, is part of a collective process of creative product development. (CEO videogame firm)

In this context, proximity is vital for firm innovation. Territorial proximity is required for both learning and collaborative processes. In sum, this firm reflects an important context-specific trait for its innovation processes.

5.2. A plurality of innovation cultures

The above results reveal a plurality of specific cultures of innovation. Some universal traits are also identified, as we highlighted in the previous section. The differences stress context-specific aspects such as the firm's cognitive expertise, the sector, the territory and particular institutional arrangements regarding core innovation processes: collaboration and learning processes. A culture of innovation understood as the combination of traits related to learning and collaboration, as suggested by Jucevicius (2007), therefore seems relevant and appropriate. Moreover, the other dimensions of the culture of innovation, as defined here, are similar in all three cases, although some differences are evident. For example, 'openness to novelty' (dimension 1) shows differences due to product development terms in all three cases: from very long-term (10 years) in the biotechnology firm (analytic) to very short-term (few months) in the videogames firm (symbolic).

Rather than a single culture in innovative micro firms, it seems more appropriate to speak about plural cultures of innovation with some common traits. On the one hand, the common traits seem to be present in all innovative organizations. 'Openness to novelty' (dimension 1), 'acceptance of diversity and critical thinking' (dimension 3) and 'entrepreneurial spirit' (dimension 6) are observed in all case studies and confirmed by similar observations from interviews. This finding is also consistent with specialized empirical research that considers these traits as part of the general modernization process of organizations, with wider implications in the population of regions and countries (Wieland, 2006). On the other hand, core innovation issues, such as learning and collaboration processes, highlight differences between resulting cultures of innovation

Table 4. Cultures of innovation informed by main dimensions.

Case studies/dimensions	case 1: Analytic knowledge-based firm	Case 2: Synthetic knowledge-based firm	Case 3: Symbolic knowledge-based firm
1. Openness to change	Importance of state-of-the-art	Constant adaptation to change	Continuous adaptation
	Few new products because of long development terms (up to 10 years)	Anticipating to change within 3 years for new product development	Frequent new product launches that need few months to deliver
2. Willingness to cooperate and share knowledge	High costs of innovation limits knowledge sharing	Knowledge and information is shared with certain limits	Open knowledge sharing with users in communities without limits
	Formal and normative collaboration	Frequent collaborations also for gaining credibility	Informal collaboration
	High impact of intellectual capital vs. low impact of social capital	High impact of social and intellectual capital	High impact of social and creative capital
3. Acceptance of diversity and critical, divergent and creative thinking	Diversity limited to the boundaries of the team	Diversity both inside and outside the team	Wide diversity inside and outside the team: multidisciplinary
	Homogeneous profiles due to high specialization	Heterogeneous profiles in multidisciplinary teams	Stress on unity of team
4. Lifelong and collective learning mindset	Very structured, organized and documented process	Interactive learning processes	Interactive learning processes through community and users
	High access barriers	Emphasis on problem solving applying knowledge from different sources	Open culture with free access to knowledge that is recombined
	Emphasis on the individual	Emphasis on the network	Emphasis on the team
	Low importance of proximity, global knowledge networks	Importance of proximity and network learning	Importance on learning through failure and self-taught learning, very context-specific
5. Risk tolerance	Very calculated risk, no tolerance	Calculated risk, tolerance	High risk tolerance
6. Entrepreneurial spirit	No differences observed	No differences observed	No differences observed
Cultures of innovation	Internally oriented with strong normative and formal features	External oriented towards networks and collaboration	Community driven by users' experience

regarding internal and external features, and the relevance of social, intellectual and creative capital in each case.

Finally, the role of social capital in each of these cultures is clearly different, as reflected in micro firms' open innovation strategies. Different types of capital are involved (social, intellectual and creative) in each case study. Social capital seems to be important for firms with a synthetic and symbolic knowledge base, but not so much for firms with an analytical knowledge base, where intellectual capital is a fundamental and constituent asset. Intellectual and social capital are equally important for these firms. In contrast, for the symbolic knowledge-based firm, both creative capital and social capital are decisive for interactions with the community. Table 4 shows an overview of the specific cultures of innovation as discussed in this section.

5.3. Cultures of innovation and firms' open innovation strategies

Our observations point to two key findings in terms of the links of these results with firms' open innovation strategies: on the one hand, the existence of closed innovation strategies in analytical knowledge-based micro firms that foster an internally oriented culture of innovation with strong normative and formal features. The high cost of innovation limits openness. Collaboration with external partners only exists through formal confidentiality and IPR agreements. Open innovation appears to be more useful for small companies in their marketing phases than in other phases, such as R&D activities, which are more appropriate for large firms. In these cases, small firms would benefit from patenting, despite the inconvenience of associated costs (Hossain, 2015).

On the other hand, an open innovation strategy is clearly present in the other two types of cultures of innovation, albeit in different ways. The external network and collaboration-oriented culture that defines synthetic knowledge-based firms relies on both formal and informal institutions. Here, protection is required for certain phases of (technological) development, in order to avoid placing new product developments at risk. But this culture also enhances knowledge sharing through participation in open online communities and professional workshops. A more balanced open innovation strategy helps these firms to interact in global markets, and to combine IPR and open knowledge at different stages of their innovation processes. So, synthetic knowledge-based firms typically follow an open innovation approach (Chesbrough, 2003), although they would benefit from incorporating cultural observations in micro firms.

In symbolic knowledge-based firms, with a typical community-driven culture of innovation, open innovation seems to be a common strategy for connecting with users and learning through their experience. No protection other than the registration of trademarks is considered. Creativity and recombination of existing knowledge imply the existence of multidisciplinary teams and their interactions with communities. A wide open innovation strategy thus explains the culture of innovation of this kind of firm.

Finally, it is worthwhile mentioning that innovative micro firms, in contrast with larger firms, cope with a bounded capacity for knowledge selection and absorption, which limits their open innovation potential. Maintaining intensive external networks demands resources and the valuable time of qualified and creative human resources, which are very scarce in micro firms. Also, the protection of intellectual property or the regulation of shared knowledge, when required, involves costs and specialized management, hard to get for micro firms.

6. Conclusions and implications

In this article, observations of Spanish innovative micro firms from a peripheral region have been used in order to identify the social and cultural mechanisms that shape their innovation processes. The research strategy is based on a cross-fertilization of theoretical approaches and the triangulation of different data sources. Mainstream innovation literature has been combined with contributions from cultural and institutional sociology. The empirical work has benefited from the triangulation of information, with a combination of different data sources that facilitate the observation of the richness and complexity of innovation dynamics in micro firms, especially the functioning of cultural factors.

The contributions of this paper are threefold. First, a conceptual contribution is made through the development of an operational definition of the notion of culture of innovation and its main dimensions. Second, the empirical findings contribute to the discussion on homogeneity versus plurality of cultures of innovation. Third, the results facilitate the observation of cultural and social mechanisms that shape the innovation dynamics in micro firms, and the diversity of open innovation strategies. The outcomes suggest, in general, that the debate on open innovation strategies could benefit with the consideration of an operational cultural dimension, as provided here, in future research.

The results show that not all dimensions of the culture of innovation have the same relevance for micro firms' innovation strategies. The dimensions with greater explanatory capacity are those associated with the fundamental processes of innovation: collaboration and learning. Both processes involve myriad interactions that depend on the openness versus closeness of the collaboration and learning interactions between actors, the degree of formal versus informal protection and sharing, and the importance of creative versus structured procedures, amongst others. The values and skills associated with these fundamental processes of collaboration and learning form a plurality of cultures of innovation. Future research should address strategies in order to provide a right balance between learning and cooperation and ways to implement them.

The outcomes reveal the presence of several traits in all innovative companies: 'openness to novelty' (dimension 1), 'acceptance of diversity' (dimension 3) and 'entrepreneurial spirit' (dimension 6). This points towards the universal aspects of a culture of innovation. The combination of other traits forms specific cultural profiles of innovation: 'willingness to cooperate and share knowledge' (dimension 2); 'lifelong and collective learning mindset' (dimension 4) and 'risk tolerance' (dimension 5). This explains the existence of context-specific cultures of innovation in a plural and specific sense.

In summary, the first case study of an analytical knowledge-based firm reveals an internal oriented, normative and formal culture of innovation. The second case study of a synthetic knowledge-based firm shows an externally oriented network culture of innovation. The third case study of a symbolic knowledge-based firm displays a community-driven culture of innovation.

The plurality of cultures of innovation that emerges throughout the case studies can be seen as models or types of culture. As such, the results have implications for regions that wish to promote a culture of innovation. At firm level, strategies and practices could be directed towards increasing firms' capacity for collaboration and learning as fundamental processes for innovation. The findings of this research are also useful for policymakers seeking to design sectorial policy instruments involving, for example, upgrading micro firms towards more robust, bigger firms that can cope more easily with open innovation challenges. Intellectual property assessments or facilitating productive partnerships between small firms and government-funded industry or research centres could be provided. The outcomes of this study also suggest parallels with other peripheral regions with similar socioeconomic traits. In this sense, the findings provide useful insights for policymakers concerned with promoting a culture of innovation and with analysing the cultural dimensions of regional innovation performance and capacities or a culture of innovation amongst local small firms.

Notes

1. This table is based on a review of mainstream literature and earlier reviews on the connections between culture, innovation and firm performance (Bueschgens, Bausch, & Balkin,

2013; Crossan & Apaydin, 2010; Hogan & Coote, 2014; McLean, 2005; van der Panne et al., 2003). Most earlier reviews concern the organizational level, with some exceptions that focus on the macro (regional) level (Trippl & Toedtling, 2008) or several levels of analysis (Castro & García, 2014).

2. The Canary Islands are Spain's outermost region and are located in the Atlantic Ocean, close to the northwest coast of Africa and Morocco. They mainly have a service economy, which is highly dependent on tourism (30% of the region's GDP). The region has one of the lowest rates of innovation performance in the European Union (Annoni, Dijkstra, & Gargano, 2017).

3. The survey covered the seven Canary Islands. The questionnaire was structured in five dimensions: (1) general characteristics of the company; (2) firms' innovation activities and attitudes; (3) use of ICT; (4) assessment of the regional context; and (5) entrepreneurs' personal traits. The methodology and the findings of this survey are found in González de la Fe et al. (2012). One of the main goals of the survey was to identify the subsector of micro firms carrying out activities in the knowledge economy, mainly in high-tech and intensive knowledge sectors.

4. Innovativeness of micro firms is measured according to the frequency and intensity of innovation activities: 'Non innovative' firms are those which almost never introduce innovative products or services in the market. 'Moderate innovators' are those with an average of three innovative activities in the last three years. 'Active innovators' are firms that have implemented at least four innovative products or services in the market in the last three years. Over 70% of this group has done so more than once.

5. An overwhelming part of active innovators belongs to the service sector, especially tourism and the more traditional commercial sectors.

6. We checked for visibility and reputation in the media, and whether these firms had received awards or public recognition.

7. In analytic knowledge base firms, codified knowledge prevails and innovations are produced by creating new knowledge through scientific research and formal models, often in collaboration with research centres. In synthetic knowledge, base firms tacit knowledge prevails and innovations arise through a novel combination of existing knowledge and applied problem-solving engineering processes. In symbolic knowledge, base firms' innovation occurs by a recombination of existing knowledge in new ways, relying on tacit and practical crafts and skills (Asheim & Coenen, 2005).

Disclosure statement

No potential conflict of interest was reported by the authors.

ORCID

Madelon van Oostrom ⓘ http://orcid.org/0000-0001-6505-3101

References

Acs, Z. (2006). How is entrepreneurship good for economic growth? *Innovations: Technology, Governance, Globalization, 1*(1), 97–107. doi:10.1162/itgg.2006.1.1.97

Amin, A., & Thrift, N. (1995). Globalisation, institutional thickness and the local economy. *Managing Cities: The New Urban Context, 12*, 91–108.

Annoni, P., Dijkstra, L., & Gargano, N. (2017). *The EU regional competitiveness index 2016.*

Argote, L., & Ingram, P. (2000). Knowledge transfer: A basis for competitive advantage in firms. *Organizational Behavior and Human Decision Processes, 82*(1), 150–169. doi:10.1006/obhd. 2000.2893

Asheim, B., & Coenen, L. (2005). Knowledge bases and regional innovation systems: Comparing Nordic clusters. *Research Policy*, *34*(8), 1173–1190. doi:10.1016/j.respol.2005.03.013

Asheim, B., & Isaksen, A. (2002). Regional innovation systems: The integration of local 'sticky' and global 'ubiquitous' knowledge. *The Journal of Technology Transfer*, *27*(1), 77–86.

Benito Hernández, S., Platero Jaime, M., & Rodríguez Duarte, A. (2012). Factores determinantes de la innovación en las microempresas españolas: La importancia de los factores internos/ Determinants of innovation in Spanish micro-enterprises: The importance of internal factors. *Universia Business Review*, *33*, 104.

Bessant, J., & Tidd, J. (2007). *Innovation and entrepreneurship*. Chichester: John Wiley & Sons.

Bosma, N., van Praag, M., Thurik, R., & de Wit, G. (2004). The value of human and social capital investments for the business performance of startups. *Small Business Economics*, *23*(3), 227–236. doi:10.1023/B:SBEJ.0000032032.21192.72

Bourdieu, P. (1986). The forms of capital. In N. W. Biggart (Ed.), *Readings in Economic Sociology* (pp. 280–291). Oxford: Blackwell.

Bueschgens, T., Bausch, A., & Balkin, D. B. (2013). Organizational culture and innovation: A meta-analytic review. *Journal of Product Innovation Management*, *30*(4), 763–781. doi:10.1111/jpim.12021

Casper, S., & Van Waarden, F. (2005). *Innovation and institutions*. Cheltenham: Edward Elgar.

Castro, E., & García, A. (2014). La relación entre cultura e innovación : tres ámbitos de análisis. In B. Laspra & E. Muñoz (Eds.), *Culturas científicas e innovadoras. Progreso Social* (pp. 237–254). Eudeba.

Chesbrough, H. (2003). *Open innovation: The new imperative for creating and profiting from technology*. Boston, MA: Harvard Business Press.

Chesbrough, H. (2012). Open innovation: Where we've been and where we're going. *Research-Technology Management*, *55*(4), 20–27. doi:10.5437/08956308X5504085

Cohen, W. M., & Levinthal, D. A. (1990). Absorptive capacity : A new perspective on learning and innovation. *Administrative Science Quarterly*, *35*(1), 128–152. doi:10.2307/2393553

Cooke, P., Gomez Uranga, M., & Etxebarria, G. (1997). Regional innovation systems: Institutional and organisational dimensions. *Research Policy*, *26*(4–5), 475–491. doi:10.1016/S0048-7333 (97)00025-5

Crossan, M. M., & Apaydin, M. (2010). A multi-dimensional framework of organizational innovation: A systematic review of the literature. *Journal of Management Studies*, *47*(6), 1154–1191. doi:10.1111/j.1467-6486.2009.00880.x

DiMaggio, P. (1997). Culture and cognition. *Annual Review of Sociology*, *23*(263), 25.

DiMaggio, P., & Powell, W. (1983). The iron cage revisited: Institutional isomorphism and collective rationality in organizational fields. *American Sociological Review*, *48*(2), 147–160. doi:10.2307/2095101

Drucker, P. (2014). *Innovation and entrepreneurship*. Routledge.

Dyer, J., Gregersen, H., & Christensen, C. (2011). *The innovator's DNA: Mastering the five skills of disruptive innovators*. Boston, MA: Harvard Business Press.

Edquist, C. (2001). The systems of innovation approach and innovation policy : An account of the state of the art. 1–24.

Edquist, C. (2005). Systems of innovation: Perspectives and challenges. In *The Oxford handbook of innovation* (pp. 181–208). Oxford: Oxford University Press.

Fagerberg, J., & Verspagen, B. (2009). Innovation studies – The emerging structure of a new scientific field. *Research Policy*, *38*(2), 218–233. doi:10.1016/j.respol.2008.12.006

Fernández-Esquinas, M. (2012). Hacia un programa de investigación en sociología de la innovación. *Arbor. Revista de Pensamiento, Ciencia y Cultura*, *188*(753), 5–18.

Fernández-Esquinas, M., & Pinto, H. (2014). The role of universities in urban regeneration: Reframing the analytical approach. *European Planning Studies*, *22*(7), 1462–1483. doi:10.1080/09654313.2013.791967

Fernández-Esquinas, M., Pinto, H., Yruela, M. P., & Pereira, T. S. (2016). Tracing the flows of knowledge transfer: Latent dimensions and determinants of university–industry interactions. *Technological Forecasting and Social Change*, *113*(part), 266–279. doi:10.1016/j.techfore.2015.07.013

Ferrary, M., & Granovetter, M. (2009). The role of venture capital firms in Silicon Valley's complex innovation network. *Economy and Society, 38*(2), 326–359. doi:10.1080/03085140902786827

Florida, R. (2005). *The flight of the creative class*. New York, NY: Harper Business.

Freel, M. S. (2005). Patterns of innovation and skills in small firms. *Technovation, 25*(2), 123–134. doi:10.1016/S0166-4972(03)00082-8

García Carpintero, E., Albert-Martínez, A., Granadino, B., & Plaza, L. M. (2014). Análisis de la colaboración entre las empresas biotecnológicas españolas con actividades de I+D y el sistema público de I+D. *Revista española de Documentación Científica, 37*(2), e041. doi:10.3989/redc. 2014.2.1106

Godin, B. (2008). *Innovation: The history of a category*. Project on the Intellectual History of Innovation Working, (1), pp. 1–67.

González de la Fe, T., Hernández Hernández, N., & Van Oostrom, M. (2012). Innovación, cultura y tamaño: la microempresa en una región ultraperiférica. *Arbor, 188*(753), 113–134. doi:10.3989/ arbor.2012.753n1008

Granovetter, M. (1985). Economic action and social structure: The problem of embeddedness. *American Journal of Sociology, 91*(3), 481–510. doi:10.1086/228311

Granovetter, M. S. (1973). The strenght of weak ties. *American Journal of Sociology, 78*, 1360–1380. doi:10.1086/225469

Gray, C. (2006). Absorptive capacity, knowledge management and innovation in entrepreneurial small firms. *International Journal of Entrepreneurial Behavior & Research, 12*(6), 345–360. doi:10.1108/13552550610710144

Himanen, P. (2001). *La ética del hacker y el espíritu de la era de la información*. Barcelona: Ediciones Destino.

von Hippel, E. (2005). Democratizing innovation: The evolving phenomenon of user innovation. *Journal f{ü}r Betriebswirtschaft, 55*(1), 63–78. doi:10.1007/s11301-004-0002-8

Hofstede, G. (1980). *Culture's consequences: International differences in work-related values*. Beverly Hills, CA: Sage.

Hofstede, G. (2011). Dimensionalizing cultures: The Hofstede model in context, *Online Readings in Psychology and Culture, 2*(1), 1–26. doi:10.9707/2307-0919.1014

Hogan, S. J., & Coote, L. V. (2014). Organizational culture, innovation, and performance: A test of Schein's model. *Journal of Business Research, 67*(8), 1609–1621. doi:10.1016/j.jbusres.2013.09. 007

Hossain, M. (2015). A review of literature on open innovation in small and medium-sized enterprises. *Journal of Global Entrepreneurship Research, 5*(1). doi:10.1186/s40497-015-0022-y

Hussler, C. (2004). Culture and knowledge spillovers in Europe: New perspectives for innovation and convergence policies? *Economics of Innovation and New Technology, 13*(6), 523–541. doi:10.1080/1043859042000234302

James, A. (2005). Demystifying the role of culture in innovative regional economies. *Regional Studies, 39*(9), 1197–1216. doi:10.1080/00343400500389968

Jaruzelski, B., Loehr, J., & Holman, R. (2011). *Why culture is key. The global innovation 1000*, Strategy+Business, Winter *2011*(65).

Jucevicius, G. (2007). Innovation culture: The contestable universality of the concept. *Social Sciences, 58*(4), 7–19.

Jucevicius, G. (2009). The innovation culture in modern Lithuanian organizations: Values, attitudes and practices, *Social Sciences, 63*(1), 38–45.

Jucevicius, G. (2010). *Culture vs. Cultures of innovation: Conceptual framework and parameters for assessment*. ICICKM proceedings of the 7th internationl conference on intellectual capital, knowledge management and organizational learning, Hong Kong.

Lundvall, B. A., & Borrás, S. (1997). *The globalising learning economy: implications for innovation policy*.

Malerba, F. (2005). Sectoral systems of innovation: A framework for linking innovation to the knowledge base, structure and dynamics of sectors. *Economics of Innovation and New Technology, 14*(1–2), 63–82. doi:10.1080/1043859042000228688

Manley, K. (2003). Frameworks for understanding interactive innovation processes. *The International Journal of Entrepreneurship and Innovation*, *4*(1), 25–36. doi:10.5367/000000003101299375

Marcati, A., Guido, G., & Peluso, A. M. (2008). The role of SME entrepreneurs' innovativeness and personality in the adoption of innovations. *Research Policy*, *37*(9), 1579–1590. doi:10.1016/j.respol.2008.06.004

McLean, L. D. (2005). Organizational culture's influence on creativity and innovation: A review of the literature and implications for human resource development. *Advances in Developing Human Resources*, *7*(2), 226–246. doi:10.1177/1523422305274528

Nelson, R., & Winter, S. (1982). *An evolutionary theory on economic change*. Cambridge, MA: The Belknap Press of Harvard University Press.

van der Panne, G., van Beers, C., & Kleinknecht, A. (2003). Success and failure of innovation: A literature review. *International Journal of Innovation Management*, *07*(3), 309–338. doi:10.1142/S1363919603000830

Pilon, S., & DeBresson, C. (2003). *Local culture and regional innovative networks: New hypotheses and some propositions.*

Portes, A. (2013). *Sociología económica. Una investigación sistemática*. Madrid: Centro de Investigaciones Sociológicas (CIS).

Ruef, M. (2002). Strong ties, weak ties and islands: Structural and cultural predictors of organizational innovation. *Industrial and Corporate Change*, *11*(3), 427–449. doi:10.1093/icc/11.3.427

Sackmann, S. (1997). *Cultural complexity in organizations: Inherent contrasts and contradictions*. London: Sage.

Schwartz, S. H. (1994). Are there universal aspects in the structure and content of human values? *Journal of Social Issues*, *50*(4), 19–45. doi:10.1111/j.1540-4560.1994.tb01196.x

Spillane, J. P. (2012). *Distributed leadership*. John Wiley & Sons.

Swidler, A. (1986). Culture in action: Symbols and strategies. *American Sociological Review*, *51*(2), 273. doi:10.2307/2095521

Tellis, G. J., Prabhu, J. C., & Chandy, R. K. (2009). Radical innovation across nations : The preeminence of corporate culture, *Journal of Marketing*, *73*(1), 3–23. doi:10.1509/jmkg.73.1.3

Tether, B. S., Mina, A., Consoli, D., & Gagliaardi, D. (2005). A literature review on skills and innovation. How does successful innovation impact on the demand for skills and how do skills drive innovation? *Policy*, (September) 1–124.

Trippl, M., & Toedtling, F. (2008). *Regional innovation cultures.*

Vossen, R. W. (1998). Relative strengths and weaknesses of small firms in innovation. *International Small Business Journal*, *16*(3), 88–94. doi:10.1177/0266242698163005

Werker, C., Ooms, W., & Caniëls, M. (2014). *The role of personal proximity in collaborations : The Case of Dutch nanotechnology*. DRUID society conference 2014 CBS copenhague, June 16–18.

Wieland, T. (2006). *Innovation culture, technology policy and The uses of history*. International ProACT conference. Innovation pressure, 15–17 March 2006, Tampere, Finland.

Zelizer, V. (2010). *Economic lives: How culture shapes the economy*. Princeton, NJ: Princeton University Press.

The 'Enterprise of Innovation' in hard times: corporate culture and performance in Italian high-tech companies

Francesco Ramella

ABSTRACT
This article deals with the strategies that Italian innovative manufacturing companies have deployed in recent years. Italy has, in fact, been hit particularly severely by the international crisis, which has induced a sharp decline in employment and a narrowing of the productive base. That said, we know very little about the strategies used by Italian entrepreneurs to cope with the economic downturn, especially the more innovative ones. To address this topic, the author has used a sample of over 400 Italian companies with European patents in the sectors of mechanical engineering and high technology (European Patent Office (EPO) companies), which were investigated by means of a panel survey: a longitudinal study carried out on the same companies at different times (2010 and 2012). The analysis conducted in this article has two main goals: (1) to describe the socio-economic and territorial characteristics of EPO companies and their strategies in the years of the crisis and (2) to examine the influence of a 'collaborative corporate culture' on company performance. What emerges from the research into EPO companies is the complementarity of resources useful for innovation and economic performance among (a) the internal and external relations of the organization; (b) the variety of knowledge and the cohesion of relationships and (c) the short and long networks of collaboration. In conclusion, successful company strategies are those which – thanks to a collaborative company culture – are able to exploit the 'embedded complementarity of innovative resources'.

1. Introduction

One of the central themes in the literature on economic innovation is the ability of companies to cooperate in this particular area, especially where small and medium ones are concerned. There are two sides to this issue: one internal, one external. While the first concerns the endowment of human capital and organizational strategies that facilitate collaboration and innovative creativity, the second regards the possibility of accessing resources external to the company. These are two sides of the same coin, so to speak, since obtaining the best results from the latter depends on both the 'absorptive capacity' of the company and the territorial endowment of resources and local collective goods. If, on the one hand, external resources increase the 'requisite variety' of knowledge, on the other, internal resources boost the 'capacity to make productive use' of such knowledge.

Innovation studies often tend to emphasize that innovation is the result of a combination of various ideas. Picking up on the suggestion of Schumpeter (1912), various authors have defined innovation as a problem-solving process of a combinatorial type, that is, oriented towards the search for new combinations of known elements. With reference to technological change in particular, stress is placed on the importance of the circulation of knowledge in increasing the variety of experiences and ideas available to companies. In short, attention is focused on the 'socio-cognitive dimension' of innovation. This perspective, however, is a reductive one. The search for new technical solutions, in fact, is only one aspect of the phenomenon in question – which is broader and more complex.

Firstly, economic innovation is not limited to technological change. Following Pavitt's (2005, p. 88) observation, we can conceive it as a process that involves 'matching technological opportunities with market needs and organizational practices'. Secondly, these combinatorial processes are embedded in social and economic relations, that is, in learning networks which are organizationally and territorially structured. Thirdly, the socio-cognitive aspect of innovation is closely linked to the 'socio-normative dimension' – which comprises the internal cohesion of project teams and the social capital available to the company. Both these dimensions are important: the assortment of cognitive resources (variety of knowledge) that facilitate the search for innovative combinations, and the presence of socio-normative resources (cohesion and social capital) that facilitate the exchange of ideas and interactive learning processes inside and outside the company. In other words, innovation actors inside the companies (be they entrepreneurs, researchers, employees, etc.) make use of organizational relationships and personal ties which convey cognitive resources of variety, as well as normative resources of cohesion and trust.

From this point of view, the study of 'corporate culture' – which includes both the socio-cognitive and socio-normative dimensions – is particularly important. With 'corporate culture', I refer to the system of meanings and shared practices that guide both the internal relations, between management and employees, and external relations with other actors (companies, customers, suppliers, research centres, local governments, etc.). Corporate culture consists of two interrelated aspects: (1) the cognitive and normative 'dispositions' that guide behaviour and (2) the organizational and relational 'practices' that convey these dispositions and embed them internally.

The first aspect ('dispositions') can be compared to what in the social sciences – with reference to individuals – is called 'attitude', that is, a particular dispositional state based on a combination of knowledge, values and beliefs that define the style of the company and direct the decisions and behaviour of the management on specific issues. These dispositions – which are more or less shared and supported throughout the organization – have a structured character connected both to contextual factors (linked to the production sector, region and country in which the companies operate) and to factors of a more idiosyncratic kind (related to the specific experience and skills accumulated in the company's history).

The second aspect ('practices'), on the other hand, draws on two strands of the literature on innovation and creativity which emphasize the organizational and interactional aspects underlying the cognitive and normative dimensions. While one strand explores the relationship between organizational design and the ways in which companies learn and innovate (Arundel, Lorenz, Lundvall, & Valeyre, 2007), the other proposes a 'cultural network analysis' of socio-cognitive spaces. The latter brings together the study of cultural structures – understood as group skills and cognitive styles that are developed through social relations – and the study of groups' social structures – understood as networks of belonging and interaction (De Vaan, Stark, & Vedres, 2015).

Seen in light of these studies, corporate culture forms an analytical bridge between structure and agency, as well as between reproduction and change. On the one hand, in fact, it embodies dispositions of action shaped by the socio-economic context and previous experience, which tend to reproduce the company's routine strategies. On the other hand, however, these same dispositions – subjected to new economic challenges – can steer management behaviour in the direction of innovation. Paraphrasing Giddens, there therefore exists a constitutive 'dualism' in corporate culture connected to the fact that it is not only 'structured', but also 'structuring'.

This article will address the theme of corporate culture and cooperative attitudes by means of data deriving from an empirical research on a sample of Italian manufacturing companies with European patents – companies that have been forced to respond to the acute challenge presented by the economic downturn of recent years. Italy has, in fact, been hit particularly severely by the international crisis, which has induced a sharp decline in employment and a narrowing of the productive base. However, we know very little about the strategies that Italian entrepreneurs, especially the more innovative ones, have deployed in order to cope with the crisis.

To address this topic, I have used a sample of over 400 innovative Italian companies, with patents granted between 1995 and 2004 (i.e. before the crisis) by the European Patent Office (EPO) in the sectors of mechanical engineering and high technology.[1] These companies were investigated by means of a panel survey: a longitudinal study carried out on the 'same' firms at 'different' times (at the beginning of 2010 and at the end of 2012).[2] The analysis carried out in this article has two main goals: (1) to describe the socio-economic and territorial characteristics of EPO companies and their strategies in the years of the crisis and (2) to examine the influence of a 'collaborative corporate culture' on company performance. As a proxy for this latter dimension, I will use the attitude of the EPO companies in terms of building cooperative relationships both internally, through a 'strategic integration' approach that valorizes human capital and organizational flexibility, and externally, through innovative partnerships with other actors.

The article is organized as follows. In Sections 2 and 3, I will present – concisely and with no claims to exhaustiveness – some studies that have stressed the importance of territorial proximity and organizational strategies in order to understand the economic and innovative performance of companies. In Section 4, I will provide the details about the research design and the methodology. In Sections 5 and 6, I will illustrate the distinctive profile of EPO companies. Finally, in the last two sections (7 and 8), I will analyse the performance of the latter and draw some conclusions of a more general nature.

2. Contextual factors: the geography of innovation

Innovation does not happen everywhere. It tends to agglomerate in certain places rich in resources strictly linked to the socio-institutional context (universities, research centres, advanced services, etc.). The spatial dimension is important for innovation for three main reasons. The first is that the introduction of new products and production processes involves interaction and exchange among numerous actors (companies, governments and research centres); in other words, it is configured as a joint process of creation and/or application of new knowledge which is facilitated by spatial proximity (Asheim & Gertler, 2005).

The second reason relates to the importance of 'local collective competition goods' which create external economies: that is to say, special benefits for companies because they both lower production costs and increase innovative capacity. These externalities can be either tangible or intangible: the former includes infrastructure and local services; the latter, both cognitive and normative resources, such as tacit, contextualized knowledge, conventions, norms of reciprocity and local social capital (Crouch, Le Galès, Trigilia, & Voelzkow, 2001).

The third reason is linked to knowledge spillovers – the, more or less voluntary, circulation of information and knowledge produced in the activity of research and innovation. Knowledge spillovers produce positive externalities which also benefit actors that have not contributed to producing the knowledge. As a result, the innovative performance of companies depends not only on the resources that they invest in research (within the company itself), but also on those invested by other companies and other actors in the same sector or related sectors, as well as by universities, research centres, etc. The appropriation of these spillovers is linked, however, to proximity to the source of new knowledge; and this proximity becomes even more important the more 'tacit knowledge' is also used in the innovation (Polanyi, 1966).

In fact, this territorial expertise, rather than disappearing, actually assumes particular importance against the backdrop of globalization processes. The more codified knowledge circulates easily through global networks, the more tacit knowledge becomes a strategic asset, generating a competitive advantage that is difficult to imitate (Maskell & Malmberg, 1999). In short, the production and dissemination of – economically significant – new knowledge often take place at a local level, in territorial systems of innovation, through the dynamics of learning through interacting (Lundvall & Johnson, 1994).

Various strands of the literature have contributed to the rediscovery of the 'territories of innovation'. Some economists have explored either the existence of 'geographically bounded' spillovers, or the 'localized effects of university research' due to the human capital conveyed by star scientists. Others have worked on systems of innovation at the national and regional levels and on the competitive advantages created by agglomeration economies (Ramella, 2016).

In general, however, economists have mostly underlined the cognitive aspects of the circulation of information and knowledge and the importance of territorial proximity in facilitating this circulation. In the most recent years, however, economic geographers have gradually 'relativized' and 'socialized' the concepts of distance and proximity and transformed them into relational terms (Rodríguez-Pose, 2011). Recent studies have attempted to make these categories less static and more processual, transforming them into a continuum of multilevel relations – that is, relations which take place on different territorial levels. In other words, there is a 'relational stretching' of the distance/proximity dyad, with the result that these concepts lose their exclusive anchorage to the dimension of geographical space. In this way, distance is socialized: different types of relationship between the actors render territorial proximity more or less important, and proximity thus becomes a multidimensional concept (Boschma, 2005).

Finally, sociologists have enhanced understanding of how innovation is socially constructed at different territorial and analytical levels. At the macro- (global and national) and meso- (regional and local) levels of analysis, they have underlined the importance of the socio-institutional context and of the 'modes of regulation', exploring the links among different varieties of capitalism and their regime of innovation. At the micro-level, they have analysed the social embeddedness of economic activities, underlining the influence of networks of interactions among innovative actors (Ramella, 2016).

3. Agency and relational factors: entrepreneurial strategies

That said, the emphasis placed on the territorial and systemic aspects of innovation should not over-restrict the space attributed to 'agency and relational factors' – in other words, to entrepreneurial strategies. As has been pointed out, a common error in various institutional and systemic approaches is to read the behaviour of the actors – the companies, for instance – only through the characteristics of the contexts in which they operate (Gertler, 2010, p. 5). But companies have a certain strategic autonomy with regard to the institutional contexts to which they pertain: they are not exclusively 'rule-takers'; they are also 'rule-makers' (Crouch, Schröder, & Voelzkow, 2009). They derive a substantial degree of freedom from the reflexive re-elaboration of the repertoire of skills and experience that they have inherited from their own past. And they do so in a way that is partly independent of the industry and the country in which they operate. Berger (2005) described this approach as the 'dynamic legacies model'.

The study of innovation cannot, therefore, leave the choices made by companies, and their competitive and organizational strategies, out of consideration. With regard to the latter, for example, certain studies link the innovative capacity of companies to the specific organizational designs that they adopt. Research carried out by Lester and Piore (2004) on case studies in the fields of mobile phones, medical appliances and clothing shows that the most important innovations derive from an organizational and management approach of an 'interpretive' type. The authors contrast two different procedural approaches to problem-solving: analytical and interpretive. 'Analytical processes' are those that can be applied when the problems to be solved and the possible results are well known. 'Interpretive processes', however, are more appropriate when neither the decision alternatives nor the possible outcomes are known in advance. Solutions must, therefore, be sought by exploring the frontier of innovation. In the latter case, the activity of discovering new solutions proceeds through 'interpretive conversations' between people who pertain to different organizational areas and work teams. Managerial activity, therefore, is aimed at promoting the open exchange of communication and integrating a variety of resources in order to cross predetermined cognitive and organizational boundaries. The results of Lester and Piore's study shed light on how the creation of these 'interpretive spaces' – open to the contribution of a plurality of subjects – produces the best results.

The three case studies analysed by Stark (2009) – through ethnographic research on the media and on finance in the USA, and on the machine tool sector in Hungary – also bring out this interpretive aspect in relation to innovation. This is especially true when organizations find themselves operating in competitive environments characterized by scenarios of radical uncertainty. In these contexts, the best performance is obtained by 'heterarchical organizations', which are able to take advantage of the uncertainty by nurturing an ongoing capacity for innovation. These organizations tend to question organizational routine systematically and intentionally, and to foster co-presence and dialogue between different evaluative criteria deriving from different units and skills. 'Heterarchy', therefore, represents a strategy that seeks to 'organize dissonance' by exploiting the intelligence dispersed within an organization and coordinating it, without suppressing the presence of different principles of evaluation and valorization. The interactive coexistence of dissonant elements generates 'creative frictions', and these foster the innovative recombination of resources.

If, on the one hand, this perspective on business reclaims the analytical independence of 'agency factors' (in terms of firms' strategies and organizational design), it does not, on the other, mean isolating the companies from the context in which they operate. On the contrary, what is really interesting is to see how companies are able to exploit the opportunities or compensate for the obstacles which are present in the context by developing 'interactive learning networks' (relational factors) and how they can do so both internally and externally.

In fact, in recent years, emphasis has been placed on the development of organizational forms that are not only more flexible, but also more open to collaboration with other actors, including businesses, universities, local agencies, etc. The rapidity of technological change, the uncertainty of its evolutionary trajectories, growing international competition and the pluralization of knowledge sources have made companies more dependent on external resources. Inter-organizational partnerships (alliances between companies, collaboration with universities, etc.) have therefore multiplied, especially in the field of research and innovation. And this has focused the attention of innovation studies on the social and economic networks that support them (Powell & Grodal, 2005).

In conclusion, the different business strategies (agency and relational factors) help to explain the significant heterogeneity of performance observed both in territories and in production sectors (contextual factors). That being said, we nonetheless know relatively little about the behaviour of the most innovative companies during the international economic crisis.

4. A piece of research on innovative Italian companies

Italy is a particularly interesting case for the analysis of the issues mentioned in the two preceding sections, and for two reasons: firstly, because it embodies a regionalized model of capitalism with a strong territorial agglomeration of innovation (Burroni & Trigilia, 2011; Ramella & Trigilia, 2010a, 2010b; Trigilia & Burroni, 2009) and, secondly, because its production structure has been greatly modified by the crisis, and it therefore becomes interesting to determine whether and how the adoption of a particular management strategy – collaborative in nature – has helped some firms to cope with this radical challenge.

With regard to the first point, as is well known, Italy is the second largest manufacturing country in Europe. Perhaps less well known is the fact that this also applies to medium-high and high-technology sectors. When these productive sectors are grouped together, it turns out that, in 2012, Italy was first in Europe in terms of number of companies, second in terms of volume of employment and third in terms of turnover and value added (calculations based on Eurostat data). This indicates an extremely respectable productive potential that, however, does not seem able to translate into an equivalent capacity for innovation, as the data on patenting clearly highlight. In general, Italian patenting intensity is fairly low, standing at around two-thirds of the European average (70 patents per million inhabitants vs. 109). But it is the country's performance in high-tech sectors that is, in fact, far from satisfactory, where it manages to reach only a quarter of the EU average (2.8 vs. 10.5). In other words, the gap increases precisely in the production sectors where the deficiencies of the national/regional systems of innovation have a stronger and more negative impact.

As regards the second point, it should be borne in mind that the blow delivered by the international economic crisis to the Italian manufacturing system was a particularly severe one. There has been not only a significant slowdown in economic growth, but also a drastic reduction in employment and investment.[3] And yet, less negative signals also emerged in the years of crisis, such as an increase in the percentage of companies taking a proactive approach by investing in innovation.[4] Analysing the profile of innovative companies, especially in high-technology areas, may therefore prove interesting in terms of defining the ingredients (external and internal) that explain this improved performance. Precisely to investigate this question, a survey was carried out on Italian companies with European patents in the fields of mechanical engineering and high technology (EPO companies).

4.1. The research design and methodology

The data discussed in this article derive from research on the geography of innovation in Italy, in the areas of high and medium-high technology, which was carried out over a period of five years: from the beginning of 2008 to the end of 2012. The research was divided into three parts: (a) territorial analysis of patent activity; (b) study of companies with European patents and (c) an investigation of inventors. Although in the next sections I will mainly comment on data coming from the survey on enterprises, I shall also use information derived from the other two parts of the research. It is, therefore, necessary to provide some details on all of them.

(a) *The territorial analysis: the European patents*
During the first phase of research, the geography of innovation in Italy was analysed. The main goal was to delineate the key socio-economic characteristics of the most innovative territories, which we labelled 'innovation leading systems'. To this end, we used as our indicator the number of patent applications filed by Italian enterprises, individuals and public organizations between 1995 and 2004 with the European agency for the protection of intellectual property rights. The information on the patents was collected through the database of the EPO (http://ep.espacenet.com). To identify the high- and medium-high technology sectors, we used the Eurostat-OECD classification (manufacturing industries classified according to their global technological intensity), which divides manufacturing into four classes according to a descending order of technology intensity. The geographical localization of these patents was then reconstructed at a particularly precise territorial (subregional) level, that of 'local labour systems'. These are the territorial units created

by the Italian National Institute of Statistics (ISTAT), on the basis of 'home to work commuting', that is, by identifying areas where there is a high 'self-containment' of daily population movements for reasons of work.

(b) *The survey of EPO companies*

(b1) In the second phase of the research, the analytical focus shifted from the territories to the organizational and relational characteristics of companies. The reference in this part of the survey was to high-technology and mechanical engineering companies. A panel survey method was used: the same businesses were interviewed in two successive stages. To identify the universe of reference, 5313 European patents granted to Italian recipients in the mechanical engineering and high-technology fields were analysed. This base was converted into a list of 1504 active companies, to which a questionnaire was electronically administered (CAWI method: computer-assisted web interviewing).

(b2) The first research stage (EP0-survey 2010) was carried out in early 2010, and 407 companies responded – in whole or in part – to the questionnaire, a response rate of 27%. The second stage (EP0-survey 2012) was replicated in late 2012 using (a) the 'same' sample of companies that had responded to the first survey and (b) the 'same' investigation techniques. A total of 155 companies responded to the second interview, a response rate equal to 40% of the companies that were still active/available. Analysis of the profile of the companies that did not respond to the questionnaire did not show any systematic distortion of the sample compared to the universe of reference. In the first survey, a sample audit was carried out (407 companies) compared to the universe (1504 companies) based on the geographical localization and industrial sector of the companies. In the second survey, in addition to the previous two variables, the sample (155 companies) was also compared to the universe (407 companies) according to the size class of the employees. In all cases, the sample/universe deviations were always very limited, comprising between 3% and 8% (the latter percentage refers to the second survey, and the comparison of class size).

(c) *The inventors*

(c1) The survey (Inventors Survey)

Finally, in the third phase of the research, using information contained in the patent files on the authors of the inventions, we examined the individual profiles of the latter and the organizational and relational contexts in which the discoveries were made. To this end, we carried out a survey between June and July 2009 which involved 739 inventors. The contact data were extracted from a sample of Italian patents selected from those granted by the EPO. To select the patents from which to derive the names of the inventors, a mixed sample design (probabilistic and non-probabilistic) was used. A total of 2825 patents were selected overall, from which a list of 2681 'useful contacts' was derived for the survey (disregarding those contacts who were untraceable, deceased, etc.). In all, 739 inventors completed the questionnaire (a response rate of 28%). The survey was conducted by means of electronically administered questionnaires (CAWI method).

(c2) The qualitative interviews

To give the study more detail, we also selected a smaller (territorially stratified) sample of inventors in the fields of mechanical engineering and pharmaceuticals. Thirty semi-structured interviews were carried out in the central and northern regions (15 for the pharmaceutical sector and 15 for mechanical engineering) with, in patent terms, the most prolific inventors. In all, 23 interviews were conducted in the South (11 for the pharmaceutical sector and 12 for mechanical engineering) with inventors with more than one patent, resident in one of the following three regions: Campania, Puglia and Sicily.

5. The profile of EPO companies

Having completed the presentation of the overall research design, we now focus on what is our main interest in this article: the EPO companies. As mentioned in the previous section, 407 companies responded – in whole or in part – to the first questionnaire (EP0-survey 2010), with a total of 1478 patents, an average of 3.6 per firm. Their territorial origin was concentrated in the more developed regions of Italy: 43% were located in the North-West and 50% – especially those involved with mechanical engineering – in the Central and North-East regions, the so-called Third Italy.

Their biographical and structural profile highlights the solidity of the EPO companies. Almost 80% had been active for over 20 years. Although there was a clear prevalence of small and medium-sized companies (under 250 employees), about half were medium-large (over 50 employees) and had a good turnover (over 10 million euros) and high labour productivity (with a turnover per employee of around 257,000 euros). In the main, they were companies that catered to national and international markets, providing – particularly in the engineering sector – intermediate and capital goods (machinery and components) that other companies used to produce goods destined for final consumers.

The markets in which they operated were characterized by a high level of competition and radical uncertainty, and human capital was one of the key resources with which to address these competitive scenarios: 49% of entrepreneurs were university graduates and half of the employees had a high-school diploma or a certificate of higher education. Internal training was also given a great deal of attention. Overall, these were solid companies with a good level of production performance. And this is the first distinctive aspect of EPO companies. To see this clearly, it is only necessary to compare their profiles with the average profile present in the same sectors at a national level (Table 1).

Among the EPO companies, micro-businesses with fewer than 10 workers were seriously under-represented: just 9%, while in Italy they exceed 80%. Conversely, medium and large companies (over 50 employees) were over-represented: 55% against an Italian average that approaches only 4%. Where size was similar, performance was higher in terms of turnover, labour productivity and export capacity. The gap was particularly significant for smaller companies. Those with fewer than 20 employees had a turnover 6 times higher than other Italian companies operating in the same sectors, while labour productivity and export shares were nearly double. Such performance levels are extremely important, since they highlight high competitive capacity linked – as we shall see – to innovation.

The EPO companies invested heavily in research and development (R&D). On average in the mechanical engineering sector, a 5% share of the turnover is devoted to this area, while for high-technology companies the figure is 7%. These are considerable resources, especially as regards the first of the two sectors. Research work is carried out by specific project teams, present in 79% of EPO companies (source: EP0-survey 2010). The work of the teams is overseen by senior managerial figures, who ensure the coordination and

Table 1. Profile of EPO companies compared to average national values.

	EPO companies			National companies		
	High technology	Mechanical engineering	Total	High technology	Mechanical engineering	Total
Employees						
Up to 9 employees	10.1	8.7	9.1	88.8	75.8	81.3
10–49 employees	31.9	38.1	36.3	8.7	19.8	15.1
50–249 employees	37.7	31.2	33.1	2.0	3.8	3.1
250 employees and more	20.3	22.0	21.5	0.5	0.6	0.5
Total	100.0	100.0	100.0	100.0	100.0	100.0
Up to 19 employees						
Turnover (thousand euros)	2,116	2,524	2,419	289	567	444
Turnover per employee (thousand euros)	181	268	244	104	130	121
% of turnover on exports	44.0	42.5	42.9	14.3	24.8	21.8
20 employees and more						
Turnover (thousand euros)	352,108	57,538	142,339	34,860	21,273	24,974
Turnover per employee (thousand euros)	378	215	262	254	248	250
% of turnover on exports	53.4	63.8	60.7	36.5	52.6	46.5

Source: EPO-survey 2010; ISTAT *Conti economici delle imprese*, 2010, our elaborations.

integration of the various projects. Team organization follows a precise model, characterized by cohesion and flexibility: coordination by one or more people is accompanied, as regards researchers, by a strong tendency towards self-management in their work. These, therefore, are small, highly cohesive work groups, within which however researchers enjoy a considerable level of autonomy in carrying out their duties.

Informal discussions with colleagues – especially those working for the same company – play a particularly important role. These ongoing dialogues represent the hidden ingredient in what we might call the 'dialectic of discovery'. This is a subtle weft of conversation (more or less formalized), exchanges of ideas, lively discussions and occasional clashes, which does not exclude playfulness, that leads the group work towards the invention (which may or may not be patented).

> These discussions (…) are usually never organized. They take place in the canteen, or after 5.00 pm, or over a pizza, when we're chatting about how a particular machine should be made (mechanical sector).[5]

These conversations accompany the process of discovery both in the generative phase of invention – that is, in the work done before the discovery – and in the later phase of verification and development of the new idea hatched at the crucial moment of 'insight'.

> When an idea comes to you, it doesn't immediately come all wrapped up and finished, with the colours and details all in place. Instead, you have this nebulous, confusing stuff that you can't represent or build. So then comes a phase when the nebulous, out-of-focus stuff has to be clarified. And talking to others can be very useful to move this idea on from the nebulous phase to the stage where it becomes clear and defined (mechanical sector).

It is not only the ongoing confrontation with close colleagues that is important, however; so too is the cooperation with, and flow of information through, the various teams present in the same organization. And this requires a specific corporate culture and an organizational approach able to generate positive-sum games and nourish mutual trust, so as to avoid what one interviewee called the 'closed drawer' trap.

> Office relationships are important. (...) You can't have the 'closed drawer' philosophy going around, because that way you'll never get anywhere (mechanical sector).

> You'd try and do something together with the laboratories and then you'd come back and re-discuss everything. (...) In one laboratory there could also be people working on different types of projects, but there was always a discussion going on (pharmaceutical sector).

Alongside these elements, however, the role played by the plurality of skills and knowledge available should not be forgotten. The variety of cognitive resources[6] is, in fact, crucial for the success of inventions and their subsequent development. In 59% of cases, the skills of researchers were defined by interviewees as 'kindred': all the team members belonged to the same scientific field, but with quite different specializations. In 30% of companies, however, the skills were highly 'heterogeneous' and involved the collaboration of researchers from a variety of scientific and technological fields. Finally, in the remaining 11% of cases, there were teams with very 'homogenous' skills (source: Inventors Survey).

The variety of internal skills influenced the absorptive capacity of the project teams and, more generally, of the companies themselves (Cohen & Levinthal, 1990). The presence of a plurality of specializations, in fact, increased their ability to absorb information from outside. To acquire the knowledge useful to them, companies make extensive use of different sources of information: some information comes from the company itself or from other companies within the same group ('internal sources'); other information is derived from relationships with suppliers, customers, competitors, etc. ('external market sources') and more again arrives from relationships with research institutes, universities, consultants, etc. ('external technico-scientific sources'). In general, the EPO companies mainly made use of the first two types of channels. But what most differentiated them was the use of knowledge from the scientific and technological community, which was superior not only in high-tech sectors and in the larger companies, but also in those with a greater endowment of researchers and with more diverse skills in project teams.

A variety of internal resources (the extent and plurality of skills), therefore, significantly influenced innovative capacity. In general, a deficit in variety greatly hindered the production of new and truly creative ideas, which require, in addition to synergy within the team, organizational models that allow the circulation of various types of knowledge derived by the company from both internal and external sources.

> (The most innovative companies are those where) information circulates, both vertically and horizontally. Success is information plus integration, because sometimes it's opposing knowledge and skills that create the solution. (...) Working time has to be broken up, to create discontinuity in the routine; and this generates stress, generates ideas ... in fact, I'd say that ideas are produced under stress. (...) And that's why we need to have teams with different knowledge and different skills (mechanical sector).

As can be seen, these observations are very much in line with the interpretive approach to problem-solving highlighted by Lester and Piore, and with the heterarchical organizational forms described by David Stark. These results are also confirmed in studies on organizations at the cutting edge of scientific research (Hollingsworth, Hollingsworth, & Hage, 2008).

6. The social and territorial embeddedness of EPO companies

As previously mentioned, however, organizational flexibility and internal skills alone are not enough to ensure good innovative performance. Since the mid-1990s, innovation studies have shown growing interest in inter-organizational relationships due to the exponential increase in collaborative relations between companies, especially those in the hightech sectors (Hagedoorn, 2002, pp. 479–482), and the diffusion of business strategies based on 'open innovation' (Chesbrough, 2003).

Collaborative practices of this kind are widespread among Italian EPO companies. Overall, 70% of those surveyed had at least one 'innovative partnership': 59% of them had at least one partnership with other companies (mainly small and medium size) and 54% with a research centre or university (source: EP0-survey 2010). These are extraordinarily high figures, as is clear from comparison with national averages. In Italy, in fact, in the same period in which we conducted the survey, only 13% of innovative companies had cooperation agreements for innovation with external partners: this was the lowest percentage in Europe, where on average recorded values were 25% (CIS, 2010). While percentages rise in the high-technology sector, they still place Italy among the lowest positions in the European ranking. The point to emphasize, therefore, is 'the pervasiveness of innovative partnerships', which represent a highly distinctive element of EPO companies.

But what kind of collaborations are they? Most of them involve partners located at a certain geographical distance: in other words, they are based on 'long networks' (extraregional) that make it possible for companies to acquire 'non-redundant' knowledge and skills – that is, resources and information different from those already in possession of the company and which are not available in the surrounding area. In all, 42% of the EPO companies had partnerships with national companies and 34% with foreign companies; 34% with national universities or research centres and 17% with foreign institutions. This does not mean that short networks – relations with local/regional companies and universities – were not significant: 48% had at least one collaboration of this kind (source: EP0-survey 2010). However, long networks should not be seen as being in opposition to short networks, since in most cases they coexist and nourish each other. In fact, among the companies with at least one partnership, those that combined regional/local and extra-regional collaborations represented the majority: 56.3%. Companies with 'only' regional/local collaborations amounted to 14%, while those that had 'only' extraregional collaborations amounted to 29.7%.

Similarly, it would be a mistake to identify these innovative partnerships, which convey a variety of resources, with relationships governed exclusively by the market. Interviewees were asked to rank innovative partnerships with other companies, distinguishing between those with whom they had an occasional kind of relationship based solely on the logic of the market ('market ties') and those with whom they had established relationships over a period of time and where trust played a major role ('socio-economic ties'). In two-thirds of cases, it was this second type of relationship that prevailed. And this was regardless of the sector, the size of the company and the geographical location of the partner. Our research, therefore, clearly shows the predominant role of – long-lasting and trust-based – 'strong ties' in the structuring of innovative partnerships, both local and non-local. In fact, not only the importance of tacit knowledge, but also the risks of opportunism related to the use of more codified knowledge make the fiduciary aspect particularly significant for this type of transaction.

However, these 'interactive learning networks', which, as said, distinguish EPO companies, should not be isolated from the internal characteristics of the firms, since they affect performance only through the mediation of precise organizational strategies. This is clearly shown by an index that detects an organizational model based on and supporting companies' 'strategic integration'. This index brings together two dimensions: (a) the endowment of human capital and (b) the organizational flexibility and cohesion. It is derived from both semantic (affinity of content) and statistical (factor) analysis conducted on five variables: (V1) the percentage of graduate employees; (V2) the presence of internal training; (V3) the operational autonomy of the research team; (V4) the autonomy of the team's researchers and (V5) the existence of a strong employee commitment to the company's goals.[7]

In other words, the index highlights a corporate culture oriented to collaboration, which is based, on the one hand, on a valorisation of the company's human capital and, on the other, on a flexible and decentralized organizational model involving the participation of researchers and employees. These, therefore, are learning organizations (Arundel et al., 2007), and this also leads to the activation of external collaborations. In the case of the EPO companies, in fact, high scores on the 'strategic integration' index were associated – even taking productive sectors and dimensions into account – with a greater number of external innovative partnerships (Table 2) and – as we will see – with a better level of economic performance.

To this must be added the fact already mentioned in the second section: that is, that the embeddedness of innovation also has a clear territorial matrix. EPO companies are highly agglomerated in urban areas, and most of them belong to 'innovation-leading systems' in the mechanical engineering and high-tech sectors which register the vast majority of Italian patenting activities in the two sectors. Identification of the social and economic characteristics of innovation territories was one of the objectives of the first part of our research (see Section 4) and revealed an environmental profile highly qualified not only from an economic-productive point of view, but also in terms of the endowment of local collective goods.[8]

What makes the innovation-leading systems in the sectors of mechanical engineering and high technology stand out? Compared to other local economic systems (control group) – endowed with good entrepreneurial and productive resources in the two sectors, but with

Table 2. Innovative partnerships.

Level of strategic integration	Medium-low	High
No external collaborations	23.9	15.1
From 1 to 5	41.1	31.4
Over 5	35.0	53.5
Total	100.0	100.0
No. cases	180	172

Source: EPO-survey 2010.
Notes: Collaborations with companies, universities and research centres based on the index of strategic integration (% values). For details, see methodological appendix.

Table 3. Local collective goods present in the territorial area where EPO companies are located (% values).

% of EPO companies that answered that	Are present in the territory in which they are located	Are important for the success of their innovations (score > 5 – scale 1/10)
Private services for research and innovation	69.0	53.2
Private services for legal and commercial consultancy	82.7	54.0
Universities and public research centres	86.5	65.2
Specialized financial services for innovative activities	65.6	51.3
Possibility of collaboration with other companies	76.8	66.1
Possibility of collaboration with clients	80.7	79.9
Good endowment of human resources	77.7	80.6
Good communication and logistic infrastructure	75.5	73.2
Good quality of public services	54.5	60.2
Good standard of living	87.1	77.8

Source: EPO-survey 2010.

a far lower patenting capacity – what most differentiates the leading systems is the quality of the local collective goods. In fact, in order to develop a highly innovative local system, besides an adequate economic and entrepreneurial base, the support of a strong institutional structure is also necessary; the latter comprises a good endowment of human capital and university centres, a developed infrastructure network, advanced services and a high quality of life. The importance of 'contextual factors' also finds precise confirmation in the evaluations given by our interviewees regarding the quality and importance of collective goods present in their territory (Table 3).

7. Innovative and economic performances

This brings us to the performance of EPO companies during the years of the economic crisis. The R&D activities carried out in the preceding years had produced positive economic results on the whole. In fact, almost a third of the turnover of EPO companies derived from patented products. There is, however, no automatic link among research, patenting, innovation and economic performance. Patent activity is often regarded as a proxy for 'innovative output'. In reality, it indicates above all the attitude of companies to research. Firstly, it shows technological capacity and 'inventive output' and, secondly, competitive strategies (not all patents are marketed, since their main purpose is sometimes to block the competition rather than contribute to innovation). It is advisable, therefore, to keep patent activity distinct from 'company innovation' – the introduction, in other words, of new products and new technological solutions relating to processes, organization and marketing designed to improve the company's competitiveness and market position.

That said, besides research, the EPO companies had also produced many innovations. In the last three-year period, almost all of them had introduced a new product or service on the market (89%); nearly three-quarters of them had introduced process (71%) and organizational (74%) innovations; half of them, innovations in marketing (50%)

(source: EP0-survey 2010). Once again, these are extraordinarily high values when one considers that, between 2008 and 2010, only 31% of 'Italian companies' with more than 10 employees managed to achieve some form of product/service or process innovation (European average, 39%) (CIS, 2010).

Finally to be considered is economic performance. Despite the economic crisis, in the three years studied by the first survey (2007–2009), EPO companies showed positive results on average: employees increased by 8% and turnovers by 19%. Only in 2009 did the turnover remain static. To be noted is that, in the same period, Italian industrial companies suffered heavy setbacks: in the first half of 2009, the index of industrial production fell by 23%, with a peak of 36% in the manufacturing of the machinery and mechanical equipment sector; in the second half, the decline was slower but still significant (–14% and –28%, respectively).

The second survey, which covered the next three-year period (2010–2012), also confirmed the good performance of EPO companies. Only 6% of them ceased activity (compared to a national average of 18%). All the other companies that agreed to respond to the new questionnaire continued to carry out innovative activity, producing good economic results: 41% significantly increased resources devoted to research and development; 45% increased their turnover and 19% remained stable; 45% increased the number of their employees and 49% maintained previous levels (only 6% reduced staff).

EPO companies, therefore, continued to perform well even in the worst period of the global economic crisis. Among the more than 400 companies that responded to the initial survey, however, a marked heterogeneity in performance is visible, especially with regard to the trend in turnover and productivity. Those that suffered most in the crisis were the mechanical engineering companies, the largest and the most exposed to international markets. Conversely, small and medium companies – especially in high-tech sectors – achieved better results.

The factors that explain economic performance and innovative performance, however, are significantly different. The ability to achieve a high output of innovation relates to the techno-scientific configuration of the company: high levels of education among employees; the presence of a reasonable number of researchers; good internal collaborative relations; the circulation of non-redundant knowledge gained through external sources; and a rich network of innovative partnerships. To these characteristics may then be added the relatively recent origin of the company and a patenting strategy clearly aimed at the productive exploitation of the discoveries made.

As regards economic performance, together with some of the variables mentioned before, other elements also become relevant, mainly ones connected to organizational and entrepreneurial choices: in particular, the performance on extra-regional markets, and the ability to address the demand of public administrations (especially for medium-to-large companies), large companies (for small companies) and final consumers. Also important is the commercial success of one of the patents obtained.[9]

But what matters most – and this is the point to which I would like to draw attention in this article – is the presence of a collaborative corporate culture, both externally and internally. In fact, both in the first phase of the crisis (EP0-survey 2010) and in the one that followed (EP0-survey 2012), innovative partnerships significantly improved the occupational performance of the EPO companies (Table 4). And this is especially true of those that avoided the 'trap of localism', often by combining short and long networks.

Table 4. Innovative partnerships and occupational performances of companies (% values).

Percentage of companies that increased number of employees during the period	2007–2009	2010–2012
Innovative partnerships		
None	25.0	37.9
At least one	39.3	51.8
Geographical location of partnerships		
Only regional	30.4	33.3
Regional and extra-regional	43.0	53.7
Only extra-regional	36.4	55.2
No. cases	225	141

Source: EPO-survey 2010 and EPO-survey 2012.
Note: For details, see methodological appendix.

Table 5. The economic–occupational performances of companies according to entrepreneurial and organizational strategies (% values).

Companies with	Increase in number of employees		High economic performance 2007–2009
	2007–2009	2010–2012	
No innovative partnership	25.0	37.9	27.3
At least one partnership, with			
Low strategic integration	35.2	40.4	46.9
High strategic integration	42.7	64.8	54.9
No. cases	225	141	166

Source: EPO-survey 2010 and EPO-survey 2012.
Notes: The class of 'high economic performance' refers to the median of the distribution of the index of economic performance. For more details, see note 10 in the text and the methodological appendix.

The ability to capitalize on external resources, however, is strongly influenced by the organizational model that has been chosen internally. Companies with high 'strategic integration' not only have a greater number of innovative partnerships, but also achieve better economic performance.[10] An interesting interaction effect may be observed between these two aspects of corporate culture: in fact, companies that combine a high level of internal integration and external partnerships – that possess, in other words, a corporate culture of collaboration – are those that register the best occupational and economic results (Table 5).

The importance of corporate culture and, in particular, the internal organizational strategy is also confirmed by multivariate statistical analysis (logistic regression) carried out on the companies that provided data on employment trends between 2010 and 2012. For reasons of analytical parsimony, a model was tested which consisted of few

Table 6. Logistic regression that predicts if a company has increased employment in the period 2010–2012.

	Nagelkerke R^2	χ^2	df	Sig.	No. cases included
Summary of model	.407	33.91	4	.000	93
Variable in equation	B	E.S.	df	Sig.	Exp (B)
Presence of innovation (2007–2009)	0.311	1.329	1	.815	1.364
Innovative partnerships (2007–2009)	−0.088	0.872	1	.919	0.915
Strategic integration (2007–2009)	1.924	0.543	1	.000	6.850
Variation in employees (2007–2009)	2.238	0.579	1	.000	9.371
Constant	−2.755	1.528	1	.071	0.064

Source: EPO-survey 2010 and EPO-survey 2012.
Note: For details see methodological appendix.

variables; nevertheless, it made it possible to classify 75% of the EPO companies correctly (as opposed to 50% in the model with only the intercept). The analysis shows that whether companies increased or did not increase employment during the hardest years of the crisis can be predicted by the combination of four variables, only two of which, however, are significant: the occupational trend in the previous period (2007–2009) and the strategic integration of the companies (Table 6).

8. Conclusions: the embedded complementarities of innovation

The results of the two surveys on Italian companies with European patents in the mechanical engineering and high-tech sectors provide clear answers to the questions asked at the beginning of this article regarding their distinctive characteristics and their behaviour during the international economic crisis. What are the specific features that differentiate EPO companies from the others? Firstly, they are 'solid companies' with a skilled workforce, operating in highly competitive and uncertain markets. Even though the majority of them are small or medium-sized companies, compared to the national average, medium-large companies are over-represented. Secondly, they are 'highly innovative' research-intensive companies that introduce many innovations on the market. Thirdly, they are 'deeply embedded at both the social and territorial levels'. The uncertainty of the competitive environment is, in fact, dealt with through the socio-economic embeddedness of their activities.

One of the features that most distinguishes EPO companies is their propensity for 'innovative partnerships': external collaborations for research and innovation purposes. Such partnerships are fairly generalized in these companies, as is the use of external sources of information. Innovation, as we have seen, also has a clear territorial embeddedness. Most EPO companies belong to the leading innovative systems in mechanical engineering and high technology; that is, they operate in local contexts that are highly qualified in both economic and socio-institutional terms. That said, their innovative partnerships are not confined exclusively to a local level. The companies with the best innovative performance manage to combine the advantages of short networks (local and regional) with those of long networks (extra-regional). But also the latter are socially embedded. The majority of innovative partnerships, in fact, do not respond to purely economic and market logic, but are based on collaborations in which reciprocal trust plays a major role.

Another aspect that emerges from the research is the 'importance of the socio-organizational dimension'. An organization that supports its research teams with the appropriate means and allows them full independence, by creating working groups based on flexible coordination methods and a good mix of research integration and researcher autonomy, will significantly enhance inventive/innovative performance. This last, therefore, does not depend exclusively on the characteristics of individual researchers and not even on the simple sum of those in the research team. Rather, it is manifest as an emergent property of (often informal) group interactions that are facilitated by an appropriate organizational structure.

The fourth and last element that distinguishes EPO companies is their 'high economic performance'. These are companies with high levels of turnover, productivity and exporting, which have been able to maintain a substantial dynamism even during the most difficult years of the economic crisis. And this is due to the proactive behaviour of the preceding period, especially in the area of research and innovation. That said, the link between innovation and economic performance is not automatic: even among EPO companies, revenue exhibits a high level of heterogeneity. This heterogeneity depends on variable manufacturing, managerial and market expertise, which is not necessarily associated with the technico-scientific skills and innovative capacity present within a company.

In any case, a significant role is played by what I have called a 'collaborative corporate culture'. In particular, positive results in terms of employment and turnover require a strong 'strategic integration': a good endowment of human capital and organizational practices that valorize both work autonomy and company flexibility and cohesion. It is this 'internal organizational design' that augments the effectiveness of 'external innovative partnerships'. In addition to the importance of the organizational dimension, I also want to emphasize the close relationship between the cognitive and fiduciary aspects in innovation processes. The socio-normative component is often neglected in innovation studies, especially those conducted from an economic perspective. However, the generation of new knowledge and its economic valorization depend on the social capital that the company may have internally, as well as in its external relations. Internal cohesion does not necessarily imply homogeneity of knowledge and judgement criteria, nor an absence of conflict. It is, however, the condition that makes it possible to successfully integrate the variety of resources available both inside and outside the company.

That said, what emerges from the research into EPO companies is the complementarity of resources useful for innovation and economic performance among (a) the internal and external relations of the organization; (b) the variety of knowledge and cohesion of relationships and (c) the short and long networks of collaboration. In conclusion, successful company strategies are those which – thanks to a collaborative company culture – are able to exploit the 'embedded complementarity of innovative resources'.

What lessons of a more general kind can be drawn from the results of this research? Some, as we have seen, concern the management and organizational strategies useful for promoting improved business performance. Others, instead, concern the public actors and policies useful in supporting a long-term development strategy. Research, in fact, confirms the strategic importance of local collective goods and the 'systemic' nature of innovation. In light of these assumptions, therefore, the policies shown to be particularly appropriate are those that aim to strengthen and improve the national/regional system of innovation and the collaboration among the various actors involved therein (companies, research centres, universities, funding agencies, etc.). In contrast, over the last 20 years, the policy mix adopted by Italy (and the other Mediterranean countries) has been focused on direct support to companies (European Commission, 2013. Moreover, during the crisis, government policies – also taking into account the constraints imposed by the EU – have focused on the reduction of public expenditure rather than on research funding, advanced training and the endowment of public goods for innovation. This 'low road to competitiveness' is thus likely to produce a further weakening of the Italian capacity for innovation. The crisis, instead, could have represented an appropriate moment for strategically rethinking development policies, by interpreting it as an opportunity to solve the structural problems of the national system of innovation and to promote more systemic policies for innovation and long-term growth.[11]

Notes

1. These production sectors account for the majority of Italian patents in Europe: the mechanical engineering sector covers 31% and the high-tech sector 24%. Patents are a well-established indicator in the scientific literature (especially in the economic field) that studies innovative output. For a discussion of the analytical potential, as well as the limitations, of this indicator, see Ramella and Trigilia (2010a).
2. These two surveys form part of a larger investigation into the geography of innovation in high technology in Italy that I have carried out with Carlo Trigilia (Ramella & Trigilia, 2010a, 2010b). For details, see Section 4.
3. Giving the per capita GDP of the EU a value of 100, in 2000 Italy had a value of 120. In 2014, this fell to 98, with a reduction of fully 22 percentage points.
4. For greater detail regarding the effects of the economic crisis on Italy and the Mediterranean countries, see Donatiello and Ramella (2017).
5. This quotation, and those that follow, come from the interviews with inventors that we carried out in the third part of our research into the geography of innovation in Italy (see Section 4).
6. In other words, the extent and plurality of knowledge and skills available within the company or acquired through external relations.
7. Factor analysis was conducted with the SPSS statistical program, using the method of main components and oblique rotation (direct oblimin). The analysis led to the extraction of two factors that together explained 50.1% of the variance. The Kaiser–Meyer–Olkin (KMO) test registered a sufficient, even if not good, value equal to 0.53, while the Bartlett sphericity test gave a significant result ($p \leq .01$). On the basis of this analysis, two indices were built. The first – organizational flexibility and cohesion – was based on three variables ($v3 + v4 + v5$) and assumed the maximum value when there was simultaneous occurrence of team autonomy, researcher autonomy and employee involvement. The second – 'human capital' – was based on two variables ($v1 + v2$) and assumed the maximum value in the case of the coexistence of a high endowment of graduates and training activities. The two indices were then aggregated into the strategic integration index (range of variation 0–2), which was used exclusively for typological purposes – that is, to identify an organizational type characterized by high levels of human capital/organizational flexibility and cohesion (index scores ≥ 1.5).
8. This part of the study was carried out using ecological variables, a series of indicators and indices, highly disaggregated at the territorial level, and deriving from a plurality of sources. For data sources and the ecological results of the analysis, see Biagiotti (2010).
9. With reference to these aspects, again see Ramella and Trigilia (2010a).
10. To assess the 'economic performance', an index was built, in an additive way, from the following variables (the weighting coefficients employed are in parentheses): (1) labour productivity (turnover per employee) in 2009 (0.47); (2) variation in labour productivity between 2007 and 2009 (0.40) and (3) variation in turnover between 2007 and 2009 (0.48). These variables were identified from a factorial analysis (principal component analysis, varimax rotation method) that led to the extraction of a factor explaining 57.4% of variance. The KMO test recorded a value of 0.61, and the result of Bartlett's sphericity test was significant ($p \leq .001$).
11. Only in the past year has there been some evidence that a rethinking in this direction is beginning; for example, with the 'Piano Nazionale Industria 4.0' (National Industry Plan 4.0) launched by the Italian government to encourage – through an integrated approach – the digitization of manufacturing sectors.

Disclosure statement

No potential conflict of interest was reported by the author.

References

Arundel, A., Lorenz, E., Lundvall, B.-Å., & Valeyre, A. (2007). How Europe's economies learn: A comparison of work organization and innovation mode for the EU-15. *Industrial and Corporate Change, 16*(6), 1175–1210. doi:10.1093/icc/dtm035

Asheim, B. T., & Gertler, M. S. (2005). The geography of innovation: Regional innovation systems. In J. Fagerberg, D. C. Mowery, & R. R. Nelson (Eds.), *The Oxford handbook of innovation* (pp. 291–317). New York, NY: Oxford University Press.

Berger, S. (2005). *How we compete*. New York, NY: Currency/Doubleday.

Biagiotti, A. (2010). I sistemi locali leader nei brevetti. In F. Ramella, & C. Trigilia (Eds.), *Imprese e territori dell'Alta Tecnologia in Italia* (pp. 75–97). Bologna: Il Mulino.

Boschma, R. A. (2005). Proximity and innovation: A critical assessment. *Regional Studies, 39*(1), 61–74. doi:10.1080/0034340052000320887

Burroni, L., & Trigilia, C. (Eds.). (2011). *Le città dell'innovazione. Dove e perché cresce l'alta tecnologia in Italia*. Bologna: Il Mulino.

Chesbrough, H. W. (2003). *Open innovation: The new imperative for creating and profiting from technology*. Boston, MA: Harvard Business School Press.

CIS. (2010). *Types of co-operation partner for product and process innovation*. Author. Retrieved from http://epp.eurostat.ec.europa.eu/portal/page/portal/science_technology_innovation/data/database

Cohen, W. M., & Levinthal, D. A. (1990). Absorptive capacity: A new perspective on learning and innovation. *Administrative Science Quarterly, 35*(1), 128–133. doi:10.2307/2393553

Crouch, C., Le Galès, P., Trigilia, C., & Voelzkow, H. (2001). *Local production systems in Europe. Rise or demise?* Oxford: Oxford University Press.

Crouch, C., Schröder, M., & Voelzkow, H. (2009). Regional and sectoral varieties of capitalism. *Economy and Society, 38*(4), 654–678. doi:10.1080/03085140903190383

De Vaan, M., Stark, D., & Vedres, B. (2015). Game changer: The topology of creativity. *American Journal of Sociology, 120*(4), 1144–1194. doi:10.1086/681213

Donatiello, D., & Ramella, F. (2017). The innovation paradox in Southern Europe. Unexpected Performance During the Economic Crisis. *South European Society and Politics*. doi:10.1080/13608746.2017.1327339

European Commission. (2013). Lessons from a decade of innovation policy. What can be learnt from the INNO Policy Trend Chart and the Innovation Union Scoreboard. Retrieved from: http://ec.europa.eu/DocsRoom/documents/5220/attachments/1/translations/en/renditions/pdf

Gertler, M. S. (2010). Rules of the game: The place of institutions. *Regional Economic Change, 44*(1), 1–15. doi:10.1080/00343400903389979

Hagedoorn, J. (2002). Inter-firm R&D partnerships: An overview of major trends and patterns since 1960. *Research Policy, 31*(4), 477–492. doi:10.1016/S0048-7333(01)00120-2

Hollingsworth, R., Hollingsworth, E. J., & Hage, J. (2008). *Fostering scientific excellence: Organizations, institutions, and major discoveries in biomedical science*. New York, NY: Cambridge University Press.

Lester, R. K., & Piore, M. J. (2004). *Innovation. The missing dimension*. Cambridge, MA: Harvard University Press.

Lundvall, B.-Å., & Johnson, B. (1994). The learning economy. *Journal of Industry Studies, 1*(2), 23–42. doi:10.1080/13662719400000002

Maskell, P., & Malmberg, A. (1999). Localised learning and industrial competitiveness. *Cambridge Journal of Economics, 23*(2), 167–186. doi:10.1093/cje/23.2.167

Pavitt, K. (2005). Innovation processes. In J. Fagerberg, D. C. Mowery, & R. R. Nelson (Eds.), *The Oxford handbook of innovation* (pp. 86–114). New York, NY: Oxford University Press.

Polanyi, M. (1966). *The tacit dimension*. New York, NY: Anchor Books.

Powell, W. W., & Grodal, S. (2005). Networks of innovators. In J. Fagerberg, D. C. Mowery, & R. R. Nelson (Eds.), *The Oxford handbook of innovation* (pp. 56–85). New York, NY: Oxford University Press.

Ramella, F. (2016). *Sociology of economic innovation*. London: Routledge.

Ramella, F., & Trigilia, C. (Eds). (2010a). *Imprese e territori dell'Alta Tecnologia in Italia* [High-tech companies and their territories in Italy]. Bologna: Il Mulino.
Ramella, F., & Trigilia, C. (Eds). (2010b). *Invenzioni, inventori e territori in Italia* [Inventions and inventors in Italy]. Bologna: Il Mulino.
Rodríguez-Pose, A. (2011). Economists as geographers and geographers as something else: On the changing conception of distance in geography and economics. *Journal of Economic Geography, 11*(2), 347–356. doi:10.1093/jeg/lbq034
Schumpeter, J. A. (1912). *Theorie der wirtschaftlichen Entwicklung.* Leipzig: Duncker & Humblot. Eng. trans. (1980). *The theory of economic development.* London: Oxford University Press.
Stark, D. (2009). *The sense of dissonance.* Princeton, NJ: Princeton University Press.
Trigilia, C., & Burroni, L. (2009). Italy: Rise, decline and restructuring of a regionalized capitalism. *Economy and Society, 38*(4), 630–653. doi:10.1080/03085140903190367

Methodological appendix

Explanatory notes for the tables in the text

Table 2
Innovative partnerships. Collaborations with companies, universities and research centres
This category refers to the following questions in the questionnaire:

a. Can you tell us how many companies you have co-operated with on research and innovation activities in the past three years (2007-2009)?
b. And how many universities and research centres have you co-operated with in the past three years?

Index of strategic integration
The variables in the index refer to the following questions in the questionnaire:

1. V1 What percentage of employees have a qualification of the kind indicated? (undergraduate and postgraduate degree, high-school diploma, vocational school diploma, middle-school certificate)
2. V2 Have any staff training activities been carried out during the past three years (2007-2009)?
1. V3-V4. How would you define the style of working present within these project teams?
   a. V3 The teams have a high level of operational autonomy with regard to the company.
   b. V4 Each team member has a high degree of autonomy in carrying out specific tasks.
2. V5 How would you define the relationship between employees and company management (ownership and management)? Answer B.
   a. There is a clear distinction of roles with respect to the various responsibilities.
   b. There is close cooperation with a strong involvement in all the objectives of the company.
   c. Relationships are difficult because of poor mutual cooperation.

Table 4
Innovative partnerships
See the comment above on Table 2.
Occupational performance
This category refers to the following items in the questionnaire:
Total number of employees on 31/12/2007; 31/12/2009; 31/12/2010; at the end of 2012.

Table 5
In the two surveys, to elicit the turnover, the following question was asked:
What has been the turnover in the past three years? (EP0-survey 2010: 2007, 2008, 2009. EP0-survey 2010: 2010, 2011 and 2012).

For the other variables, see the comments to the previous tables.

Table 6

The table shows the results of a binomial logistic regression which I conducted on the 93 companies for which all relevant information was available. As the 'dependent variable', I used the employment trends between 2010 and 2012: the first class included the companies in which the number of employees had remained stable or decreased, and the second those in which it had increased. I preferred to use this variable, rather than that related to the variation in turnover, as it had fewer missings.

As regards the 'independent variables', I used four dichotomous predictors: (1) companies with at least one innovative partnership in the period 2007–2009; (2) companies with at least one innovation in the period 2007–2009 (see below); (3) companies with high strategic integration in the period 2007–2009 and (4) companies that increased employment in the period 2007–2009.

Other regressions performed – for control purposes – with variables related to market strategies (% of foreign sales) and intensity of research produced similar results.

Variable 2 refers to companies that gave an affirmative answer to at least one of the following questions in the questionnaire:

In the past three years, has the company introduced:

1. Innovations in Products/Service?
   a. Technologically new (or significantly improved) products?
   b. Technologically new (or significantly improved) services?.
2. 4. Innovations in Processes?
   a. Technologically new (or significantly improved) production processes?
   b. Systems of logistics, distribution methods or external supply of technologically new (or significantly improved) products or services?
   c. Other technologically new (or significantly improved) processes concerning the management of purchasing, maintenance and support activities, management of administrative and information systems, accounting activities?
3. Organizational innovations?
   a. New (or significantly improved) management techniques to enhance the use and exchange of information, knowledge and technical skills and internal work?
   b. New forms of work organization, such as the definition of new divisional or business units, the reduction of hierarchical levels, the decentralization of company decision making?
   c. Changes in relationships with other companies or public institutions, such as new production and commercial agreements, partnerships, sub-contracting agreements or outsourcing?
4. Marketing innovations?
   a. Significant changes in the aesthetic characteristics of the products, including those relating to packaging?
   b. New (or significantly improved) marketing techniques and practices or distribution of products or services, such as electronic commerce, franchising, direct sales or distribution licenses?

For the other variables, see the comments on the previous tables.

A new approach to business innovation modes: the 'Research, Technology and Human Resource Management (RTH) model' in the ICT sector in Belarus

Natalja Apanasovich, Henar Alcalde-Heras and Mario Davide Parrilli

ABSTRACT

Echoing previous contributions on 'STI and DUI innovation modes' (science and technology-based innovation, and innovation based on learning-by-doing, by-using and by-interacting), this study discusses their role in small and medium-sized enterprise (SME) ability to develop novel products. In particular, the RTH model (based on Research, Technology and Human Resource Management) is proposed so as to describe the most effective approach taken by innovative SMEs. On these bases, the STI and DUI modes are changed for a more empirical identification of business innovation modes centred on differentiating among three separate drivers of innovation: Research (R), non-research and development (R&D) Technology (T) and Human Resource management (HRM). The study focuses on analysing how different drivers of innovation can be effectively aggregated within a firm to support its ability to produce innovation. We propose a new research instrument – RTH model – and test on a sample of SMEs in the ICT sphere that operates in a technology-follower country in transition, Belarus. The results of the econometric analyses show insightful outcomes, that is, the novelty of product innovation is more sensitive to the Technology and HRM drivers than to the Research driver.

1. Introduction

In recent years, the debate on business modes of innovation has attracted a noteworthy interest among international scholars. However, their country-based analyses on the modes of innovation (derived from the literature on innovation systems, that is, Cooke, Heidenreich, & Braczick, 2004; Lundvall, 1992) have been mainly tested in market economies (Amara, Landry, Becheikh, & Ouimet, 2008; Aslesen, Isaksen, & Karlsen, 2012; Fitjar & Rodriguez-Pose, 2013; Jensen, Johnson, Lorenz, & Lundvall, 2007; Isaksen & Nilsson, 2013; Malaver & Vargas, 2013; Nunes & Lopes, 2015; Parrilli & Alcalde Heras, 2016; Parrilli & Elola, 2012). These studies have shown that firms that combine science and technology-based innovation (STI) and learning-by-doing, by-using, and by-interacting (DUI) modes of learning are more likely to innovate than those relying on the STI and DUI mode taken separately. This happens in Denmark (Jensen et al., 2007), Norway and Sweden (Aslesen et al., 2012; Isaksen & Nilsson, 2013, p. 2) and Canada (Amara et al., 2008). However, other studies developed in Spain (Gonzalez-Pernia, Parrilli, and Peña-Legazkue, 2015; Parrilli & Elola, 2012), China (Chen, Chen, & Vanhaverbeke, 2011), Portugal (Nunes & Lopes, 2015) and Colombia (Malaver & Vargas, 2013) show more ambiguous results. This might lead to some context-specific interpretation of the importance of innovation modes that we aim at exploring in further depth. In the context of post-Soviet transition economies (PSTE), the study of the effect of modes of innovation on firm performance has been developed to a limited extent (Apanasovich, Alcalde Heras, & Parrilli, 2016), thus motivating the present research endeavour. The peculiarities of these countries are, on the negative side, the lack of financial capital, innovation management experience and state-of-the-art technology, while, on the positive side, a rather high level of educated human capital (Aidis, Estrin, & Mickiewicz, 2008; Fink, Haiss, & Vukšić 2009; Rees & Miazhevich, 2009). Together with former cultural and/or institutional interpretations of innovations system's paradoxes (Asheim & Gertler, 2005; Edquist, 2005), this work promotes a novel hypothesis regarding the importance of human resources and technological context-specificities in transition economies.

Since our study was aimed to contribute to the ongoing debate on modes of innovation (Aslesen et al., 2012; Jensen et al., 2007; Parrilli & Elola, 2012), Isaksen and Karlsen (2012), Isaksen and Nilsson (2013), Nunes and Lopes (2015), Gonzalez-Pernia et al. (2015) and Apanasovich et al. (2016) traditionally focused on small and medium-sized enterprises (SMEs), we decide to analyse this particular group of enterprises. Business research and empirical evidence shows that SMEs are a key competitive actor in most national and regional economies (Becattini, Bellandi, & De Propris, 2009; Cooke, 2001; Rammer, Czarnitzki, & Spielkamp, 2009). These firms are critical for a dynamic market economy, as they are commonly recognized as nimbler than larger enterprises, thus can easily explore new types of activities (Rammer et al., 2009).

Different studies focused on innovation in this type of firms as a means to increase their competitive capacity and that of their countries (Acs & Audretsch, 1990). They concluded that the innovation capacity of SMEs is hindered by their scale limitations and the lack of financial and specialized human resources (see also Pavitt, 1998). Furthermore, in a context of uncertainty, new opportunities arise and innovation becomes determinant for survival. Within this new business milieu, our second contribution is to identify and weigh aspects of the innovation process, such as the key innovation drivers, profiles and modes adopted by SMEs in PSTE.

A third contribution of this study is the context-embedded selection of business innovation drivers that helps to explain why some firms are more innovative than others. The literature is relatively silent on how to connect the 'R', 'T' and 'H' drivers in one mode of innovation (Isaksen & Karlsen, 2012). In this regard, the novelty of our study is that it goes beyond the analysis of modes of innovation and proposes a more fine-grained tool to identify 'real-life' innovation profiles and modes of innovation, and their impact on the novelty of product innovation. In order to explain the logic behind this argument, we present the elements of the RTH model (see Appendix 1). More specifically, each innovation profile implies a specific combination of the three drivers in different 'theoretical' proportions. Firms with similar innovation profiles are then grouped into 'practice-based' clusters, which are defined as representative 'modes of innovation'. The interrelation between innovation profiles and modes of innovation enables the identification of the most effective (and real) innovation mode, which involves particular levels of each driver.

We test the aforementioned research tool in the original context of transition economies (i.e. Belarus) on a sample of SMEs in the ICT sphere. In our exploratory work, we have selected the ICT sector because of its rapid growth and great potential to contribute to the Belarusian economy. In 2016, this sector demonstrated significant export growth. The average annual growth of IT services is about 20–30%. There are successful examples of the Belarusian IT companies and start-ups that have received recognition of millions of users worldwide: Wargaming (World of Tanks, the world-famous 'Tank Battle'), MAPS.ME (offline map of the world), 'Masquerade' (MSQRD) and Viber messenger. The Belarusian Company EPAM Systems is listed on the New York Stock Exchange. As a consequence, the ICT industry is a good case for a preliminary study in which we explore the reasonableness of the proposed interpretive model (i.e. RTH).

This paper is structured as follows. In Section 2, we discuss the main streams of research focusing on the sources of innovation within the business innovation mode literature. The description of the RTH model of innovation and our research propositions are provided in Section 3. The empirical Section 4 describes the sample, variables and econometric techniques employed. Section 5 presents the results of the statistical and econometric analysis, whereas the final section summarizes the findings and discusses the implications for research and policy-making.

2. The debate on STI and DUI innovation modes

The model we propose with this work (see next Section 3) is based upon (and derived from) a sub-strand of the literature on innovation systems. In particular, the selected topic refers to the type of knowledge bases and innovation approaches developed by businesses in different countries and regions (Archibugi & Lundvall, 2001; Asheim & Coenen, 2005; Lundvall, 1992, 2007; Parrilli & Alcalde Heras, 2016). Specifically, it frames the behaviour of firms within country or regional perspectives – and their cultural idiosyncrasies – that should be considered when analysing the business contribution to the innovation output of their regional and/or national economies (Parrilli, Fitjar, & Rodriguez-Pose, 2016). On these bases, Jensen et al. (2007) explicitly identified the STI mode through which firms can improve their innovation capabilities through a stronger connection to science that provides a platform for the firm's technological learning and innovation. The majority of innovation activities and research-based projects that characterize the STI mode of innovation take place in research and development (R&D) departments, universities and research institutes. Therefore, the key inputs for innovation are investments in R&D, scientific human capital and collaboration with scientific partners (Cohen & Levinthal, 1989; Griliches, 1979; Romer, 1994). However, this mode cannot explain the capacity of economies such as Denmark and Norway to demonstrate high innovation output despite their more limited R&D investments vis-à-vis other highly R&D investing countries. In contrast, a second approach to business innovation stresses the importance of practice and interaction-based innovation that relies on DUI (Chen et al., 2011; Fitjar & Rodriguez-Pose, 2013; Jensen et al., 2007). Specifically, learning-by-doing is based upon the accumulation of experience (Arrow, 1962); learning-by-using machines and technological equipment allows to acquire competences by deploying relevant state-of-the-art technologies (Rosenberg, 1982) and learning-by-interacting involves collaborations between various organizations that provide access to different kinds of knowledge and market information, and impact positively on the development of novel innovation (Alcalde, 2014; Fu, Diez, & Schiller, 2013; Lundvall, 1992; Von Hippel, 1988).

This debate has recently stressed that these 'primordial' modes are not mutually exclusive. Scholars argue that these modes might complement each other in the production of higher outcomes in terms of both innovation and economic performance (Aslesen et al., 2012; Chen et al., 2011; Jensen et al., 2007; Isaksen and Karlsen, 2012; Parrilli & Alcalde Heras, 2016). Specifically, positive evidence has been found in Norway and Sweden (Aslesen et al., 2012; Isaksen & Karlsen, 2012; Isaksen & Nilsson, 2013), Portugal (Nunes & Lopes, 2015), China (Chen et al., 2011) and Spain (Gonzalez-Pernia et al., 2015; Parrilli & Alcalde Heras, 2016). Table 1 provides information about the country comparison in terms of the most effective mode of innovation. In the majority of studies that analyse the STI and DUI modes of innovation, the STI + DUI mode is the most effective mode. At the same time, these countries differ a lot in the levels of development of such modes (Nielsen, 2011; UN, 2013). However, as posited by Isaksen and Karlsen (2012), the afore-mentioned studies do not specify how firms mix the two modes of innovation to increase their own performance. In this regard, our research focuses on analysing how different drivers of innovation can be effectively aggregated within a firm to support its capacity to produce innovation, as well as the novelty of such innovations.

3. The RTH model of innovation

Jensen et al. (2007) established an original classification of the STI, DUI and mixed STI + DUI modes of innovation. Regarding the characteristics of human resources, while the STI mode encourages the power of highly educated scientific employees to exploit codified knowledge and collaborate with other researchers, the DUI mode requires experienced

Table 1. Literature review on innovation modes.

Study	Country	Economy	The most effective mode
Jensen et al. (2007)	Denmark	Market, North Europe	STI + DUI
Aslesen et al. (2012), Isaksen and Karlsen (2012), Isaksen and Nilsson (2013)	Norway, Sweden	Market, North Europe	STI + DUI
Nunes and Lopes (2015)	Portugal	Market, South Europe	STI + DUI
Parrilli and Elola (2012), Gonzalez-Pernia et al. (2015) Parrilli and Alcalde Heras (2016)	Spain	Market, South Europe	STI (product innovation), STI + DUI
Amara et al. (2008)	Canada	Market, North America	STI + DUI
Chen et al. (2011)	China	Emerging country	STI + DUI in high-tech DUI in low-tech
Malaver and Vargas (2013)	Colombia	Emerging country	STI (product innovation)
Apanasovich et al. (2016)	Belarus	Transition, post-soviet	STI + DUI (product innovation), DUI (organizational innovation)

Source: Adapted from Apanasovich (2016) and Parrilli et al. (2016).

and skilled managers, technicians and other employees who can adapt solutions that respond to the needs of lead customers (Isaksen & Karlsen, 2012). The DUI mode can be perceived as a set of Human Resource Management (HRM) practices (Laursen & Foss, 2012, p. 13) because it includes specific indicators such as teamwork, integration of function, softened demarcations (decentralization), education/training systems and communication policy that involve the whole organization. These indicators should not be underestimated, as there is growing evidence available to suggest that HRM practices are positively related to the generation of innovation (Beugelsdijk, 2008; Oke, Walumbwa, & Myers, 2012; Shipton, Fay, West, Patterson, & Birdi, 2005). Beugelsdijk (2008) shows that HRM practices can foster both radical and incremental innovation: for example, training and performance-based pay promote incremental innovations, while radical innovations can be achieved by task autonomy and flexible working hours. Using longitudinal data from UK manufacturing firms, Shipton et al. (2005) demonstrate that effective HRM systems (e.g. incorporating sophisticated approaches to recruitment, appraisal and training) have the potential to promote organizational innovation. As we show in this work, this is particularly relevant to characterize the context and opportunities of PSTE.

As pointed out before, previous studies did not focus on how SMEs mix effectively the STI and DUI modes of innovation or what the effective proportion of their drivers is. In our attempt to close this gap, and realizing the particular specificities derived from HRM, we propose the RTH model that allows revealing the actual proportions of innovation drivers in SME innovation profiles and, later, help to identify the most effective mode of innovation. This three-driver model fills the gap by connecting the set of classical economic drivers of innovation such as Research and Technology (Cohen & Levinthal, 1989; Greunz, 2005; Romer, 1994) with HRM (Beugelsdijk, 2008; Oke et al., 2012; Shipton et al., 2005). Our RTH model benefits from Research (level of scientific development), Technology (level of technological development) and HRM (HRM practices and interaction) innovation drivers (Table 2). The literature is relatively silent on how to separate research and technology; they are usually approximated by the same indicators within the STI mode (Jensen et al., 2007; Parrilli & Elola, 2012). This separation is particularly important at the country level. In fact, the separation of the 'R' from the 'T' may be relevant not only in the context of countries in transition but also for catching-up/emerging economies and developed countries. One of the main reasons why we decided to separate the 'R' from 'T' driver is that in practice firms can innovate in two quite distinct forms. Firstly,

Table 2. Description of RTH drivers.

RTH drivers	Academic categorizations	Seminal contribution	Categories description
Research	Science	Romer (1994)	Basic Research Scientific collaboration
Technology	Learning-by-doing Learning-by-using Learning-by-technical interacting	Arrow, (1962); Rosenberg (1982)	Manufacturing Operations management Product development and customization Technical collaboration
HRM	Human resources practices Learning-by-internal interacting Learning-by-market interacting	Shipton et al. (2005); Lundvall (1992)	HRM practices Internal collaboration Market-based collaboration

Source: Own elaboration.

technological innovation can be connected to the purchase and installation of new machinery and the effective use of new equipment (Palacín & Radosevic, 2011). In our view, this is very likely to occur in emerging and transition economies. Secondly, other enterprises can benefit from R&D activities and outcomes, for example, patents (R driver) conducted either by themselves or by public institutions and large enterprises. This second option is very likely to occur in the most advanced economies. For this expected divergence, in our work, these two drivers are not bundled together in the innovation mode taken by individual firms. As said above, their intensity is very likely to be determined by the technological context-specificity (i.e. country level of development) and the firms' ability to absorb this knowledge.

3.1. The 'R' driver

The Research driver targets innovation based on R&D, human capital (scientifically trained personnel with PhD and MSc degrees in S&T who work full time in innovation projects) and research collaborations. Business R&D teams increase the absorptive capacity of a company (Cohen & Levinthal, 1990). External R&D activities are considered as a main source of innovation in SMEs (Alcalde Heras, 2014; Rammer et al., 2009). The firm expenditure in R&D can be considered as a long-term investment and if such investments do not have a direct commercial application, they can, however, generate a cash flow in the following years or even later on (Rosenberg, 1990). However, investing in R&D involves high costs and risks, thus firms carefully weigh up all the pros and cons and find a proper balance between the expected benefits from successful R&D activities and the costs and probability of failure and loss of invested capital (Rammer et al., 2009).

Nevertheless, SMEs benefit a lot in terms of innovation activities from a stronger connection to science (Fabrizio, 2009; Fleming & Sorenson, 2004; Parrilli & Elola, 2012). A large amount of such activities take place in collaboration with the centres that produce new knowledge; for example, R&D departments, research-intensive small firms and universities. Such interactions promote positive spillovers (Audretsch, 2003) and the generation of codified/scientific knowledge that a firm uses to produce radical technological innovation (Parrilli & Alcalde Heras, 2016). Therefore, we can conclude that the Research driver, which emphasizes the importance of science and considers investments in R&D, scientific human capital, infrastructure and interaction with research partners, would impact positively on the development of novel products (Cohen & Levinthal, 1989; Fabrizio, 2009; Jong & Slavova, 2014; Romer, 1994).

However, when focusing on PSTE, we must consider certain peculiarities which lead to reformulate previous arguments. They managed to preserve their scientific and engineering potential originated in the Soviet past (Yegorov, 2009); however, the lack of financial capital, innovation management experience and state-of-the-art technology (Apanasovich et al., 2016; Fink et al., 2009; Rees & Miazhevich, 2009) does not facilitate the conversion of basic research into final product innovations. As posited in Apanasovich et al. (2016), PSTE do not fit into the global trend of rising expenditures on R&D, while such economies invest more in acquisition of basic machinery and equipment than in R&D. When comparing expenditure on innovation activities of PSTE, for example, Belarusian enterprises invest 81% of total expenditures on innovation activities in purchasing machinery, equipment and software (among Russian enterprises it is 90% of this type of expenditure). In contrast, Danish and Swedish enterprises spend respectively 81% and 83% of total business innovation expenditure in R&D (Belstat, 2011). The high share of expenditures in machinery and equipment can be explained by the fact that PSTEs are catching-up economies whose technological and innovation system operates behind the technology frontier (Alam, Casero, Khan, & Udomsaph, 2008; Radosevic, 2011; Varblane, Dyker, Tamm, & von Tunzelmann, 2007). Belarus has been chosen for our empirical analysis as a representative of PSTE because it shares most economic and political features with this group of countries. As it was argued by Apanasovich et al. (2016), Belarusian SMEs that rely on experience-based learning – DUI mode – are more likely to generate product innovation than those relying on the STI mode. This implies that the innovation capacity of such countries (PSTE) is more likely to be determined by the rate of absorption of new technologies and knowledge from abroad, and the effective use of machinery, that is, DUI drivers (Apanasovich et al., 2016; UNECE, 2011).

For these set of reasons, in our first proposition, we argue that in PSTE, in contrast to market economies, the Research driver is not likely to have a significant impact on the novelty of product innovation.

3.2. The technological 'T' driver

The relationship between science and technology was discussed in Rosenberg's book (1982). He questioned the statement that science precedes technological development and stated that technology is not only the application of scientific knowledge. Technology is 'knowledge of techniques, methods and designs' and 'if the human race had been con-fined to technologies that were understood in a scientific sense, it would have passed from the scene long ago' (Rosenberg, 1982, p. 143). Technologies are not compulsory and direct products of science because they have to satisfy customer needs. 'One of the stylized facts coming out of research on the relation between science and technology is that in most areas, the results of scientific research are not directly useful for technological advance' (Jensen et al., 2007, pp. 682–683). Hervas-Oliver, Garrigos-Albors, & Gil-Pechian (2011) analyse SMEs innovation in the context of a technology-follower country (Spain). They find that R&D activities are separated from non-R&D (including non-R&D technological) activities. Innovative SMEs do constantly scan markets for new tech-nologies that might help to further develop and apply new ideas. The Technology driver includes important components such as the technological base (Adler & Shenhar, 1990) and the technological competences (Rammer et al., 2009; Ritter & Gemünden, 2004) that firms and their experts and technicians identify and value as a means to develop new products and processes. The 'technological base' implies the technological know-how that enables a firm to develop and manufacture new products using the appropriate process technologies, and to benefit from opportunities that require prompt actions invol-ving technology (Adler & Shenhar, 1990). The development of the technological base includes adopting more or less familiar technologies that hasten the technological process (Chen et al., 2011; Isaksen & Karlsen, 2012; Rosenberg, 1982). 'Technological competence' implies a firm's ability to understand and use relevant state-of-the-art tech-nology, build and deploy that know-how effectively, explore new ways of solving technical problems, produce and deliver goods and services that will help firms to generate inno-vations that outperform competitors and increase profitability (Rammer et al., 2009;

Ritter & Gemünden, 2004). Such competences have a positive impact on innovation and product development (Patel & Pavitt, 1997; Ritter & Gemünden, 2003). Technologies have direct commercial applications and aim at responding to market demand. In a nutshell, it is an instrument for producing marketable goods and services. Crosby (2000) argues that international flows of capital and ideas are so intensive that there is no necessity to conduct large amounts of R&D in small countries. Such countries can purchase new technology and know-how.

Due to the fast rate of technological change, there is a need for constant monitoring of the-state-of-the-art technologies. The 'T' driver in our model can be approximated with indicators such as monitoring and acquisition of up-to-date machinery, equipment and sophisticated technologies, engineering capabilities, and the interaction with technology organizations (Adler & Shenhar, 1990; Cooper & Kleinschmidt, 1986; Patel & Pavitt, 1997; Ritter & Gemünden, 2004). The rapid growth in complexity and cost of new technologies has promoted the emergence of technical collaborations (Sen & Egelhoff, 2000). This type of interaction with technological agents (i.e. technical consortia, technology centres and engineering companies) leads to the development of technological capabilities which may impact on the creation of novel products (Hagedoorn, 1993; Sen & Egelhoff, 2000).

Our study goes beyond intramural R&D, considering the fact that in catching-up economies in transition SMEs do not perform high levels of investments in R&D; however, they implement high expenditures in machinery and equipment (Belstat, 2011). This happens because these countries, which operate behind the technology frontier, try to reduce the technological gap they face vis-à-vis technological leading countries. Thus, they innovate through new technology acquisition and application, learning-by-doing and by-using- (Alam et al., 2008; Apanasovich, 2016; Radosevic, 2011; Varblane et al., 2007).

On these bases, in our second proposition, we argue that Belarusian (PSTE) SMEs that rely on experience-based learning developed with usage of new technology (the 'T' driver) are likely to have a significant and positive impact on the novelty of product innovation.

3.3. The 'H' driver

The third HRM driver of innovation comprises 'HRM practices' (Beugelsdijk, 2008; Laursen & Foss, 2012; Shipton et al., 2005) and 'interaction' (Jensen et al., 2007; Ritter & Gemünden, 2004; Spithoven, Vanhaverbeke, & Roijakkers, 2013). 'HRM practices' involve methods of organizing work responsibilities and decision-making, employees' training, extensive lateral and vertical communication channels and the use of reward and recognition systems. According to Shipton et al. (2005, p. 119), such practices manage the 'three stages of the organizational learning cycle – the creation, transfer and implementation of knowledge'. It was shown by Rammer et al. (2009) that SMEs that do not apply in-house R&D can obtain a similar innovation performance by applying appropriate HRM practices to facilitate innovation processes. In this regard, the implementation of innovation-focused HRM practices influences positively the innovation performance in a firm and contributes to a sustained competitive advantage (Beugelsdijk, 2008; Oke et al., 2012; Shipton et al., 2005). Managerial skills can be more important for innovation than access to modern technology (Cooper, 1999; Varblane et al., 2007).

Amabile (1998, p. 6) raised the question of motivation of scientists that can have outstanding education and a great facility for generating new knowledge, but if they lack 'the motivation to do a particular job', they 'simply won't do it'; 'their expertise and creative thinking will either go untapped or be applied to something else'. The capacity to generate innovations is largely dependent on the way employees are motivated to perform research activities and commercialize their results. In addition, HR policies that include rewards and recognition systems that promote innovation activities are likely to facilitate an innovative organizational culture. Such a culture tends to back up a firm's innovation strategy because it creates an environment that can be characterized as innovation encouraging, and provides the freedom to experiment and the openness to new ideas (Oke et al., 2012). The notion that all employees are innovators enables one of the largest Chinese steel manufacturing companies to achieve an extraordinary innovation output (Chen et al., 2011).

Beugelsdijk (2008) demonstrates that HRM practices can foster innovations with different degrees of novelty. Lorenz (2012) argues that if creativity and labour market mobility are mediated by an appropriate HRM, they can generate a range of radical knowledge outputs. Creativity is expected to be supported and fostered by the creation and promotion of complex jobs within a firm (Beugelsdijk, 2008). Such jobs are associated with high levels of autonomy, variety of skills, significance and feedback (Beugelsdijk, 2008; Lorenz & Lundvall, 2011). The literature on HRM suggests that providing training facilities may create a positive employee attitude and commitment to promote sustainable development (Cooper, 1999). By the same token, education and complex jobs, creativity and innovation can be promoted by teamwork (Nonaka & Takeuchi, 1995), especially cross-functional teamwork (Cooper, 1994; Lau & Ngo, 2004). Currently, innovation processes involve different areas and functions working together as a project team. Team meetings provide employees with a broad range of information and may be organized to search for and to discuss new ideas and perspectives. The involvement of employees in decision-making improves the business innovation propensity (Cosh, Fu, & Hughes, 2012). Several authors applied quantitative methodology to delve with the HRM contribution to innovation performance (Beugelsdijk, 2008; Shipton et al., 2005); however, the link between HRM practices and innovation performance has not yet been clearly explained (Laursen & Foss, 2012).

The 'H' driver of our model includes both internal and external market 'interactions' related to the manager's ability to involve other market agents in the innovation process (Lundvall, 1992; Ritter & Gemünden, 2004). Internal interaction arises as part of the company logic and communication works in both directions: top-down and bottom-up (vertical communication) and between different company departments (horizontal communication) (Cooper, 1999; Hinds & Kiesler, 1995). Market interactions capture the firm's capacity to interact with its business environment. Market partnerships involve a high degree of heterogeneity, which is represented by agents within the supply chain and outside. Interactions within the supply chain – mainly with suppliers and clients – are fundamentally formal (Fitjar & Rodriguez-Pose, 2013) and aimed at improving the delivery of components and products in order to boost their competitiveness. These interactions are expected to be more directly related to problem-solving and will help firms to exploit better their current knowledge pool and search for new product solutions. Collaboration with clients is especially keen on getting market information and, in some cases, the direct involvement of clients and so as to create teams that lead to more successful innovations (Amara & Landry, 2005; Atuahene-Gima, 1995) and a stronger marker orientation to the final product (Cooper, 1994). In the same way, collaborations with suppliers are valuable sources of information to develop or improve products by reducing risks and lead times in product development, while enhancing flexibility, product quality and market adaptability (Chung & Kim, 2003).

However, it was found that competitors cooperation is oriented towards carrying out basic research and establishing standards (Bayona, García-Marco, Huerta, 2001; Tether, 2002) to solve common problems that are outside the competitor's area of influence – for instance, a regulatory change (Tether, 2002). Knowledge spillovers are more an unintended consequence of the relationship than its main purpose, as firms try to avoid direct transfer to rivals, but cannot control indirect transfer (Von Hippel, 1988, p. 295). Therefore, interaction with rivals seems to have a poor impact on innovation (Tomlinson & Fai, 2013) and a detrimental effect on the propensity of firms to innovate (Fitjar & Rodriguez-Pose, 2013). However, independently from the purpose of this collaboration, market interactions capture managers' ability to connect with close business environments, which later impact on the firm's ability to exploit current capabilities and knowledge domains.

Thus, the 'H' driver can be approximated with indicators such as some HRM practices (e.g. training, communication, and reward systems), internal interaction (i.e. teamwork) and market collaboration (i.e. actors along the supply chain and with competitors).

When focusing on the context of transition economies, the introduction of the 'H' driver becomes essential due to its high levels of human capital (Aidis et al., 2008), particularly high in tertiary education. In these countries, managers focus on adopting effectively Western managerial approaches, experience and practices, which often arise from cooperation with supply chain partners located abroad (Miazhevich, 2007). As it is corroborated by Kuznetsov and Yakavenka (2005), these managers possess advanced skills and knowledge that allow them appreciating the value of imported concepts, knowledge and organizational practices. Therefore, high human capital, specific knowledge based on work experience and market interactions would increase the business absorptive capacity (Vinding, 2006), and contribute to the development of novel products.

For these reasons, in our third proposition, we argue that in the context of Belarus/PSTE, at least in the ICT sector, the 'H' driver is likely to have a positive and significant impact on the novelty of product innovation.

The three above-mentioned propositions are summarized in Figure 1.

4. Data and methods

This study focuses on drivers and modes of innovation specific to SMEs in transition economies. However, due to the lack of available data related to HRM practices and Technology drivers, we conducted a specific survey of Belarusian ICT firms located in Minsk and its capital region. We select the ICT sector due to the great opportunities it involves for the economy. As recognized in the EU smart specialization strategy, the development of a competitive ICT sector represents an enabling technology, as it tends to generate positive spillovers in the rest of economic sectors due to the development of ICT. The ability to

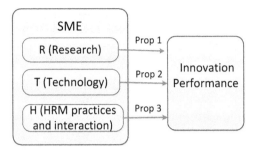

Figure 1. The theoretical RTH model in a PSTE. Source: own elaboration. Note: Expected result.

disseminate ICT technologies increases the productivity of many sectors (e.g. traditional manufacturing, health and automotive) and shifts upwards the territorial innovation frontier. Therefore, the ICT sector represents an opportunity to update the technological competences of PSTE. In Soviet times, Minsk was one of the main ICT centres in USSR. In this city, computer production facilities and design institutes were concentrated in a way that enable Belarus to supply 60% of the USSR demand for computer production. With the independence, the country inherited one of the highest standards of scientific and technological potential of the former Soviet Union. Nowadays, highly skilled experts educated within local universities contribute to the success of the Belarusian ICT industry.

The ICT high potential for producing innovation is also recognized by Belarus policymakers (SPID, 2011). In fact, during the last years, the ICT sector (formed in early 2000s) has received strong governmental support in Belarus and it has become one of the top-priority economic sectors. As a result, Belarus today is one of ICT leaders in the Eastern European region (Maznyuk & Sergiychuk, 2010), and Minsk is one of the largest centres of offshore programming in the area of the former USSR. The main outputs of the companies are software services for clients, application development, solutions and ICT consulting services, and are successfully exporting their software products and services to North American and European high-tech markets (export share exceeds 80%).

We sent the questionnaire to all 245 ICT companies that were registered in Minsk and its region at the time of the survey. Contact addresses were obtained from 'Regist Belarus' government database. The survey was conducted through a web-based questionnaire and personal e-mails sent to the all 245 IT firms based in the Minsk capital area. Eighty-two firms completed the questionnaire. The response rate is 33%. In order to restrict the sample to SME firms, we followed the European Commission Recommendation (2003) criteria based on the number of employees. Therefore, we excluded companies with less than 10 employees and firms with more than 250 employees from the analysis. The final sample is composed of 51 IT firms. According to Hair et al. (2003) a multiple regression can be effective with a minimum sample of 50 and a minimum ratio of observations to variables is 5:1 (the preferred ratio is 15:1 or 20:1). In our analysis, the ratio of observations is 17:1. For this reason, our sample is valid. Moreover, the goal of this study is not to make strong generalizations, but to develop a new research instrument (RTH model) and demonstrate how it operates.

The sequential empirical validation of RTH model consists of three stages (Figure 2) that help to identify the most effective mode of innovation according to innovation output. In the first stage, we identify the key drivers of innovation, and propose indicators to identify each driver and analyse the relationship between drivers and innovation output. Secondly, we build various innovation profiles (possible combination of the drivers of innovation) that should help to describe the features of innovative firms, and visualize them using the mosaic plot. In the third stage, we perform a cluster analysis to determine the optimal number of innovation modes.

4.1. Drivers of innovation

In the first stage, we study drivers of innovation and analyse their impact on innovation output.

4.1.1. Dependent variables

The dependent variable in our study is the novelty of product innovation (IO). In this, we follow the classification of product innovation used in the Community Innovation Surveys (CIS, 2008) and in the literature (Parrilli & Elola, 2012; Vega-Jurado, Gutiérrez-Gracia, Fernández-de-Lucio, & Manjarrés-Henríquez, 2008) that distinguish between: whether a firm introduced new or significantly improved goods and services that were (1) only new to this firm or (2) new to market (the product may have already been available in other markets). However, in order to capture the novelty in a more detailed way, we rely on the Oslo Manual and build an ordinal variable that spans across: (1) new-to-firm, (2) new-to-national market and (3) new-to-international market innovation (Table 3). The rationale behind this classification is that in transition and in developing countries, there is a substantial difference between national and international markets that needs to be taken into account.

4.1.2. Independent variables

The Research, Technology, and HRM drivers are independent variables in our study. We propose three groups of indicators to identify each driver (Table 4). The first driver, Research (R), contains three indicators that reflect the scientific approach and state that innovation is a result of R&D (Jensen et al., 2007). The 'T' driver represents a non-R&D technological driver, which emphasizes knowledge of techniques and methods

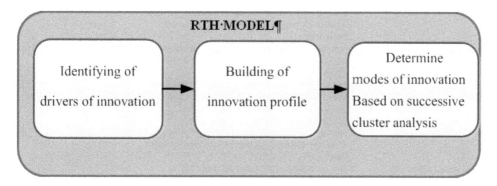

Figure 2. Stages of empirical validation. Source: own elaboration.

Table 3. Description of the dependent variable.

Variables	Description	Literature
Product innovation		
New-to-firm innovation	Sales of innovative products that are new to firm (1)	Apanasovich et al. (2016); Chen et al. (2011); Fitjar and Rodriguez-Pose (2013); Jensen et al. (2007) Parrilli and
New-to-market	Sales of innovative products that are new to national market (2)	Elola (2012)
New-to-international market	Sales of innovative products that are new to international markets (3)	

(Rosenberg, 1982), technological competences (Rammer et al., 2009; Ritter & Gemünden, 2004) and know-how that enable a firm to develop and manufacture new products using the appropriate process technologies (Hagedoorn, 1993; Sen & Egelhoff, 2000).

Table 4. Indicators of the R, T, H drivers and descriptive statistics.

Indicators	Description	Mean	Std.Dev.	Min.	Max.
The Research driver					
Expenditures on R&D (R1)	Expenditures on R&D as share of total revenue, Likert scale	1.88	1.11	1.00	5.00
Scientifically trained personnel (R2)	A firm employs scientifically trained personnel (master and PhD degree), Likert scale	1.90	0.90	1.00	4.00
Interaction with research organizations (R3)	A firm cooperates with universities, scientific institutes, research centres, Likert scale	1.90	1.12	1.00	5.00
The Technology driver					
Monitoring of new technology in the market (T1)	A firm is constantly monitoring new technology appearance in the market, Likert scale	3.55	1.35	1.00	5.00
Purchase of technology, patents or external knowledge (T2)	The frequency of purchasing patents, external knowledge or licensing of patents and non-patented inventions, know-how and other types of knowledge from other enterprises or organizations, Likert scale	2.61	1.36	1.00	5.00
Production facilities (T3)	A firm possesses state-of-the-art production facilities, Likert scale	2.63	1.40	1.00	5.00
Technological competence (T4)	The ability to develop and adapt current and new technologies, Likert scale	3.04	1.52	1.00	5.00
Interaction with technology organizations (T5)	Interaction and collaboration exist with technology centres, engineering companies and technical alliances, Likert scale	2.31	1.29	1.00	5.00
The HRM driver					
Reward systems (H1)	The reward and recognition systems encourage innovation and reinforce entrepreneurial behaviour and teamwork, Likert scale	2.61	1.42	1.00	5.00
Training (H2)	A firm organizes training aimed to acquire and develop skills that are crucial to introduce new or significantly improved products and processes, Likert scale	2.71	1.36	1.00	5.00
Organizing work (H3) responsibilities and decision-making	A firm has implemented new methods of organizing work responsibilities and delegation of decisions (decentralized form), Likert scale	2.53	1.29	1.00	5.00
Extensive lateral and vertical communication (H4)	Communication works in both directions: top-down and bottom-up (vertical communication) and between different company departments (horizontal communication), Likert scale	2.43	1.33	1.00	5.00
Internal collaboration (H5)	Teamwork and collaboration between employees arises spontaneously as part of the company logic, Likert scale	2.80	1.39	1.00	5.00
Market collaboration (H6)	A firm cooperates with customers and pilot-customers, suppliers, competitors, distributors, Likert scale	2.98	1.32	1.00	5.00

The HRM driver stresses that innovation is the result of HRM practices (Beugelsdijk, 2008; Laursen & Foss, 2012; Shipton et al., 2005) and interactions (Jensen et al., 2007; Lundvall, 1992; Ritter & Gemünden, 2004).

Our survey questionnaire was designed using a Likert-type scale. Consistently with previous studies in the field (Apanasovich et al., 2016; Parrilli & Elola, 2012), we extracted key qualitative information, classified and treated it on a quantitative basis.

The value of indicators varies from 1 to 5 that can be seen in the descriptive Table 4. The highest value of mean is 3.55 (T1 driver, quite high) and the smallest is 1.88 (R1 driver, quite low, something that is later confirmed with the inferential analysis). Each indicator was transformed into an ordinary scale and the final variable that characterizes the R driver was calculated. This variable was set to 1 ('low' level) when the sum of R indicators exceeded zero but was less or equal to 5. Medium' level (2) was assigned when the sum of R indicators exceeded 5 but was less than or equal to 10. When the sum possessed a value greater than 10, the 'high' level (3) was assigned. The same procedure was performed to transform variables describing the T and H drivers. The explanatory table of variable transformation is presented in Table 5.

Thus, the RTH model implies three innovation drivers (independent variables) and three levels for each driver (Figure 3). Variance inflation factors for R, T, H variables are 1.08, 1.45, 1.43, respectively. All variables are less than 10, meaning that there is no multicollinearity.

4.1.3. Regression analysis

In order to analyse the relationship between the 'R', 'T' and 'H' drivers of innovation output, we perform a regression analysis. Since the outcome is measured as an ordinal

Table 5. The explanatory table of transformation of variables.

	Indicators	Measure used in survey	Measure of indicators (transformational scale)	Measures of final variable in regression model
R	Expenditures on R&D (R1) Scientifically trained personnel (R2) Interaction with research organizations (R3)	Likert scale	1,2,3,4,5	If $SI = 0 < SI \leq 5$ – low level (1); If $5 < SI \leq 10$ – medium level (2); If $SI > 10$ – high level (3)
T	Monitoring of new technology in the market (T1) Purchase of technology, patents or external knowledge (T2) Production facilities (T3) Technological competence (T4) Interaction with technology organizations (T5)			If $SI = 0 < SI \leq 8$ – low level (1); If $5 < SI \leq 17$ – medium level (2); If $SI > 17$ – high level (3)
H	Reward systems (H1) Training (H2) Organizing work (H3) responsibilities and decision-making Extensive lateral and vertical communication (H4) Internal collaboration (H5) Market collaboration (H6)			If $SI = 0 < SI \leq 10$ – low level (1); If $5 < SI \leq 20$ – medium level (2); If $SI > 20$ – high level (3)

Notes: I – value of any indicator and
SI – sum of measures of indicators (I).

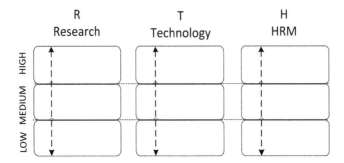

Figure 3. Categories of RTH drivers. Source: own elaboration.

scale (1, 2, 3), an ordinal regression model fits best. The ordinal regression allows the consolidation of the ordinal nature of both the dependent and independent variables.

Table 6 contains the parameters estimated for the model. The significance levels observed in this table indicate that the 'T' and 'H' drivers exert significant influence on the innovation output, but, the 'R' driver does not appear to be significant in this relationship.

Table 7 contains new estimated coefficients for the model indicating that firms with greater levels of 'T' and 'H' obtain greater innovation outputs.

Concluding the results of the regression analysis, we confirm the first proposition, that there is no statistically significant relationship between the 'R' driver and product innovation output in this particular case (ICT sector in Belarus). In contrast, the propositions related to the importance of the technological driver and the HR driver for innovation output are confirmed. ICT firms in Belarus (PSTE) are significantly influenced by these drivers, as such firms manage effectively and creatively both the human/managerial capital and the (new) technological capital so as to be able to produce significant innovation output. Of course, it is an exploratory study centred on a very specific industry

Table 6. Parameter estimates.

	Estimate	Std. error	Wald	Df	Sig.	95% Confidence interval	
						Lower bound	Upper bound
[ProdIO = 1]	−5.29	1.67	9.98	1	0.00	−8.57	−2.01
[ProdIO = 2]	−2.46	1.51	2.67	1	0.10	−5.41	0.49
[R = 1]	−0.56	1.32	0.18	1	0.67	−3.16	2.03
[R = 2]	0.00	1.42	0.00	1	1.00	−2.79	2.78
[R = 3]	0ᵃ	.	.	0	.	.	.
[T = 1]	−3.66***	1.04	12.33	1	0.00	−5.70	−1.62
[T = 2]	−2.02**	0.82	6.08	1	0.01	−3.62	−0.41
[T = 3]	0ᵃ	.	.	0	.	.	.
[H = 1]	−2.64*	1.08	5.95	1	0.02	−4.76	−0.52
[H = 2]	−1.60	0.94	2.92	1	0.09	−3.44	0.24
[H = 3]	0ᵃ	.	.	0	.	.	.

Link function: Logit
Number of observation: 51
Chi-Square: 37.73
Pseudo R^2:
  Cox and Snel: 0.523
  Nagelkerke's: 0.589
  McFadden's: 0.338
Level of significance: 0.001

Note: 0ᵃ, reference level.

Table 7. The Tracew Index parameter estimates.

	Estimate	Std. error	Wald	Df	Sig.	95% Confidence interval	
						Lower bound	Upper bound
[ProdIO = 1]	−4.95	1.10	20.09	1	0.00	−7.11	−2.78
[ProdIO = 2]	−2.16	0.87	6.18	1	0.01	−3.86	−0.46
[T = 1]	−3.77***	1.03	13.35	1	0.00	−5.79	−1.75
[T = 2]	−1.97*	0.81	5.90	1	0.02	−3.56	−0.38
[T = 3]	0ᵃ	.	.	0	.	.	.
[H = 1]	−2.66**	1.07	6.23	1	0.01	−4.75	−0.57
[H = 2]	−1.68	0.92	3.36	1	0.07	−3.49	0.12
[H = 3]	0ᵃ	.	.	0	.	.	.

Link function: Logit
Number of observation: 51
Chi-Square: 37.05
Pseudo R^2:
 Cox and Snel: 0.516
 Nagelkerke's: 0.582
 McFadden's: 0.332
Level of significance: 0.001

Note: 0ᵃ, reference level.

and a quite limited sample, and thus will need further confirmation through wider and cross-sectoral studies.

4.2. Innovation profiles

Once we categorized the 'R', 'T', 'H' drivers, we approach our second stage to reveal more precisely the innovation profile of the firms. Thus, a firm's innovation profile is a 'numerical combination' of the drivers of innovation. For example, the RTH profile (3, 2, 1) shows that the SME has a high level of the 'Research' driver, a medium level of 'Technology' and a low level of the 'HRM' driver within our framework. The RTH model implies 27 possible innovation profiles (numerical combination of three innovation drivers and three levels of each driver). The innovation profiles of the sampled firms are visualized in Figure 4 using the mosaic plot (Friendly, 1999), a graphical

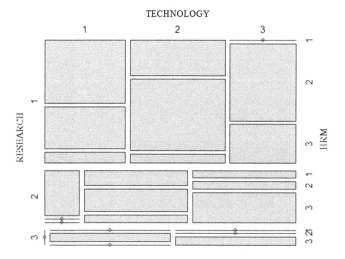

Figure 4. Mosaic plot of 'R', 'T' and 'H' drivers). Source: own elaboration.

presentation of firm innovation profiles divided into rectangles, so that the area of each rectangle is proportional to the frequencies of the various possible RTH innovation profiles. The most frequent innovation profile (15.7% of firms) is RTH (1, 2, 2). We can see that there are 17 active firm profiles (i.e. populated by firms) out of 27 possible profiles in the Minsk region.

4.3. Re-grouping the modes of innovation: empirical evidence

We identified the 'mode of innovation' as a group (cluster) of homogeneous innovation profiles extracted from 27 possible profiles.[1] To group innovation profiles in clusters (modes of innovation), we employ the hierarchical clustering algorithm (Kaufman & Rousseeuw, 1990). Cluster analysis is consistent with some influential works in this area (Fitjar & Rodriguez-Pose, 2013; Jensen et al., 2007). The Manhattan distance method was used to measure the distance between connected elements (Hastie, Tibshirani, & Friedman, 2001), and the Tracew index to determine the optimal number of clusters. The Tracew Index has been one of the most popular indices suggested for use in clustering context (Edwards & Cavalli-Sforza, 1965; Fukunaga & Koontz, 1970; Milligan & Cooper, 1985). We performed scree plot (Appendix B). The location of the elbow in the resulting plot suggests a suitable number of clusters for the k-means. Tracew index increases monotonically with solutions containing fewer clusters. The maximum of the second differences scores allowed us to determine the number of clusters. Three is the optimal number of clusters in our case (Friedman and Rubin, 1967). The dendrogram illustrated in Appendix C, provides a complete description of the hierarchical clustering in a graphical format (Hastie et al., 2001).

The three modes (groups of similar innovation profiles) of innovations are visualized in the mosaic plot (Figure 5) in different colours.

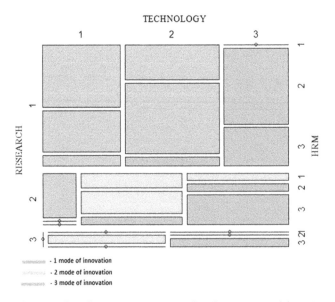

Figure 5. Three modes of innovation, mosaic plot. Source: own elaboration.

Table 8. Characteristics of business modes of innovation based on empirical clusters.

Mode	Name	Characteristics	Product innovation novelty
1 mode	Laggard organizations	Low level of 'R', 'T' and 'H' drivers	New-to-firm
2 mode	S&T organizations	Medium level of 'R' and 'T' drivers and low of 'H' driver	New-to-national market
3 mode	Creative organizations	Low level of 'R' and high level of 'T' and above medium level of 'H' driver	New-to-international market

Source: Own elaboration.

With this empirics-based assignation of firms to the archetypal innovation modes, we find the effective way in which ICT businesses boost their innovation capacity in the context of Belarus and PSTE in general. Table 8 shows that the first mode of innovation is represented by the largest amount of firms (49% of total SMEs in our sample). As each driver has a low level, we designate this mode as 'low learning mode' or laggard organizations, and mainly report new-to-firm innovation. The R&T-based firms correspond to the second group of innovation profiles or mode of innovation (16%), which rely on strong 'R' and 'T' drivers and low level of H driver, and develop new-to-national market and new-to-firm innovations. We can explain the increase in the degree of novelty of product innovation with the growth of the 'T' driver from low to medium. Finally, the creative organizations refer to the third mode (35%) characterized by low level of 'R', high level of the 'T' and above medium level of the 'H' driver, and reports the highest innovation output, that is, new-to-international market products. Overall, this set of observations is in line with what the regression analysis has shown. Increasing the business effort, on the one hand, in the acquisition and usage of new technologies, and, on the other, in the adoption of an effective HRM (including investment in upskilling the workforce) is the means that guarantee a more effective innovation capacity in the context of Belarus and other PSTE.

5. Conclusions and policy implications

In this study, we analyse the modes of innovation, adopted by SMEs with a new framework that departing from the STI and DUI framework, proposes a new approach based on empirically-grounded 'innovation profiles' and 'business innovation modes' – the RTH model of innovation. In our view, this better specifies the strategic behaviour of SMEs as it recognizes that, especially in transition economies, firms may separate the 'R' driver from the 'T' driver, and obtain a differentiated impact on the novelty of product innovation. The degree, to which Research, Technology and HRM drivers are applied, however, depends on the contextual characteristics of the country and the industrial sector. The separation of the 'R' (R&D driver) from the 'T' (non-R&D technological driver) may be relevant not only in Belarus and other PSTE, but also in the broader context of technology-follower countries (e.g. transition and emerging), and developed countries where the technological catch-up process pushes firms to invest in the first stages of scientific knowledge generation. In our case study, we found that there is a statistically significant relationship between the 'T' and 'H' drivers and the novelty of product innovation. In contrast, the 'R' driver does not relate to innovation output to a significant extent. This result leads us to make two relevant considerations. From an empirical perspective, this pattern may reflect context-specificities of a particular set of countries: the transition economies. In these countries, (IT) firms seem to have a special sensitivity for technology acquisition and the capacity to learn-by-doing and by-using. This is a more important driver than investments in R&D and highly skilled scientific human capital. From a conceptual perspective, we identify the importance of splitting the impact of R driver from T, thus breaking the former identification of a STI-type of innovation mode. This argument implies the importance to reconsider the theoretical framework that formed the debate on STI–DUI innovation modes, and to promote the search for more appropriate frameworks, for example, the RTH model, which may explain better specific country contexts. An additional novelty of our study is instrumental to the former, although more general. We go beneath the analysis of 'modes of innovation' as contemplated by Jensen et al. (2007), Isaksen and Karlsen (2010), Chen et al. (2011) among others, and propose the identification of 'innovation profiles' as a means to understand the various strategic combinations of drivers implemented by different sets of innovative firms. Firms with similar innovation profiles are then grouped into clusters which we identify as empirically based 'modes of innovation', which are different from the more abstract and perhaps more dualistic modes identified by Jensen et al. (2007).

The relationship between innovation profiles and modes of innovation helps in identifying the most effective innovation mode (and the most performing combination of drivers associated with this mode). Across Belarusian SMEs, we have identified 17 innovation profiles (whereas other 10 potential profiles were not found in the sample) that we grouped through cluster analysis in 3 archetypical modes of innovation. The first mode of innovation can be characterized as a 'low learning' mode or 'laggard organizations' due to the low levels of the 'R', 'T' and 'H' drivers. The 'low learning' cluster gathers firms that neither invest in HRM, technology nor employ scientifically trained personnel. The firms belonging to this cluster do not have highly developed forms of organizations that support technology acquisition or HRM practices, and do not cooperate with researchers and value chain partners. In general, they can mostly develop no innovations or new-to-firm type of innovations. The second mode has a rather high level of 'R' and 'T', and a low level of 'H' driver. As the value of 'T' has grown in comparison with the first mode, the degree of novelty of product innovation has also increased. As a result, these SMEs are able to produce, in addition to new-to-firm, new-to-national-market innovations. We identified this mode as the 'S&T-based mode' of innovation. The third mode is characterized by low level of 'R' and high level of 'T' and above the average level of 'H'. Firms in this cluster report the highest innovation output among the revealed modes, that is, manage to produce new-to-international market products and services. Firms belonging to this mode are characterized as 'creative organizations'.

From a practical perspective, the new research instrument – the RTH model – for analyzing innovation processes across firms can be used not only by researchers, but also by policy-makers and managers. It enables the exploration of detailed innovation profiles across SMEs and the modes of innovation applied at the industry, region and country level. Policy-makers can use the concept of 'modes of innovation' to develop strategies and programmes aimed at improving the innovation capacities of regions and sectors. The RTH model enables the exploration of the industry-based mode of innovation. Based on the RTH model, company managers can recognize the exact innovation profile that helps to develop and implement strategies, make strategic decisions and exploit their company's limited resources in the most appropriate way. Thus, identifying the best combination of drivers that promote product innovation helps to create a more conducive environment for innovation-based development, thus enhancing the competitiveness of SMEs.

Our work is not exempt of limitations. In order to show how the RTH model operates, we use data that represent one ICT sector (that requires specific knowledge base) in a technology-follower country in transition. On the grounds of the analysis of data collected by the National Statistical Committee of the Republic of Belarus, that adopts a CIS-type of format, a wider set of Belarusian and other transition countries' SMEs might be studied in a set of representative manufacturing industries: metallic construction, furniture, apparel, footwear, bread and apparel. The lack of very meaningful indicators of HRM and T drivers in Belstat statistics might lead to conduct a specific survey that enables a wider access to relevant data, with the potential to extract results of interest for a larger universe of businesses and countries. It might be extremely adequate to collect data from several sectors both in technology-follower countries and in technology-leader countries as a means to test the consistence of the RTH model in different country contexts. In conclusion, our study aims at encouraging further research and policy analysis on business modes of innovation.

Note

1. The explanation of the term 'innovation profile' is provided in a descriptive Table 1.

Disclosure statement

No potential conflict of interest was reported by the authors.

References

Acs, Z. J., & Audretsch, D. B. (1990). *Innovation and small firms*. Cambridge, MA: MIT Press.

Alcalde Heras, M. D. H. (2014). Building product diversification through contractual R&D agreements. *R&D Management, 44*(4), 384–397. doi:10.1111/radm.12075

Adler, P. S., & Shenhar, A. (1990). Adapting your technological base: The organizational challenge. *Sloan Management Review, 32*(1), 25–37.

Aidis, R., Estrin, S., & Mickiewicz, T. (2008). Institutions and entrepreneurship development in Russia: A comparative perspective. *Journal of Business Venturing, 23*, 656–672.

Alam, A., Casero, P. A., Khan, F., & Udomsaph, C. (2008). *Unleashing prosperity: Productivity growth in Eastern Europe and the former Soviet Union*. Washington, DC: World Bank.

Amabile, T. M. (1998). How to kill creativity. *Harvard Business Review, 76*(5), 76–87.

Amara, N., & Landry, R. (2005). Sources of information as determinants of novelty of innovation in manufacturing firms: Evidence from the 1999 statistics Canada innovation survey. *Technovation, 25*(3), 245–259. doi:10.1016/S0166-4972(03)00113-5

Amara, N., Landry, R., Becheikh, N., & Ouimet, M. (2008). Learning and novelty of innovation in established manufacturing SMEs. *Technovation, 28* (7), 450–463. doi:10.1016/j.technovation.2008.02.001

Apanasovich, N. (2016). Modes of innovation: A grounded meta-analysis. *Journal of the Knowledge Economy, 7*(3), 720–737. doi:10.1007/s13132-014-0237-0

Apanasovich, N., Alcalde Heras, H., & Parrilli, M. D. (2016). The impact of business innovation modes on SME innovation performance in post-Soviet transition economies: The case of Belarus. *Technovation, 57–58*, 30–40. doi:10.1016/j.technovation.2016.05.001

Archibugi, D., & Lundvall, B. Å. (2001). *The globalising learning economy: Major socio-economic trends and European innovation policy*. Oxford: Oxford University Press.

Arrow, K. J. (1962). The economic implications of learning by doing. *The Review of Economic Studies*, 29(3), 155–173. doi:10.2307/2295952

Asheim, B., & Gertler, M. (2005). The geography of innovation: Regional innovation systems. In J. Fagerberg, D. Mowery & R. Nelson (Eds.), *The oxford handbook of innovation* (pp. 291–317). New York: Oxford University Press.

Asheim, B. T., & Coenen, L. (2005). Knowledge bases and regional innovation systems: Comparing Nordic clusters. *Research Policy*, 34, 1173–1190. doi:10.1016/j.respol.2005.03.013

Aslesen, H. W., Isaksen, A., & Karlsen, J. (2012). Modes of innovation and differentiated responses to globalisation – A case study of innovation modes in the Agder Region, Norway. *Journal of the Knowledge Economy*, 3, 389–405. doi:10.1007/s13132-011-0060-9

Atuahene-Gima, K. (1995). An exploratory analysis of the impact of market orientation on new product performance a contingency approach. *Journal of Product Innovation Management*, 12 (4), 275–293. doi:10.1016/0737-6782(95)00027-Q

Audretsch, D. (2003). Standing on the shoulders of old midgets: The US small business innovation program. *Small Business Economics*, 20, 129–135. doi:10.1023/A:1022259931084

Bayona, C., García-Marco, T., & Huerta, E. (2001). Firms' motivations for cooperative R&D: An empirical analysis of Spanish firms. *Research Policy*, 30, 1289–1307. doi:10.1016/S0048-7333 (00)00151-7

Becattini, G., Bellandi, M., & De Propris, L. (2009). *A handbook of industrial districts*. Cheltenham: Edward Elgar.

Belstat. (2011). *Statistical book science and innovation activity*. Minsk: National Statistical Committee of the Republic of Belarus.

Beugelsdijk, S. (2008). Strategic human resource practices and product innovation. *Organization Studies*, 29(6), 821–847. doi:10.1177/0170840608090530

Chen, J., Chen, Y., & Vanhaverbeke, W. (2011). The influence of scope, depth and orientation of external technology sources on the innovative performance of Chinese firms. *Technovation*, 31(8), 362–373. doi:10.1016/j.technovation.2011.03.002

Chung, S. A., & Kim, G. M. (2003). Performance effects of partnership between manufacturers and suppliers for new product development: The supplier's standpoint. *Research Policy*, 32(4), 587–603. doi:10.1016/S0048-7333(02)00047-1

Community Innovation Surveys. (2008). *Community innovation survey*. Dublin: Forfas.

Cohen, W. M., & Levinthal, D. A. (1989). Innovation and learning: The two faces of R&D. *The Economic Journal*, 99(397), 569–596. doi:10.2307/2233763

Cohen, W. M., & Levinthal, D. A. (1990). Absorptive capacity: A new perspective on learning and innovation. *Administrative Science Quarterly*, 35, 128–152. doi:10.2307/2393553

Cooke, P. (2001). Regional innovation systems, clusters, and the knowledge economy. *Industrial and Corporate Change*, 10(4), 945–974. doi:10.1093/icc/10.4.945

Cooke, P., Heidenreich, M., & Braczick, S. (Eds.). (2004). *Regional innovation systems*. London: Routledge.

Cooper, R. G. (1994). Perspective: Third-generation new product processes. *Journal of Product Innovation Management*, 11(1), 3–14. doi:10.1016/0737-6782(94)90115-5

Cooper, R. G. (1999). From experience: The invisible success factors in product innovation. *Journal of Product Innovation Management*, 16(2), 115–133. doi:10.1016/S0737-6782(98)00061-7

Cooper, R. G., & Kleinschmidt, E. J. (1986). An investigation into the new product process: Steps, deficiencies, and impact. *Journal of Product Innovation Management*, 3(2), 71–85. doi:10.1016/ 0737-6782(86)90030-5

Cosh, A., Fu, X., & Hughes, A. (2012). Organisation structure and innovation performance in different environments. *Small Business Economics*, 39(2), 301–317. doi:10.1007/s11187-010-9304-5

Crosby, M. (2000). Patents, innovation and growth. *Economic Record*, 76(234), 255–262. doi:10. 1111/j.1475-4932.2000.tb00021.x

Edquist, C. (2005). Systems of innovation: Perspectives and challenges. In J. Fagerberg, D. Mowery & R. Nelson (Eds.), *The Oxford handbook of innovation* (pp. 181–208). New York: Oxford University Press.

Edwards, A. W. F., & Cavalli-Sforza, L. (1965). A method for cluster analysis. *Biometrics*, *21*(2), 362–375. doi:10.2307/2528096

European Union Commission. (2003). Commission recommendation of 6 May 2003 concerning the definition of micro, small and medium-sized enterprises. *Official Journal of the European Union*, *46*, 36–41.

Fabrizio, K. R. (2009). Absorptive capacity and the search for innovation. *Research Policy*, *38*, 255–267. doi:10.1016/j.respol.2008.10.023

Fink, G., Haiss, P., & Vukšić, G. (2009). Contribution of financial market segments at different stages of development: Transition, cohesion and mature economies compared. *Journal of Financial Stability*, *5*(4), 431–455. doi:10.1016/j.jfs.2008.05.002

Fitjar, R. D., & Rodriguez-Pose, A. (2013). Firm collaboration and modes of innovation in Norway. *Research Policy*, *42*(1), 128–138. doi:10.1016/j.respol.2012.05.009

Fleming, L., & Sorenson, O. (2004). Science as a map in technological search. *Strategic Management Journal*, *25*, 909–928. doi:10.1002/smj.384

Friedman, H. P., & Rubin, J. (1967). On some invariant criteria for grouping data. *Journal of the American Statistical Association*, *62*(320), 1159–1178. doi:10.1080/01621459.1967.10500923

Friendly, M. (1999). Extending mosaic displays: Marginal, conditional, and partial views of categorical data. *Journal of Computational and Graphical Statistics*, *8*(3), 373–395.

Fu, W., Diez, J. R., & Schiller, D. (2013). Interactive learning, informal networks and innovation: Evidence from electronics firm survey in the Pearl River Delta, China. *Research Policy*, *42*, 635–646. doi:10.1016/j.respol.2012.09.006

Fukunaga, K., & Koontz, W. L. G. (1970). A criterion and an algorithm for grouping data. *IEEE Transactions on Computers*, *C-19*(10), 917–923. doi:10.1109/T-C.1970.222799

Gonzalez-Pernia, J. L., Parrilli, M. D., & Peña-Legazkue, I. (2015). STI–DUI learning modes, firm–university collaboration and innovation. *The Journal of Technology Transfer*, *40*, 475–492.

Greunz, L. (2005). Intra-and inter-regional knowledge spillovers: Evidence from European regions. *European Planning Studies*, *13*(3), 449–473. doi:10.1080/09654310500089746

Griliches, Z. (1979). Issues in assessing the contribution of research and development to productivity growth. *Bell Journal of Economics*, *10*(1), 92–116.

Hagedoorn, J. (1993). Understanding the rationale of strategic technology partnering: Nterorganizational modes of cooperation and sectoral differences. *Strategic Management Journal*, *14*(5), 371–385. doi:10.1002/smj.4250140505

Hair, J. F., Black, W., Babin, B., & Anderson, R. (2010). *Multivariate Data Analysis. A Global Perspective*. New Jearsey: Pearson Prentice Hall.

Hastie, T., Tibshirani, R., & Friedman, J. (2001). *The elements of statistical learning*. New York, NY: Springer.

Heras, H. A. (2014). Collaboration patterns and product innovation in the Basque country. Does a firm's nationality matter? *Journal of Entrepreneurship, Management and Innovation*, *10*(3), 29–56.

Hervas-Oliver, J. L., Garrigos-Albors, J., & Gil-Pechian, I. (2011). Making sense of innovation by R&D and non-R&D innovation in low-technology context. *Technovation*, *31*(9), 427–446. doi:10.1016/j.technovation.2011.06.006

Hinds, P., & Kiesler, S. (1995). Communication across boundaries: Work, structure, and use of communication technologies in a large organization. *Organization Science*, *6*(4), 373–393. doi:10.1287/orsc.6.4.373

Isaksen, A., & Karlsen, J. (2010). Different modes of innovation and the challenge of connecting universities and industry: case studies of two regional industries in Norway. *European Planning Studies*, *18*(12), 1993–2008. doi:10.1080/09654313.2010.516523

Isaksen, A., & Karlsen, J. (2012). Combined and complex mode of innovation in region cluster development: Analysis of the light-weight material cluster in Raufoss, Norway. In B. T. Asheim & M. D. Parrilli (Eds.), *Interactive learning for innovation: A key drive within clusters and innovation systems* (pp. 115–136). Basingstroke: Palgrave-Macmilan.

Isaksen, A., & Nilsson, M. (2013). Combined innovation policy: Linking scientific and practical knowledge in innovation systems. *European Planning Studies, 21*(12), 1919–1936. doi:10.1080/09654313.2012.722966

Jensen, M. B., Johnson, B., Lorenz, E., & Lundvall, B. A. (2007). Forms of knowledge and modes of innovation. *Research Policy, 36*, 680–693. doi:10.1016/j.respol.2007.01.006

Jong, S., & Slavova, K. (2014). When publications lead to products: The open science conundrum in new product development. *Research Policy, 43*(4), 645–654. doi:10.1016/j.respol.2013.12.009

Kaufman, L., & Rousseeuw, P. J. (1990). *Finding groups in data: An introduction to cluster analysis* (1st ed.). New York, NY: John Wiley.

Kuznetsov, A., & Yakavenka, H. (2005). Barriers to the absorption of management knowledge in Belarus. *Journal of Managerial Psychology, 20*(7), 566–577. doi:10.1108/02683940510623380

Lau, C. M., & Ngo, H. Y. (2004). The HR system, organizational culture and product innovation. *International Business Review, 13*, 685–703. doi:10.1016/j.ibusrev.2004.08.001

Laursen, K., & Foss, N. J. (2012). *Human resource management practices and innovation. Handbook of Innovation Management.* Oxford, UK: Oxford University Press. Retrieved from http://www.druid.dk/laursen/files/Handbook_of_Innovation_ Management_LaursenFoss.pdf.

Lorenz, E. (2012). Labour market institutions, skills, and innovation style: A critique of the varieties of capitalism perspective. In B. T. Asheim & M. D. Parrilli (Eds.), *Interactive learning for innovation: A key driver within clusters and innovation systems* (pp. 72–89). Basingstoke: Palgrave Macmillan.

Lorenz, E., & Lundvall, B. A. (2011). Accounting for creativity in the European Union: A multi-level analysis of individual competence, labour market structure, and systems of education and training. *Cambridge Journal of Economics, 35*(2), 269–294. doi:10.1093/cje/beq014

Lundvall, B. A. (1992). *National innovation system: Towards a theory of innovation and interactive learning.* London: Pinter.

Lundvall, B. A. (2007). National systems of innovation: Analytical concept and development tool. *Industry and Innovation, 14*, 95–119. doi:10.1080/13662710601130863

Malaver, F., & Vargas, M. (2013). *Aprendizaje y formas de innovar: una lectura critica.* University of Deusto, San Sebastian, Mimeo.

Maznyuk, V., & Sergiychuk, I. (2010). *Central and Eastern Europe IT outsourcing review 2010.* Kiev: Central and Eastern European Outsourcing Association.

Miazhevich, G. (2007). Official media discourse and the self-representation of entrepreneurs in Belarus. *Europe-Asia Studies, 59*(8), 1331–1348.

Milligan, G. W., & Cooper, M. C. (1985). An examination of procedures for determining the number of clusters in a data Set. *Psychometrika, 50*(2), 159–179. doi:10.1007/BF02294245

Nielsen, L. (2011). *Classifications of countries based on their level of development: How it is done and how it could be done* (Working Paper IMF).

Nonaka, I., & Takeuchi, H. (1995). *The knowledge creating company.* Oxford: Oxford University Press.

Nunes, S., & Lopes, R. (2015). Firm performance, innovation modes and territorial embeddedness. *European Planning Studies, 23*(9), 1796–1826. doi:10.1080/09654313.2015.1021666

Oke, A., Walumbwa, F. O., & Myers, A. (2012). Innovation strategy, human resource policy, and firms' revenue growth: The roles of environmental uncertainty and innovation performance. *Decision Sciences, 43*(2), 273–302. doi:10.1111/j.1540-5915.2011.00350.x

Palacín, J., & Radosevic, S. (2011). Recent economic and innovation performance. In J. Kubiš (Ed.), *The innovation performance review of Belarus* (pp. 1–18). New York, NY: United Nations.

Parrilli, M. D., & Alcalde Heras, H. (2016). STI and DUI innovation modes: Scientific-technological and context-specific nuances. *Research Policy, 45*(4), 747–756. doi:10.1016/j.respol.2016.01.001

Parrilli, M. D., & Elola, A. (2012). The strength of science and technology drivers for SME innovation. *Small Business Economics, 39*(4), 897–907. doi:10.1007/s11187-011-9319-6

Parrilli, M. D., Fitjar, R. D., & Rodriguez-Pose, A. (2016). Business innovation modes: A review from a country perspective. In M. D. Parrilli, R. D. Fitjar, & A. Rodriguez-Pose (Eds.), *Innovation drivers and regional innovation strategies* (pp. 197–218). New York, NY: Routledge.

Pavitt, K. (1998). The social shaping of the national science base. *Research Policy, 27*(8), 793–805. doi:10.1016/S0048-7333(98)00091-2

Patel, P., & Pavitt, K. (1997). The technological competencies of the world's largest firms: Complex and path-dependent, but not much variety. *Research Policy, 26*(2), 141–156. doi:10.1016/S0048-7333(97)00005-X

Radosevic, S. (2011). Science-industry links in central and Eastern Europe and the commonwealth of independent states: Conventional policy wisdom facing reality. *Science and Public Policy, 38* (5), 365–378. doi:10.3152/030234211X12924093660435

Rammer, C., Czarnitzki, D., & Spielkamp, A. (2009). Innovation success of non-R&D-performers: Substituting technology by management in SMEs. *Small Business Economics, 33*(1), 35–58. doi:10.1007/s11187-009-9185-7

Rees, C. J., & Miazhevich, G. (2009). Socio-cultural change and business ethics in post-Soviet countries: The cases of Belarus and Estonia. *Journal of Business Ethics, 86*(1), 51–63. doi:10. 1007/s10551-008-9817-x

Ritter, T., & Gemünden, H. G. (2003). Network competence: Its impact on innovation success and its antecedents. *Journal of Business Research, 56*(9), 745–755. doi:10.1016/S0148-2963(01)00259-4

Ritter, T., & Gemünden, H. G. (2004). The impact of a company's business strategy on its techno-logical competence, network competence and innovation success. *Journal of Business Research, 57*(5), 548–556. doi:10.1016/S0148-2963(02)00320-X

Romer, P. M. (1994). The origins of endogenous growth. *Journal of Economic Perspectives, 8*(1), 3–22. doi:10.1257/jep.8.1.3

Rosenberg, N. (1982). *Inside the black box: Technology and economics.* Cambridge: Cambridge University Press.

Rosenberg, N. (1990). Why do firms do basic research (with their own money)? *Research Policy, 19* (2), 165–174. doi:10.1016/0048-7333(90)90046-9

Sen, F. K., & Egelhoff, W. G. (2000). Innovative capabilities of a firm and the use of technical alli-ances. *IEEE Transactions on Engineering Management, 47*(1), 174–183. doi:10.1109/17.846785

Shipton, H., Fay, D., West, M., Patterson, M., & Birdi, K. (2005). Managing people to promote inno-vation. *Creativity and Innovation Management, 14*(2), 118–128. doi:10.1111/j.1467-8691.2005. 00332.x

SPID. (2011). *The state programme for innovative development of the Republic of Belarus for 2011–2015.* Minsk: Republic of Belarus.

Spithoven, A., Vanhaverbeke, W., & Roijakkers, N. (2013). Open innovation practices in SMEs and large enterprises. *Small Business Economics, 41*(3), 537–562. doi:10.1007/s11187-012-9453-9

Tether, B. S. (2002). Who co-operates for innovation, and why: An empirical analysis. *Research Policy, 31*(6), 947–967.

Tomlinson, P. R., & Fai, F. M. (2013). The nature of SME co-operation and innovation: A multi-scalar and multi-dimensional analysis. *International Journal of Production Economics, 141*(1), 316–326. doi:10.1016/j.ijpe.2012.08.012

UN. (2013). *World Economic Situation and Prospects (WESP). Country classification.* Retrieved from https://www.un.org/development/desa/dpad/publication/world-economic-situation-and-prospects-2013/

UNECE. (2011). *Innovation performance review of Belarus, Government, Minsk.* Retrieved from http://www.unece.org/ceci/2011/ipr.html

Varblane, U., Dyker, D., Tamm, D., & von Tunzelmann, N. (2007). Can the national innovation systems of the new EU member states be improved? *Post-Communist Economies, 19*(4), 399–416. doi:10.1080/14631370701680048

Vega-Jurado, J., Gutiérrez-Gracia, A., Fernández-de-Lucio, I., & Manjarrés-Henríquez, L. (2008). The effect of external and internal factors on firms' product innovation. *Research Policy, 37*(4), 616–632. doi:10.1016/j.respol.2008.01.001

Vinding, L. A. (2006). Absorptive capacity and innovative performance: A human capital approach. *Economics of Innovation and New Technology, 15*(4-5), 507–517. doi:10.1080/ 10438590500513057

Von Hippel, E. (1988). *The sources of innovation.* New York, NY: Oxford University Press.

Yegorov, I. (2009). Post-Soviet science: Difficulties in the transformation of the R&D systems in Russia and Ukraine. *Research Policy, 38*(4), 600–609.

Appendix 1

Concept	Definition	Details/explanation
Driver of innovation	The driving force that allows to create, implement and develop innovation	Research (R), Technology (T) and HRM (H)
Innovation profile	The combination of drivers of innovation, indicating the extent/weight to which SME relies on these drivers	E.g.: Profile RTH (3,2,1) shows, e.g. SME that have a high level of 'R', medium 'T' and low level of H driver, and among others.
Mode of innovation	A firm's innovation strategy, a group/cluster of innovation profiles	E.g.: Laggard organizations, S&T organizations, and Creative organizations.
Model of innovation	Theoretical framework representing the relation between innovation performance and its critical drivers	E.g.: RTH model (Figure 1)

Source: Own elaboration.

Appendix 2. Tracew index.

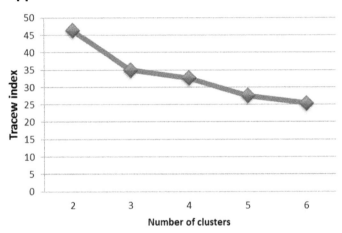

Source: Own elaboration.

Appendix 3. Cluster dendrogram.

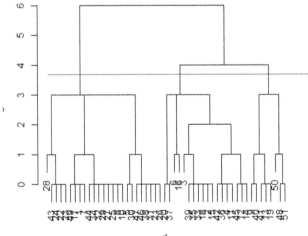

Source: Own elaboration.

Strengthening SMEs' innovation culture through collaborations with public research organizations. Do all firms benefit equally?

Julia Olmos-Peñuela, Ana García-Granero, Elena Castro-Martínez and Pablo D'Este

ABSTRACT

The purpose of this paper is to explore whether collaborating with public research organizations (PROs) contributes to strengthening the innovation culture of small and medium sized enterprises (SMEs). We examine to what extent their innovation culture is reinforced by collaborations with research organizations and investigate the type of organizational strategies that enhance this effect of collaboration. The empirical study is based on a survey of firms that collaborate with the largest Spanish PRO, Spanish National Research Council (CSIC). Our results indicate that SMEs differ greatly in their capacity to strengthen their innovation culture through collaboration with research organizations. We show also that firms with formal innovation plans that develop internal and external search strategies are more likely to improve their innovation culture as a result of collaboration with PROs. These findings provide managers with new insights into how to strengthen their firms' innovation culture through collaboration with research organizations.

1. Introduction

The innovation literature identifies a range of factors likely to influence the innovation performance of firms (Freeman, 1974; Mansfield, 1991). It shows that the creation of an appropriate organizational culture is one factor that contributes to innovation success. Pavitt (1991) studies large firms and highlights, among other aspects, flexibility, communication, customer relationships, flows of ideas and proposals as strengths of an innovative firm. The firm culture can also contribute by mobilizing internal resources, improving communication and knowledge sharing and setting incentive structures oriented towards innovation (Martins & Terblanche, 2003).

Although several studies investigate the relevance of the firm's innovation culture, we know little about how an organizational innovation culture is built and nurtured. In line with work on open innovation, we investigate how collaboration with external agents can contribute to this process. With a few exceptions (i.e. Martins & Terblanche, 2003), studies of firms' innovation culture pay little attention to how external actors can contribute to its enhancement.

In this paper, we are interested in the role of research organizations as potential contributors to the firm's innovation culture. Since innovation processes often involve exploration and experimentation and tolerance for risk, firms are collaborating with research organizations in order to get access to state-of-the-art research, ideas for product and process developments and opportunities to strengthen capabilities (Miotti & Sachwald, 2003).

The focus in this paper is on small and medium sized enterprises (SMEs). Huizingh (2011) points out that more research is needed in order to identify how SMEs benefit from their collaborations with external agents. Van de Vrande, De Jong, Vanhaverbeke, and De Rochemont (2009) highlight that smaller firms increased collaboration with external partners is especially relevant because smaller firms often suffer from limited resources. Thus, it is important to examine to what extent collaboration with research organizations provide the key resources needed to build and strengthen the firm's innovative culture.

We examine Spanish SMEs with established collaborations with scientists affiliated to the Spanish National Research Council (CSIC), the largest public research organization (PRO) in Spain. We exploit a large-scale survey of Spanish firms with at least one formal contract with CSIC researchers during the period 1999–2010. The survey asked about firms' general, organizational and management strategies and innovation activities; reasons for working with CSIC such as corporate strategy, search for solution to technical problems and access to knowledge and complementary capabilities; the types of activities conducted in collaboration with CSIC; results in the form of corporate strategy, process, product and organizational innovations, access to CSIC knowledge and competences, access to contact networks; and the experience of SMEs in terms of satisfaction with or obstacles to collaboration. This survey was the first comprehensive questionnaire administered to the group of companies that have cooperated with CSIC over an extended period.

Most existing studies use secondary sources, such as PITEC,[1] to examine among other factors, benefits to collaboration, and tend to provide general information on new products, new processes, patents, etc. Designing our own survey allowed us to focus on other type of benefits derived from such collaborations, such as strengthening the firm's innovation culture, and to collect other fine-grained information.

In this study we address the following questions: (1) To what extent do SMEs strengthen their innovation culture through their collaborations with research organizations? (2) What type of SMEs benefit most? Our paper contributes to the literature in several ways. First, studies of innovation culture focus mainly on what happens within the firm's boundaries. However, our study draws on the open innovation literature and suggests that their innovation culture can be also enhanced by leveraging external sources of knowledge. Second, we add to the open innovation literature by showing that SMEs benefit from cooperation with research organizations in terms not only of new products and processes but also a stronger innovation culture. Third, we contribute to work on absorptive capacity by highlighting that Research and Development (R&D) is not the only facilitator of open innovation and that firms need a formal innovation plan and a particular search strategy.

The paper is organized as follows. Section 2 presents the conceptual framework high-lighting the importance of an innovative culture and the potential benefits to the firm of collaborating with a research organization. Section 3 formulates the research questions addressed and examines the factors that allow firms to benefit from a stronger innovation culture as a result of their collaborations with research organizations. Section 4 describes data used in the analysis and Section 5 presents the main empirical results. Section 6 is a discussion and conclusion.

2. Literature review

2.1. The importance of firm's innovation culture

The concept of organizational culture refers to a set of values and beliefs (norms) of behav-iour expected from firm members. It defines how the organization should conduct its activities (Barney, 1986; Schein, 1992). It is acknowledged that individual employees are an organization's main source of value and that their actions ultimately affect the whole organization (Grant, 1996). There is also a consensus on the role played by the social context and culture in which these individuals act and which can support or hinder their activities and accomplishment of organizational goals (Menzel, Aaltio, & Ulijn, 2007). A strong firm culture provides shared values, rules and norms, which shape employees' behaviours and ensure that everyone is oriented to achieving the firm's goals (Colquitt, Lepine, & Wesson, 2009; Robbins, 1996).

The influence on employees of an organizational culture is particularly important for firms aimed at promoting innovation processes given the uncertain, unpredictable and risky nature of innovation. Such organizations need to balance conflicting incentives when promoting innovation activities. They need to have in place an incentive system that rewards a favourable attitude to the introduction and application of new ideas, in order to signal that innovative behaviour is desirable in the organization. On the other hand, firms need to accept that employees' innovative behaviour can challenge established practices and routines (Janssen, 2003). An organizational culture that is favourable to innovation should be sufficiently flexible to cope with the potential conflicts that might arise and to balance reward systems which favour risk-taking with reassurances that failures or challenges to existing norms will not be penalized (Yuan & Woodman, 2010).

Innovation culture has been defined in various ways. Dobni (2008) defines it as a multi-dimensional context that includes the intention to be innovative, the infrastructure to support innovation, a market orientation and an environment conducive to innovation (Dobni, 2008, p. 540). Herzog and Leker (2010, p. 325), in their analysis of open and closed innovation strategies, define innovation culture as an important firm or business unit subculture, which takes account of the different dimensions related to shared basic values, and organization-wide norms and practices to support innovation. Brettel and Cleven (2011) view innovation culture as an intangible strategic resource that can be assessed by the following four dimensions: an orientation towards technological inno-vation, a learning orientation, a willingness to take risks and a future market orientation. Martín-de-Castro, Delgado-Verde, Navas-López and Cruz-González (2013, p. 353) describe innovation culture as employee shared values, beliefs and assumptions which facilitate the product innovation process. Bader, Vanbrabant, and Enkel (2014, pp. 3–4) consider innovation culture to be a firm environment that promotes a market orientation and organizational learning, supports openness to new solutions, technologies, markets and risk-taking, and tolerates failure. Common to all these definitions is that innovation culture involves several dimensions related to the promotion of new ideas and employees' innovation capacity, market orientation, organizational learning and risk-taking.

Thus, firms that encourage employees' to contribute new ideas and share knowledge, and which are tolerant of mistakes and changes to organizational routines, exhibit a high innovation culture. However, while some studies of innovation culture refer to openness to new solutions and the importance of communication (i.e. Bader et al., 2014; Martins & Terblanche, 2003), few emphasize the role of external agents for enhancing innovation culture. We turn on this issue in the following section.

2.2. Benefits from collaborations with research organizations

External partners, such as suppliers, customers and research organizations (universities and research centres), constitute alternative sources of information and knowledge for firms in search of innovative ideas (Brettel & Cleven, 2011; Laursen & Salter, 2004; Sánchez-González & Herrera, 2010). Innovation is rarely the outcome of an isolated search process and many firms need to source the resources of external partners. The open innovation approach suggests that external sources are sometimes more relevant than internal sources of knowledge for innovation (Chesbrough, 2003).

Among external partners, research organizations are one of the most important sources of information and knowledge (Amara & Landry, 2005; Becheikh, Landry, & Amara, 2006) due to their large repositories of knowledge and expertise, highly qualified workforce and exploration capabilities (Santoro & Chakrabarti, 2002). Specifically, research organizations provide firms with complementary knowledge, technologies and skills which facilitate complex and risky activities and provide opportunities for bi-directional learning (Un, Cuervo-Cazurra, & Asakawa, 2010). Thus, co-operation with research organizations can enhance the firm's chances of introducing a technological breakthrough or radical innovation, and explorative activities beyond its range of in house competencies (Miotti & Sachwald, 2003).

Previous studies highlight the benefits for firms of collaborations with research organizations. They point to technological innovations (new products and processes) and, especially, radical innovations (Belderbos, Carree, Diederen, Lokshin, & Veugelers, 2004; Brettel & Cleven, 2011; Lööf & Broström, 2008; Monjon & Waelbroeck, 2003). Most empirical work focuses on technological innovation as the potential result of a firm collaboration with a research organization. Few discuss whether such collaboration contributes to strengthening the firm's innovation culture. This is surprising since research organizations employ researchers with deep knowledge in their area of expertise and personal characteristics related to innovation such as creativity, enthusiasm, communication skills, ability to learn and to take risks, and ability to work in multicultural teams and to develop projects (Amabile, 1998; Durette, Fournier, & Lafon, 2016; Kelley & Caplan, 1993; Roberts & Fusfeld, 1981). Thus, it might be expected that the firm's innovation culture would be strengthened by its interactions with the scientific community.

3. Main research question and hypotheses

3.1. Strengthening the firm's innovation culture as a result of collaborations with research organizations

Firms and research organizations operate under different systems. Research organizations are based on the principles of 'public science', and free, rapid and objective dissemination of research outputs; firms rely on 'private science' principles such as appropriation and private commercialization of research results (Manjarrés-Henríquez, Gutiérrez-Gracia, Carrión-García, & Vega-Jurado, 2009; Partha & David, 1994; Stephan, 1996). These divergent principles entail differences in terms of goals, incentives, structures and resources. Academic and commercial activities require different skills and abilities; the former focus on how to conduct rigorous research, the latter seek commercial accomplishments (Ambos, Mäkelä, Birkinshaw, & D'Este, 2008; D'Este & Patel, 2007).

These differences can produce tensions and difficulties in relation to collaboration, but also can amplify the chances of learning. Collaborations with research organizations are related to exploratory learning, which enables problem-solving (Koza & Lewin, 1998), the ability to manage unfamiliar knowledge and skills, experimentation and tolerance for risk (Bierly & Daly, 2007). These attributes can strengthen the firm's innovation culture. Employees' interactions with scientists can increase the employees' orientation to innovation and ultimately the firm's innovation culture. In the case of SMEs, this is particularly relevant. SMEs' scarce resources make them more prone to collaborate with PROs, resulting in a higher potential for learning (Van de Vrande et al., 2009). We investigate to what extent SMEs strengthen their innovation cultures as a result of collaborations with research organizations. This addresses our first research question.

3.2. Formal innovation plan

Firms do not benefit equally from collaborations with research organizations (Cohen & Levinthal, 1990). More R&D intensive firms will benefit more from collaborations with research organizations. Studies using absorptive capacity as their main theoretical framework, consider R&D to be a condition required to benefit fully from the knowledge held by research organizations, but ignore the role of other firm organizational practices (Colombo, Rabbiosi, & Reichstein, 2011).

The presence (and relevance) in the firm of innovation objectives can be an incentive for collaboration with a research organization. The implementation of a strategy and plan oriented towards innovation reflects the firm's innovation priorities by setting out the firm's innovation objectives. Some studies emphasize a strategic plan for the implementation of open innovation (Kutvonen, 2011; Lazzarotti & Manzini, 2009; Sakkab, 2002). An innovation plan can add value to the firm by building prepared minds and encouraging creative minds (Beinhocker & Kaplan, 2002). First, a formal innovation plan ensures that decision-makers and employees have a shared understanding of the firm's innovation goals and the activities required to achieve them (prepared minds). Second, implementing an innovation plan does not guarantee creativity and innovation outputs, but signals the firm's direction and priorities and establishes conditions and incentives to stimulate proactive innovative behaviour from employees (creative minds).

We argue that SMEs with formal innovation plans are more likely to encourage prepared and creative minds, both of which will benefit from the knowledge acquired through external collaborations. In their interactions with research organizations, these firms will be better prepared to learn how to generate a favourable climate, to promote new ideas, to be flexible, to engage in teamwork and to work on innovation. In other words, these SMEs are more likely to strengthen their innovation cultures through collaborations with research organizations. We hypothesize that:

> H1: SMEs that have articulated a formal innovation plan are more likely to strengthen their innovation culture as a result of collaborations with research organizations.

3.3. Search strategy

Firms with a formal search strategy are likely to benefit more from their collaborations with PROs. Search strategies refer to how the firm organizes and manages its search processes (Laursen & Salter, 2004). These activities are related to the firm's efforts to scan the environment in order to identify and process information and knowledge for innovation. Scholars have theorized about search strategy categorisations (Rosenkopf & Nerkar, 2001; Rothaermel & Deeds, 2004). They may be internal or external. Internal search strategies reflect the choice to mobilize and access knowledge from within the firm (i.e. seeking for and encouraging employees' ideas); external search strategies are associated with accessing and exploiting knowledge from external sources (Rosenkopf & Nerkar, 2001).

Laursen and Salter (2004) argue that the extent to which firms rely on different types of information sources constitutes an important driver of collaboration with universities. The authors suggest that open search strategies have a strong influence on the probability of using university knowledge in the firm's innovation activities. In other words, firms that adopt an 'open' approach to innovative search are more likely to use universities as a source of innovation.

We argue that firms with a search strategy will be more likely to gain from collaborating with a research organization. Also, experience of collaborating with external sources for innovation, and managing a portfolio of collaborations is likely to have positive spillovers. That is, an external search strategy implies that the firm is capable of activating the complementarities between the information and knowledge obtained from different actors (other firms, customers, clients, universities, etc.) to enhance its capacity to benefit from collaborations with research organizations. Similarly, having in place an internal search strategy implies that the firm has a set of routines to activate the screening of ideas and knowledge from within the firm, which will have an impact in the firm's capacity to benefit from collaborations with research organizations. In SME settings, the higher need for resources leads to consideration of networks to extend technological competences (Lee, Park, Yoon, & Park, 2010) and identifying complementarities among different sources of knowledge is critical for success. Therefore, we expect that SMEs with active search strategies will benefit more from collaborations with research organizations in terms of innovation culture. We hypothesize that:

> H2a: SMEs with an active internal search strategy are more likely to strengthen their innovation culture as a result of collaborations with research organizations.

H2b: SMEs with an active external search strategy are more likely to strengthen their innovation culture as a result of collaborations with research organizations.

3.4. Formal innovation plan and search strategy

Given the complexity involved in activating and maintaining an active search strategy (e.g. implementing an internal suggestion box or managing a network of collaborations), the articulation of a formal plan is an important tool to reduce this complexity. Formality refers to establishing routines and protocols for action (Damanpour, 1991). This helps articulating risky activities, complex tasks and conflicts of interests which might arise as the result of broad collaboration. On the one hand, having a formal plan encourages a mental attitude among employees towards innovation as critical for the firm and makes them open to new ideas (Beinhocker & Kaplan, 2002) (e.g. from scientists in research organizations). On the other hand, it helps in the planning of innovation activities and management of collaboration networks. Although these activities can be beneficial based on the synergies created by the interactions among different actors, they can be difficult to manage. Formal plans help simplify the management of broad collaboration networks.

Based on the above, we argue that firms with formal innovation plans and active search strategies are more likely and better prepared to benefit from their collaborations with research organizations. These two elements (innovation plan and search strategy) will be self-reinforcing and will contribute to a stronger innovation culture as a result of collaborations with research organizations. We suggest that SMEs with formal innovation plans and active search strategies will benefit more from their collaborations with research organizations in terms of a stronger innovation culture. We hypothesize that:

H3a: SMEs with formal innovation plans and active internal search strategies are more likely to strengthen their innovation cultures as a result of collaborations with research organizations.

H3b: SMEs with formal innovation plans and active external search strategies are more likely to strengthen their innovation culture as a result of collaborations with research organizations.

4. Methodology

4.1. Population, sample and data source

The empirical study is based on a large-scale survey aimed at obtaining a better understanding of the impact of collaborations between firms and PROs. We focus on the largest Spanish PRO – CSIC. CSIC has 14,050 employees distributed across over a hundred research institutes throughout the Spanish territory. CSIC's main mission is development and promotion of research to achieve both scientific and technological progress (CSIC, 2012).[2]

The population for this study is 1891 Spanish firms that established at least one (among 5334) formal research contract with CSIC during the period 1999–2010. Data were collected via a questionnaire that asked general questions about firm's characteristics and the management of innovation activities, and specific questions related to their collaboration with CSIC, motivations for collaboration and the benefits obtained. The questionnaires were mostly administered to the person responsible for the collaboration contract with CSIC, since it was assumed they would be best placed to assess its impact and results. Where this was not possible, the manager with knowledge on the collaborations established with CSIC was approached. Note that the sample includes firms that have collaborated with CSIC, which means that the firms in our sample have some distinct features (e.g. higher levels of R&D investment) compared to the whole population of Spanish firms.[3]

The questionnaire was pre-tested to ensure it was understandable to potential respondents. The questionnaire was administered face to face with the firm respondent (mostly R&D or technical managers). The fieldwork was conducted between 1 October 2010 and 31 January 2011, on a sample of 794 Spanish firms who agreed to participate (a response rate of nearly 42%).

We conducted a Harman's one-factor test to assess the occurrence of common method bias in the data collected. We found this was not a concern since the test results were within the boundaries recommended by Podsakoff and Organ (1986). Also, the questionnaire information was complemented by data from the Iberian balance sheet analysis system database (SABI), on firm age, firm size and firm sector. Our firm sample included the 756 firms for which we had information from both sources (the questionnaire and SABI). Since our interest is in SMEs, the final sample includes 610 firms. Table 1 presents the sample distribution based on firm size, R&D intensity and firm sector.

4.2. Dependent variable

We are interested in whether SMEs reinforce their innovation culture through collaboration with CSIC. Therefore, instead of focusing on the benefits related to product and process innovation (Aschhoff & Schmidt, 2008; Lööf & Broström, 2008), we consider innovation culture as a potential benefit from collaborating with a PRO.

Table 1. Sample distribution by industrial sector, size and R&D intensity.

Variables	N (%)
Industrial sector	
Energy and water supply	3 (0.49)
Mining	15 (2.46)
Construction	23 (3.77)
Services	267 (43.77)
Agriculture, forestry and fishing	32 (5.25)
High technology	27 (4.43)
Low technology	172 (28.20)
Medium-high technology	71 (11.64)
Size	
Micro	141 (23.11)
Small	257 (42.13)
Medium	212 (34.75)
R&D intensity	
Does not develop	70 (11.74)
Occasionally	131 (21.98)
On a regular basis	395 (66.28)
Total (N)	*610**

* When percentages do not add up to 100% is due to missing values.

Our dependent variable captures the extent to which the firm strengthened its innovation culture as a result of interactions with PROs. We constructed this variable using information from the questionnaire responses regarding the benefits obtained by the firm from collaborating with CSIC. Specifically, respondents were asked whether the firm increased its innovation culture as a consequence of its collaborations with CSIC, and the importance of this benefit to the firm. Importance was scored on a 4-point Likert scale ranging from 1 'none' to 4 'very much' (Valmaseda-Andia, Albizu-Gallastegi, Fernandez-Esquinas, & Fernandez-de-Lucio, 2015). This measure captures the firm's perception of the extent to which collaborating with CSIC contributed to strengthening its innovation culture. Since our sample is composed of firms with a history of collaboration with CSIC and firms that are familiar with R&D activities (see Table 1), we consider that (and as observed in the pre-test) firm perception is a reliable measure of the improvement to their innovation culture. We label this variable: 'improved innovation culture'.

Although this variable is measured on the basis of responses to a single-item, we provide some reassurance about the reliability of the indicator, in terms of its construct validity. We examined the link between the responses to the question asking about strengthening the firm's innovation culture as a result of collaborations with CSIC and responses to other questions in the survey asking about aspects related to the degree of the firm's commitment to organizational practices associated with innovation culture such as knowledge sharing and a horizontal decision-making structure. More precisely, we explore whether firms report regular use of organizational practices oriented to: (i) encouraging new ideas; (ii) creating inter-departmental working teams and (iii) encouraging employees to participate in decision-making (decentralization of decision-making).

Table 2 shows that the proportion of firms that report major improvements to the innovation culture as a result of collaboration with PROs is systematically (and significantly) larger among firms that regularly engage in the organizational practices described above. For instance, we observe that 42% of firms, which regularly use a decentralized process of decision-making, report high improvements to their innovation culture, compared to 34% of those firms that do not involve their employees in decision-making.

Table 2. Proportion of firms reporting high values for 'improved innovation culture' (%), by type of organizational practices.

	'High' improved innovation culture	N
(i) Encouraging new ideas		
Frequent use	41% (188/455)	455
Sporadic or no use	29% (33/114)	114
Total observations		569*
(ii) Creating inter-departmental teams		
Frequent use	43% (160/376)	376
Sporadic or no use	32% (60/186)	186
Total observations		562*
(iii) Decentralization of decision-making		
Frequent use	42% (143/338)	338
Sporadic or no use	34% (77/227)	227
Total observations		565*

* Totals do not amount to 610 observations due to missing values. Chi-Square test (i): 2.97 ($p < .10$); (ii): 0.47 ($p < .05$); (iii): 1.26 ($p < .05$).

4.3. Independent variables

4.3.1. Innovation plan
The independent variable for firm's 'innovation plan' is captured by the existence of a formal innovation plan. Specifically, respondents were asked about their firm's innovation plan based on the responses to the four following options: (a) firm has no innovation plan; (b) firm is expecting to develop an innovation plan; (c) firm is currently developing an innovation plan; (d) firm has a formal innovation plan in place. We created a binary variable to distinguish between those firms in the process of developing an innovation plan or firms that have an innovation plan in place; and those firms with no innovation plan or planning its implementation. We created the binary variable 'innovation plan' which takes the value 1 if the firm has an innovation plan or is implementing 1 and 0 otherwise.

4.3.2. Search strategy
In relation to the independent variable related to 'search strategy' for innovation, respondents were asked to indicate the importance of different sources of information to improve the firm's innovation processes. The sources of information are internal (i.e. firm's internal knowledge) and diverse external sources (i.e. suppliers, clients, competitors, consultants, laboratories or R&D private institutes, universities and public research bodies, technology centres, conferences, congresses, fairs and professional meetings, regional and national government, and professional and industry associations). Their importance was scored on a 4-point Likert scale ranging from 1 'none' to 4 'very much'.

To construct the search strategy variables, we distinguish between internal and external search (sources within the firm or outside the firm's boundaries). Following Laursen and Salter (2006), external search strategies can be differentiated according to the number of different information and knowledge sources that the firm draws on for its innovation activities (range of external sources); and the extent to which firms draws intensively on different information sources (depth). In our empirical study, we investigate internal and external search strategies by focusing on search depth and control for the range of external sources. Thus, we created two independent variables for search strategy: 'internal search depth' and 'external search depth'.

'Internal search depth' was constructed as a variable ranging from 1 to 4, which captures the importance to the firm of drawing on internal sources of information for innovation, meaning the extent to which the firm relies on information and knowledge from firms' employees and internal R&D activities.

'External search depth' relates to the importance to the firm on external knowledge sources. It was constructed by coding each external source (initially ranging from 1 to 4) into a binary variable, which takes the value 1 if the firm reports the external source as very important for innovation and 0 otherwise. We added the nine binary variables obtained to construct our independent variable 'external search depth', which takes the value 0 if the firms does not consider any external sources to be very important, and 9 if it considers all nine external sources of information to be very important.

4.4. Control variables

Control variables (such as range of external sources, R&D intensity, previous experience of collaboration, firm age, size and sector) were also included in the regression analysis. First, we measure the 'range of external sources' as the variety of external sources used by the firm to innovate, constructed by combining the nine external sources identified. The first step was coding each external source (ranging initially from 1 to 4) into a binary variable, which takes the value 1 if the firm relies on a particular source for innovation and 0 otherwise. The second step was adding up the nine variables to construct the variable 'range of external sources', which takes the value 9 if the firm relies on every external source and 0 if it does not rely on any of them. Second, we measure technological capacity ('R&D intensity') on a 1–3 scale, where the value 1 indicates that the firm does not conduct internal R&D, 2 indicates that the firm conducts occasional R&D activity and 3 indicates regular internal R&D activity. Third, we capture 'experience of collaboration' through a binary variable that takes the value 1 if the firm indicates that CSIC is its most frequent external collaboration partner and 0 otherwise. Fourth, we control for firm 'age' through a continuous variable that counts the number of years since the firm's foundation. Fifth, firm 'size' is captured by a continuous variable for the number of firm employees. We use a logarithmic transformation to match this variable with a normal distribution. Finally, we control for 'industrial sector'. The firms in our sample belong to a wide range of sectors. Therefore, we created a binary variable for each sector, which takes the value 1 if the firm belongs to that sector and 0 otherwise. The sectors considered are: construction, energy and water supply, mining, services, agriculture, forestry and fishing, high technology manufacturing, low technology manufacturing and medium-high technology manufacturing.

4.5. Analysis

To address our first research question, we conducted a descriptive analysis to explore the extent to which firms' collaboration with CSIC strengthens their innovation culture. In order to explore how collaboration with a PRO can lead to an improved firm innovation culture, we performed an ordered logistic regression. More specifically, we consider 'improved innovation culture' as our dependent variable and include firm's 'innovation plan, internal search depth and external search depth' as the main independent variables. We pay particular attention to firms' deliberate efforts to formulate and formalize an innovation plan and the firms' search strategy to improve their innovation processes. We estimate three different specifications to test our hypotheses (see results section).

Table 3 presents the descriptive statistics and bivariate correlations of the independent variables and control variables. The correlation matrix indicates weak correlation coefficients. Table 3, column 6 reports the Variance Inflation Factor (VIF) values, which indicate whether two independent variables have a strong linear relationship. All VIF values are much lower than 10, which suggests that multicollinearity is not a concern in the regression analysis (Field, 2009; Neter, Kutner, Nachtsheim, & Wasserman, 1996). In addition, we use mean centred variables to evaluate the moderating effects in order to reduce multicollinearity problems.

5. Results

5.1. Descriptive results

The descriptive statistics computed for the variable 'improved innovation culture' indicate that 38% of the firms surveyed report that, as a result of collaborating with CSIC, their

Table 3. Descriptive statistics and correlations.

	Mean	SD	Min	Max	VIF	1	2	3	4	5	6	7
(1) Innovation plan	0.53	0.50	0.00	1.00	1.12							
(2) Depth internal search	3.55	0.62	1.00	4.00	1.09	0.16***						
(3) Depth external search	2.14	2.08	0.00	9.00	1.11	0.15***	0.32***					
(4) Range of external sources	8.27	1.37	0.00	9.00	1.09	0.11***	0.21***	0.29***				
(5) R&D intensity	2.59	0.66	1.00	3.00	1.10	0.35***	0.13***	0.12***	0.09***			
(6) Experience in collaborations	0.15	0.35	0.00	1.00	1.04	−0.05	−0.07*	−0.03	−0.06	−0.09*		
(7) Firm age	24.24	18.13	2.00	209.00	1.10	0.01	0.01	0.06	0.08*	0.05	−0.03	
(8) Firm size	3.33	1.20	0.69	5.52	1.17	0.22***	0.06	0.04	0.13***	0.19***	−0.19***	0.34***

Notes: Industrial sector dummies not reported. $N = 513$.
*$p < .10$.
***$p < .01$.

innovation cultures improved. This result indicates that SMEs can strengthen their innovation cultures from collaboration with PROs. However, since not all firms benefit equally from collaborating with a PRO, we want to distinguish what characterizes (in terms of innovation plan and search strategies) those SMEs whose innovation culture benefits the most from collaborating with CSIC.

5.2. Regression results

Table 4 presents the results of the ordered logit model. We ran three different models to test our three hypotheses. Model 1 is our baseline model and includes the three independent variables – 'innovation plan', 'internal search depth' and 'external search depth' – and the control variables. Model 1 tests hypotheses 1, 2a and 2b. Models 2 and 3 include the same variables as the baseline model plus the interaction between innovation plan and one type of search strategy. Thus, Model 2 includes the interaction 'innovation plan * internal search depth' (H3a) and Model 3 includes the interaction 'innovation plan * external search depth' (H3b). The inclusion of these interactions is aimed at exploring whether search strategies exerts a moderating effect between formal innovation plan and increasing the firm's innovation culture.

The results of Model 1 show that having a formal innovation plan determines the extent to which firms take advantage of collaboration with a PRO to strengthen their innovation culture. Specifically, 'innovation plan' has a significant positive effect on improving innovation culture, which supports hypothesis 1 and suggests that those firms with a formal innovation strategy may benefit more from collaboration with external research bodies.

Table 4. Ordered logit regression analysis. Dependent variable 'improved innovation culture'.

Independent variables	Model 1		Model 2		Model 3	
Innovation plan	0.58***	(0.20)	0.58***	(0.20)	0.59***	(0.20)
Internal search depth	0.08	(0.15)	−0.21	(0.20)	0.09	(0.15)
External search depth	0.07	(0.05)	0.07	(0.05)	−0.01	(0.07)
Range of external sources	0.27***	(0.08)	0.27***	(0.08)	0.27***	(0.08)
R&D intensity	0.29**	(0.15)	0.28*	(0.15)	0.29*	(0.15)
Experience in collaborations	0.61**	(0.25)	0.61**	(0.25)	0.63**	(0.25)
Firm age	0.02***	(0.01)	0.02***	(0.01)	0.02***	(0.01)
Firm size	−0.20**	(0.09)	−0.19**	(0.09)	−0.20**	(0.09)
Energy and water supply	0.27	(1.03)	0.57	(1.04)	0.41	(1.03)
Mining	−1.62**	(0.78)	−1.55**	(0.77)	−1.58**	(0.78)
Services	−0.65	(0.47)	−0.58	(0.46)	−0.61	(0.46)
Agriculture, forestry and fishing	−0.37	(0.58)	−0.23	(0.58)	−0.33	(0.58)
High technology	−0.99*	(0.59)	−0.99*	(0.58)	−0.98*	(0.58)
Low technology	−0.80*	(0.48)	−0.72	(0.48)	−0.80*	(0.47)
Medium-high technology	−0.68	(0.52)	−0.56	(0.52)	−0.65	(0.52)
Innovation plan * Internal search depth			0.66**	(0.30)		
Innovation plan * External search depth					0.15*	(0.09)
cut1	2.73***	(0.95)	−0.35	(0.46)	−0.40	(0.46)
cut2	3.31***	(0.95)	0.24	(0.46)	0.19	(0.46)
cut3	5.49***	(0.97)	2.43***	(0.48)	2.38***	(0.48)
N	489		489		489	
Log likelihood	70.91***		75.84***		73.60***	

Note: Standard errors in parentheses. Sector category of reference is construction.
*p < .10.
**p < .05.
***p < .01.

However, the search strategies considered (our independent variables) do not affect the dependent variable. There is no evidence of a significant relationship for the two search strategies: 'external search depth' and 'internal search depth'. Thus, the data do not support hypotheses 2a and 2b that the innovation cultures of SMEs with active internal and external in depth search strategies benefit more from collaboration with PRO. Regarding the control variables, the results indicate that a wider range of external sources, higher levels of R&D intensity, more experience of collaborating with CSIC and firm age are significantly and positively related to more improvements to the firm's innovation culture from collaboration with CSIC. Also, the variable 'firm size' shows a negative significant association with an increased innovation culture.

Models 2 and 3 test hypotheses 3a and 3b that having an innovation plan and an explicit search strategy might be complementary and self-reinforcing, and that firms with both elements in place will benefit more from collaborating with CSIC in terms of improving their innovation culture. Model 2 shows that the coefficient of the relationship between the interaction 'innovation plan * internal search depth' and 'improved innovation culture' is significant and positive. The results of Model 3 show that the coefficient of the relationship between the interaction 'innovation plan * external search depth' and 'improved innovation culture' is significant and positive. These results suggest that, even if depth of internal search and depth of external search do not have a direct significant effect on improving the firm's innovation culture, in combination with a formal innovation plan, the effect is significant and positive for strengthening the firm's innovation culture. Graphically, Figure 1 depicts the moderating effect of 'innovation plan' on 'improved innovation culture' when 'internal search depth' varies. At high levels of 'internal search depth', the effect of an 'innovation plan' on 'improved innovation culture' is higher. Figure 2 depicts the moderating effect of 'innovation plan' on improving 'innovation culture' when 'external search depth' varies. At high levels of 'external search depth' the

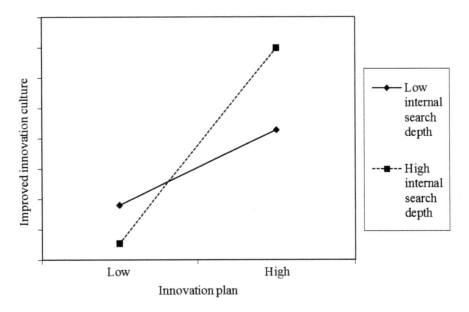

Figure 1. Moderator effect of internal search depth.

effect of 'innovation plan' on 'improved innovation culture' is higher. Thus, hypotheses 3a and 3b on the moderating role of internal and external search strategies are supported.

6. Discussion and conclusions

The effect of an innovation culture on performance has been discussed extensively in the literature. However, the conditions causing an innovation culture to emerge or increase require more research attention (Hogan & Coote, 2014). Work on PRO–firm collaboration stresses that research has been skewed towards analysing the benefits in the form of technological innovations (i.e. Arza & Vazquez, 2010; Bishop, D'Este, & Neely, 2011), but overlooks other aspects such as enhancement of the innovation culture. In this paper, we focused on SMEs' collaborations with external agents to compensate for a lack of resources (Huizingh, 2011; Van de Vrande et al., 2009). Our exploratory study addressed whether and under what conditions SMEs could enhance their innovation culture through collaborations with research organizations. We focused, in particular, on the roles of a formal innovation plan and an active search strategy.

Our results show that more than a third of SMEs that collaborated with research organizations experienced an increase in their innovation culture. This means that these firms focus on practices that encourage innovative behaviours among employees and the generation of new ideas including those that might challenge the organizational status quo.

The results indicate also that SMEs with a formal innovation plan are more likely to promote the conditions to embrace an innovation culture from collaborations with research organizations. Systematised guidelines promoting innovation signal to employees that innovation is supported by top management. Our results show that those firms with a formal innovation plan are able to exploit collaboration with research organizations to improve their innovation cultures. This is akin to the finding in the literature on

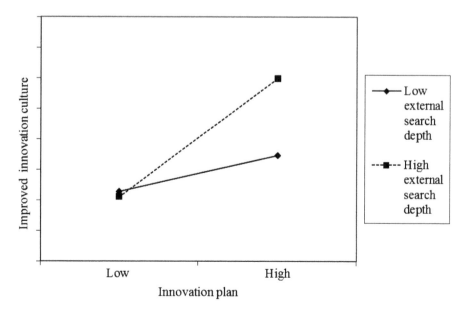

Figure 2. Moderator effect of external search depth.

absorptive capacity that similar levels of prior knowledge, skills, capabilities and culture between firm and collaboration partner are necessary to fully exploit the collaboration (Cohen & Levinthal, 1990; Lane & Lubatkin, 1998).

Our findings indicate also the relevance of search strategies to enable SMEs to obtain the most advantage from their collaborations with research organizations. The firm does not benefit directly from a search strategy; however, the existence of search strategies combined with an innovation plan has a positive effect. While the depth of search does not exert a significant direct effect on the firm's innovation culture, they have a significant and positive moderating effect on the interaction between having a formal innovation plan and strengthening the innovation culture. In other words, when firms follow an in depth search strategy, they draw intensively on internal and external sources of knowledge and innovation, which reinforces the effect of a formal innovation plan on the firm's innovation culture. In sum, firms that want to benefit more from their collaboration with research organizations should implement a formal innovation plan and exploit both internal and external sources of information.

In relation specifically to the effects of firm size, previous experience and age, on the management of innovation culture: Our results suggest that smaller SMEs benefit more from cooperation with research organizations in terms of strengthening their innovation culture, supporting our theoretical argument that smaller firms benefit more from PRO collaboration since it provides them with resources and knowledge not available within the firm. Also, the smaller the firm, the simpler the necessary organizational arrangement, resulting in higher levels of discretion among both managers and employees in the creation of an innovation culture. Firms with past experience of collaboration with CSIC gain more benefit in terms of strengthening their innovation culture; repeated collaboration over time generates a higher ability to absorb the knowledge and skills provided by the teaching partner. It is also interesting that older firms obtain more benefits for their innovation culture from collaborating with a PRO. This suggests that older firms might be keener to collaborate with research organizations and to improve their innovation culture since older organizations tend to suffer from organizational rigidity and inertia.

Interpretation of the results would be inadequate without taking full acknowledgement of the limitations of the paper. First, we acknowledge that a single-item has been used to proxy for improved innovation culture, but the data-gathering methodology, the characteristic of our sample and our *post hoc* analysis alleviates this limitation. Second, the study uses cross-sectional data, which do not allow conclusions to be made about causal relationships. Third, we rely on data from only one country (Spain), which does not allow for generalization to other countries or contexts. Future studies should extend the analysis to other countries with a similar industrial structure to Spain, in order to allow for comparisons across countries, validate our findings and allow generalization. Future research on innovation culture and its foundations should focus especially on SMEs and micro firms given their relevance in southern countries' industrial structures.

Our findings could be helpful for managers. Formalizing an innovation plan and putting in place an active and deep search strategy are two organizational practices which could be pursued easily. If SME managers want to become more 'innovative' thanks to their firms' collaborations with a PRO, they should pursue these practices. It is important to take innovation seriously and have a formalized plan combined with an active search strategy based on a strong firm commitment.

Notes

1. The Spanish version of the Community Survey Innovation (CIS).
2. For more details on CSIC characteristics at the time of the study, see Olmos-Peñuela, Benneworth and Castro-Martínez (2014).
3. Eighty-nine per cent of the sample firms conducted occasional or regular R&D activities, which is a much higher percentage than the one obtained from the Spanish Innovation Surveys.

Acknowledgements

The authors acknowledge CSIC and other IMPACTO project researchers (from INGENIO and IESA institutes) for their hard and very satisfactory work and also to the firms, whose questionnaire answers allowed developing the database. The authors would like to thank two anonymous reviewers for their constructive comments. Any errors or omissions remain the authors' responsibility.

Disclosure statement

No potential conflict of interest was reported by the authors.

Funding

This work was supported by the Spanish National Research Council (CSIC) under the IMPACTO project and by the Spanish Ministry of Economy and Competitiveness [grant number CS02013-48053-R].

References

Amabile, T. M. (1998). How to kill creativity. *Harvard Business Review*, 76(5), 77–87. Retrieved from http://gwmoon.knu.ac.kr/Lecture_Library_Upload/HOW_TO_KILL_CREATIVITY.pdf.
Amara, N., & Landry, R. (2005). Sources of information as determinants of novelty of innovation in manufacturing firms: Evidence from the 1999 statistics Canada innovation survey. *Technovation*, 25(3), 245–259. doi:10.1016/S0166-4972(03)00113-5
Ambos, T. C., Mäkelä, K., Birkinshaw, J., & D'Este, P. (2008). When does university research get commercialized? Creating ambidexterity in research institutions. *Journal of Management Studies*, 45(8), 1424–1447. doi:10.1111/j.1467-6486.2008.00804.x
Arza, V., & Vazquez, C. (2010). Interactions between public research organisations and industry in Argentina. *Science and Public Policy*, 37(7), 499–511. doi:10.3152/030234210X512728
Aschhoff, B., & Schmidt, T. (2008). Empirical evidence on the success of R&D cooperation—Happy together? *Review of Industrial Organization*, 33(1), 41–62. doi:10.1007/s11151-008-9179-7
Bader, K., Vanbrabant, L., & Enkel, E. (2014, June). *Drivers of firm openness: innovation culture and strategic direction as stimulating factors*. Paper presented at the meeting of European Academy of Management, Valencia. ISBN: 978-84-697-0377-9.
Barney, J. B. (1986). Organizational culture: Can it be a source of sustained competitive advantage? *Academy of Management Review*, 11(3), 656–665. doi:10.5465/AMR.1986.4306261

Becheikh, N., Landry, R., & Amara, N. (2006). Lessons from innovation empirical studies in the manufacturing sector: A systematic review of the literature from 1993–2003. *Technovation, 26* (5), 644–664. doi:10.1016/j.technovation.2005.06.016

Beinhocker, E. D., & Kaplan, S. (2002, June). Tired of strategic planning. *The McKinsey Quarterly*. Retrieved from http://www.mckinsey.com/business-functions/strategy-and-corporate-finance/our-insights/tired-of-strategic-planning.

Belderbos, R., Carree, M., Diederen, B., Lokshin, B., & Veugelers, R. (2004). Heterogeneity in R&D cooperation strategies. *International Journal of Industrial Organization, 22*(8), 1237–1263. doi:10.1016/j.ijindorg.2004.08.001

Bierly, P. E., & Daly, P. S. (2007). Alternative knowledge strategies, competitive environment, and organizational performance in small manufacturing firms. *Entrepreneurship Theory and Practice, 31*(4), 493–516. doi:10.1111/j.1540-6520.2007.00185.x

Bishop, K., D'Este, P., & Neely, A. (2011). Gaining from interactions with universities: Multiple methods for nurturing absorptive capacity. *Research Policy, 40*(1), 30–40. doi:10.1016/j.respol.2010.09.009

Brettel, M., & Cleven, N. J. (2011). Innovation culture, collaboration with external partners and NPD performance. *Creativity and Innovation Management, 20*(4), 253–272. doi:10.1111/j.1467-8691.2011.00617.x

Chesbrough, H. W. (2003). *Open innovation: The new imperative for creating and profiting from technology*. Boston, MA: Harvard Business School Press.

Cohen, W. M., & Levinthal, D. A. (1990). Absorptive capacity: A new perspective on learning and innovation. *Administrative Science Quarterly, 35*, 128–152. doi:10.2307/2393553

Colombo, M. G., Rabbiosi, L., & Reichstein, T. (2011). Organizing for external knowledge sourcing. *European Management Review, 8*(3), 111–116. doi:10.1111/j.1740-4762.2011.01018.x

Colquitt, J., Lepine, J. A., & Wesson, M. J. (2009). *Organizational behaviour: Improving performance and commitment in the workplace*. New York, NY: McGraw-Hill.

CSIC. (2012). *Memoria anual del CSIC 2011*. Madrid: Consejo Superior de Investigaciones Científicas.

Damanpour, F. (1991). Organizational innovation: A meta-analysis of effects of determinants and moderators. *Academy of Management Journal, 34*(3), 555–590. doi:10.2307/256406

D'Este, P., & Patel, P. (2007). University–industry linkages in the UK: What are the factors underlying the variety of interactions with industry? *Research Policy, 36*(9), 1295–1313. doi:10.1016/j.respol.2007.05.002

Dobni, C. B. (2008). Measuring innovation culture in organizations: The development of a generalized innovation culture construct using exploratory factor analysis. *European Journal of Innovation Management, 11*(4), 539–559. doi:10.1108/14601060810911156

Durette, B., Fournier, M., & Lafon, M. (2016). The core competencies of PhDs. *Studies in Higher Education, 41*(8), 1355–1370. doi:10.1080/03075079.2014.968540

Field, A. (2009). *Discovering statistics using SPSS* (3rd ed.). London: Sage.

Freeman, C. (1974). *The economics of industrial innovation*. Harmondsworth: Penguin Books.

Grant, R. M. (1996). Prospering in dynamically-competitive environments: Organizational capability as knowledge integration. *Organization Science, 7*(4), 375–387. doi:10.1287/orsc.7.4.375

Herzog, P., & Leker, J. (2010). Open and closed innovation: Different innovation cultures for different strategies. *International Journal of Technology Management, 52*(3/4), 322–343. doi:10.1504/IJTM.2010.035979

Hogan, S. J., & Coote, L. V. (2014). Organizational culture, innovation, and performance: A test of Schein's model. *Journal of Business Research, 67*(8), 1609–1621. doi:10.1016/j.jbusres.2013.09.007

Huizingh, E. K. (2011). Open innovation: State of the art and future perspectives. *Technovation, 31* (1), 2–9. doi:10.1016/j.technovation.2010.10.002

Janssen, O. (2003). Innovative behaviour and job involvement at the price of conflict and less satisfactory relations with co-workers. *Journal of Occupational and Organizational Psychology, 76* (3), 347–364. doi:10.1348/096317903769647210

Kelley, R., & Caplan, J. (1993). How bell-labs creates star performers. *Harvard Business Review, 71* (4), 128–139. Retrieved from https://hbr.org/1993/07/how-bell-labs-creates-star-performer.

Koza, M. P., & Lewin, A. Y. (1998). The co-evolution of strategic alliances. *Organization Science, 9* (3), 255–264. doi:10.1287/orsc.9.3.255

Kutvonen, A. (2011). Strategic application of outbound open innovation. *European Journal of Innovation Management, 14*(4), 460–474. doi:10.1108/14601061111174916

Lane, P. J., & Lubatkin, M. (1998). Relative absorptive capacity and interorganizational learning. *Strategic Management Journal, 19*(5), 461–477. doi:10.1002/(SICI)1097-0266(199805)19:5<461 ::AID-SMJ953>3.0.CO;2-L

Laursen, K., & Salter, A. (2004). Searching high and low: What types of firms use universities as a source of innovation? *Research Policy, 33*(8), 1201–1215. doi:10.1016/j.respol.2004.07.004

Laursen, K., & Salter, A. (2006). Open for innovation: The role of openness in explaining innovation performance among UK manufacturing firms. *Strategic Management Journal, 27*(2), 131–150. doi:10.1002/smj.507

Lazzarotti, V., & Manzini, R. (2009). Different modes of open innovation: A theoretical framework and an empirical study. *International Journal of Innovation Management, 13*(4), 615–636. doi:10. 1142/S1363919609002443

Lee, S., Park, G., Yoon, B., & Park, J. (2010). Open innovation in SMEs—An intermediated network model. *Research Policy, 39*(2), 290–300. doi:10.1016/j.respol.2009.12.009

Lööf, H., & Broström, A. (2008). Does knowledge diffusion between university and industry increase innovativeness? *The Journal of Technology Transfer, 33*(1), 73–90. doi:10.1007/ s10961-006-9001-3

Manjarrés-Henríquez, L., Gutiérrez-Gracia, A., Carrión-García, A., & Vega-Jurado, J. (2009). The effects of university–industry relationships and academic research on scientific performance: Synergy or substitution? *Research in Higher Education, 50*(8), 795–811. doi:10.1007/s11162-009-9142-y

Mansfield, E. (1991). Academic research and industrial innovation. *Research Policy, 20*(1), 1–12. doi:10.1016/0048-7333(91)90080-A

Martín-de Castro, G., Delgado-Verde, M., Navas-López, J. E., & Cruz-González, J. (2013). The moderating role of innovation culture in the relationship between knowledge assets and product innovation. *Technological Forecasting and Social Change, 80*(2), 351–363. doi:10.1016/ j.techfore.2012.08.012

Martins, E. C., & Terblanche, F. (2003). Building organisational culture that stimulates creativity and innovation. *European Journal of Innovation Management, 6*(1), 64–74. doi:10.1108/ 14601060310456337

Menzel, H. C., Aaltio, I., & Ulijn, J. M. (2007). On the way to creativity: Engineers as intrapreneurs in organizations. *Technovation, 27*(12), 732–743. doi:10.1016/j.technovation.2007.05.004

Miotti, L., & Sachwald, F. (2003). Co-operative R&D: Why and with whom?: An integrated framework of analysis. *Research Policy, 32*(8), 1481–1499. doi:10.1016/S0048-7333(02)00159-2

Monjon, S., & Waelbroeck, P. (2003). Assessing spillovers from universities to firms: Evidence from French firm-level data. *International Journal of Industrial Organization, 21*(9), 1255–1270. doi:10.1016/s0167-7187(03)00082-1

Neter, J., Kutner, M. H., Nachtsheim, C. J., & Wasserman, W. (1996). *Applied linear statistical methods.* Chicago, IL: Irwin.

Olmos-Peñuela, J., Benneworth, P., & Castro-Martínez, E. (2014). Are 'STEM from Mars and SSH from Venus'? Challenging disciplinary stereotypes of research's social value. *Science and Public Policy, 41*(3), 384–400. doi:10.1093/scipol/sct071

Partha, D., & David, P. A. (1994). Toward a new economics of science. *Research Policy, 23*(5), 487–521. doi:10.1016/0048-7333(94)01002-1

Pavitt, K. (1991). Key characteristics of the large innovating firm. *British Journal of Management, 2* (1), 41–50. doi:10.1111/j.1467-8551.1991.tb00014.x

Podsakoff, P. M., & Organ, D. W. (1986). Self-reports in organizational research: Problems and prospects. *Journal of Management, 12*(4), 531–544. doi:10.1177/014920638601200408

Robbins, S. P. (1996). *Organizational behaviour: Concepts, controversies, applications* (7th ed.). Englewood Cliffs, NJ: Prentice Hall.

Roberts, E. B., & Fusfeld, A. R. (1981). Staffing the innovative technology-based organization. *Sloan Management Review, 22*(3), 19–34. Retrieved from http://search.proquest.com/docview/1302987321/citation/AC3B06C634DF4620PQ/1?accountid=14777.

Rosenkopf, L., & Nerkar, A. (2001). Beyond local search: Boundary-spanning, exploration, and impact in the optical disk industry. *Strategic Management Journal, 22*(4), 287–306. doi:10.1002/smj.160

Rothaermel, F. T., & Deeds, D. L. (2004). Exploration and exploitation alliances in biotechnology: A system of new product development. *Strategic Management Journal, 25*(3), 201–221. doi:10.1002/smj.376

Sakkab, N. (2002). Connect & develop complements research & develop at P&G. *Research-Technology Management, 45*(2), 38–45. doi:10.1080/08956308.2002.11671490

Sánchez-González, G., & Herrera, L. (2010). The influence of R&D cooperation on innovatory effort. *Innovation, 12*(3), 337–354. doi:10.5172/impp.12.3.337

Santoro, M. D., & Chakrabarti, A. K. (2002). Firm size and technology centrality in industry–university interactions. *Research Policy, 31*(7), 1163–1180. doi:10.1016/S0048-7333(01)00190-1

Schein, E. H. (1992). *Organizational culture and leadership.* San Francisco, CA: Jossey-Bass.

Stephan, P. E. (1996). The economics of science. *Journal of Economic Literature, 34*(3), 1199–1235. Retrieved from http://www.jstor.org/stable/2729500

Un, C. A., Cuervo-Cazurra, A., & Asakawa, K. (2010). R&D collaborations and product innovation. *Journal of Product Innovation Management, 27*(5), 673–689. doi:10.1111/j.1540-5885.2010.00744.x

Valmaseda-Andia, O., Albizu-Gallastegi, E., Fernandez-Esquinas, M., & Fernandez-de-Lucio, I. (2015). Interaction between the Spanish firms and the CSIC: Motivations, mechanisms and benefits from the firm's perspective. *Revista Española de Documentación Científica, 38*(4), 1–17. doi:10.3989/redc.2015.4.1263

Van de Vrande, V., De Jong, J. P., Vanhaverbeke, W., & De Rochemont, M. (2009). Open innovation in SMEs: Trends, motives and management challenges. *Technovation, 29*(6), 423–437. doi:10.1016/j.technovation.2008.10.001

Yuan, F., & Woodman, R. W. (2010). Innovative behavior in the workplace: The role of performance and image outcome expectations. *Academy of Management Journal, 53*(2), 323–342. doi:10.5465/AMJ.2010.49388995

Innovative culture in district innovation systems of European ceramics SMEs

Daniel Gabaldón-Estevan ⓘ and Josep-Antoni Ybarra

ABSTRACT
We need to understand the dynamics of current local production systems in the form of industrial districts and, particularly, how culture and innovation are interlinked. In this paper, we argue that the district innovation system approach, which covers the innovation systems and industrial district literatures, provides a set of ideas useful for understanding the role of culture in innovation in industrial districts. We study the role of innovation culture in two of the most important European ceramics industrial districts in Italy and Spain. Specifically, we analyse how, within a given district system, the innovation culture, networks and social structure, and their inter-relations, influence the interactions among those agents actively participating in the development, diffusion or adoption of innovation. We identify the cultural elements that are decisive in these innovation systems and whether these elements are substantially equal between the two countries or whether there are differences in their cultures, processes and innovation systems. Our main finding is that the cultural dynamics in district innovation systems differs among countries.

1. Introduction

Since Granovetter's (1985, p. 481) comment on the role of social relations in economic activity that 'economic action is embedded in structures of social relations, in modern industrial society', the focus has been on concepts from sociology to understand how innovation is achieved. This interest in the role of culture, agents, networks and institutions has been directed towards both emerging sectors and new modes of economic interaction (Manzo & Ramella, 2015), and established sectors (Beugelsdijk, 2010; Brown & Ulijn, 2004; Casson, 2003; Day, 2009; Vallejo, 2011). Although sociological concepts are being applied quite widely, their use is at the same time selective and ignores controversial issues such as power, legitimization and conflict (Ramella, 2015). Specifically, in our case, the analysis is aimed at understanding the role of innovative culture[1] in how the values, norms, cognitive frames, roles and institutions, social structures, networks and relations in a given industrial district affect the interactions among agents participating actively in the development, diffusion and adoption of innovation.

The innovation systems approach has assumed more importance in debates over the determinants of innovation, and has implications also for innovation policy (Edquist, 2004). This approach identifies the agents and their connections in different territorial contexts such as the national (Freeman, 1995; Lundvall, 1992; Nelson, 1993), regional (Cooke, 2001; Cooke & Morgan, 1993; Cooke, Uranga, & Etxebarria, 1997) and local (Anselin, Varga, & Acs, 1997; Camagni, 1991), in different sectors (Breschi & Malerba, 1997; Freeman, 1982, 1987; Malerba, 1999; Nelson & Winter, 1982; Rosenberg, 1982) and in different technologies (Callon, 1992; Carlsson & Stankiewicz, 1991; Hughes, 1984), all of which has improved our understanding of how innovation processes function.

In response to this heterogeneity, there is a considerable body of recent research devoted to understanding this socio-technical transitions phenomenon and, especially, from a multi-level perspective (MLP) (Geels, 2002). An MLP structures the analysis at three heuristic levels: socio-technical regime, socio-technical niche and socio-technical landscape (Geels, 2002; Geels & Schot, 2010). Regime refers to the dominant cognitive, regulatory or normative structures that have emerged around a technology. Niche defines the protected space that allows a specific technological innovation to develop. Landscape captures the exogenous context of a socio-technical system.

However, these boundaries may not be appropriate for an analysis of the most significant relationships in specific contexts such as industrial districts (Gabaldón-Estevan, Fernández-de-Lucio, & Molina-Morales, 2012). The industrial districts approach (Becattini, 1979; Bellandi, 1996, 2002; Pyke & Sengenberger, 1992; Pyke, Becattini, & Sengerberger, 1992) offers an appropriate unit of analysis to study the relations and role of community and culture in industrial districts. However, in existing work on industrial districts, innovation is not the central focus. In the present paper, we study the role of culture in innovation, in the context of the district innovation system (DIS), a concept that is useful to understand the overlapping elements, which can be identified in the industrial district literature (e.g., the atmosphere and elements of the cognitive frame such as tacit knowledge) and the innovation systems literature (e.g., different actors' linkages, systemic functions and failures). We acknowledge a tendency towards conceptual fragmentation within innovation systems studies and recognize that the separation among the concepts of regional, sectoral and DISs is very tenuous. However, we consider DIS to be an appropriate framework and unit of analysis for the present study.

The paper is organized as follows. We provide a synthesis of the industrial districts and innovation systems literatures, which underpin the DIS concept (Section 2). The theoretical part (Section 3), following a description of the case study methodology applied, analyses the role of innovative culture in two European ceramic tile districts – in Sassuolo, Italy and Castellon, Spain. Section 4 presents the results and these are discussed in Section 5, and some policy implications are derived in Section 6. The paper concludes in Section 7.

2. Background

DIS is a concept that emphasizes the relevance of territory when an industry adopts the industrial district form, but is dependent also on other innovation system elements. It encompasses the relevance of both the innovation systems concept, especially from a sectoral perspective, and the industrial district tradition. We examine these two perspectives on industrial development using different, but complementary tools. DIS emphasizes the relevance of territory when an industry adopts the industrial district form, but we show that other elements in the innovation system are also important (Gabaldón-Estevan et al., 2012).

Specifically, a DIS is defined as

> a system of relationships within an industrial district where externalities facilitate firms'
> innovation processes (…) An industrial district is understood as a social entity, which,
> while linked to a territory, usually does not conform to the limits of a specific administration.
> District innovation system emphasizes the relevance of territory, that is, when an industry
> adopts the district form, but is also dependent on other elements in the innovation
> system. Consequently the district innovation system is made up of a set of institutions,
> firms and promotion mechanisms that offer continuous support to district firms. The district
> innovation system involves interconnections and cooperation among elements within the
> same environment for the purposes of innovation. (Gabaldón-Estevan, 2016, p. 83)

The types of networks established in a DIS can favour different types of knowledge transfer because of the variety of connections and the localized character of social capital. Frequent contacts between companies are useful for the development of incremental innovations, which require deep knowledge in certain areas (Fagerberg, 2003; Granovetter, 1985). However, these types of contacts (strong ties) seem not to be conducive to the development of breakthrough (radical) innovations. This is because such contacts provide information that, given the frequency of the contacts, tends to be redundant (Granovetter, 1985) and, also, because these stable networks can exhibit symptoms of path dependency (Pavitt, 1984) derived from a shared perception of reality (group thinking). Thus, a culture of participation in a network of weak ties may be a more useful strategy for firms that want the freedom to change their orientation (Fagerberg, 2003). This applies especially to small and medium-sized enterprises (SMEs) which need to compensate for their limited domestic resources by establishing strong external interactions. However, the increasing complexity of the knowledge base required for innovation means that even large companies rely increasingly on external sources for their innovation activities (Andersson, Forsgren, & Holm, 2002).

Kline and Rosenberg (1986) highlighted that innovation should not be understood as homogeneous, as well defined and displayed, or available at a specific time. In most cases, innovations undergo important developments, which can introduce drastic changes that affect their economic significance. The numerous future improvements made to an initial invention can result in a product that is more important economically than the initial invention. Along these lines, Nelson and Rosenberg (1993) suggest that the Schumpeterian innovative company that first brings a product to market is usually not the firm that ultimately captures most of the rents associated with that innovation. Successful innovation is less a matter of invention and more a matter of design and adaptation. Thus, innovative activity depends on the interactions among all the organizations in the DIS.

The systemic view involves a series of conditions that merit consideration. First, it considers that agents and institutions should be measured in terms of their contribution to innovation. A fundamental aspect of the improvements in the innovation process involves reviewing and redesigning the links between the parts of the system. In this view, it is assumed that there are imperfections in the market for innovations, whose resolution requires political interventions. Power is distributed unevenly among companies; innovation good practice does not spread automatically among companies, and market failures can include the failure of organizations to coordinate, connect and meet system needs, etc. (Woolthuis, Lankhuizen, & Gilsing, 2005). On the other hand, it is assumed that the institutional framework differs from one territory to another and that certain phases of the process are best outsourced to companies in a specific country or territory. In short, innovation systems need to ensure the flow of information across the interfaces between companies, research centres, entrepreneurs, investors, consulting firms, patenting agencies, local organizations and other intermediaries (Lundvall & Borrás, 2005).

From a DIS perspective, innovation is conceived as an interactive process in which a multitude of different agents (customers, companies and other organizations such as universities, research centres, government agencies, financial organizations, etc.) conform and participate in the innovative culture. Since companies do not innovate in isolation, but interact with other companies and other organizations and system elements, the networks that connect the different elements in the system and the exchange mechanisms involved are paramount.

In relation to the unit of analysis, sectoral systems of innovation (SSI), although a relevant contribution to the discipline and part of our conceptual framework, is limited to the notion of industrial sector (defined in terms of product). SSI refers to those companies, agents and institutions linked to the sectoral activity, regardless of their location. However, the concept of DIS emphasizes the types of external relationships generated by the relationships already existing within a territory. Malerba (1999, p. 9) allows some room for manoeuvre: 'high cumulativeness within specific locations is more likely to be associated with low appropriability conditions and spatially localized knowledge spillovers'.

This is in line with our district view. However, it indicates that, when considering the agents involved in an SSI, the unit of analysis might differ across sectors (Malerba, 1999, p. 15). Malerba (1999, p. 17) states also that, in some sectors, networks can create local or regional innovation and production systems and that 'A tradition closer to sectoral systems are the studies on regional or local systems: very often in fact a local system overlaps with a sector (see, for example, the studies of industrial districts and the machinery industry)' (Malerba, 1999, p. 30).

The main contributors to industrial district theory reject the sectoral level of analysis and consider it inadequate to explain the main phenomena affecting the development of local production systems. Becattini (1979), drawing on Marshall (1997), concludes that the industrial district is an indivisible unit, an atom, from which industrial research must start. In addition, spatial location and the multi-sectoral nature characterizing the Marshallian industrial district (MID) provide greater stability than industry, sector or technology in situations of intensive change thanks to the innovative culture conformed by values, norms, cognitive frames, roles and institutions. The greater the number of transitions in the MID, the stronger its identity (Becattini, 1979).

Again, from a systems perspective, it has been emphasized that the interconnection that facilitates interactions and synergies among resource poor companies can compensate for these lacking resources. For instance, Hobday (1991) describes the main mechanisms that help these companies: (i) reliance on organizations in the network allows small business groups to maintain frontier technologies (ii) accumulation of skills and collective learning occurs within the network, which benefits all participants since information is a social or common good[2]; (iii) promotion of flows of key individuals between companies; (iv) combination and recombination of skills to resolve bottlenecks; (v) reduced time and costs of innovation; (vi) entry to the industry, via the network, of new innovative companies and (vii) increased flexibility and enabled by networks. Overall, these mechanisms generate intragroup competition which promotes imitation and spillover effects that benefit all participants and enables adaptations to innovations at no cost (Dei Ottati, 1994). These characteristics are in line with the competitive advantage of district economies, which derives from the highly interconnected set of 'economies external to the companies, but internal to the district' (Dei Ottati, 2006, p. 74). They can be summarized as (1) efficient use of resources, particularly labour and intermediate inputs and (2) innovation resulting from the accumulation of specialized human capital, competitive dynamics and rapid dissemination of information.

Thus, in the context of this paper, the notion of DIS is understood as a system of relationships that generates externalities for businesses through an innovative culture. From this perspective, the unit of analysis to examine the DIS should include not only the businesses and organizations that make up the industrial district, but also those elements of the SSI (e.g., technologies and products) with which it interacts, regardless of whether these are located within or outside the same national (or regional) innovation system. We show that the Castellon ceramic tile district has important relations with major operators in Sassuolo, Italy. Therefore, which agents and organizations fall within the DIS unit of analysis depends on their contribution to the generation of innovations in the district. This allows our analysis of industrial activity based on a single product (the ceramic tile) to include other relevant district activities (e.g., frits, glazes and ceramic colours and metal-mechanics). We extend the classification of industrial activity based only on technology, which is relatively transitory in the development of an industry (Becattini, 1979), to avoid substantial technological change undermining our unit of analysis (Ybarra, 2007). Nevertheless, as Becattini (1979) points out, the feeling of belonging to an industry (as an element of the culture and collective psychology), which underpins the definition of MID, is useful to limit our unit of analysis and allow us to go beyond the local community to include the sectoral network structure. This allows retrospective study of a production unit (Figure 1).

To sum up, a DIS is a system of relationships within an industrial district, in which externalities facilitate firms' innovation processes (Gabaldón-Estevan et al., 2012). The advantage of the DIS approach is that it overcomes the potential limitations of the district concept by capturing and explaining the innovation processes occurring within it, while taking account also of the unique specificities that characterize and differentiate the industrial district at other levels of analysis.

3. Methodology

This article exploits and builds on evidence accumulated during the period 2004–2016 on MID (Ybarra, 2006, 2007) and the European ceramic tile industry specifically (see Gabaldón-Estevan, 2016 for a review). Extensive case study analyses of the ceramic tile industries in the autonomous regions of Valencia and the north of Italy provide an

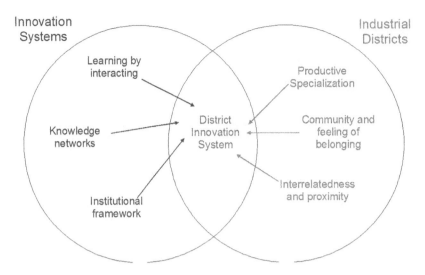

Figure 1. District innovation system. Source: Gabaldón-Estevan et al. (2012).

understanding of the links between innovation and cooperation among firms in a particular industrial district, and the providers of technology and advanced services to several districts. We conducted research on innovation in the European ceramic tile industrial districts, starting in 2004, based on analysis of secondary statistical data on the sector, and 40 semi-structured interviews[3] with representatives from the ceramic industrial districts in Sassuolo in Italy and Castellon in Spain (see Gabaldón-Estevan, 2016).

In the present paper, we revisit our earlier research and focus here on the role of the innovation culture on the performance of the ceramic tile DIS, adopting a comparative approach. It is important to highlight that this comparison allows us to study the cultural elements of industrial districts that help SMEs to achieve competitive advantage, by facilitating a certain type of innovation, such as incremental innovation in so-called traditional sectors (furniture, machinery, etc.), or commercial innovation in medium or low-tech products, based on symbolic knowledge associated to design and craftsmanship (fashion, food, etc.).

4. The Italian and the Spanish DISs

The European ceramic tile industry produces ceramic floor and wall tiles, decorative pieces, frits, glazes and colours and the machinery and equipment required for their production. It is involved in other activities related to the ceramic tile process and is a world leader in design and innovation related to new functionalities. It exports around a third of its production (Gabaldón-Estevan, 2016).

The Italian and Spanish ceramic tile DIS are clustered around Sassuolo in Italy and Castelló de la Plana in Spain. However, their configuration and predominant types of companies differ (Meyer-Stamer, Maggi, & Seibel, 2001; Molina-Morales, 2008).

The Italian ceramic tile district is a leader in design and was the main exporter until the recent economic crisis. The Spanish ceramic tile district developed as a result of expansion in Italy and partial delocalization of Italian companies, especially colours, frits and glazes providers. Italian ceramic tile companies tend to be bigger and more dynamic than their Spanish counterparts. The machinery used in the sector (see Figure 2) is produced by a very important metal-mechanics industry in Italy, which also produces machinery used in the food, pharmaceutical and automotive sectors (Russo, 1985).

The Spanish ceramic tile district has benefited from many years of intensive construction in Spain and from exporting activity based on its ability to produce a product of equivalent quality to that produced in Italy, but at a lower price (Giacomini, 2007). However, following the 2007 economic crisis, competence from emerging economies, especially China, became a concern for both districts (Russo, 2004). In terms of machinery,

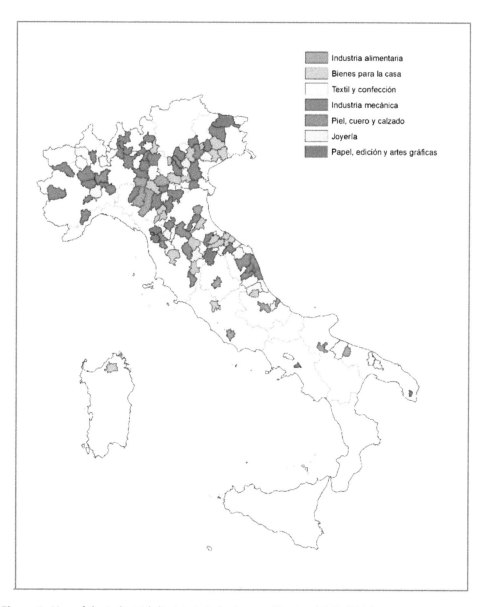

Figure 2. Map of the industrial districts in Italy. Source: Sforzi and Boix (2016).

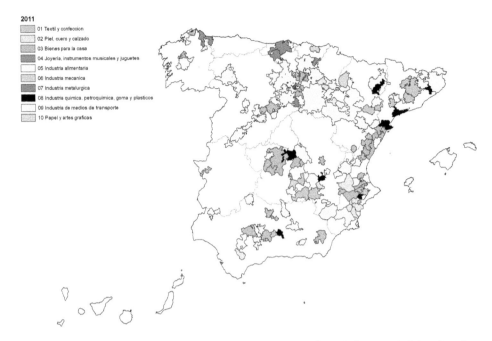

2011
- 01 Textil y confeccion
- 02 Piel, cuero y calzado
- 03 Bienes para la casa
- 04 Joyeria, instrumentos musicales y juguetes
- 05 Industria alimentaria
- 06 Industria mecanica
- 07 Industria metalurgica
- 08 Industria quimica, petroquimica, goma y plasticos
- 09 Industria de medios de transporte
- 10 Papel y artes graficas

Figure 3. Map of the Spanish industrial districts. Source: Boix, Sforzi, Galletto and Llobet (2015).

the Spanish district is an importer of Italian products since it has only a small subsector specialized in machinery for glazes. However, Spain has an important subsector of frits, glazes and ceramic colours, due in part to the partial delocalization of the industry from Italy as a consequence of the latter's stricter environmental regulations (Gabaldón-Estevan, Criado, & Monfort, 2014). Figure 3 shows that neighbouring Spanish ceramic tile industry clusters are relatively isolated since there are no complex systems providers able to transfer innovations from other sectors.

5. Results

International evolution of production and consumption of ceramics shows that innovative strategies are being adopted in the sector. The emerging countries (China, India, Brazil or Mexico) are assuming world leadership in both the production and consumption of ceramics, and the traditional tile producing countries are focusing on specialization and/or differentiation. Their ability to adapt to change and innovation is essential (see Tables 1–3).

Demand for ceramics is polarized. On the one hand, emerging economies have massive demand for ceramic products, but increasingly this is being satisfied by domestic production (especially in the cases of China, Latin American and Brazil). On the other hand, there are countries where demand for mass produced products has fallen and been replaced by demand for differentiation and individualized and/or market-oriented commercial model(s). In this second case, the possible production possibilities matter; logistics, design and personalized marketing are influenced by innovation. The split between standardization and specialization rests on the capacity for innovation. So, what is needed for innovation? The industry culture and the productive and technological relations within it matter in this respect.

Table 1. World main ceramic tiles manufacturers, 2011–2015. Source: Baraldi (2016), p. 50.

Rank	Country	2011 (Sq.m Mill.)	2012 (Sq.m Mill.)	2013 (Sq.m Mill.)	2014 (Sq.m Mill.)	2015 (Sq.m Mill.)	% On 2015 world production	% avar. 15/14
1	China	4800	5200	5700	6000	5970	48.3	−0.5
2	Brazil	844	866	871	903	899	7.3	−0.4
3	India	617	691	750	825	850	6.9	3.0
4	Spain	392	404	420	425	440	3.6	3.5
5	Vietnam	380	290	300	360	440	3.6	22.2
6	Italy	400	367	363	382	395	3.2	3.4
7	Indonesia	320	360	390	420	370	3.0	−11.9
8	Turkey	260	280	340	315	320	2.6	1.6
9	Iran	475	500	500	410	300	2.4	−26.8
10	Mexico	221	231	230	230	242	2.0	5.2
Total		8709	9189	9864	10,270	10,226	82.8	−0.4
Total world		10,626	11,224	11,958	12,373	12,355	100.0	−0.1

There is debate in the international literature over the most useful innovation model – science, technology and innovation or doing, using and interacting (DUI) (Jensen, Johnson, Lorenz, & Lundvall, 2007). Each of these emphasizes aspects related to open or closed innovation (Chesbrough, 2006). The openness of the DIS means it can involve other sectors, activities and territories especially through shared cognitive frames but where shared values, norms, roles and institutions also play a part. A closed DIS means that the innovative activity derives mainly from internal and inbred resources, of course here the shared culture is also present, but there is a shortage of diversity. This has serious implications for innovation opportunities and the cost of innovation activity. The distinction between open and closed innovation exemplifies the differences that exist between Italy and Spain in terms of implementing innovations in ceramics. In Italy, innovations are created in dedicated departments in companies with capabilities for process and product innovation. In addition, innovations are often a response to stated needs or the result of strategic collaborations among companies, innovative suppliers and business innovation departments. Some of the most important innovations involve technological improvements to production processes (furnaces, atomization) for machinery and marketing (marketing and image of the product).

Table 2. World main ceramic tiles exporters, 2011–2015. Source: Baraldi (2016), p. 51.

Rank	Country	2012 (Sq.m Mill.)	2013 (Sq.m Mill.)	2014 (Sq.m Mill.)	2015 (Sq.m Mill.)	% On 2015 national production	% On 2015 world exports	% avar. 15/14	Value 2015 (million €)	Average export price (€/sq.m)
1	China	1086	1148	1110	1089	18.2	39.8	−1.9	n.a.	n.a.
2	Spain	296	318	339	378	85.9	13.8	11.5	2452	6.5
3	Italy	289	303	314	317	80.2	11.6	0.9	4318	13.7
4	India	33	51	92	122	14.4	4.5	32.6	498	4.1
5	Iran	93	114	109	112	37.3	4.1	2.8	380	3.4
6	Turkey	92	88	85	77	24.1	2.8	−8.9	451	5.9
7	Brazil	59	63	69	77	8.6	2.8	11.0	265	3.4
8	Mexico	63	64	62	61	25.2	2.2	−1.6	320	5.2
9	EAU	54	58	55	54	71.1	2.0	−1.8	297	5.5
10	Poland	42	48	42	42	30.4	1.5	0.0	222	5.3
Total		2107	2255	2277	2329	24.2	85.1	2.2		
Total world		2524	2666	2695	2735	22.1	100.0	1.5		

Table 3. World main ceramic tiles importers, 2011–2015. Source Baraldi (2016), p. 52.

Rank	Country	2011 (Sq.m Mill.)	2012 (Sq.m Mill.)	2013 (Sq.m Mill.)	2014 (Sq.m Mill.)	2015 (Sq.m Mill.)	% On 2015 national consumption	% On 2015 world imports	% Var. 15/14
1	USA	131	139	160	159	175	68.9	6.4	9.9
2	Saudi Arabia	134	155	155	149	174	66.2	6.4	16.8
3	Iraq	80	105	121	102	106	99.1	3.9	3.9
4	Germany	90	89	89	95	100	83.3	3.7	5.3
5	France	110	107	96	99	99	87.6	3.6	0.0
6	South Korea	63	61	65	76	85	63.9	3.1	11.8
7	Nigeria	47	61	84	90	70	86.4	2.6	−22.2
8	UAE	50	52	53	54	64	74.4	2.3	18.5
9	Philippines	31	38	46	53	60	61.9	2.2	13.2
10	Thailand	46	52	68	49	56	29.2	2.0	14.3
Total		782	859	937	926	989	68.4	36.2	6.8
Total world		2346	2524	2666	2695	2735	22.5	100.0	1.5

In the Spanish case, companies that do not have a research department approach external partners to work on innovations, which also might benefit these external companies. This makes the innovation appear to be reacting to a need.[4] In Spain, cooperation is limited to the same sector and uses the resources of external agents (such as universities and the technology institutes), which are the main sources of information on existing opportunities. The most important innovation in the Spanish case is the frits process, an essential and strategic aspect of the design of ceramic pieces. Design, glaze and colour are essential aspects of ceramic pieces. Ceramics companies do not employ designers, but depend on external frits companies, which offer this service.

The opportunities for innovation in Italy compared to Spain tend to stem not from differences in their DIS, but from how this system is conceived. Thus, in the Italian case, the DIS is an open system, related to other systems and other sectors, while the Spanish DIS is closed. In Italy there are external elements for innovations that might be directly or indirectly adopted, for instance economies of demonstration, induction or testing. In the Spanish case, innovation opportunities derive from prioritization and centralization of the innovation process as a closed and previously determined process, with a beginning and a fixed goal.

In addition, in Italy private actors and business firms are important for innovation, they are more involved in the innovation culture, while in Spain innovation relies on universities and technology organizations. In Italy, the mechanics, the machines, are essential for innovation in ceramics. In Spain, innovation involves frits. The Italian innovation sector is ahead of that in Spain and involves more actors.

Open innovation systems, such as those adopted in Italian ceramics, are proactive as well as not only to relate to the particular sector. The challenge in Italy is how to manufacture the product in the shortest possible time for potential clients (Germany demands delivery in 3–4 days). The need to import raw materials causes production delays. This is an area that requires innovation. Improvements to logistics and transportation would benefit the industry. It would imply changes to storage and distribution platforms, similar to what occurred in the case of agri-food products from Emilia Romagna in Italy.

Mechanical activities related to ceramics are essential for production process innovations; Italy is the world supplier of ceramics machinery. In Italy, it is a horizontal activity whose production is used in many other sectors and activities than ceramics. The advances made in parallel sectors improve production processes and can be adapted and adopted at reasonable cost and minimum effort. Because they share a similar innovative culture across sectors we can talk about an open innovation system.

There is a third aspect, which is related to image, marketing and internationalization of the sector. Italy launched an aggressive marketing strategy. Italian tiles have qualities that tiles from other countries cannot match and which are associated with a high-quality product (see average export price in Table 2). Italian designs are distinctive and involve work and effort. They derive from innovative commercial forms and concepts and give Italian ceramics an advantage in foreign markets. The association of Italian products with a higher aesthetic value has of course a cultural ground. But where does the quality image stem from in the case of ceramics? It is clear that transversal knowledge on marketing and internationalization in other markets than ceramics is available within the DIS. Training centres and universities offer specific courses, taught by a range of agents. Innovation involves every aspect even those outside of production, as they are just as necessary as any other element to reach the consumer.

Finally, in the Italian case, the innovation system is open and proactive in terms of processes and knowledge and involves agents external to the sector, located across the territory, in other companies and organizations but sharing an innovative culture. In Spain, innovation focuses on improvements to product manufacturing and achieving a high-quality product, which can be costly, and more narrowly focus on the production process.

6. Policy implications

These findings have significant implications for the DIS. We know that the innovation opportunities offered by the DIS derive not just from financial resources but also from the quality and quantity of the agents involved in the system. However, the DIS goes beyond what is facilitated by formal and informal participation of agents and institutions (e.g. social capital). In our view, the existing knowledge could be used more broadly, beyond the activity for which it initially was conceived if a shared innovative culture is promoted. Thus, transversal applied technological knowledge, tacit or formal, that is useful for a sector and an activity, can transcend to others. In other words, the knowledge in the sector has a greater range of applicability beyond that sector. As a result, knowledge-related intangibles increase the innovative capacity of the DIS. The DIS could become a tool to allow analysis and implementation of innovation processes; the existence of intangible transversal technological elements could accelerate or slow the innovation system – whether sectoral or regional.

In order to understand the closed and/or open opportunities offered by the DIS, and to exploit the opportunities available, requires examination of the value chain and the relations with other activities. We need to investigate whether these activities develop in isolation or in interaction with others and the possibilities for exploiting complementarities and application opportunities. Activities that are being conducted in close proximity allow innovative solutions to be shared by several actors, sectors and activities, either immediately or with some simple adaptations.

Knowledge transfer is relatively straightforward in these cases and may require only application of engineering knowledge. If we focus on the environmental aspects related to raw materials supply and energy efficiency, innovation in product types, such as production of ceramic Lamina, becomes important. The production of ceramic Lamina reduces raw materials and energy use by one-third compared to traditional production systems. In turn, this involves other aspects, such as degrowth,[5] which increasingly involves the environment and use of materials and energy resources. Finally, as far as future innovation is concerned, transport and logistics are relevant to advantage in the international market. These types of innovations can exploit cross-cutting knowledge from other sectors, adapted to ceramics. The sectors most likely to benefit from open innovation are agribusiness, capital goods and machinery. Thus, in an open innovation system, characterized by a shared innovative culture, the tacit knowledge in the territory provides a robust basis for invention.[6]

7. Conclusions

The advantage of comparative research is that it highlights aspects that might not seem to be valuable. When comparing innovation models in a particular sector, such as ceramics, and in two different contexts, such as Italy and Spain, elements that per se may seem irrelevant or invisible are highlighted.

Innovation models based on the incorporation of science and technology into processes and products can be counterpoised (or in some cases are complementary) to models of relationships with customers and suppliers that drive innovation based on DUI.

The results of the innovation models in the Spanish and Italian ceramics industries show that the Italian model is an open model of innovation that allows the development of innovations applicable not just to ceramics, but also to other sectors such as logistics, mechanics and marketing. The closed Spanish innovation model achieves more limited results focused only on ceramics and frits.

Our results show that there can be transversal application of the cognitive frame (tacit and/or formal knowledge) that is useful for more than one sector and activity. This is enabled by an open innovation system, which increases the possibilities for innovation exponentially. An open innovation system requires not only a diversity of agents across sectors but a shared innovative culture as well. In our case, this was confirmed by knowledge developed in ceramics that was extended to other areas related to the supply of raw materials and energy efficiency. The application of this knowledge was extended also to agribusiness, capital goods and machinery. Thus, in an open system of innovation that exploits the tacit knowledge in the territory, the DIS promotes innovation across sectors through innovation culture. The promotion of production relations, forums, meetings and mutual visits, and the complementarities among activities are essential if innovation is to be developed in a generalized way without huge cost or effort.

The comparative research also presents some limitations especially regarding the degree of generalization of the results. Also cultural differences being so rooted in respective societies it is not easy to disentangle what is specific from the region and what from the sector. Consequently, further research should be directed to apply the DIS perspective in other MID-like sectors.

Notes

1. It is important, first, to clarify Portes's (2001; 2007) distinction between the cultural and the social as differentiated dimensions of reality (Fernández Esquinas, 2012). The cultural

dimension comprises values, norms, cognitive frames, roles and institutions while the social structure is made up of power, social classes, hierarquies and organizations.
2. Recall that learning is an important cognitive element of the cultural dimension frame.
3. Interviewees included managers in ceramic, electro-mechanical and glaze companies, representatives of employers' and workers' associations, representatives of public organizations specialized in technology or trade, managers of research organizations responsible for innovation and development in the industry, and academic researchers. The interviews provided information on the tile production process, on the roles of relevant actors in the tile districts, on how innovations are produced and disseminated in the market, and the participation and motivation of different actors in the innovation processes. They also provided more general information, such as global production trends, emergence of new competitors and trade.
4. For these companies deregulation of employment, promotion of anti-dumping measures and failure to comply with environmental standards can be more important than innovation for achieving sectoral competitiveness.
5. Degrowth fosters a reduction of energy and material throughput, needed in order to face the existing biophysical constraints. It challenges the omnipresence of market-based relations in society and the growth-based roots of the social imaginary replacing them by the idea of frugal abundance. It is also a call for deeper democracy, applied to issues which lie outside the mainstream democratic domain, like technology. Finally, it implies an equitable redistribution of wealth within and across the Global North and South, as well as between present and future generations (Demaria, Schneider, Sekulova, & Martinez-Alier, 2013).
6. Several examples confirm this. Atomization is an essential process in the modern manufacture of ceramics and derives from the agri-food and pharmaceuticals sectors. It can be described as a horizontal innovation that has transferred across sectors due to the proximity of agents. This applies also to continuous kiln ceramic production, which originated in biscuit manufacture.

Disclosure statement

No potential conflict of interest was reported by the authors.

ORCID

Daniel Gabaldón-Estevan http://orcid.org/0000-0003-2086-5012

References

Andersson, U., Forsgren, M., & Holm, U. (2002). The strategic impact of external networks: Subsidiary performance and competence development in the multinational corporation. *Strategic Management Journal, 23,* 979–996. http://onlinelibrary.wiley.com/doi/10.1002/smj.267/full
Anselin, L., Varga, A., & Acs, Z. (1997). Local geographic spillovers between university research and high technology innovations. *Journal of Urban Economics, 42,* 422–448. http://EconPapers.repec.org/RePEc:eee:juecon:v:42:y:1997:i:3:p:422-448
Baraldi, L. (2016). World production and consumption of ceramic tiles. *Tile International, 3,* 48–54.
Becattini, G. (1979). Dal Settore Industriale al Distretto Industriale. Alcune considerazioni sull'unitá di indagine in economia industriale. *Revista di Economia e Politica Industriale, 1,* 7–14.
Bellandi, M. (1996). Innovation and change in the Marshallian industrial district. *European Planning Studies, 4*(3), 357–368.
Bellandi, M. (2002). Italian industrial districts: An industrial economics interpretation. *European Planning Studies, 10*(4), 425–437. doi:10.1080/09654310220130158

Beugelsdijk, S. (2010). Entrepreneurial culture, regional innovativeness and economic growth. In *Entrepreneurship and culture* (pp. 129–154). Berlin: Springer.

Boix, R., Sforzi, F., Galletto, V., & Llobet, J. (2015). Sistemas locales de trabajo y distritos industriales en España 2011–2011. Paper presented at the meeting of Reunión Annual de Clusters y Distritos Industriales, 28–29.

Breschi, S., & Malerba, F. (1997). Sectoral systems of innovation: Technological regimes, Schumpeterian dynamics and spatial boundaries. In C. Edquist (Ed.), *Systems of innovation* (pp. 130–156). London: Frances Pinter.

Brown, T. E., & Ulijn, J. M. (Eds.). (2004). *Innovation, entrepreneurship and culture: The interaction between technology, progress and economic growth*. Cheltenham: Edward Elgar.

Callon, M. (1992). The dynamics of techno-economic networks. In R. Coombs & V. Walsh (Eds.), *Technical change and company strategies: Economic and sociological perspectives* (pp. 72–102). San Diego, CA: Harcourt Brace Jovanovich.

Camagni, R. (1991). 'Local Milieu', uncertainty and innovation networks: Towards a new dynamic theory of economic space. In R. Camagni (Ed.), *Innovation networks: Spacial perspectives* (pp. 121–143). London: Belhaven Press.

Carlsson, B., & Stankiewicz, R. (1991). On the nature, function and composition of technological systems. *Journal of Evolutionary Economics, 1*(2), 93–118.

Casson, M. (2003). Entrepreneurship, business culture and the theory of the firm. In *Handbook of entrepreneurship research* (pp. 223–246). Berlin: Springer.

Chesbrough, H. W. (2006). *Open innovation: The new imperative for creating and profiting from technology*. Boston, MA: Harvard Business Press.

Cooke, P. (2001). Sistemas de innovación regional: conceptos, análisis & tipología. At M. Olazaran and M. Gómez (coords.) *Sistemas regionales de innovación* (pp. 73–91). Bilbao: Universidad del País Vasco.

Cooke, P., & Morgan, K. (1993). The network paradigm: New departures in corporate and regional development. *Environment and Planning D: Society and Space, 11*, 543–564.

Cooke, P., Uranga, M. G., & Etxebarria, G. (1997). Regional innovation systems: Institutional and organisational dimensions. *Research Policy, 26*(4), 475–491.

Day, R. H. (2009). The technology evolving culture: Character and consequence. In *Schumpeterian perspectives on innovation, competition and growth* (pp. 25–34). Berlin: Springer.

Dei Ottati, G. (1994). Cooperation and competition in the industrial district as an organization model. *European Planning Studies, 2*(4), 463–483.

Dei Ottati, G. (2006). El "efecto distrito": algunos aspectos conceptuales de sus ventajas competitivas. *Economía Industrial, 1*(359), 73–79.

Demaria, F., Schneider, F., Sekulova, F., & Martinez-Alier, J. (2013). What is degrowth? From an activist slogan to a social movement. *Environmental Values, 22*(2), 191–215. doi:10.3197/096327113X13581561725194

Edquist, C. (2004). Systems of innovation: Perspectives and challenges. In J. Fagerberg, D. Mowery, & R. R. Nelson (Eds.), *Oxford handbook of innovation* (pp. 181–208). Oxford: Oxford University Press.

Fagerberg, J. (2003). Innovation: A guide to the literature. *Working Papers on Innovation Studies* 20031012, Oslo: Centre for Technology, Innovation and Culture, University of Oslo.

Fernández Esquinas, M. (2012). Hacia un programa de investigación en sociología de la innovación. *Arbor. Revista de Pensamiento, Ciencia y Cultura, 188*(753), 5–18. doi:10.3989/arbor.2012.753n1001

Freeman, C. (1982). *The economics of industrial innovation*. London: Pinter.

Freeman, C. (1987). *Technology and economic performance: Lessons from Japan*. London: Pinter.

Freeman, C. (1995). The 'national system of innovation' in historical perspective. *Cambridge Journal of Economics, 19*(1), 5–24.

Gabaldón-Estevan, D. (2016). Innovation diffusion in the European ceramic tile industry supply chain. In R. Addo-Tenkorang, J. Kantola, P. Helo, & A. Shamsuzzoha (Eds.), *Supply chain strategies and the engineer-to-order approach* (pp. 76–97). Hershey: IGI Global. doi:10.4018/978-1-5225-0021-6.ch005

Gabaldón-Estevan, D., Criado, E., & Monfort, E. (2014). The green factor in European manufacturing: A case study of the Spanish ceramic tile industry. *Journal of Cleaner Production, 70*, 242–250. doi:10.1016/j.jclepro.2014.02.018

Gabaldón-Estevan, D., Fernández-de-Lucio, I., & Molina-Morales, F. X. (2012). Sistemas distrituales de innovación. *Arbor, 188*(753), 63–73. doi:10.3989/arbor.2012.753n1005

Geels, F. W. (2002). Technological transitions as evolutionary reconfiguration processes: A multilevel perspective and a case-study. *Research Policy, 31*(8–9), 1257–1274. doi:10.1016/S0048-7333(02)00062-8

Geels, F. W., & Schot, J. (2010). The dynamics of transitions: A socio-technical perspective. In J. Grin, J. Rotmans, & J. Schot (Eds.), *Transitions to sustainable development. New directions in the study of long term transformative change* (pp. 11–104). New York, NY: Routledge.

Giacomini, P. (2007). World production and consumption of ceramic tiles. *Tile International, 4*, 40–54.

Granovetter, M. (1985). Economic action and social structure: The problem of embeddedness. *American Journal of Sociology, 91*(3), 481–510.

Hobday, M. (1991). Dynamic networks, technology diffusion and complementary assets: Explaining U.S. decline in semiconductors. *DRC Discussion Papers, 78*. Falmer (UK): Science Policy Research Unit, University of Sussex.

Hughes, T. (1984). The evolution of large technological systems. In W. Bijker, T. Hughes, & T. Pinch (Eds.), *The social construction of technological systems: New directions in the sociology and history of technology* (pp. 51–82). Cambridge: MIT Press.

Jensen, M. B., Johnson, B., Lorenz, E., & Lundvall, BÅ. (2007). Forms of knowledge and modes of innovation. *Research Policy, 36*(5), 680–693. doi:10.1016/j.respol.2007.0

Kline, S. J., & Rosenberg, N. (1986). *An overview of innovation*. Washington, DC: National Academy Press.

Lundvall, B. A. (1992). *National systems of innovation: Towards a theory of innovation and interactive learning*. London: Pinter.

Lundvall, B. A., & Borrás, S. (2005). Science, technology, and innovation policy. In J. Fagerberg, D. C. Mowery, & R. R. Nelson (Eds.), *The Oxford handbook of innovation* (pp. 599–631). New York: Oxford University Press.

Malerba, F. (1999). Sectoral systems of innovation and production. *DRUID Conference on: National Innovation Systems, Industrial Dynamics and Innovation Policy, Rebuild*. Retrieved from http://www.druid.dk/uploads/tx_ picturedb/ds1999-69.pdf

Manzo, C., & Ramella, F. (2015). Fab labs in Italy: Collective goods in the sharing economy. *Stato e mercato, 35*(3), 379–418. doi:10.1425/81605:y:2015:i:3:p:379-418

Marshall, A. (1997). *Principles of economics*. New York: Prometheus Books.

Meyer-Stamer, J., Maggi, C., & Seibel, S. (2001). *Improving upon nature. Creating competitive advantage in ceramic tile clusters in Italy, Spain, and Brazil*. Duisburg: Institute for Development and Peace Gerhard-Mercator University of Duisburg.

Molina-Morales, F. X. (2008). Los distritos industriales en la Europa mediterránea: las diferencias entre Italia & España. In V. Soler (coor.), *Los distritos industriales* (pp. 183–201). El Ejido (Almería): Cajamar Caja Rural Intermediterránea.

Nelson, R. R. (Ed.). (1993). *National innovation systems*. New York: Oxford University Press.

Nelson, R. R., & Rosenberg, N. (1993). Technical innovation and national systems. In R. Nelson (Ed.), *National innovation systems* (pp. 3–21). New York: Oxford University Press.

Nelson, R. R., & Winter, S. G. (1982). *An evolutionary theory of economic change*. Cambridge, MA: Belknap Press.

Pavitt, K. (1984). Sectoral patterns of technical change: Towards a taxonomy and a theory. *Research Policy, 13*(6), 343–373.

Portes, A. (2001). The resilient significance of class: A nominalist interpretation. In D. E. Davis (Ed.), *Political power and social theory* (pp. 249–284). Bingley: Emerald Group Publishing Limited.

Portes, A. (2007). Instituciones y desarrollo: una revisión conceptual. *Desarrollo Económico. Revista de Ciencias Sociales, 184*, 475–504.

Pyke, F., Becattini, G., & Sengerberger, W. (comps.) (1992). *Los distritos industriales & las pequeñas empresas. I. Distritos industriales & cooperación interempresarial en Italia*. Madrid: Ministerio de Trabajo & Seguridad Social.

Pyke, F., & Sengenberger, W. (Eds.). (1992). *Industrial districts and local economic regeneration* (13–23). Geneva: International Labour Organisation.

Ramella, F. (2015). *Sociology of economic innovation*. London: Routledge.

Rosenberg, N. (1982). *Inside the black box: Technology and economics*. Cambridge: Cambridge University Press.

Russo, M. (1985). Technical change and the industrial district: The role of interfirm relations in the growth and transformation of ceramic tile production in Italy. *Research Policy, 14*(6), 329–343.

Russo, M. (2004). *The ceramic industrial district facing the challenge from China*. Dipartimento di Scienze Sociali, Cognitive e Quantitative. Modena: Università degli Studi di Modena e Reggio Emilia.

Sforzi, F., & Boix, R. (2016). *I distretti industriali marshalliani tra continuità e cambiamento: un confronto Italia-Spagna*. Paper presented at the 37th AISRe Conference, Ancona (Italy), 20–22 September.

Vallejo, M. C. (2011). A model to study the organizational culture of the family firm. *Small Business Economics, 36*(1), 47–64. doi:10.1007/s11187-009-9175-9

Woolthuis, R. K., Lankhuizen, M., & Gilsing, V. (2005). A system failure framework for innovation policy design. *Technovation, 25*(6), 609–619. doi:10.1016/j.technovation.2003.11.002

Ybarra, J. A. (2006). La experiencia española en distritos industriales. Realidad de un concepto para la pyme & el territorio. *Economía Industrial, 359*, 89–94. http://hdl.handle.net/10045/13535

Ybarra, J. A. (2007). *La innovación en el sector del juguete de la Comunidad Valenciana*. Valencia: Fundación Premios Rey Jaime I. Presidencia de la Generalitat Valenciana.

Entrepreneurial process in peripheral regions: the role of motivation and culture

Francisco J. García-Rodríguez, Esperanza Gil-Soto, Inés Ruiz-Rosa and Desiderio Gutiérrez-Taño

ABSTRACT
The entrepreneurial potential of a region is a key factor in linking innovation to the market, thus leading to economic growth. This is especially important in peripheral regions that are characterized by low innovative dynamism. This paper analyses the entrepreneurial process in a European peripheral region, the Canary Islands, Spain. It attempts to determine possible cultural specificities and the role of motivation in the entrepreneurial process. To do this, an analysis of entrepreneurial intention (EI) is framed within the theory of planned behaviour and using motivation, opportunity and ability theory. An empirical study was carried out using a sample of 1457 university students participating in the Global University Entrepreneurial Spirit Students' Survey project. Results indicate that motivation influences EI directly and indirectly through an individual's attitude towards entrepreneurial behaviour. The perception of business opportunities is also a significant antecedent of entrepreneurial motivation. Consequently, entrepreneurial education and policies to foster entrepreneurship in peripheral regions should not attempt to transform individuals' attitudes towards entrepreneurship directly, but rather focus on improving motivation using intensive pedagogical strategies in creativity that go beyond mere informative content. Methodologies and content focused on recognizing opportunities and problem-solving would also be effective elements in educational programmes of entrepreneurship.

Introduction

The study of innovation's positive impact on the economic growth of regions and countries is a classic theme in academic literature (Damanpour, 1991; Damanpour & Scheneider, 2006; Drucker, 1986; Hult, Hurley, & Knight, 2004; Schmiedeberg, 2008). Much effort has been invested in trying to understand the dynamics of the innovation process and the policies and incentives that drive or hinder its development (Asheim, 2009; Piñero, Rodríguez-Monroy, & Arbola, 2012; Van Oostrom, 2015).

However, when regional development is analysed, at least at European level, it is clear that 'no one size fits all' (Asheim, Moodyson, & Tödtling, 2011; Tödtling & Trippl, 2005).

It is not possible; therefore, to perform homogeneous analyses, since each region has specific features in terms of its innovative capacity, and the impact investments in innovation would generate in terms of economic growth. From this point of view, Asheim et al. (2011) distinguish between metropolitan, industrial and peripheral regions. The latter are characterized by low-level innovative activity due to a lack of dynamic firms and knowledge-generating organizations, a 'thin' and less specialized structure of knowledge suppliers, educational institutions and poorly developed networks of these suppliers.

By contrast, metropolitan regions are innovation centres that benefit from economies of scale and agglomeration as well as a high density of knowledge centres, clusters and support institutions. Industrial regions also have a high level of expertise in certain key industries around which knowledge-generating organizations and educational institutions can focus.

Among the dynamics that determine regional character regarding its innovative potential, cultural specificities have been shown as some of the most important elements (Clifton, Gärtner, & Rehfeld, 2011). However, few studies have systematically analysed this connection, with the exception of the seminal analysis of Saxenian (1994), which compared the impact of sociocultural aspects in the success of Silicon Valley as an innovative region with the so-called Route 128 in Boston. The author concludes that the culture of interaction between the actors in the Californian region was the decisive factor for its great innovative dynamism. In this sense, Keeble and Wilkinson (2000) also highlight the impact of cultural influences on learning processes and innovation in European high-tech regions.

Therefore, in explaining the dynamics of innovation, the institutional and organizational contexts in different regions must be considered, as well as the processes of generation and exploitation of knowledge and interactions between different actors (Autio, 1998; Cooke, Heidenreich, & Braczyk, 2004; Doloreux, 2002; Tödtling & Trippl, 2005). The importance of these institutional and cultural specificities is reinforced by the need for modern innovation policies to be based not only on promoting investment in R&D (driven by supply), but also on promoting demand from users (Asheim, 2009).

Among the institutional and cultural aspects that can influence innovation and regional economic development, the degree of entrepreneurial potential in the territory should be highlighted as one that generates innovation and promotes economic growth. There need to be entrepreneurs with the ability to link innovation to the market, generating value, creating demand and the resulting economic growth (Audretsch & Keilbach, 2004; González, Peña, & Vendrell, 2012; Guerrero & Peña-Legazkue, 2013).

It can be argued that a country or region's competitiveness is based on its investment in research and technological development (R&D) and its ability to generate and attract skilled human capital. It is also essential to have 'the existence of a business network that is able to tap into the sources of knowledge and technology at its disposal to produce new products and services that have acceptance in the global marketplace' (COTEC Foundation, 2015, p. 21). For peripheral regions, this poses additional difficulties, in that most studies agree that individuals' motivation for entrepreneurial activities in non-core regions is mainly need-driven (Baumgartner, Pütz, & Seidl, 2013; Kalantaridis, 2004). Thus, following the terminology of Liñán, Fernández-Serrano, and Romero (2013), it is mainly necessity entrepreneurship rather than opportunity entrepreneurship. There is also a tendency for the most talented entrepreneurs from the periphery to migrate to the core regions (Kaufmann & Malul, 2015).

It is therefore important to understand the cultural and institutional specificities of a country or region in which entrepreneurial activities are carried out, since these can be barriers and obstacles to transferring innovative efforts into economic development (Guerrero & Peña-Legazkue, 2013). Overcoming these limitations is essential to access the benefits of a virtuous circle that could increase regions' economic prosperity through investment in innovation, which in turn can improve potential innovative and entrepreneurial activity (Audretsch & Peña, 2012; González, Martiarena, Navarro, & Peña, 2009).

Empirical studies have demonstrated how the cultural aspects of a specific region can affect entrepreneurial intention (hereinafter EI) even more than economic variables (García-Cabrera & García-Soto, 2008; García-Rodríguez, Gil-Soto, Ruiz-Rosa, & Sene, 2015; Hofstede et al., 2004; Liñán, Urbano, & Guerrero, 2011; Wennekers, Thurik, Van Stel, & Noorderhaven, 2007), in that the former tend to present a more permanent character than the latter. For Mueller and Thomas (2001), the concept of 'culture' is associated with the system of fundamental values and principles specific to a particular group or society that, at the same time, give rise to certain personality traits and individual motivations that are not reproduced in other societies. Hofstede (1984) distinguishes four dimensions when analysing cultural differences among countries or regions: power distance, uncertainty avoidance, individualism–collectivism in a country, and masculinity–femininity. Later, Hofstede (1991) added a fifth dimension: individuals' orientation towards the short/long term.

For a given region, it is clear that having university education contributes to the innovative potential and impact of the region's economic development, not only through classic knowledge transfer, but also by providing leadership for the creation of entrepreneurial thinking, actions and institutions (Guerrero, Cunningham, & Urbano, 2015; Guerrero, Urbano, & Fayolle, 2016). Therefore, it is particularly interesting to analyse the dynamics of the entrepreneurial process and the possible existence of institutional obstacles or cultural barriers among university students (Guerrero & Peña-Legazkue, 2013).

Together with cultural aspects, individual motivation is an important explanatory factor in the entrepreneurial process. It is related to the so-called theories of needs, which identify individuals' internal stimuli (hunger, fear, etc.) that guide their behaviour, and 'incentive theories', which suggest that individuals develop one behaviour or another in search of external objectives or prizes (Carsrud & Brännback, 2011; Fayolle, Liñán, & Moriano, 2014).

Taking into account the above aspects, this paper analyses the entrepreneurial process in a European peripheral region, the Canary Islands, Spain. It attempts to determine possible cultural specificities and provides an integrated view of motivation's role in EI and its antecedents. It adopts the perspective based on the approach of Shapero and Sokol (1982) and the theory of planned behaviour by Ajzen (1991). Attitude towards entrepreneurial behaviour, subjective norms and perceived behavioural control are assumed to be antecedents of EI. This view is complemented by the so-called motivation, opportunity and ability (MOA) theory, originally adopted by MacInnis and Jaworski (1989), which determines the impact of motivation on EI either directly or indirectly through its antecedents.

The model is tested on a sample of undergraduates, who participated in the Global University Entrepreneurial Spirit Students' Survey (GUESSS) project.

After having contextualized the importance of potential entrepreneurs to regions, especially peripheral ones and highlighting specific cultural features, the second section of the paper explains entrepreneurial process and motivation from a theoretical perspective and puts forward the working hypotheses. Subsequently, an empirical analysis is carried out among university students in the Canary Islands, Spain, a European peripheral region. Results show the main relational links between motivation and EI. Finally, the most relevant conclusions are drawn, from both academic and applied perspectives.

The role of motivation and cultural aspects in the entrepreneurial process

The entrepreneurial process

The phenomenon of entrepreneurship, as a process that occurs over time (Gartner, Shaver, Gatewood, & Katz, 1994), begins long before the moment when an individual sets up a business. Thus, as with all behaviours, it requires a planning process even to reach the stage of EI. This intention, therefore, is prior to the creation of a business and can be considered one of the best predictors of entrepreneurship (Ajzen, 1987, 1991, 2001, 2002; Krueger & Brazeal, 1994).

This perspective runs parallel to the conviction predominantly supported by the literature since the 1980s, stating that it is not nature but nurture that makes an entrepreneur. Therefore, entrepreneurship is associated with learning processes, maturing and possible changes in individuals' abilities and personal capacities (Minniti & Bygrave, 2001).

In this sense, entrepreneurs' abilities are not fixed personality traits or characteristics; instead, their abilities can change over time, develop and be learnt through experience (Gibb, 1993, 2000). This is the context in which entrepreneurship can be explained based on the theory of attitudes (Robinson, Stimpson, Huefner, & Hunt, 1991) and studies such as the one by McCline, Bhat, and Baj (2000). The basic idea is that the concept or the attitude of an individual is dynamic and changing. Individuals respond to external incentives, and therefore it is more appropriate to explain entrepreneurship this way rather than in a more static way associated with personality traits.

Among the various theoretical models proposed to describe and explain the entrepreneurial process, it is worth mentioning Shapero and Sokol's work (1982) and Ajzen's (1991) theory of planned behaviour. Both models have been widely tested and validated in numerous scientific studies, particularly noteworthy are the ones by Krueger and Brazeal (1994), Peterman and Kennedy (2003) and Souitaris, Zerbinati, and Al-Laham (2007).

According to this perspective, the decision to initiate a new entrepreneurial activity depends on three elements: the perception of desirability, feasibility and the individual's willingness to act. Krueger and Brazeal (1994) differentiate between an individual's entrepreneurial potential, which can remain in a 'latent' state and his/her EI, which is a reaction to a relevant event that can cause a change in behaviour. Thus, the perceived desire, perceived feasibility and propensity to act are antecedents of EI (Shapero & Sokol, 1982). To these three elements, Azjen's 'subjective norms' can be added, which support the entrepreneur's behavioural setting.

To the degree personal and social factors influence entrepreneurial conduct, in contrast to the approach of Shapero and Sokol (1982), the theory of planned behaviour (Ajzen, 1991, 2001) has become consolidated as the most commonly used approach in recent research into EI (Liñán & Fayolle, 2015; Moriano, Gómez, Laguna, & Roznowski, 2008).

To sum up, the theory of planned behaviour holds that EI depends on the influence of three variables: attitude towards entrepreneurship, subjective norms and perceived behavioural control (Ajzen, 1991, 2001). In the latter variable, Ajzen (2001) incorporates two dimensions: self-efficacy (belief in one's own capacity to organize and perform behaviour) and controllability (belief in one's control of his/her conduct).

This theoretical model has had wide empirical testing with the works of Liñán and Chen (2009), Souitaris et al. (2007), Peterman and Kennedy (2003), Audet (2002, 2004), Krueger, Reilly, and Carsrud (2000), Kolvereid (1996) and Tkachev and Kolvereid (1999) being worthy of particular mention.

Motivation in the entrepreneurial process

However, the research focus on EI within the field of entrepreneurship as the best predictor of behaviour has meant that another key element in the entrepreneurial process has been left aside: motivation (Carsrud & Brännback, 2011). The entrepreneurial process may not be linear, but instead could be better understood as behaviour directed towards the search for objectives at distinct levels of deliberation. These objectives serve as sources of external motivation (Lawson, 1997).

There are essentially two perspectives in motivational theories: one based on economics and the other on psychology (Fisher, 1930), which attempt to answer three questions: What activates a person? What makes the individual choose one behaviour over another? Why do different people respond differently to the same motivational stimuli? (Carsrud & Brännback, 2011).

Among the main theories that support the study of motivation in entrepreneurship, there are 'incentive theories' based on the idea that individuals develop one kind of behaviour or another in search of objectives and external prizes created to incentivize. There are also the 'theories of needs' that rely on the existence of internal stimuli in individuals that guide their behaviour (Carsrud & Brännback, 2011; Fayolle et al., 2014). Theories of needs applied to the entrepreneurial process hold that individuals have intrinsic needs that generate internal tensions, which motivate them to act. In this way, motivation will influence the antecedents of EI and finally EI itself (Fayolle et al., 2014; Solesvik, 2013).

Motivation can be an important explanatory element both of EI's antecedents (Solesvik, 2013), as well as influencing the relationship between EI and the decision to be an entrepreneur (Carsrud & Brännback, 2011; Fayolle et al., 2014). Various studies have demonstrated the existence of relationships between several motivational variables and EI (Chen, Greene, & Crick, 1998; Souitaris et al., 2007). More recently, Hui-Chen, Kuen-Hung, and Chen-Yi (2014) have proposed an integrated model of the entrepreneurial process, finding that motivation affects EI through attitudes and perceived behavioural control. From the perspective of 'incentive theories', motivation could play a key role in transforming EI into the actual setting up of a business activity by being the missing link between intention and behaviour (Carsrud & Brännback, 2011; Edelman, Brush, Manolova, & Greene, 2010).

On the other hand, another important concept that has emerged recently in the field of entrepreneurship, related to but different from motivation, is individual values (Fayolle et al., 2014). These can be considered as general principles that show certain stability over a long period and guide the conduct of the individual (Schwartz, 2011).

Formulating hypotheses

Based on the above, and, in particular, on the recent works of Solesvik (2013) and Hui-Chen et al. (2014), motivation would be expected to influence EI positively. This could occur both directly and indirectly through its antecedents and to the extent that the entrepreneurial process is not linear but rather a search for objectives (Carsrud & Brännback, 2011; Lawson, 1997). In this sense, a significant number of studies have demonstrated that motivation is directly linked to entrepreneurs (Caird, 1991; Durand & Shea, 1974; Morris & Fargher, 1974; Robinson et al., 1991). In accordance with Fayolle et al. (2014), it would be possible to relate the theory of motivation based on need with greater EI owing to the internal tension generated, which is then channelled through the antecedents of the intention, making it possible to propose the following hypothesis:

> H1. Motivation has a positive impact on (a) EI, (b) personal attitude, (c) perceived behavioural control and (d) subjective norms.

MacInnis and Jaworski (1989) were the authors who originally proposed the MOA theory. This theory has had a varied academic path. It has been applied to diverse areas to try to explain behaviours of choice among companies and individuals (Binney, Hall, & Shaw, 2003; Gruen, Osmonbekov, & Czaplewski, 2005, 2006, 2007; Rothschild, 1999; Siemsen, Roth, & Balasubramanian, 2008). Therefore, in this case, as well as in motivation, it will be necessary to consider it as an explanatory element of EI and EI's antecedents: opportunity and individuals' ability.

Opportunities will be external factors that favour or hamper the achievement of individuals' desires (Binney et al., 2003). Therefore, from the perspective of becoming an entrepreneur, if opportunities do not exist, it is unlikely that the desired behaviour will be achieved despite great motivation on the part of an individual. It is also necessary to consider individuals' abilities, that is, their competencies that would favour the setting up of a business activity, since these will help individuals feel ready to achieve their goals (Binney et al., 2003; Rothschild, 1999).

Thus, it is possible to put forward the following hypotheses:

> H2. Opportunity has a positive impact on (a) EI, (b) motivation, (e) personal attitudes, (f) perceived control of behaviour and (g) subjective norms.

> H3. Abilities have a positive impact on (a) EI, (b) motivation, (c) opportunity, (e) personal attitudes, (f) perceived behavioural control and (g) subjective norms.

In addition, various studies based on Ajzen's (1991) theory of planned behaviour have shown a positive relationship between EI and personal attitudes and perceived control (Audet, 2002, 2004; Finisterra Do Paço et al., 2011; Kolvereid, 1996; Krueger et al., 2000; Liñán & Chen, 2009; Souitaris et al., 2007; Tkachev & Kolvereid, 1999), thus, making it logical to propose that:

H4. Personal attitudes have a positive impact on (a) EI.

H5. Perceived control of behaviour has a positive impact on (a) EI.

Finally, Liñán and Chen (2009) show that many previous works on the theory of planned behaviour did not include the subjective norms variable in the analysis, so bearing in mind studies that did (Kolvereid, 1996; Tkachev & Kolvereid, 1999), it is reasonable to expect that:

H6. Subjective norms have a positive impact on (a) EI, (e) personal attitudes and (f) perceived control of behaviour.

Empirical work

Regional context, data gathering and sample description

Canary Island is a Spanish fragmented island territory with a surface area of 7447 km^2. It is considered a peripheral region by the European Union, geographically located in the African continent, on the eastern edge of the mid-Atlantic, at the southern limit of the temperate zone, with the Sahara Desert to the east. Its mild, warm climate combined with the political and socio-economic stability of the region has meant that its tourism sector has developed to become the leading international tourist destination during the winter season receiving almost 12 million visitors in 2014. However, this polarized economic activity is not enough to create sufficient employment, as current unemployment in the Canary Islands stands at over 30%.

According to the COTEC Foundation (2015), the Canary Islands ranks as the second region with least resources devoted to R&D in Spain in 2013 (0.52% of GDP). Moreover, it should be noted that Spain's R&D expenditure represented 1.24% of GDP, which remains well below the average for OECD (2005) countries (2.4%) and the EU-28 (1.92%). This is why the Canary Islands constitutes a representative example of a European peripheral region.

The data to carry out this study come from answers to a questionnaire as part of the GUESSS project with students from the University of La Laguna in Canary Islands. GUESSS is an international research project that attempts to analyse EI and its antecedents for students at a global level. In its sixth edition, data were gathered from over 700 universities in 34 different countries, between October 2013 and March 2014, with Spain participating for the first time in the analysis.

The GUESSS project aims to carry out a comprehensive analysis not only of the psychological characteristics of future entrepreneurs but also specific attitudes, personal antecedents and situational variables. The main contribution of the project has been to homogenize methodology, so that comparisons can be made between different countries, significantly enhancing the study of EI among students. The sixth edition, corresponding to 2013, contained 12 blocks that have been translated and validated by experts in entrepreneurship, from both academic and applied areas.

At the University La Laguna, the questionnaire was sent to all the students (20,729) by email in November 2013 and 1457 responses were obtained over the two months in which the fieldwork took place. The questionnaire was in electronic format and was self-administered with assistance using the Qualtrics programme. The sample consisted of 37.5%

men and 64.3% women; regarding age, 81.5% were between 18 and 24 years, 12.5% between 25 and 30 years and 5.9% over 30 years. There were 80.6% studying undergraduate degrees, 18.4% were doing postgraduate studies and 0.8% doctorate students. Out of the total sample, 25.7% were studying business, economics and law, 42.5% science and medicine, and 31.8% social sciences.

Differences in variables such as age, gender and educational level could influence the predictive ability of the model for the sample. In order to assess their impact and determine whether these control variables influence indicators of the MOA model constructs, an analysis of variance was carried out for each of the three classification variables. The ANOVA results for the three age groups (18–24, 25–30 and >30) and educational level (degree, master and doctorate) and the analysis of mean difference in gender (men and women) led to the conclusion that there is no association between independent variables or any of the three control variables since no significant statistical F values ($p > .05$) were obtained.

In addition, the majority of the students in the sample (91.7%) were not working regularly and in 30.2% of the cases, one or both of their parents were self-employed. In addition, 6% of the sample intended to become entrepreneurs on finishing their studies and 36.3% indicated EI in the future (five years).

The measurement scales used in this research were not prepared ad hoc but used those proposed in the GUESSS model project, whose theoretical foundations are based on the theory of planned behaviour by Ajzen (1991). All scales have been widely validated in previous studies, for example, Liñán and Chen (2009) for Personal Attitude and Entrepreneurial Intention scales. This confirms the validity of the content used to fulfil the objectives and the hypotheses of the analysis model (Figure 1). In addition, for the

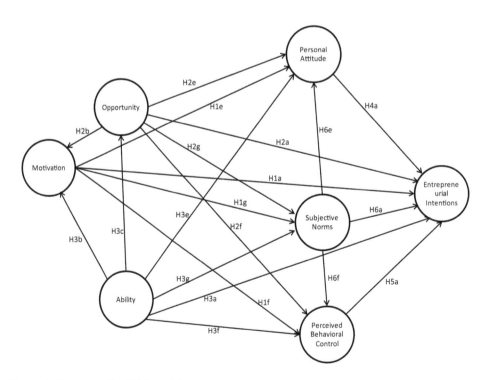

Figure 1. Constructs for MOA model.

opportunity variable, the questionnaire items refer to the opportunity to initiate an activity after finishing studying and within five years of finishing.

Data analysis

Structural equations were chosen to analyse the data, using the technique of partial least-squares (PLS) (Fornell & Cha, 1994). This technique is designed to reflect the theoretical and empirical characteristics of social sciences and behaviour, in which theories frequently lack sufficient support and there is little information available (Wold, 1979). Specifically, SmartPLS 2.0 was used (Ringle, Wende, & Will, 2005).

The general recommendations regarding the theoretical support for a model of PLS have been followed; the sifting of data and the analysis of the psychometric properties of all the variables of the model before beginning the analysis; examining relationships and effects; standard errors and the predictive power of the model to guarantee its validity. The PLS method allows hypotheses to be tested at the same time as admitting measurements with single and multiple items and the use of formative and reflective indicators (Fornell & Bookstein, 1982).

Following the criteria of Chin (1998) regarding the items used for each of the constructs of the proposed model, we find that all the indicators of the latent variables are reflective, since an increase in one of the indicators in one direction means that the rest change in a similar way.

To assure the validity of the PLS technique, two steps are required (Barclay, Higgins, & Thompson, 1995). First, the measurement model is evaluated and then the structural one. The evaluation of the measurement model is performed by ensuring the reliability of each item, the reliability of constructs, the average variance extracted (AVE) and the discriminatory validity of the indicators that measure the latent variables. The structural model is validated by confirming up to what point the causal relations are consistent with the available data (Real, Leal, & Roldán, 2006).

In the model proposed in this study, there are seven first-order constructs, as observed in Figure 1.

The analysis begins by evaluating the individual reliability of the constructs examining the factor loading, composite reliability (CR) and AVE (Chin, 1998; Fornell & Larcker, 1981). Table 1 shows these measures as well as each of the items used. The factor loadings are all over .707, indicating that at least 50% of the variance of the construct is reflected in the indicator (Chin, 1998). CR is always greater than .7, which is required in the initial stages of research, and is also higher than the stricter value of .8 required for basic research (Nunnally, 1978).

As for AVE, for the indicators of each construct, these should be greater than .5, which explains 50% or more the indicator's variance (Fornell & Larcker, 1981). This condition was comfortably met in all cases.

To ensure discriminatory validity, the square roots of AVEs are compared (i.e. the diagonal values in Table 2) with the correlations between constructs (i.e. the elements that are outside the diagonal in the table).

All the constructs are reflective and mainly relate to their own measures rather than to other constructs (Table 3). Additionally, crossed factor loadings have been analysed and it has been confirmed that they are not significant regarding their relation with factor loadings (Chin, 1998).

Table 1. Construct properties of model.

Constructs and items		Mean	STD	λ	AVE	CR	α
Ability							
Please indicate your level of competence in performing the following tasks (1 = very low competence, 7 = very high competence)							
Q6.3_1	Identifying new business opportunities	4.49	1.43	.975	.952	.994	.993
Q6.3_2	Creating new products and services	4.34	1.49	.976			
Q6.3_3	Applying my personal creativity	5.01	1.49	.969			
Q6.3_4	Managing innovation within a firm	4.68	1.50	.983			
Q6.3_5	Being a leader and communicator	5.02	1.53	.976			
Q6.3_6	Building up a professional network	4.62	1.54	.975			
Q6.3_7	Commercializing a new idea or development	4.64	1.55	.977			
Q6.3_8	Successfully managing a business	4.84	1.55	.974			
Els							
Please indicate your level of agreement with the following statements (1 = strongly disagree, 7 = strongly agree)							
Q6.1a_1	I am ready to do anything to be an entrepreneur	3.77	1.73	.936	.930	.988	.985
Q6.1a_2	My professional goal is to become an entrepreneur	3.99	1.86	.968			
Q6.1a_3	I will make every effort to start and run my own firm	3.99	1.89	.979			
Q6.1a_4	I am determined to create a firm in the future	4.00	1.93	.980			
Q6.1a_5	I have very seriously thought of starting a firm	3.91	2.01	.952			
Q6.1a_6	I have the strong intention to start a firm someday	3.97	2.04	.972			
Motivation							
How important are the following factors when you decide on your future career path? (1 = not important at all, 7 = very important)							
Q4_1	To have a challenging job	5.28	1.40	.892	.759	.969	.963
Q4_10	To take advantage of your creative needs	5.67	1.40	.921			
Q4_2	To have an exciting job	5.75	1.25	.928			
Q4_3	Freedom	5.77	1.16	.936			
Q4_4	Independence	5.68	1.24	.924			
Q4_5	To be your own boss	4.43	1.68	.610			
Q4_6	To have power to make decisions	5.51	1.27	.684			
Q4_7	To have authority	5.02	1.47	.887			
Q4_8	To realize your dream	6.34	1.11	.944			
Q4_9	To create something	5.47	1.54	.917			
Opportunity							
Which career path do you intend to pursue right after completion of your studies, and which career path five years after completion of studies? I want to be an entrepreneur working in my own firm							
OP1	Opportunity on finishing studies	1.71	1.37	.970	.918	.957	.912
OP2	Opportunity five years after	3.11	2.74	.946			
Personal attitude							
Please indicate your level of agreement with the following statements (1 = strongly disagree, 7 = strongly agree)							
Q6.1b_1	Being an entrepreneur implies more advantages than disadvantages to me	4.11	1.65	.955	.948	.989	.986
Q6.1b_2	A career as entrepreneur is attractive for me	4.28	1.79	.977			
Q6.1b_3	If I had the opportunity and resources, I would become an entrepreneur	5.07	1.79	.979			
Q6.1b_4	Being an entrepreneur would entail great satisfaction for me	4.76	1.83	.982			
Q6.1b_5	Among various options, I would rather become an entrepreneur	4.26	1.87	.976			
Perceived behavioural control							
Please indicate your level of agreement with the following statements (1 = strongly disagree, 7 = strongly agree)							
Q6.1c_1	I am usually able to protect my personal interests	5.36	1.22	.968	.916	.987	.985
Q6.1c_2	When I make plans, I am almost certain to make them work	5.38	1.21	.971			
Q6.1c_3	I can pretty much determine what will happen in my life	3.91	1.56	.945			
Q6.1c_4	For me, being an entrepreneur would be very easy	3.60	1.61	.951			
Q6.1c_5	If I wanted to, I could easily pursue a career as entrepreneur	3.33	1.59	.939			
Q6.1c_6	As entrepreneur, I would have complete control over the situation	5.04	1.59	.957			
Q6.1c_7	If I become an entrepreneur, the chances of success would be very high	4.34	1.43	.967			
Subjective norms							
If you would pursue a career as an entrepreneur, how would people in your environment react? (1 = very negatively, 7 = very positively)							
Q6.2_1	Your close family	5.54	1.51	.982	.969	.990	.984
Q6.2_2	Your friends	5.67	1.31	.992			
Q6.2_3	Your fellow students	5.40	1.41	.980			

Note: CR = composite reliability; AVE = average variance extracted; α = Cronbach's alpha.

Table 2. AVE and correlations between model constructs.

	Ability	Els	Motivation	Opportunity	Personal attitude	Perceived behavioural control	Subjective norms
Ability	*.976*						
Els	.708	*.965*					
Motivation	.389	.499	*.871*				
Opportunity	.790	.712	.660	*.958*			
Personal attitude	.768	.903	.480	.737	*.974*		
Perceived behavioural control	.855	.750	.435	.758	.828	*.957*	
Subjective norms	.858	.720	.416	.751	.808	.919	*.985*

Notes: All correlations are significant to the level of $p < .01$.
The diagonal shows the square root of AVE.

Table 3. Table of crossed correlations.

	Ability	Els	Motivation	Opportunity	Personal attitude	Perceived behavioural control	Subjective norms
OP1	.269	.336	.680	**.970**	.334	.324	.318
OP2	.187	.180	.565	**.946**	.208	.241	.243
Q4_1	.354	.431	**.892**	.594	.420	.390	.361
Q4_10	.377	.472	**.921**	.610	.450	.404	.387
Q4_2	.352	.449	**.928**	.630	.436	.403	.387
Q4_3	.345	.446	**.936**	.638	.434	.404	.393
Q4_4	.331	.446	**.924**	.613	.428	.388	.380
Q4_5	.261	.351	.610	.328	.330	.279	.266
Q4_6	.255	.324	.684	.407	.312	.273	.250
Q4_7	.346	.457	.887	.564	.440	.388	.371
Q4_8	.366	.460	.944	.661	.446	.418	.404
Q4_9	.377	.481	.917	.597	.461	.406	.388
Q6.1a_1	.679	**.936**	.491	.305	.858	.738	.705
Q6.1a_2	.683	**.968**	.490	.283	.887	.726	.701
Q6.1a_3	.692	**.979**	.487	.272	.882	.728	.698
Q6.1a_4	.693	**.980**	.480	.262	.879	.728	.697
Q6.1a_5	.679	**.952**	.467	.252	.851	.709	.676
Q6.1a_6	.682	**.972**	.469	.250	.866	.713	.689
Q6.1b_1	.725	.857	.465	.292	**.955**	.788	.774
Q6.1b_2	.753	.891	.466	.278	**.977**	.809	.784
Q6.1b_3	.762	.873	.477	.301	**.979**	.820	.801
Q6.1b_4	.750	.888	.472	.286	**.982**	.812	.789
Q6.1b_5	.756	.887	.458	.264	**.976**	.803	.785
Q6.1c_1	.831	.719	.432	.309	.798	**.968**	.913
Q6.1c_2	.835	.717	.432	.310	.800	**.971**	.914
Q6.1c_3	.791	.690	.404	.287	.762	**.945**	.854
Q6.1c_4	.810	.716	.403	.269	.785	**.951**	.852
Q6.1c_5	.794	.707	.390	.265	.770	**.939**	.833
Q6.1c_6	.824	.729	.423	.287	.808	**.957**	.892
Q6.1c_7	.843	.746	.426	.282	.822	**.967**	.896
Q6.2_1	.848	.718	.406	.289	.799	.905	**.982**
Q6.2_2	.855	.715	.417	.297	.806	.914	**.992**
Q6.2_3	.834	.694	.406	.294	.781	.895	**.980**
Q6.3_1	**.975**	.704	.377	.236	.760	.834	.841
Q6.3_2	**.976**	.698	.379	.237	.755	.830	.837
Q6.3_3	**.969**	.682	.386	.245	.744	.838	.841
Q6.3_4	**.983**	.701	.382	.234	.759	.839	.839
Q6.3_5	**.976**	.686	.382	.242	.748	.840	.841
Q6.3_6	**.975**	.684	.379	.237	.743	.832	.832
Q6.3_7	**.977**	.693	.376	.235	.746	.828	.837
Q6.3_8	**.974**	.691	.373	.238	.751	.836	.837

Results

Figure 2 shows the results of the analysis of the structural model, including the explained variance of the constructs (R^2) and standardized coefficients (β). The PLS method makes no distribution assumptions about parameters' estimation, which is why it is more appropriate than traditional parameter techniques to ensure significance and evaluate the model (Chin, 1998). Another difference between analytical approaches using covariance structure or PLS is that in the latter, there is no single measure to guarantee the goodness of fit (GoF) of the model (Hulland, 1999). Thus, in PLS, the structural model is examined using the values for R^2, the Q^2 test for predictive relevance and the size of the path coefficients. Finally, the stability of estimations is examined using t-statistics that are obtained by bootstrapping with 500 samples.

Table 4 shows the hypotheses that were proposed, coefficient paths and observed t values with their significance from the bootstrap test. Additionally, the direct effects and the proportion of explained variance are shown, as well as Q^2 constructs.

Regarding the explained variance (R^2) of the EI latent variable (Table 4), the structural model shows an adequate predictive power, since 82% of the variance is explained. As well as examining R^2, the model is evaluated by observing the predictive relevance Q^2 of the models' constructs (Geisser, 1974). This test measures to what degree observed values are reproduced by the model and their estimated parameters (Chin, 1998). A Q^2 greater than 0 implies that the model has predictive relevance, whereas if the value is below 0, it indicates that the model lacks predictive relevance. The results shown in

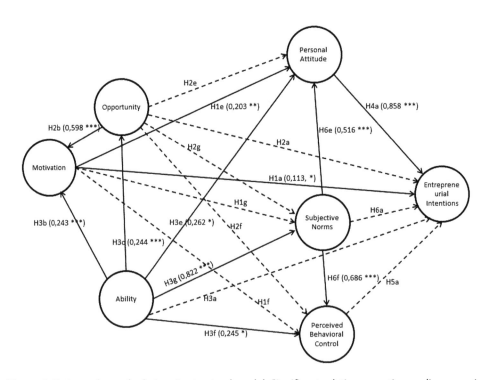

Figure 2. Estimated causal relations in structural model. Significant relation = continuous line; non-significant relation = dashed line.

Table 4. Direct, indirect and total effects, variance explained and test Q^2.

Hypothesis	Relacion	Direct effect	Sig.	T statistic	Correlation coefficients	Variance explained	Total effect	Q^2
Els						.823		.751
H3a	AB → EI	.077	ns	0.903	.710	.055	.714	
H1a	MO → EI	.113	*	1.726	.498	.056	.314	
H2a	OP → EI	−.042	ns	1.112	.281	−.012	.115	
H4a	PA → EI	.858	***	11.222	.903	.775	.858	
H5a	PBC → EI	.031	ns	0.261	.750	.023	.041	
H6a	SN → EI	−.102	ns	0.888	.720	−.074	.347	
Motivation						.488		.365
H3b	AB → MO	.243	***	3.443	.389	.094	.391	
H2b	OP → MO	.598	***	5.814	.657	.393	.594	
Opportunity						.060		.052
H3c	AB → OP	.244	***	3.700	.244	.060	.246	
Personal attitude						.282		.653
H3e	AB → PA	.262	*	2.011	.769	.202	.859	
H1e	MO → PA	.203	**	2.666	.480	.097	.236	
H2e	OP → PA	−.059	ns	1.219	.292	−.017	.112	
H6e	SN → PA	.516	***	3.903	.808	.417	.503	
Perceived behavioural control						.864		.770
H3f	AB → PBC	.245	*	1.993	.855	.210	.859	
H1f	MO → PBC	.053	ns	1.217	.435	.023	.090	
H2f	OP → PBC	.001	ns	0.030	.300	.000	.097	
H6f	SN → PBC	.686	***	5.677	.919	.631	.670	
Subjective norms						.748		.721
H3g	AB → SN	.822	***	14.441	.859	.707	.860	
H1g	MO → SN	.057	ns	0.891	.416	.024	.056	
H2g	OP → SN	.060	ns	1.343	.298	.018	.094	

Note: Level of significance: ***$p < .001$; **$p < .01$; *$p < .05$; ns, non-significant.

Table 4 confirm that the measurement model is appropriate, and that the structural model has predictive relevance.

Finally, to guarantee the quality of the model, the PLS approach has recently developed the GoF test. This is defined as the 'geometric mean' of the average communality and the average R^2 for endogenous constructs (Tenenhaus, Vinzi, Chatelin, & Lauro, 2005; Wetzels, Odekerken-Schröder, & Van Oppen, 2009), with average communality being measured using the AVE in PLS. In our case, for the complete model (Table 5), we obtained a GoF value of .746. This comfortably exceeds the value of .36 proposed by Wetzels et al. (2009) that considers the most unfavourable situation for this test: a sample with large effects.

Therefore, in relation to the proposed hypotheses in the model, the following conclusions can be drawn:

- H1a and H1e are confirmed. These establish, respectively, that motivation has a positive impact on EI ($\beta = .113$, $p < .05$) and personal attitude ($\beta = .203$, $p < .01$).
- By contrast, H1f and H1g are not confirmed, so the existence of relations between motivation and perceived behavioural control cannot be claimed ($\beta = .053$, n.s.) and neither between motivation and subjective norms ($\beta = .057$, n.s.).
- H2b is confirmed. This establishes that opportunity has a positive impact on motivation ($\beta = .598$, $p < .001$).

Table 5. GoF test.

	AVE	R^2	GoF
EIs	.930	.823	
Motivation	.759	.488	
Opportunity	.918	.060	
Personal attitude	.948	.698	
Perceived behavioural control	.916	.864	
Subjective norms	.969	.748	
	.907	.613	.746

- However, H2a, H2e, H2f and H2g are not confirmed. Therefore, there are no relations between opportunity and EI ($\beta = -.042$, n.s.), personal attitude ($\beta = -.059$, n.s.), perceived control ($\beta = .001$, ns) and subjective norms ($\beta = .060$, n.s.).
- H3b, H3c, H3e–H3g are confirmed. They establish, respectively, that ability has a positive impact on motivation ($\beta = .243$, $p < .001$), opportunity ($\beta = .244$, $p < .001$), personal attitude ($\beta = .262$, $p < .05$), perceived behavioural control ($\beta = .245$, $p < .05$) and subjective norms ($\beta = .822$, $p < .001$).
- By contrast, H3a is not confirmed. Therefore, no relation can be claimed between ability and EI ($\beta = .077$, ns).
- H4a is confirmed. This hypothesis states that personal attitude has a positive impact on EI ($\beta = .858$, $p < .001$).
- However, H5a cannot be confirmed. So, no relation between perceived behavioural control and EI can be claimed ($\beta = .031$, n.s.).
- H6e and H6f, respectively, establish that subjective norms have a positive impact on personal attitudes ($\beta = .516$, $p < .001$) and on perceived behavioural control ($\beta = .686$, $p < .001$).
- To the contrary, H6a was not confirmed and, therefore, no relationship can be claimed to exist between subjective norms and EI ($\beta = -.102$, n.s.).

Discussion of results

This paper has analysed, from an integrated perspective, the entrepreneurial process in undergraduates in the Canary Islands, Spain, a European peripheral region, and the role of motivation and cultural specificities in forming EI. The results partially confirm those from previous studies, demonstrating the existence of relations between diverse motivational variables and EI (Chen et al., 1998; Souitaris et al., 2007).

Additionally, the application of motivational and needs theories to the entrepreneurial process can be partially accepted. This is particularly true, in the sense that EI is positively affected by individuals' attempts to reduce certain internal tensions, through greater EI, which is channelled through some of their antecedents (Fayolle et al., 2014; Solesvik, 2013).

As mentioned above, this is only partial insomuch as motivation indirectly affects EI through attitude though not through perceived behavioural control and subjective norms. These results differ from those obtained by Solesvik (2013) and Hui-Chen et al. (2014), who found an indirect effect through all these three variables.

This difference in results could be due to possible cultural differences in regions like those analysed here (García-Rodríguez et al., 2015; Liñán & Chen, 2009), which means that further testing would be necessary in different sociocultural contexts. Thus, it may be that in peripheral regions such as the one analysed, the subjective norms are so strongly rooted in young people that they are difficult to change through motivation.

In addition, it is worth highlighting that motivation also directly affects EI positively, which coincides with the results obtained by Hui-Chen et al. (2014) in their integrated model of the entrepreneurial process. However, a direct and significant relationship between abilities and personal attitude occurs which can be observed in this study, unlike previous works like Hui-Chen et al. (2014). This seems to indicate that in the context analysed, the acquisition of entrepreneurial abilities eventually has an impact, albeit indirectly, in EI.

Conclusions and limitations

The results obtained have important consequences for entrepreneurial education and policies in peripheral regions and, specifically, in the attention that should be paid to motivation. Thus, it seems that by improving young people's motivation to be entrepreneurs, their EI would also increase, on the one hand, through direct influence and on the other, thanks to the impact of an improvement in personal attitude. This confirms the importance of motivational–inspirational content in actions to promote entrepreneurship, in line with the approaches of Souitaris et al. (2007), and demonstrates the limited effectiveness of approaches only aimed at changing individuals' attitudes.

It seems that rather than attempting to directly transform individuals' attitudes towards entrepreneurship, it would be more efficient to focus on improving their motivation using intensive pedagogical strategies in creativity that go beyond mere informative content. Education could be particularly important in peripheral regions, for example, inspiring stories of successful entrepreneurs. These stories can convey to young people a vision of entrepreneurial activity in the region itself that is viable, desirable and attractive and thus help break entrepreneurship brain drain from the region (Kaufmann & Malul, 2015).

In connection with the above, it is worth noting the role of opportunity in motivation. Thus, the perception of opportunities for entrepreneurship would indirectly influence motivation in a positive sense. Consequently, it would seem that including methodologies and content focused on recognizing opportunities and problem-solving in educational programmes of entrepreneurship could also be an efficient element.

It also appears that investments in entrepreneurship training (abilities) for young people in peripheral regions could have a high impact on EI, to the extent that it has the power to transform their attitudes. Therefore, policies that invest in human capital in the field of entrepreneurship would be highly recommended in this type of peripheral contexts.

Looking to the future, it would be useful to repeat this study in other regions, peripheral as well as in metropolitan and industrial ones to carry out comparative studies. This would help determine to what extent the characteristics of the entrepreneurial process found here are linked to the peripheral nature of the region and can, therefore, be extrapolated to other similar ones or follow other patterns. In this sense, there is empirical evidence on the relevance of the socio-demographic context in motivation and individuals' personalities (Liñán & Chen, 2009). Second, as in the majority of EI studies, it would be interesting to incorporate the time factor (Audet, 2002), particularly since cross-sectional studies cannot make strong conclusions about causality because they do not allow causal relations to be tested, and common method variance is also likely to be a problem. Finally, despite the theory of planned behaviour by Ajzen (1991) still being a valid point of reference for the study of EI (Liñán & Fayolle, 2015), researchers should not only study variables that make up an entrepreneur's psychological profile but should also determine the relative importance of other cognitive and contextual variables. These could influence directly or indirectly antecedents of EI and individuals' 'posteriori' behaviour and could provide potential advances in this field.

Disclosure statement

No potential conflict of interest was reported by the authors.

References

Ajzen, I. (1987). Attitudes, traits, and actions: Dispositional prediction of behavior in personality and social psychology. *Advances in Experimental Social Psychology, 20*(C), 1. doi:10.1016/S0065-2601(08)60411-6

Ajzen, I. (1991). The theory of planned behavior. *Organizational Behavior and Human Decision Processes, 50*(2), 179–211. doi:10.1016/0749-5978(91)90020-T

Ajzen, I. (2001). Nature and operation of attitudes. *Annual Review of Psychology, 52*, 27–58. doi:10.1146/annurev.psych.52.1.27

Ajzen, I. (2002). Perceived behavioral control, self-efficacy, locus of control, and the theory of planned behavior. *Journal of Applied Social Psychology, 32*(4), 665–683. doi:10.1111/j.1559-1816.2002.tb00236.x

Asheim, B. (2009). La política regional de innovación de la próxima generación: cómo combinar los enfoques del impulso por la ciencia y por el usuario en los sistemas regionales de innovación. *Ekonomiaz, 70*, 86–105

Asheim, B., Moodyson, J., & Tödtling, F. (2011). Constructing regional advantage: Towards state-of-the-art regional innovation system policies in Europe? *European Planning Studies, 19*(7), 1133–1139. doi:10.1080/09654313.2011.573127

Audet, J. (2002). *A longitudinal study of the entrepreneurial intentions of university students*. Trois-Rivières: Dép. des Sciences de la gestion et de l'économie, Université du Québec à Trois-Rivières.

Audet, J. (2004). L'impact de deux projets de session sur les perceptions et intentions entrepreneuriales d'étudiants en administration. *Journal of Small Business and Entrepreneurship, 17*(3), 223–240. doi:10.1080/08276331.2004.10593321

Audretsch, D. B., & Keilbach, M. (2004). Entrepreneurship capital and economic performance. *Regional Studies, 38*(8), 949–959. doi:10.1080/0034340042000280956

Audretsch, D. B., & Peña, I. (2012). Entrepreneurial activity and regional competitiveness: An introduction to the special issue. *Small Business Economics, 39*(3), 531–537. doi:10.1007/s11187-011-9328-5

Autio, E. (1998). Evaluation of RTD in regional systems of innovation. *European Planning Studies, 6*(2), 131–140. doi:10.1080/09654319808720451

Barclay, D., Higgins, C., & Thompson, R. (1995). The partial least squares (PLS) approach to causal modeling: Personal computer adoption and use as an illustration. *Technological Studies, 2*(2), 285–309.

Baumgartner, D., Pütz, M., & Seidl, I. (2013). What kind of entrepreneurship drives regional development in European non-core regions? A literature review on empirical entrepreneurship research. *European Planning Studies, 21*(8), 1095–1127. doi:10.1080/09654313.2012.722937

Binney, W., Hall, J., & Shaw, M. (2003). A further development in social marketing application of the MOA framework and behavioral implications. *Marketing Theory*, *3*(3), 387–403. doi:10. 1177/147059310333001

Caird, S. (1991). Testing enterprise tendency in occupational groups. *British Journal of Management*, *12*, 177–186. doi:10.1111/j.1467-8551.1991.tb00025.x

Carsrud, A. L., & Brännback, M. (2011). Entrepreneurial motivations: What do we still need to know? *Journal of Small Business Management*, *49*(1), 9–26. doi:10.1111/j.1540-627X.2010. 00312.x

Chen, C. C., Greene, P. G., & Crick, A. (1998). Does entrepreneurial self-efficacy distinguish entre-preneurs from managers? *Journal of Business Venturing*, *13*(4), 295–316. doi:10.1016/S0883-9026(97)00029-3

Chin, W. W. (1998). Issues and opinion on structure equation modeling. *MIS Quarterly*, *22*(1), 7–16i.

Clifton, N., Gärtner, S., & Rehfeld, D. (2011). Companies, cultures, and the region: Interactions and outcomes. *European Planning Studies*, *19*(11), 1857–1864. doi:10.1080/09654313.2011.618683

Cooke, P., Heidenreich, M., & Braczyk, H.-J. (Eds.). (2004). *Regional innovation systems* (2nd ed.). London: UCL Press.

Damanpour, F. (1991). Organizational innovation: A meta-analysis of effects of determinants and moderators. *Academy of Management Journal*, *34*, 555–590. doi:10.2307/256406

Damanpour, F., & Scheneider, M. (2006). Phases of the adoption of innovations in organizations: Effects of environment, organization and top managers. *British Journal of Management*, *17*, 215–236. doi:10.1111/j.1467-8551.2006.00498.x

Doloreux, D. (2002) What we should know about regional systems of innovation. *Technology in Society*, *24*(3), 243–263. doi:10.1016/S0160-791X(02)00007-6

Drucker, P (1986). *La innovación y el empresariado innovador: la práctica y los principios*. Barcelona: Edhasa.

Durand, D., & Shea, D. (1974). Entrepreneurial activity as a function of achievement motivation and reinforcement control. *Journal of Psychology*, *88*, 57–63. doi:10.1080/00223980.1974. 9915713

Edelman, L., Brush, C. G., Manolova, T., & Greene, P. (2010). Start-up motivations and growth intentions of minority nascent entrepreneurs. *Journal of Small Business Management*, *48*(2), 174–196. doi:10.1111/j.1540-627X.2010.00291.x

Fayolle, A., Liñán, F., & Moriano, J. (2014). Beyond entrepreneurial intentions: Values and motiv-ations in entrepreneurship. *International Entrepreneurship and Management Journal*, *10*. doi:10. 1007/s11365-014-0306-7

Finisterra Do Paço, A. M., Ferreira, J. M., Raposo, M., Rodrigues, R. G., & Dinis, A. (2011). Behaviours and entrepreneurial intention: Empirical findings about secondary students. *Journal of International Entrepreneurship*, *9*(1), 20–38. doi:10.1007/s10843-010-0071-9

Fisher, I. (1930). *The theory of interest*. New York, NY: MacMillan.

Fornell, C., & Bookstein, F. L. (1982). Two structural models: LISREL and PLS applied to consumer exit-voice theory. *Journal of Marketing Research*, *19*, 440–452. doi:10.2307/3151718

Fornell, C., & Cha, J. (1994). *Partial least squares*. In R. P. Bagozzi (Eds.), *Advanced methods of mar-keting research* (pp. 52–78). Cambridge, MA: Blackwell.

Fornell, C., & Larcker, D. F. (1981). Evaluating structural equation models with unobservable vari-ables and measurement error. *Journal of Marketing Research*, *18*, 39–50. doi:10.2307/3151312

Fundación COTEC para la innovación tecnológica. (2015). *Tecnología e innovación en España*. Madrid: Author.

García-Cabrera, A. M., & García-Soto, M. G. (2008). Cultural differences and entrepreneurial behaviour: An intra-country cross-cultural analysis in Cape Verde. *Entrepreneurship and Regional Development*, *20*(5), 451–483. doi:10.1080/08985620801912608

García-Rodríguez, F. J., Gil-Soto, E., Ruiz-Rosa, I., & Sene, P. M. (2015). Entrepreneurial intentions in diverse development contexts: A cross-cultural comparison between Senegal and Spain. *International Entrepreneurship and Management Journal*, *11*(3), 511–527. doi:10.1007/s11365-013-0291-2

Gartner, W. B., Shaver, K. G., Gatewood, E., & Katz, J. A. (1994). Finding the entrepreneur in entre-preneurship. *Entrepreneurship Theory and Practice, 18*(3), 5–9.

Geisser, S. (1974). A predictive approach to the random effects model. *Biometrica, 61*, 101–107. doi:10.1093/biomet/61.1.101

Gibb, A. (1993). The enterprise culture and education. *International Small Business Journal, 11*(3), 11–34. doi:10.1177/026624269301100301

González, J. L., Martiarena, A., Navarro, M., & Peña, I. (2009). Estudio sobre la capacidad de innovación y actividad emprendedora en el ámbito sub-nacional: el caso de la Comunidad Autónoma del País Vasco. *Investigaciones Regionales, 15*, 55–87.

Gibb, A. (2000). SME policy, academic research and the growth of ignorance: Mythical concepts, myths, assumptions, rituals and confusions. *International Small Business Journal, 18*(3/71), 13–35. doi:10.1177/0266242600183001

González, J. L., Peña, I., & Vendrell, F. (2012). Innovation, entrepreneurial activity and competitive-ness at a sub-national level. *Small Business Economics, 39*(3), 561–574. doi:10.1007/s11187-011-9330-y

Gruen, T. W., Osmonbekov, T., & Czaplewski, A. J. (2005). How e-communities extend the concept of exchange in marketing: An application of the motivation, opportunity, ability (MOA) theory. *Marketing Theory, 5*(1), 33–49. doi:10.1177/1470593105049600

Gruen, T. W., Osmonbekov, T., & Czaplewski, A. J. (2006). eWOM: The impact of customerto- cus-tomer online know-how exchange on customer value and loyalty. *Journal of Business Research, 59*(4), 449–456. doi:10.1016/j.jbusres.2005.10.004

Gruen, T. W., Osmonbekov, T., & Czaplewski, A. J. (2007). Customer-to-customer exchange: Its MOA antecedents and its impact on value creation and loyalty. *Journal of the Academy of Marketing Science, 35*(4), 537–549. doi:10.1007/s11747-006-0012-2

Guerrero, M., Cunningham, J., & Urbano, D. (2015). Economic impact of entrepreneurial univer-sities' activities: An exploratory study of the United Kingdom. *Research Policy, 44*(3), 748–764. doi:10.1016/j.respol.2014.10.008

Guerrero, M., & Peña-Legazkue, I. (2013). Entrepreneurial activity and regional development: An introduction to this special issue. *Investigaciones Regionales, 26*(2013), 5–15.

Guerrero, M., Urbano, D., & Fayolle, A. (2016). Entrepreneurial activity and regional competitive-ness: Evidence from European entrepreneurial universities. *The Journal of Technology Transfer, 41*(1), 105–131. doi:10.1007/s10961-014-9377-4

Hofstede, G. (1991). *Cultures and organizations: Software of the mind*. London: McGraw-Hill.

Hofstede, G., Noorderhaven, N. G., Thurik, A. R., Wennekers, A., Uhlaner, L., & Wildeman, R. E. (2004). Culture's role in entrepreneurship: Self-employment out of dissatisfaction. In T. E. Brown & J. Ulijn (Eds.), *Innovation, entrepreneurship and culture: The interaction between tech-nology, progress and economic growth* (pp. 162–203). Nothampton: Edward Elgar Publishing.

Hofstede, G. H. (1984). *Culture's consequences: International differences in work-related values*. London: Sage.

Hui-Chen, C., Kuen-Hung, T., & Chen-Yi, P. (2014). The entrepreneurial process: An integrated model. *International Entrepreneurship and Management Journal, 10*, doi:10.1007/s11365-014-0305-8

Hulland, J. (1999). Use of partial least squares (PLS) in strategic management research: A review of four recent studies. *Strategic Management Journal, 20*(2), 195–204. doi:10.1002/(SICI)1097-0266(199902)20:2<195::AID-SMJ13>3.0.CO;2-7

Hult, G. T., Hurley, R. F., & Knight, G. A. (2004). Innovativeness: Its antecedents and impact on business performance. *Industrial Marketing Management, 33*, 429–438. doi:10.1016/j.indmarman.2003.08.015

Kalantaridis, C. (2004). Entrepreneurial behaviour in rural contexts. In L. Labrianidis (Ed.), *The future of Europe's rural peripheries* (pp. 62–86). Aldershot: Ashgate.

Kaufmann, D., & Malul, M. (2015). The dynamic brain drain of entrepreneurs in peripheral regions. *European Planning Studies, 23*(7), 1345–1356. doi:10.1080/09654313.2014.929639

Keeble, D., & Wilkinson, F. (Eds.). (2000). *High-technology clusters, networking and collective learn-ing in Europe*. Aldershot: Ashgate.

Kolvereid, L. (1996). Prediction of employment status choice intentions. *Entrepreneurship Theory and Practice, 21*(1), 47–57.

Krueger, N. F., & Brazeal, D. V. (1994). Entrepreneurial potential and potential entrepreneurs. *Entrepreneurship Theory and Practice, 18*, 91–91.

Krueger, N. F., Reilly, M. D., & Carsrud, A. L. (2000). Competing models of entrepreneurial intentions. *Journal of Business Venturing, 15*(5), 411–432. doi:10.1016/S0883-9026(98)00033-0

Lawson, R. (1997). Consumer decision making within a goal-driven framework. *Psychology and Marketing, 14*(5), 427–449. doi:10.1002/(SICI)1520-6793(199708)14:5<427::AID-MAR1>3.0. CO;2-A

Liñán, F., & Chen, Y. (2009). Development and cross-cultural application of a specific instrument to measure entrepreneurial intentions. *Entrepreneurship Theory Practice, 33*(3), 593–617. doi:10. 1111/j.1540-6520.2009.00318.x

Liñán, F., & Fayolle, A. (2015). A systematic literature review on entrepreneurial intentions: Citation, thematic analyses, and research agenda. *International Entrepreneurship and Management Journal*, 1–27. doi:10.1007/s11365-015-0356-5

Liñán, F., Fernández-Serrano, J., & Romero, I. (2013). Necessity and opportunity entrepreneurship: The mediating effect of culture. *Revista de Economía Mundial, 33*. Retrieved from http://hdl. handle.net/11441/16481

Liñán, F., Urbano, D., & Guerrero, M. (2011). Regional variations in entrepreneurial cognitions: Start-up intentions of university students in Spain. *Entrepreneurship and Regional Development, 23*(3&4), 187–215. doi:10.1080/08985620903233929

MacInnis, D. J., & Jaworski, B. J. (1989). Information processing from advertisements: Toward an integrative framework. *Journal of Marketing, 53*(10), 1–23. doi:10.2307/1251376

McCline, R. L., Bhat, S., & Baj, P. (2000). Opportunity recognition: An exploratory investigation of a component of the entrepreneurial process in the context of the health care industry. *Entrepreneurship Theory and Practice, 25*, 81–144.

Minniti, M., & Bygrave, W. D. (2001). A dynamic model of entrepreneurial learning. *Entrepreneurship Theory and Practice, 25*(5), 16.

Moriano, J. A., Gómez, A., Laguna, M., & Roznowski, B. (2008). *Validación de un cuestionario para medir la intención emprendedora. Una aplicación en España y Polonia*. In F. J. Morales, C. Huici, A. Gómez, & E. Gaviria (Eds.), *Método, teoría e investigación en psicología social* (pp. 101–122). Madrid: Prentice Hall.

Morris, J. L., & Fargher, K. (1974). Achievement drive and creativity as correlates of success in small business. *Australian Journal of Psychology, 26*(3), 217–222. doi:10.1080/00049537408255232

Mueller, S. L., & Thomas, A. S. (2001). Culture and entrepreneurial potential: A nine-country study of locus of control and innovativeness. *Journal of Business Venturing, 16*(1), 51–75. doi:10.1016/ S0883-9026(99)00039-7

Nunnally, J. (1978). *Psychometric theory*. New York, NY: McGraw-Hill.

OECD. (2005). *Oslo manual. Guidelines for collecting and interpreting innovation* (3rd ed.). Paris: OECD.

Peterman, N. E., & Kennedy, J. (2003). Enterprise education: Influencing students' perceptions of entrepreneurship. *Entrepreneurship Theory y Practice, 28*(2), 129–144. doi:10.1046/j.1540-6520. 2003.00035.x

Piñero, A., Rodríguez-Monroy, C., & Arbola, M. (2012). Vinculación y evaluación de políticas públicas de I + D+i para dinamizar la innovación en las PYMIS. *Interciencia, 37*, 883–890.

Real, J. C., Leal, A., & Roldán, J. L. (2006). Information technology as a determinant of organizational learning and technological distinctive competencies. *Industrial Marketing Management, 35*(4), 505–521. doi:10.1016/j.indmarman.2005.05.004

Ringle, C., Wende, S., & Will, A. (2005). *Smart-PLS Version 2.0 M3*. Retrieved from http://www. smartpls.de

Robinson, P. B., Stimpson, D. V., Huefner, J. C., & Hunt, H. K. (1991). An attitude approach to the prediction of entrepreneurship. *Entrepreneurship Theory and Practice, 15*, 13–31.

Rothschild, M. L. (1999). Carrots, sticks, and promises: A conceptual framework for the management of public health and social issue behaviors. *Journal of Marketing, 63*(4): 24–37. doi:10.2307/1251972

Saxenian, A. (1994). *Regional advantage: Culture and competition in Silicon Valley and Route 128.* Cambridge, MA: Harvard University Press.

Schmiedeberg, C. (2008). Complementarities of innovation activities: An empirical analysis of the German manufacturing sector. *Research Policy, 37*, 1492–1503. doi:10.1016/j.respol.2008.07.008

Schwartz, S. H. (2011). Studying values: Personal adventure, future directions. *Journal of Cross-Cultural Psychology, 42*(2), 307–319. doi:10.1177/0022022110396925

Shapero, A., & Sokol, L. (1982). The social dimensions of entrepreneurship. *Encyclopedia of Entrepreneurship,* 72–90.

Siemsen, E., Roth, A. V., & Balasubramanian, S. (2008). How motivation, opportunity, and ability drive knowledge sharing: The constraining-factor model. *Journal of Operations Management, 26*(3), 426. doi:10.1016/j.jom.2007.09.001

Solesvik, M. (2013). Entrepreneurial motivations and intentions: Investigating the role of education major. *Education + Training, 55*(3), 253–271. doi:10.1108/00400911311309314

Souitaris, V., Zerbinati, F., & Al-Laham, A. (2007). Do entrepreneurship programmes raise entrepreneurial intention of science and engineering students? The effect of learning, inspiration and resources. *Journal of Business Venturing, 22*(3), 566–591. doi:10.1016/j.jbusvent.2006.05.002

Tenenhaus, M., Vinzi, V. E., Chatelin, Y.-M., & Lauro, C. (2005). PLS path modeling. *Computational Statistics and Data Analysis, 48*(1), 159–205. doi:10.1016/j.csda.2004.03.005

Tkachev, A., & Kolvereid, L. (1999). Self-employment intentions among russian students. *Entrepreneurship y Regional Development, 11*(3), 269–280. doi:10.1080/089856299283209

Tödtling, F., & Trippl, M. (2005). One size fits all? Towards a differentiated regional innovation policy approach, *Research Policy, 34*(8), 1203–1219. doi:10.1016/j.respol.2005.01.018

Van Oostrom, M. (2015). *Cultura de la Innovación y Microempresa en Sistemas Regionales de I + D +i. Actitudes y comportamientos innovadores en las micropymes de la Comunidad Autónoma de Canarias* (Unpublished doctoral dissertation). Universidad de La Laguna, San Cristóbal de La Laguna.

Wennekers, S., Thurik, R., Van Stel, A., & Noorderhaven, N. (2007). Uncertainty avoidance and the rate of business ownership across 21 OECD countries, 1976–2004. *Journal of Evolutionary Economics, 17*(2), 133–160. doi:10.1007/s00191-006-0045-1

Wetzels, M., Odekerken-Schröder, G., & Van Oppen, C. (2009). Using PLS path modelling for assessing hierarchical construct models: Guidelines and empirical illustration. *MIS Quarterly, 33*(1), 177–195.

Wold, H. (1979). *Model construction and evaluation when theoretical knowledge is scarce: An example of the use of partial least squares.* Genève: Cahiers du Département D'Économétrie, Faculté des Sciences Économiques et Sociales, Université de Genève.

Making visible the role of vocational education and training in firm innovation: evidence from Spanish SMEs

Eneka Albizu, Mikel Olazaran, Cristina Lavía and Beatriz Otero

ABSTRACT

The interactive learning model argues the importance of incremental innovation, linked to production activities, and the role in that innovation of qualified workers – including those with a vocational training degree – in opposition to the supremacy of scientific personnel that tends to characterize high-tech industries. However, scarcely any attention has been paid to the role of intermediary workers in innovation processes. This study, based on a survey of 1142 Spanish industrial small and medium-sized enterprises (SMEs), examines the degree to which technicians and employees with a vocational education and training (VET) profile are represented in these firms and their involvement in innovation activities. In order to identify the importance of the factors studied in a multivariate model, a binary logistic regression was performed with an index of VET workers' participation as a dependent variable, segmenting the companies by technological level. The study shows that for sectors with greatest R&D intensity, the presence of VET personnel in technical posts and the existence of external co-operation in innovation were found to triple the probability of greater participation. In more low-tech sectors, these variables continue to exercise a strong influence, but the multiplier effect of another two has also been detected, specifically the innovative capacity of the company and a greater level of involvement of operators in organizational learning practices.

1. Introduction

The interactive learning model (learning by doing; learning by using; learning by interacting) argues the importance of incremental innovation and the role in such innovation of qualified workers – including those with vocational education and training (VET) skills – as opposed to the supremacy of scientific personnel in high-tech industries (Jensen, Johnson, Lorenz, & Lundvall, 2007; Lundvall & Lorenz, 2007). However, scarcely any attention has been paid to the role of workers with intermediate qualifications in the innovation processes (cf. e.g. Moodie, 2006). In this context, the CEDEFOP (2011) study of VET impact on company performance pointed out the need to study the role of this education and training agent in industry.

Only recently have some authors begun to focus on the role of employees with a VET profile in innovation activities, linking elements from different theoretical traditions such as 'varieties of capitalism', 'high-performance work systems' and innovation studies (Toner, 2011). In this regard, some writers have noted that technical workers with intermediate qualifications are involved in the design, installation, operation and maintenance of products and processes and that they, therefore, contribute – or can contribute – to innovation in these firms (Tether, Mina, Consoli, & Gagliardi, 2005; Toner, Marceau, Hall, & Considine, 2004).

Studies conducted in Australia suggest that in the face of a historical shortage of R&D resources, VET workers – together with VET institutes linked to regional development – have played an important role in the country's innovation processes, in a context of interactive learning and a preponderance of SMEs and low-tech industries (Curtain, 2004a; Guthrie & Dawe, 2004; Toner et al., 2004).

In Europe, the only studies of this kind have been conducted in the Basque Country and Navarre (Spain), industrial regions in which regional governments have made a strong commitment to strengthening vocational studies. Following the classification of Rosenfeld (1998) on the missions of VET institutes (formal education, continuous training and company services), Albizu, Olazaran, Lavía, and Otero (2011) analysed the relations between those institutes and industrial SMEs in the Basque Country. They suggested that vocational training centres are an agent of significance within the regional innovation system, contributing through their main lines of action to improving the competitiveness of companies and to stimulating their innovation processes. Subsequently, a study by Lavía, Olazaran, Albizu, and Otero (2012) showed that companies that perform more continuous training with VET centres express greater agreement on the effects of training on motivation, productivity and worker contribution, although the levels of agreement on the direct effects on innovation of the continuous training these centres offer were somewhat lower. Recently, Lavía, Otero, Albizu, and Olazaran (2016), using a new sample from the Basque Country, have studied in more detail the presence of VET employees in industrial SMEs and their participation in innovation activities.

These studies, carried out from the perspective of regional innovation systems, show the existence of a strong link between the education system and the manufacturing fabric, essentially in terms of education and training of human capital and, to a lesser extent, continuous training and services for innovation. Nonetheless, a number of issues remain to be clarified regarding the extent of the contribution made by these employees to innovation and aspects such as the way and the circumstances in which this contribution takes place.

This study contributes new evidence to this largely understudied field, highlighting the importance of workers with intermediate qualifications (VET) in the innovation processes of SMEs. More specifically, based on a large sample of Spanish industrial SMEs, it seeks to answer the following two questions: 'Are workers with VET qualifications involved in the companies' innovation processes?' and 'Which are the specific variables that condition participation by intermediary staff in innovation?'

The document is structured as follows. Section 2 describes the conceptual framework of the research, which is based on the concept of innovation as continuous and interactive learning, located in a regional environment in which the exchange of tacit knowledge and provision of skilled labour largely take place. Section 3 explains the research methodology employed. It describes the way in which information has been gathered, together with the characteristics of the sample of companies, data processing, variables and descriptive results. Section 4 sets out the results of the study, divided into two subsections: characteristics of SMEs and VET workers' participation in innovation and a binary logistic regression performed to estimate VET employee participation according to different factors characteristic of SMEs and taking into account the technological level of the companies (high and medium high vs. medium low and low). Section 5 sets out the discussion and, finally, conclusions, implications and limitations are described.

2. Theoretical framework

In their recent review about VET skills and innovation, Toner and Woolley (2016) point out at a strong causal interrelation between higher levels of education, training and skills, and technical and organizational innovation. Within this context, VET plays a key role at both the firm and the regional/national system level in the virtuous circle connecting initial education, continuous training and capacity of the workforce to deal with technical change. The development of workers' technical skills resulting from a close relationship between the VET system and industrial needs (mainly low- and medium technology SMEs) is a key factor in new technology absorption and diffusion (Lundvall, 1998; Tödtling, Prud'homme van Reine, & Dörhöfer, 2011). Ferrier, Trood, and Whittingham (2003) and Curtain (2004b) also pointed out at the role of VET in technology adoption and diffusion.

Most of the innovations carried out by SMEs are incremental and based in the so-called DUI (doing, using, interacting) innovation mode (learning by doing, by using, by interacting), which requires continuous implication by intermediate workers in creative problem-solving and improvement activities related to operations such as assembling, installation, maintenance, purchasing and technical service. As Shapira and Rosenfeld (1996) suggested, within this type of innovation, technical skills are often applied to the manufacturing and/or commercialization of products and services which are new for the client and which are not necessarily based on the latest, state-of-the art technological knowledge available in the market.

An important part of the innovation-related activity carried out by intermediate workers from a VET background is located within industrials firms' technical areas such as R&D units, technical offices and production engineering departments. For the Australian case, Toner, Turpin, Wooley, and Lloyd (2010) found that a large proportion of the business R&D workforce (46% according to their calculations) was made up of qualified technical workers from a VET background. They perform not only tasks of support to engineers and scientists, but also creative and autonomous work involving problem-solving and adapting ideas put forward by the latter group.

Within the current competitive environment, SMEs from many industrial sectors are demanded tailor-made solutions which can be realized with the active collaboration of workers who are 'reflective practitioners and which take their experiences and knowledge as an important source for improving production' (Ruth & Deitmer, 2010, p. 424). Therefore, there is an increasing demand for high-skilled labour to deal with technical change (HM Treasury, 2004). The application of intermediate workers' skills to firms' operations becomes critical for improvements and innovations in the companies' processes. In this respect, CEDEFOP (2011) found a positive and significant relationship between VET and different performance indicators of firms which included innovation.

> H1: The presence of VET technicians in the workforce is positively related to their participation in innovation.

Several studies have shown that lower-tech industry sectors, where many SMEs are located, are important in themselves, both because of their contribution to economic growth and employment, and because of their interaction with industries with a higher R&D intensity, in that they introduce new technologies coming from the latter and make sophisticated demands on these industries (Kaloudis, Sandven, & Smith, 2005; Robertson, Smith, & von Tuzelmann, 2009)[1]. The latter study (Kaloudis et al., 2005) maintains that the continued importance of low-tech industries in the advanced economies of the OECD (Organisation for Economic Co-operation and Development) can only be explained by a continuous and ongoing technological renewal in those industries.

Among the characteristics of the low-tech innovation mode pinpointed by recent studies, one should mention the greater relative importance of innovations in processes, affecting parameters such as quality, response time and productivity, and a lower level of external co-operation in innovation (Arundel, Bordoy, & Kanerva, 2008; Heidenreich, 2009; Hirsch-Kreinsen, 2015; Kirner, Som, & Jäger, 2015). The strong impact of manufacturing personnel in innovation, including not only engineers, but also technicians, intermediary workers and operators, has also been shown with qualitative evidence (Hirsch-Kreinsen, 2008, 2015).

It has been shown that many low-tech SMEs innovate; the challenge is to increase the degree of innovation. In this regard, Freel (2005) states that, in such companies, what makes the difference in the degree of novelty of the innovation is not so much the presence of engineering personnel or scientists, but the weight of technicians and intermediary workers.

> H2: SME innovation capacity is positively related to VET workers' participation in innovation.

This study is based on the concept of innovation as an interactive learning process, internal and external to the company, linked to its ongoing manufacturing activities, within a social environment that conditions economic activity (Edquist, 1997; Lundvall, 1992). The principal type of innovation comprises gradual or incremental improvements, related to problem-solving, process optimization and development of the existing technologies. In this type of learning process, interaction and exchange of tacit knowledge between people and departments within the organization are prevalent, together with a close relationship with a small set of external agents, generally customers or suppliers (Jensen et al., 2007; Lundvall & Lorenz, 2007).

Internal and external interactive learning takes place within an institutional and cultural environment in which factors such as relations between the public and the private sector, the education and training system, the framework of labour relations and the financial system are all of great importance. Saxenian (1994) confirms that the cultural conditions supporting innovation activities must be situated within a context of interaction in which the knowledge transfer takes place.

In the case of SMEs, which are characterized by a limited base of organizational (human, financial, technological and management) resources, relationships with external agents such as customers and suppliers, and integration into the regional setting (with its educational and research infrastructures) (Kaufmann & Tödtling, 2003), are of critical importance. Training structures situated within a regional environment – one of the main resources that low-tech SMEs possess – play an important role in spreading technological knowledge among companies and workers (Tödtling et al., 2011), a prerequisite for the development of the companies' absorption capacity. Likewise, employees with responsibilities in technical departments or in the chain of command of the SMEs, culturally socialized in the region, play an important role in knowledge exchange both inside and outside the organizations (Prud'homme van Reine & Dankbaar, 2011). Such employees are involved in regional networks of collaboration and association (González de la Fe, Hernández Hernández, & van Oostrom, 2012) and share values, language, relations and experiences with staff in education and research centres and other companies from the regional area, thus assisting in the solving of innovation problems that arise in the companies.

H3: External co-operation in innovation is positively related to VET workers' participation in innovation.

The broad concept of innovation, defined as a continuous and interactive learning process, where direct workers and intermediary technicians can play an important role, makes it necessary to consider organizational aspects such as integration of functions, reduction in hierarchical levels, creation of teams with members from different occupational fields, delegation of responsibility and problem-solving autonomy (Lundvall & Nielsen, 2007; Lundvall, Rasmussen, & Lorenz, 2008).

One of the main keys to innovation culture is the central position of workers and their participation in processes of knowledge generation, transfer and absorption. The basis of the participation lies in instruments such as regular and ad hoc work teams. Work teams are an ideal setting for generating, sharing and accumulating knowledge (Janz & Prasarnphanich, 2003; Nonaka, 1994). Because these processes (generating, sharing and accumulating knowledge) are social, the work team environment encourages the generation of trust, personal ties and a collective commitment that facilitates their development. Pérez and Quevedo (2006) suggest that most innovative Spanish companies organize their R&D activities in work teams, while Jiménez-Jiménez and Sanz-Valle (2008) confirm the relationship between employee participation and teamwork with the performance of innovative activity.

Stable work teams are responsible for value-adding processes and define their own targets and mechanisms of organization (within the context of the firm) and control. As Bolland and Hofer (2001, p. 230) argue, in reference to high-tech companies, 'centralization has shifted from machines to work groups, marking a sea change from the cult of production to the dynamic of people working with other people and the provision of services'.

Ad hoc work teams include proposals such as project teams, learning communities and problem-solving groups. Thus, a formula that favours exchange of knowledge in the organization is one that assigns people to projects depending on the specific needs of each project, based on the knowledge and skills of the team's members. Involvement in different projects fosters knowledge-sharing at an organizational level and learning among project members, and is also a good scenario for developing an innovation culture. Autonomy and interdisciplinarity of work teams favour knowledge transfer

(García-Pinto, García, & Piñeiro, 2010). Thus, the involvement of employees with VET profiles in innovation activities might be related to the existence of a solid innovation culture in the company, defined as a technical and organizational style of learning.

H4: Advanced organizational practices are positively related to VET workers' participation in innovation.

3. Methodology

3.1. Data collection, sample design and data analysis

To achieve the proposed research objectives, a telephone survey was conducted among 1388 industrial SMEs (sectors 05–39 of the 2009 Spanish Standard Industrial Classification, CNAE) with between 10 and 250 employees in five regions in northern Spain: Asturias, the Basque Country, Navarre, Aragon and Catalonia. It comprises an aggregate sample of representative samples in each region. Each regional sample is a random proportional sample stratified by size (5 strata), so that, for the aggregate sample, at a 95% confidence level and under the most unfavourable assumption ($p = q$), it assumes a margin of error of 2.5%. The regions analysed, in all of which the industrial sector has greater weight than the Spanish average, represent 27.2% of the national population and 31.8% of national GDP (2010), as well as accounting for 46% of total business-sector R&D spending in Spain (2014).

Data collection was conducted from December 2013 to January 2014. The sample was taken from a real population of 113,121 companies listed in the SABI database of Spanish firms elaborated and updated by the Bureu Van Dijk company (https://sabi.bvdinfo.com/). This database was used as a sampling frame for simple selection. The individuals surveyed were managing directors or heads of human resource management and/or training areas. The survey was specifically designed by the research team.

In all, 82% of all companies surveyed have VET-profile employees in their workforce and also perform some form of innovation or improvement. These 1142 SMEs form the empirical sample on which the analysis was performed of VET profile employee participation in innovation processes.

The data were processed with SPSS v.22. As well as the descriptive and bivariate association analyses, various multivariate explorations were conducted in order to determine the best combination of explanatory variables of the original outcome variables measuring the participation of VET employees in the forms of innovation studied. Several stepwise regressions as well as some CHAID (Chi-squared Automatic Interaction Detection) segmentation analyses were carried out with a view to finding variables which discriminate detailed levels of participation and typologies characteristic of SMEs in this regard. The best representation of the relations detected was performed by a binary logistic regression on the business characteristics that cause differences between SMEs with regard to VET employee participation in innovation activities, controlling for the technological level of the companies.

3.2. Independent variables

Several variables which may have an influence upon worker participation are considered, including objective characteristics of firms such as size or industry sector. The study is based on a broad conception of innovation, which is especially well-suited for application to SMEs and low-tech companies and includes both innovation activities per se and product and process 'improvements'. Other variables studied refer to the firm's self-perception of its innovative capacity and to external co-operation for innovation. Several measures of the firms' VET staff have also been considered, such as the percentage of employees with a VET profile, the presence of higher VET graduates among them and continuous training activities carried out with VET institutes from the regional environment.

The study of intermediate worker participation in technical innovation also sought to explore the possible impact on this factor of variables related to the companies' organizational culture. The SMEs were, therefore, asked about a series of advanced work organization practices carried out by operators (the lowest level of the hierarchy). The independent variables considered and the particular indicators used are detailed in the appendix.

3.3. Characteristics of firms

Based on the stratification applied, the sample contained a predominance of small companies (47% had under 25 workers), while 29.3% had between 25 and 49 employees and only 23.7% had 50 or more. As for the technological sector (R&D intensity, based on OECD classification), 41% of the SMEs surveyed were from low-tech sectors and the majority (65.8%) were from medium-low and low-tech sectors. In all, 31% perform medium-high technology activities and 3.2% perform high technology activities. Regarding industry sector, 48% of the firms performed metal-machining activities (CNAE2009 codes 24, 25, 28, 29, 30 and 33) and the remained were distributed among other industrial activities.

This study focused on the presence and role of workers with a VET profile in the companies. The survey, therefore, asked about the percentage of staff with this level of studies. The companies were found to have an important number of workers with these qualifications: in nearly a third of the companies surveyed, over half of the staff was made up of these profiles and, in two-thirds of the companies, at least a quarter of the staff have completed these studies.

Important levels of innovation activity were found in the surveyed firms. Process improvement (carried out by 91% of the SMEs) was seen to be the most common form of innovating; 76.3% of firms perform process innovations, 77.6% organizational innovations, 82.3% marketing innovations and 83.6% product improvements. Product innovation (70.2% of SMEs) is the most selective form of innovation. Moreover, of all the companies consulted, half (50.2%) stated that they innovate in all the forms mentioned.

The companies were asked to rate their situation in innovation, or their 'innovative capacity', in relation to that of their most direct competitors: 31% considered themselves to be in a better relative position as an innovative company than their direct competitors, while the remainder said they were worse (9%) or the same (58%). Based on this, the study differentiated SMEs by greater innovative capacity ('more innovative') as against less (those which consider themselves the same or worse, 'less innovative'). In effect, the firms that declared to be more innovative were found to perform significantly higher levels of both innovation and improvement of processes and products.

It should be noted that the companies surveyed showed an important degree of external co-operation for innovation: 52.5% said they co-operated for innovation, while 46.2% said they did not; 1.3% of companies did not answer this question. The most common agents for co-operation are suppliers and customers (52.6%), followed by technology centres (47.9%), universities (32%) and other companies (30%). A greater proportion (66%) of the SMEs that have co-operated in the last four years were found to have carried out all the innovation activities considered, as compared to 32.6% of the SMEs that did not co-operate. The most innovative companies co-operate significantly to a greater extent (64%) than the less innovative ones (48%).

Regarding relationships with VET institutes, as shown by previous studies, relations between education and industry are frequent: two-thirds of the companies have relationships with VET centres (mainly students' compulsory internships), while 30% of the companies perform continuous training in the institutes.

As for variables related to the companies' organizational culture, operator involvement in certain advanced work organization practices was rather widespread in the sample studied: 89% of companies answered that their operators plan and organize the work autonomously; 78% stated that operators participate in regular structured meetings for work/process planning, evaluation and improvement and 61.4% said that these workers participate in ad hoc problem-solving teams.

3.4. Dependent variable: index of participation

The main aim of this study was to measure VET employee participation in innovation activities and to analyse the variables that impact or are related to that participation. The companies were asked about the level of VET employee involvement in each of the innovation types under consideration (when performed) using a scale of 1–4 (meaning none, a little, quite a lot and a lot). The highest VET worker participation came in process improvement activities, with 49% of SMEs giving one of the two higher ratings (quite a lot and a lot), and in process innovation (40%) and product improvement (39%). There was less participation in product (35%), organizational (32%) and marketing (18%) innovations.

In order to relate the different aspects of innovation to the level of participation and, therefore, test the research hypotheses formulated, a global weighted participation index (WPI) was defined. The index is a quantitative measure ranging from 0 (when there is no participation at all) to 24 points which rates participation in stricter innovation activities more highly. As shown in Table 1, this index totals all degrees (1–4) of participation in the different innovations, but weighs participation in product and process innovations upwards (factor = 1.5). These are the types of innovation which entail a higher degree of novelty and are carried out less frequently by the firms. In turn, a factor of 0.5 has been applied to improvement activities, which are more common among innovative SMEs and where a higher VET worker participation is detected. Organization and market innovations have not been weighted. Thus, the index is a sum of the level of participation in the six innovation activities considered, which goes from 0 (no participation detected in any of the innovation activities considered) to 24 and which values more the activities that have a higher level of novelty.

Table 1. The weighted worker participation index.

Type of participation in innovation	Score	Weighting factor
Product innovation	1 = none; 2 = a little; 3 = quite a lot; 4 = a lot	1.5
Process innovation	1 = none; 2 = a little; 3 = quite a lot; 4 = a lot	1.5
Improvement or modifications of existing products	1 = none; 2 = a little; 3 = quite a lot; 4 = a lot	0.5
Improvement or modifications of existing processes	1 = none; 2 = a little; 3 = quite a lot; 4 = a lot	0.5
Design and implementation of new work organization systems	1 = none; 2 = a little; 3 = quite a lot; 4 = a lot	1
New channels, markets, relationships	1 = none; 2 = a little; 3 = quite a lot; 4 = a lot	1

Source: Authors' elaboration.
Note: Participation index: weighted sum of participation in the six innovation activities.

Table 2. Levels of VET employee participation in innovation based on WPI.

WPI scores	N	%
None (0)	184	16.1
Low (0.5–8)	373	32.7
Medium (8.5–16)	463	40.5
High (16.5–24)	122	10.7
Total (valid)	1142	100

Source: Authors' elaboration.

The index (Table 2) shows a quite diverse distribution, with a mean of 8.77 points and a standard deviation of 5.9 (coefficient of variation: 67%). There is an important incidence of null or low participation, given that nearly 50% of SMEs scored less than 8.5 points (median) and only the highest quartile scored over 12.5. Based on this index, and in order to explore the association between overall participation and other characteristics in the companies, four intervals of scores (categories) were established to express the levels of VET employee participation in innovations.

As Table 2 shows, 16% of SMEs innovate without participation of their VET personnel. It can also be seen that the proportion of SMEs with very high levels of participation is low (10.7%), with most SMEs standing somewhere between the medium and low levels. Nonetheless, the degree of participation detected may be considered relevant. Taking into account the fact that the index weights participation in strict product or process innovation higher, there is an important incidence of 'medium' levels of participation (from the median of the index), covering 40% of the companies surveyed. Adding the high-level ones to these, one can see that 51% of the SMEs studied perform innovations with significant participation from their VET workers.

4. VET employee participation in innovation activities

4.1. Characteristics of 'SMEs' and VET worker participation in innovation

As for the basic descriptive characteristics of the companies and their type of activity, one can see that, in themselves, variables such as industry sector or size do not cause significant differences in participation. However, as Table 3 shows, for the sample as a whole, significant

Table 3. Relations between characteristics of SMEs and WPI.

	WPI level				
	None	Low	Medium	High	Total N (100%)
VET in technical departments**					
Yes	10.1	27.5	46.2	16.2	636
No	23.7	39.1	33.4	3.8	506
Co-operates in innovation**					
Yes	12.4	25.4	48.9	13.4	599
No	20.3	40.9	31.3	7.6	528
Innovative capacity**					
Yes	13.0	25.1	44.1	17.8	354
No	17.1	36.2	39.2	7.5	765
Operator involvement in ad hoc work teams**					
Less	18.4	31.5	40.1	10.0	429
Greater	8.6	20.9	53.4	17.2	268
Operator involvement in planning and organization**					
Less	20.1	33.7	38.3	7.9	582
Greater	11.4	27.5	44.8	16.3	429
Operator involvement in structured improvement meetings**					
Less	18.8	32.3	40.1	8.8	548
Greater	8.5	24.8	49.6	17.2	343

Source: Authors' elaboration.
**Chi^2 $p < .01$.

relations can be seen between such participation and the following variables: presence of VET personnel in technical departments, external co-operation by the companies in innovation, perception of the company's innovative capacity, and operator involvement in work planning/organization, regular improvement meetings and ad hoc work teams.

A first discriminatory characteristic with regard to participation is the presence of employees with VET degrees in technical departments (R&D department, technical office, and/or manufacturing and process engineering department), which is differentially associated with greater levels of participation by these workers in innovation. The presence of these workers in technical areas is quite common, extending to 56% of the companies surveyed. A relationship between this presence and high levels of participation is found in all types and subtypes of companies considered, whereas in SMEs that have no VET personnel in such activities, participation is much lower.

At the same time, with regard to external co-operation, other studies (Otero, Lavía, Albizu, & Olazaran, 2014) have empirically detected that experience of co-operation in innovation projects with external agents (business, technological or scientific) from the regional setting is a very clear characteristic of the intensity of innovation strategies by industrial SMEs. In this survey, companies were also asked about the existence of such co-operation. For this sample of SMEs that perform innovations, the extent of co-operation was found to be relevant (see discussion in Section 3.3).

Experience in co-operation always appears significantly and positively associated with VET employee participation in the innovations made by their companies, even when the size, industry and technological level of the SMEs are controlled. As Table 3 shows, for the sample as a whole, among companies that co-operate there are fewer with no participation (12% as opposed to 20% for those that do not co-operate) and more with medium levels (49% vs. 31%) and high levels (14% vs. 8%) of participation.

Similarly, the perception of the company's relative innovative capacity is found to be a characteristic related to VET employee participation in innovations. Thus, for the sample as a whole, companies with greater relative innovative activity tend to have higher levels of participation (medium and high) than those with less relative innovative activity, whereas among the latter, lower participation (low and none) of VET workers is more frequent.

Variables related to advanced organizational practices have also been found to be important. Among SMEs with less involvement in them, the incidence of null participation in innovation virtually doubles: from 8.6% to 18.4% for ad hoc teams, 11.4% to 20.1% for autonomous planning and organization and 8.5% to 18.8% (an even greater difference) for involvement in regular structured meetings. On the contrary, medium and high levels of participation were very high among the SMEs that do perform these practices, involving their operators to a greater extent: from 61% for SMEs that practise autonomous work planning and organization by operators, to 67% for involvement in regular meetings and 71% for companies that have ad hoc problem-solving teams.

Finally, it is interesting to indicate that two other relationships were found to be highly significant for low-tech SMEs only, namely higher presence of high-level VET graduates among employees (53% of firms with high participation, against 40% for firms with lower percentages of such graduates) and performance of continuous training with VET institutes from the environment (58% of the firms with high participation, against 48% for firms with no continuous training activities).

4.2. Models of worker participation in innovation

At this point, several stepwise binary logistic regressions were performed in order to identify the importance of the factors studied in a multivariate model that takes the multiple interactions between them into consideration. Considering the WPI as a dependent variable, we worked with the basic differentiation between lowest level of participation (none or low) and highest level of participation (medium and high). Eight independent variables were initially considered (all in binary mode): size of the SME, industry sector, volume of higher VET on staff, innovative capacity, presence of VET in technical positions, experience in continuous training with VET centres from the regional environment, experience in co-operation for innovation and involvement of operators in advanced organizational planning practices. All these variables were relevant for testing the hypotheses posed or had showed some effect on participation in the previous exploratory bivariate analyses. The technique was applied with essentially descriptive, rather than predictive, aims.

Table 4 shows the model obtained, with the technological sector as a classificatory segmentation variable for the SMEs. It was seen that, when controlled in the analysis, this variable helps explain the relations of participation with different aspects of SMEs' innovation culture. After controlling for the technological level of the companies, two explanatory-predictive models of differences in participation can be obtained: one somewhat simpler for medium-high and high-tech SMEs, and another somewhat broader for medium-low and low-tech ones. As the table shows, when the technological level is controlled, neither the size nor the experience in continuous training with VET centres, nor the volume of higher VET on the staff conditions the explanation of participation.

For high- and medium-high-tech companies, the variables defining the differences are the existence of VET workers in technical positions (the probability of greater

Table 4. Binary logistic regression models for estimating WPI levels of participation (lesser/greater) according to SME technological intensity.

WPI (greater)	High and medium-high technological level			Medium-low and low technological level		
	Valid N = 246			Valid N = 550		
	B	Wald sig.	Exp(B) OR	B	Wald sig.	Exp(B) OR
Metal-machining (yes)	−.843	.006	0.431	−0.630	.001	0.533
Innovative capacity (more)				0.451	.029	1.570
VET technicians (more)	1.202	.000	3.327	1.005	.000	2.731
Co-operate (yes)	0.995	.001	2.704	0.588	.002	1.801
Advanced org. practices (more)				0.866	.000	2.377
Constant	0.127	.607	1.098	−0.753	.000	0.471
Chi^2 significance	.000			.000		
Nagelkerke's R^2	.168			.190		
Hosmer–Lemeshow test sig.	.748			.947		

Source: Authors' elaboration.
Note: Variables not in equations (non-significant): size, volume of higher VET on staff, experience in continuous training.

participation triples) and external co-operation for innovation, with a similarly positive and significant impact. They are also conditioned by the industry sector: the partial influence of being metalworking companies is negative.

Medium-low and low-tech SMEs, which form a larger more varied set in the sample, show a pattern of differences in participation composed of more partial influences: the presence of VET in technical positions and external co-operation also impact participation (with the inverse influence of the metal-machining sector being maintained), but there are more variables in play. Specifically, another two characteristics of the companies would help predict greater VET employee participation: involvement in organizational learning practices (the probability of participation being double, all else being equal) and the comparative perception of the company's innovative capacity.

5. Discussion

The results obtained confirm the strong role of VET workers in innovation activities independently of the technological level of the company. For all firms, the presence of VET workers in technical areas triples the probability of a high level of involvement by those workers in innovation activities, therefore confirming the suggestions from authors who point out at the importance of VET skills for R&D and innovation (Tether et al., 2005; Toner, 2011; Toner et al., 2004). H1 has therefore been confirmed.

On the other hand, a strong relationship has been shown to exist between external co-operation for innovation (often with agents from the regional environment), which can be seen as an indicator of intensity of innovation (Otero et al., 2014), and a high level of VET employee involvement in innovation activities: the probability of such involvement almost triples for high-tech firms and doubles for low-tech firms, thus confirming H3. As stated in the theoretical framework, the importance of VET worker involvement in innovation is not limited to internal activities and goes beyond the boundaries of the organization in establishing trust-based relationships which are necessary for knowledge exchange (González de la Fe et al., 2012; Prud'homme & Dankbaar, 2011).

It has been found that a high level of VET worker participation in innovation is strongly related both to the firms' innovative capacity and to the existence of advanced organizational practices in the case of medium-low and low-technology SMEs, but not in the case of medium-high and high-technology SMEs. In the case of low-tech firms, which amount to 66% of the sample and show a much larger variety of worker participation situations, these two variables (along with those measured in H1 and H3) make a difference with respect to VET workers' involvement in innovation.

The results obtained for low-tech SMEs are especially interesting, and suggest that high VET employee involvement is a more central characteristic of their 'mode of innovation'. H2, which has been confirmed for firms of this technological level, states that there is a strong relationship between the innovative capacity of the firm and a high involvement of VET personnel in innovation activities (the probability of high involvement of VET employees in innovation being 1.6 times bigger for firms which are more innovative than their direct competitors). In parallel, also for low-tech SMEs, high involvement of VET technicians and trades in innovation is strongly related to a more participative organizational style in which operators (the lowest level of the hierarchy) have a higher level of participation in planning, evaluation and improvement activities (the probability of VET employees' high involvement more than doubles, therefore confirming H4). Thus, intermediate worker involvement appears to be a more critical factor of the innovation mode of low-tech SMEs, strongly associated with both technical and organizational aspects of an innovation culture.

In broad terms, the results obtained for low-tech firms seem quite compatible with the recent literature in aspects such as the wide reach of innovation activities (Amara, Landry, Becheikh, & Ouimet, 2008), the weaker position in product innovation (Hirsch-Kreinsen, 2015; Kirner et al., 2015), the importance of external co-operation, which is often weaker in these firms (Amara et al., 2008; Arundel et al., 2008; Heidenreich, 2009), and the factors affecting the novelty of innovation (Freel, 2005).

In our study, important levels of innovation and improvement activities have been found for low-tech SMEs, similar to those of high-tech firms, with the exception of product innovation, in which the former have a somewhat weaker position (68.4% vs. 74.7% of high-tech firms, a difference which is significant at the $p < .05$ level). Regarding external co-operation for innovation, low-tech firms have also a somewhat weaker position (4.5-point difference), which nevertheless does not reach significance levels. In this respect, the key aspect is the innovative capacity of the firms. SMEs from all technology levels which are more innovative than their direct competitors co-operate in a much higher proportion (64% against 36%) than those which are less innovative. In the case of low-technology SMEs, both external co-operation and innovative capacity have been found to be strongly related to high involvement in innovation activities by VET employees. This last result is compatible with Freel's (2005, p. 131) finding that a higher proportion of technicians in manufacturing SMEs discriminate novel from incremental innovators. It also seems to be in line with Hirsch-Kreinsen's (2015) remark that in low-tech sectors, process innovation often takes place without formal R&D, and it is potentially initiated and always conducted by staff who are responsible for ongoing functions, such as engineers, technicians, master craftsmen and even operators.

With respect to advanced organizational practices, in particular high involvement by operators in regular planning, evaluation and improvement meetings in low-tech SMEs, the results obtained seem to indicate the importance of a participative culture which reaches the production workers and operators, as well as the middle level trades and technicians. In their study of work organization and innovative performance in EU countries (not limited to SMEs), Arundel, Lorenz, Lundvall, and Valeyre (2007) have shown that the use of work teams in itself does not need to be associated with high levels of discretionary learning, and that it is in fact more related to lean forms of production (quite extended in Southern European countries such as Spain) in which work is highly constrained and problem-solving and learning are more limited (but nevertheless higher than in taylorist and traditional organization forms). In this line, studies such as Balconi (2002) and Delbridge, Lowe, and Oliver (2000) point out at important differences in work participation between skilled workers, who would have an important involvement in production management and improvement activities, and lower level operators, whose role would be very limited. In this context, the results obtained in our study about operator involvement in low-tech SMEs seem to point out at the existence in certain firms of a participatory organizational culture which complements high involvement by VET personnel in innovation activities. In other words, for those firms, both technical and organizational aspects of innovation would reinforce each other, reaching the lowest level of the hierarchy.

6. Final reflections

The VET system is an important element of the regional environment of industrial firms, especially SMEs, but so far little attention has been paid to its role in innovation. From the perspective of innovation studies, some authors have noted the importance of intermediary workers and the VET system in the innovation system, especially in less R&D-intensive sectors, but hardly any empirical measures have been carried out in this regard (Toner, 2011; Toner & Dalitz, 2012).

Studying the role of VET employees in innovation seems especially relevant in the Spanish context, characterized by a relative weakness of VET qualifications (CEDEFOP, 2010), a lower innovation level in low-tech industries (Robertson & Patel, 2007), a lack of integration between formal and continuous VET (Homs, 2008) and less widespread practices of organizational learning (Arundel et al., 2007), as compared to European countries of reference. This study, based on a survey of 1142 Spanish industrial SMEs, sought to measure the participation of employees with a VET profile in innovation, as well as analysing the different factors that influence that participation. It has been shown that 51% of the firms studied perform innovations with significant participation from their VET workers, and that this participation is especially important in process improvement, process innovation and product improvement activities.

With respect to the main question formulated in Section 1, it may be concluded that VET employee involvement is an important element in the innovation processes of SMEs in general, and that it takes on greater strategic importance in the innovating culture of low-tech SMEs, in both a technical and an organizational sense. Regarding the second research question, which deals with the specific variables that condition participation by intermediary staff in innovation, it may be concluded that in the case of low-tech SMEs, some aspects of the innovation culture, both in a technical/strategic sense of comparative advantage 'vis-à-vis' competitors and in an organizational sense (an organizational style that prioritizes operator participation), exercise a specific influence on the level of VET employee involvement in innovation, with the importance, in common with the high-tech sector, of the presence of VET employees in technical departments and of co-operation with external agents (an indicator of an intensive level in innovation) being maintained.

In our view, the results obtained in this study have certain implications for Spanish education and industry authorities. In the last three decades, education policies directed to the promotion of university education in Spain have reinforced the dualization of the labour force between university degree holders and those who do not reach post-secondary education levels, resulting in a shortage of intermediate technical skills adapted to firms' production needs. In this context, it seems necessary to push the development of the VET system more strongly in its different dimensions: formal education and relationship with the university, continuous training more adapted to industrial needs and a higher profile in technical services offered to SMEs, especially from low-technology sectors, which are outside the scope of institutional agents devoted to technology transfer (such as public research centres, universities and technology centres). As for innovating firms, they should be encouraged to recruit and train workers with a VET profile. This study has shown that VET personnel are capable of intervening (and do in fact intervene) in many of the innovations carried out by industrial SMEs. The firms should also be more aware of VET institutes' training and technological resources as knowledge diffusion agents in the regional environment.

The results obtained have certain limitations. The sample used is representative of manufacturing SMEs from the most industrialized regions in Spain, but the study carried out so far has not looked at the differences between regions, which have distinct innovation environments (education and innovation policies, industrial specialization, training structures, etc.). On the other hand, in European countries where VET is more extended, different patterns of firm behaviour might be found. Because of these reasons, and taking into account the limited attention dedicated to this topic in the innovation studies literature, further empirical research should be carried out with a view to confirming and developing the results obtained.

Note

1. Hirsch-Kreinsen (2008, p. 12) found that medium and low-tech industries accounted for 60% of employment in the manufacturing industry of EU-15 and Frietsch and Neuhäusler (2015, p. 71) make a similar estimate for Germany.

Disclosure statement

No potential conflict of interest was reported by the authors.

Funding

This work was supported by Basque Government's Department of Education, Universities and Research (IT593-13) and the Spanish Ministry of Science and Innovation (CSO2011-29410-C03-01).

References

Albizu, E., Olazaran, M., Lavía, C., & Otero, B. (2011). Relationships between vocational training centres and industrial SMEs in the basque country: A regional innovation system approach. *Intangible Capital*, 7(2), 329–355. doi:10.3926/ic.2011.v7n2.p329-355

Amara, N., Landry, R., Becheikh, N., & Ouimet, M. (2008). Learning and novelty of innovation in established manufacturing SMEs. *Technovation, 28* (7), 450–463. doi:10.1016/j.technovation. 2008.02.001

Arundel, A., Bordoy, C., & Kanerva, M. (2008). *Neglected innovators: How do innovative firms that do not perform R&D innovate?* Manchester: MERIT, Inno-Metrics Thematic Paper.

Arundel, A., Lorenz, E., Lundvall, B., & Valeyre, A. (2007). How Europe's economies learn: A comparison of work organization and innovation mode for the EU-15. *Industrial and Corporate Change, 16*(6), 1175–1210. doi:10.1093/icc/dtm035

Balconi, M. (2002). Tacitness, codification of technological knowledge and the organisation of industry. *Research Policy, 31*(3), 357–379. doi:10.1016/S0048-7333(01)00113-5

Bolland, E. J., & Hofer, C. W. (2001). *Las empresas del futuro: Cómo funcionan las compañías de alta tecnología en los Estados Unidos de América*. México: Oxford University Press.

CEDEFOP. (2010). *La modernización de la formación profesional*. Luxemburgo: Oficina de Publicaciones de la Unión Europea. Retrieved February, 2011, from http://www.cedefop. europa.eu/EN/Files/9013_es.pdf

CEDEFOP. (2011). The impact of vocational education and training on company performance (CEDEFOP Research paper, n° 19). Luxembourg: CEDEFOP.

Curtain, R. (2004a). Innovation and vocational education and training. In S. Dawe (Ed.), *Vocational education and training and innovation: Research readings* (pp. 42–58). Adelaide: National Centre for Vocational Education research.

Curtain, R. (2004b). *Vocational education and training, innovation and globalisation*. Adelaide: National Centre for Vocational Education Research. Retrieved October 5, 2016, from http:// files.eric.ed.gov/fulltext/ED495142.pdf

Delbridge, R., Lowe, J., & Oliver, N. (2000). Shopfloor responsibilities under lean teamworking. *Human Relations, 53*(11), 1459–1479.

Edquist, C. (1997). *Systems of innovation: Technologies, institutions and organizations*. London: Pinter.

Ferrier, F., Trood, C., & Whittingham, K. (2003). *Going boldly into the future: A VET journey into The National innovation system*. Leabrook: National Centre for Vocational Education Research.

Freel, M. (2005). Patterns of innovation and skills in small firms. *Technovation, 25*, 123–134. doi:10. 1016/S0166-4972(03)00082-8

Frietsch, R., & Neuhäusler, P. (2015). The development of qualification and employment structures in non-R&D-intensive industry sectors - The case of Germany. In O. Som & E. Kirner (Eds.), *Low-tech innovation* (pp. 67–78). Cham: Springer International Publishing. doi: 10.1007/978-3-319-09973-6_5

García-Pinto, A., García, J. M., & Piñeiro, P. (2010). Incidencia de las políticas de recursos humanos en la transferencia de conocimiento y su efecto sobre la innovación. *Investigaciones Económicas en Dirección y Economía de la Empresa, 16*(1), 149–163.

González de la Fe, T., Hernández Hernández, N., & van Oostrom, M. (2012). Innovación, cultura y tamaño: La microempresa en una región ultraperiférica. *Arbor, 188*(753), 113–134. doi:10.3989/ arbor.2012.753n1008

Guthrie, H., & Dawe, S. (2004). Overview. In S. Dawe (Ed.), *Vocational education and training and innovation: Research readings* (pp. 10–19). Adelaide: National Centre for Vocational Education Research.

Heidenreich, M. (2009). Innovation patterns and location of European low- and medium-technology industries. *Research Policy, 38*, 483–494. doi:10.1016/j.respol.2008.10.005

Hirsch-Kreinsen, H. (2008). 'Low technology': A forgotten sector in innovation policy. *Journal of Technology Management and Innovation, 3*, 11–19. doi:10.4067/S0718-27242008000100002

Hirsch-Kreinsen, H. (2015). Innovation in low-tech industries: Current conditions and future prospects. In O. Som & E. Kirner (Eds.), *Low-tech innovation* (pp. 17–32). Switzerland: Springer International. doi: 10.1007/978-3-319-09973-6_5

HM Treasury. (2004). *Skills in the global economy*. London: HMSO.

Homs, O. (2008). *La Formación Profesional en España. Hacia la sociedad del conocimiento*. Barcelona: Fundación La Caixa.

Janz, B. D., & Prasarnphanich, P. (2003). Understanding the antecedents of effective knowledge management: The importance of knowledge-centered culture. *Decision Sciences*, *34*(2), 351–384. doi:10.1111/1540-5915.02328

Jensen, M., Johnson, B., Lorenz, E., & Lundvall, B. (2007). Forms of knowledge and modes of innovation. *Research Policy*, *36*(5), 680–693. doi:10.1016/j.respol.2007.01.006

Jiménez-Jiménez, D., & Sanz-Valle, R. (2008). Could HRM support organizational innovation? *The International Journal of Human Resource Management*, *19*(7), 1208–1221. doi:10.1080/09585190802109952

Kaloudis, A., Sandven, T., & Smith, K. (2005). Structural change, growth and innovation: The roles of medium and low tech industries, 1980–2002. *Journal of Mental Changes*, *11*(1–2), 49–73.

Kaufmann, A., & Tödtling, F. (2003). Innovation patterns of SMEs. In B. Asheim, A. Isaksen, C. Nauwelaers, & F. Tödtling (Eds.), *Regional innovation policy for small-medium enterprises* (pp. 78–115). Cheltenham: Edward Elgar.

Kirner, E., Som, O., & Jäger, A. (2015). Innovation strategies and patterns of non-R&D-performing and non-R&D-intensive firms. In O. Som, & E. Kirner (Eds.), *Low-tech innovation* (pp. 91–112). Switzerland: Springer International.

Lavía, C., Olazaran, M., Albizu, E., & Otero, B. (2012). Formación continua en centros de FP y actividades de innovación en las pymes industriales. *Arbor*, *188*(753), 153–170. doi:10.3989/arbor.2012.753n1010

Lavía, C., Otero, B., Albizu, E., & Olazaran, M. (2016). Perfiles empresariales y participación de los trabajadores con cualificaciones intermedias en actividades de innovación: el caso del País Vasco. *Revista Española de Sociología*, *25*(3), 61–80 doi:10.22325/fes/res.25.3.2016.367.

Lundvall, B., & Lorenz, E. (2007). *Modes of innovation and knowledge taxonomies in the learning economies*. Oslo: CAS workshop on innovation in firms.

Lundvall, B. Å. (1992). *National systems of innovation: Towards a theory of innovation and interactive learning*. London: Pinter.

Lundvall, B. Å. (1998). Innovation as an interactive process: From user-producers interaction to The National system of innovation. In G. Dosi, C. Freeman, G. Silverberg, & L. Soete (Eds.), *Technical change and economic theory* (pp. 349–367). London: Pinter.

Lundvall, B. Å., & Nielsen, P. (2007). Knowledge management and innovation performance. *International Journal of Manpower*, *28*(3–4), 207–223. doi:10.1108/01437720710755218

Lundvall, B. Å., Rasmussen, P., & Lorenz, E. (2008). Education in the learning economy: A European perspective. *Policy Futures in Education*, *6*(6), 681–700. doi:10.2304/pfie.2008.6.6.681

Moodie, G. (2006). Vocational education institutions' role in national innovation. *Research in Post-Compulsory Education*, *11*(2), 131–140. doi:10.1080/13596740600768901

Nonaka, I. (1994). A dynamic theory of organizational knowledge creation. *Organization Science*, *5*(1), 14–37. doi:10.1287/orsc.5.1.14

Otero, B., Lavía, C., Albizu, E., & Olazaran, M. (2014). Innovación y cooperación en el SRI del País Vasco. *Revista Internacional de Organizaciones*, *13*, 135–161. doi:10.17345/rio13.135-161

Pérez, C., & Quevedo, P. (2006). Human resources management and its impacto n innovation performance in companies. *International Journal of Technology Management*, *35*(1–4), 11–28. doi:10.1504/IJTM.2006.009227

Prud'homme van Reine, P., & Dankbaar, B. (2011). A virtuous circle? Co-evolution of regional and corporate cultures. *European Planning Studies*, *19*(11), 1865–1883. doi:10.1080/09654313.2011.618684

Robertson, P., & Patel, P. (2007). New wine in old bottles: Technological diffusion in developed economies. *Research Policy*, *36*, 708–721. doi:10.1016/j.respol.2007.01.008

Robertson, P., Smith, K., & von Tuzelmann, N. (2009). Innovation in low- and medium-technology industries. Introduction. *Research Policy*, *38*(3), 441–446. doi:10.1016/j.respol.2008.10.019

Rosenfeld, S. (1998). *Technical colleges, technology deployment and regional development*. Modena: OECD.

Ruth, K., & Deitmer, L. (2010). The relationship between technical and vocational education and training and innovation. In E. Baker, B. McGaw, & P. Peterson (Eds.), *International encyclopedia of education* (pp. 423–428). Oxford: Elsevier.

Saxenian, A. (1994). *Regional advantage: Culture and competition in silicon valley and route 128.* Cambridge, MA: Harvard University Press.

Shapira, P., & Rosenfeld, S. (1996). *Overview of technology diffusion policies and programs to enhance the technological absorptive capabilities of small and médium enterprises.* Background paper prepared for the Organization for Economic Cooperation and Development Directorate for Science, Technology and Industry. Retrieved October 5, 2016, from https://www.scheller. gatech.edu/centers-initiatives/ciber/projects/workingpaper/1997/shapira2.pdf

Tether, B., Mina, A., Consoli, D., & Gagliardi, D. (2005). *A literature review on skills and innovation: How does successful innovation impact on the demand of skills and how do skills drive innovation?* Manchester: ESRC Centre for Research on Innovation and Competition, University of Manchester.

Tödtling, F., Prud'homme van Reine, P., & Dörhöfer, S. (2011). Open innovation and regional culture – findings from different industrial and regional settings. *European Planning Studies,* *19*(11), 1885–1907. doi:10.1080/09654313.2011.618688

Toner, P. (2011). *Workforce skills and innovation: An overview of major themes in the literature.* Paris: OECD.

Toner, P., & Dalitz, R. (2012). Vocational education and training: The 'terra incognita'of innovation policy. *Prometheus. Critical Studies in Innovation,* *30*(4), 411–426. doi:10.1080/08109028.2012. 746412

Toner, P., Marceau, J., Hall, R., & Considine, G. (2004). Innovation agents: Vocational education and training skills in the present and future Australian innovation system. In S. Dawe (Ed.), *Vocational education and training and innovation: Research readings* (pp. 84–105). Adelaide: NCVER.

Toner, P., Turpin, T., Wooley, R., & Lloyd, C. (2010). *The role and contribution of tradespeople and technicians in Australian research & development: An exploratory study.* Sydney: Centre for Innovation Studies, University of Western Sydney.

Toner, P., & Woolley, R. (2016). Perspectives and debates on vocational education and training, skills and the prospects for innovation. *Revista Española de Sociología,* *25*(3), 319–342. doi: 10. 22325/fes/res.25.3.2016.319

Appendix: Independent variables and indicators used

Variable	Definition	Indicator
Size	Number of employees	Up to 50/bigger than 50
Technological sector	R&D intensity (high, medium high, medium low, low)	High and medium high vs. medium low and low
Activity	NACE09 codes for industry	Metal-machining activities (24,25,28,29,30,33) vs. others
Product innovation	Market introduction of a good or service that is new or significantly improved with respect to its capabilities, user friendliness, components or subsystems. The new products or services differ significantly in their characteristics or intended uses from products previously produced by the firm. The product innovations must be new to the enterprise, but they do not need to be new to the market or sector. Design is an integral part of the development and implementation of product innovations (OECD Oslo Manual)	Yes/no

(Continued)

Appendix Continued.

Variable	Definition	Indicator
Process innovation	Implementation of a new or significantly improved production process, distribution method or supporting activity. This includes significant changes in techniques, equipment and/or software. Process innovations must be new to the enterprise, but they do not need to be new to the sector or market (Oslo Manual)	Yes/no
Product improvement	Modification or improvement of technical characteristics, components or materials of existing products which usually require technical drawings modification before being applied to production	Yes/no
Process improvement	Modification or improvement of existing processes which usually do not imply the design of new processes	Yes/no
Organizational innovation	Implementation of new organizational methods (including knowledge management) in the firm's business practices, workplace organization or external relations that have not been previously used by the enterprise (Oslo Manual)	Yes/no
New channels, markets and relationships	Implementation of new marketing concepts or strategies that differ significantly from the enterprise's existing marketing methods. They include the development of new marketing practices, such as targeting new markets or market segments and developing new ways of promoting products. They exclude changes that alter the product's functional or user characteristics (these are product innovations) (Oslo Manual)	Yes/no
Innovative capacity	Self-perception of the company's innovation capacity as related to direct competitors (lower/equal/higher)	Higher capacity/lower capacity (equal or lower capacity)
External cooperation	Collaboration with agents external to the firm in innovation-related projects in the last 4 years	Cooperates (yes/no)
Presence of VET workers	Percentage of VET workers in the workforce	50% or lower/more than 50%
Presence of high-level VET workers	Percentage of high-level VET workers in the workforce	50% or lower/more than 50%
Continuous training	Receives continuous training courses offered by VET institutes from the regional environment	Continuous training (yes/no)
VET technicians	Presence of VET workers in any of the following areas: (1) technical office, (2) R&D department, (3) manufacturing and process engineering	Presence of VET workers in technical areas (yes/no)
Advanced organizational practice: ad hoc work teams	Degree of operator participation: none/a little/ quite a lot/a lot	Advanced practice with VET worker participation: lower (none/little) vs. higher (quite a lot/a lot)
Advanced organizational practices: work planning and organization	Degree of operator participation: none/a little/ quite a lot/a lot	Advanced practice with VET worker participation: lower (none/little) vs. higher (quite a lot/a lot)
Advanced organizational practice: regular improvement meetings	Degree of operator participation: none/a little/ quite a lot/a lot	Advanced practice with VET worker participation: lower (none/little) vs. higher (quite a lot/a lot)

Pragmatic urbanism: London's railway arches and small-scale enterprise

Francesca Froy and Howard Davis

ABSTRACT

Marginal spaces are increasingly being taken up for commercial use in London. This includes railway arches, which are appropriated for many different social and economic activities. This article presents the findings of a study on 165 arches in three London neighbourhoods (Hackney, Bethnal Green and Bermondsey), which found the arches to host a disproportionate amount of manufacturing, in addition to concentrations of sectors such as food and drink; and taxi services. Despite being part of Britain's industrial heritage, the arches have proved highly adaptable 'hybrid' spaces supporting office, retail, wholesale and production. They are also modular – businesses move into neighbouring arches as they expand. The arches are therefore well-suited to the postfordist economy of the inner city, which incorporates a highly networked system of small-scale manufacturers and retailers that require flexible and affordable small spaces close to commercial centres. Being arranged side-by-side, and open onto the street, they support knowledge-sharing between firms, while also bringing life to neighbourhoods. The arches have a spatial/ functional configuration that might be copied in new forms of industrial development. Indeed, they suggest the possibility of a new spatial form – 'industrial streets' as opposed to industrial estates.

Once marginal spaces are increasingly coming into commercial use in UK cities. This includes spaces under railway arches – which, despite being part of the country's Victorian heritage, have proved surprisingly adaptable to current business needs. While railway arches were originally designed for a specific infrastructural purpose, they have been appropriated by different activities, hosting bars and restaurants; theatres and gyms; centres for car repair and car washes; manufacturing units, and music practice venues amongst other things.

This article presents a spatial study of railway arches in three London neighbourhoods, using the methodology of space syntax, and places it in the context of broader research on small and medium-sized enterprises (SME's), micro-businesses and the 'postfordist economy' in cities. The latter includes artisanal, small-scale manufacturing and firms engaged in symbolic production (Hutton, 2008; Scott, 2001; Soja, 2000). The appropriation of railway arches is an example of 'pragmatic urbanism' and the commercial use of marginal spaces due to high property demand. However, railway arches appear particularly well-suited to many SMEs and micro-firms, being adaptable to hybrid uses, and promoting a culture of communication that may support innovation from the bottom up. Indeed, the 'industrial streets' created by railway arches can serve as a model for other types of commercial property development.

The questions this article explores are:

- What purposes do railway arches serve? What kind of economic activities happen under them? How do they differ from other types of commercial space (e.g. industrial estates)?
- What are the spatial characteristics of the arches – individually, and in their relationship to the surrounding urban fabric?
- Why do they attract small-scale producers including SMEs?
- How are policy makers treating them; are they under threat; could they be better used?
- Are there lessons that can be learnt from the success of railway arches for the design of commercial space in cities?

In order to answer these questions, the article draws on a research project on railway arches in three London neighbourhoods: Hackney, Bermondsey and Bethnal Green (Froy, 2013), in addition to research on other marginal commercial spaces in London (Davis, 2013). In the three neighbourhoods, the arches were observed visually, to understand their primary architectural characteristics, the ways they had been modified and their immediate relationship to the street. Adjacent arches were mapped; so clusters of uses could be seen visually and quantitatively explored. Space syntax analysis was used to assess the accessibility of the arches to the broader street network. Interviews with owners and employees in the arches helped reveal perceptions as to utility and location. Interviews were also carried out with Network Rail (as a principal landlord for the arches), and with the Greater London Authority and two London borough councils (Hackney and Southwark), to understand how the arches fit into broader local economic development strategies.

The article is structured as follows: after a literature review, a descriptive section sets out a brief history of the railway arches in London, and summarizes their key spatial characteristics. An account of the principal economic uses of the arches is then contextualized within the broader theoretical literature, while the role of different policy actors is considered. The article concludes by identifying potential lessons for the broader design of commercial spaces in cities.

The theoretical context: industrial urbanism

This work lies at the intersection of studies of urban form and structure, and studies of the emergence of new economic formations in cities, focusing on SMEs and micro-firms. There has been a long history of research into what Soja calls 'industrial urbanism' (2000), focusing on urban worlds of production and the links between economic production and urban structure (Harvey, 1973; Jacobs, 1969; Scott, 1988). While manufacturing had been in decline in UK cities since the 1970s, there has been a recent reemergence, caused by a global economic shift from mass-production to postfordist economies, based on smaller-scale artisanal production and services, and the cultural and symbolic economy (Dellot, 2015; Hutton, 2008; Piore & Sabel, 1984). Postfordist economic activities appear to work well in dense city environments, where they can draw on a skilled diverse labour force and multi-layered urban markets.

Soja describes how industrial urbanism has consistently highlighted the spatiality of economic development in cities, with theorists such as Scott (1988) and Hutton (2008) focusing on the factors which lead to the concentration of SMEs in particular city districts and on the emergence of the 'new economy of the inner city'. A number of theorists have explored how the colocation of firms in particular parts of cities can lead to 'innovative milieux' and the sharing of tacit knowledge between businesses (Hall, 1998; Hessler & Zimmerman, 2008). Economists have also analysed the role of urban density in creating agglomeration economies, heightening innovation, learning and knowledge-sharing (Duranton & Puga, 2003).

However, less attention has been paid to the materiality of the built environment which hosts industry in cities (Rantisi & Leslie, 2010), and to how production finds its place alongside other land uses. While Hutton (2008) includes maps showing detailed land uses, for example, he does not look in fine grain at where production sits within urban street networks or at the nature of particular production spaces. Industrial architecture in cities has changed over the last two hundred years from spatial formations in which workshops were closely integrated with dwellings; to purpose-built buildings that were still in neighbourhoods of dwellings; to the establishment of large factories and industrial districts separate from residential neighbourhoods. The need for larger factories, along with the negative environmental impacts of production, prompted the need for cheaper land in places away from residential districts. During the twentieth century, reactions against the nineteenth-century proximity of dwelling and polluting factories resulted in policies that helped form single-use industrial districts with large factories and industrial complexes.

Most recently however, postfordist changes to production have prompted a need for building types and urban form that are different from large-scale twentieth-century models. Much new industry is cleaner, requiring less space and in closer proximity to design and sales functions. In some cases design, production, wholesale and retail are all happening under the same roof. As production has reemerged in cities, theorists have noted a blurring between manufacturing, design and retail, leading to the creation of hybrid forms of urban enterprise (Coyle, 2001; Evans, 2009). All this means that a 'mixed-use' approach may be more appropriate, in which factories and shops are intermixed, and located near residential areas.

Finding appropriate spaces for production is a challenge, however, in many cities, given the high level of competition for residential land uses which has accompanied what some have termed an 'urban renaissance' (Urban Task Force, 2005). Rosa (2014) has highlighted that enterprises are increasingly having recourse to 'residual spaces', which were not designed for their current use, including spaces such as railway arches. This can be seen as a form of pragmatic urbanism where decisions and decision-making about location, buildings and/or use are not planned in advance but come about as a result of immediate need and opportunity. Railway arches, for example, were built simply to keep the railroad tracks above ground. Masonry arches were suitable for this single purpose, and were not built with the idea that they would be used for anything else. It was only later that the architectural space they form was seen to be useful; so pragmatic considerations prompted their use for other social and business functions.

While railway arches may be chosen as a 'last resort' in the competition for space, these spaces may also offer benefits in terms of their design and location, for both old and post-fordist industries alike. To explore their spatial characteristics in more detail, this paper draws on a methodology called space syntax. Since the 1980s, space syntax has used graph analysis to better understand the relationship between urban form and the location of economic activities (e.g. Griffiths, 2017/forthcoming; Hillier & Hanson, 1984; Penn, Perdikogianni, & Motram, 2009; Vaughan, 2015). The properties of the overall street network in a city are found to influence enterprise location, in part due to the higher like-lihood of pedestrian movement happening in certain parts of the street network. Space syntax also explores spatial relationships at a microscale, for example between pedestrian movement and the number of building entrances on a street.

As far as the authors are aware, this spatial analysis of the business use of railway arches is unique. Rosa (2014) has analysed arches as assets and constraints for urban regeneration in Manchester, identifying how they became part of the symbolic discourse in a 'post-industrial' era. Apart from this, analysis on railway arches has been relatively small scale (e.g. Day, 2012; Dwyer, 2009; Haywood, 2008) and detailed analysis of business uses absent.

A spatial description of the arches

Some estimate that there may be up to 10,000 arches in London (Spittles, 2016). Network Rail owns and rents out many of them, hosting 4000 business tenants London-wide, while some are also owned and let by Transport for London. Railway arches in business use can be found in many different cities in the UK. In London, the best-known arches are found in Bankside, Bethnal Green, Bermondsey, Brixton, Elephant and Castle, Hackney, Peckham, Shoreditch and Vauxhall. Elsewhere in Europe, railway arches are found in cities such as Paris, Berlin and Rotterdam.

London's arches were mostly constructed as part of the Victorian development of the railways. Many of the railways built into London had to penetrate the existing city using creative means, such as tunnels, cuttings, embankments and viaducts (Dennis, 2008). In the south and east of the city, the use of viaducts was particularly prevalent, partly because marshy land made cuttings more difficult. The London and Greenwich Railway (1836) into London Bridge (see Figure 1), the Eastern Counties Railway (1840) into Bishopsgate and the London and Blackwall Railway (1841) into Fenchurch Street all involved long brick viaducts. By building rail tracks on elevated platforms, the railway developers preserved existing road routes and minimized the need for compensation to property owners due to loss of land (Rosa, 2014). The arches supported the heavy railway uses efficiently while also allowing water to drain. To give an idea of scale, the London and Greenwich railway involved 878 railway arches, with 10 km of viaduct running through the south-central London area (Cross River Partnership, 2003).

While some arches went across streets, thus remaining open to traffic, many were closed off and hence available for occupation. Initially it was hoped that one by-

Figure 1. The London Bridge–Greenwich railway viaduct near London Bridge, 1836. Source: Bell's Life in London and Sporting Chronicle 30 October 1836. Public Commons – no permission required.

product of the railway arch development would be housing (Knight, 1836). However the noise, pollution and vibration of the trains made them unattractive places to live. The arches were relegated to a relatively marginal set of business uses. Kellett (1969) states that Manchester's arches were let for use as smithies, marine stores, stables, mortar mills, the storage of old tubs, casks and lumber and other 'low class' trades in the late nineteenth century. Land values around them were therefore depressed, with those around the city's south junction remaining static for 20 years despite a 75% increase in the rest of the city. There is evidence, however, that arches have long functioned as local 'refuges' and spaces for bottom up economic activities in UK cities, given that they provided large spaces at little or no financial cost (Dwyer, 2009). The arches have also been adapted over history for surprising uses, such as schools for the destitute, stables for horses and makeshift air raid shelters during the Second World war (Cross River Partnership, 2003; Dwyer, 2009).

For this research, 165 different railway arches were analysed in three case study neighbourhoods, alongside less-detailed observations elsewhere in London. The specific railway arches studied included all the arches in Three Colts Lane and Dunbridge Street in Bethnal Green, Mentmore Terrace in Hackney, and Rope Walk, Enid Street and Druid Street in Bermondsey. These areas form part of the Inner London 'city fringe' (Hutton, 2008). While the Hackney and Bermondsey arches host diverse activities, including lively scenes of cultural and symbolic production and consumption; the site chosen in Bethnal Green principally hosts a sector that has more traditionally been associated with railway arches – that of car repairs. The case studies were therefore felt to offer an opportunity for comparison of how the railway arches host businesses of the old and 'new' economy.

Railway arches vary considerably in their spatial arrangement. In some cases, long lines of arches form linear spaces almost like terrace streets. One part of a viaduct in South London, for example, aligns a series of streets leading from London Bridge Station out towards South Bermondsey including Tooley Street, Druid Street, Enid Street, Lucey Way and Silwood Street. When the London and Greenwich railway was originally being built, one journalist anticipated 'the fine spectacle of a street of nearly four miles in extent' (Knight, 1836). In other parts of London, the arches are more discontinuous. They are sometimes found tucked into the corner of an intersection between the railway and a perpendicular street creating triangular yards. In other cases, railway arches are only accessible from narrow streets that run parallel to the tracks but are gated off or difficult to access from the neighbouring street.

Despite seeming uniform at first glance, railway arches are in fact fairly irregular, creating commercial spaces with varied footprints. As the railways were designed to curve around corners and split into junctions, this often created long arches, and in some cases cavernous internal spaces under the tracks. Most of the arches in London are sized between 40 and 100 m^2 but larger properties can range from 650 m^2 up to over 1000 m^2 (Cross River Partnership, 2003). Some arch spaces have a front and back that open out onto the two sides of the railway line, while others are split in the middle into two, with each side being used for different purposes. Sometimes the backs of arches are bricked up, leaving a blank façade. The arches have the benefit of existing as modular spaces that can be linked together and added to by joining together neighbouring arches, while the high ceiling heights frequently permit the construction of mezzanines. The arches often require high maintenance, however, as they are rarely watertight. The owner of the London Fields Brewery in the arches in Mentmore Terrace, Hackney employed several people, including a plumber and electrician just to maintain the arches in a fit state for their brewing processes.

Railway arches as 'industrial streets'

Railway arches show interesting properties with regard to their relationship with the street. They often have brick or metal fronts, with large entrances that can be shut by roller shutter doors. There has been a tendency in recent years to renovate arches by adding glass fronts to increase light and visibility. Both old and new arch facades are thus relatively open. This openness is reinforced by the fact that many have a direct relationship to the street, with entrances giving onto the pavement, as opposed to having a yard or car park in front of them (see Figure 2). Over 70% of the arches studied had a direct relationship with the street. The openness of the arches facilitates access and may encourage communication between arch users. It is, however, disrupted by the fact that many arches are locked up, particularly at night, leading to what Hanson would describe as a 'ruptured interface' (2000, p.113).

Where the arches are arranged linearly side by side, they create a continuous set of entrances onto the street similar to that of terraced housing. This means that the railway arches are highly 'constituted' – a term used by Hanson (2000) to refer to

Figure 2. Arches in Druid Street, Bermondsey. Source: Author's photographs.

the degree to which public space has entrances opening onto it. The Mentmore Terrace arches in Hackney, for example, show relatively high constitutedness in comparison to a neighbouring industrial estate and have a ratio of entrances/street length that is only exceeded by a local terraced street. The arches can in this sense be seen as 'industrial streets'. They are also well-embedded into their surrounding urban fabric – in the three sites studied, 60% were most likely to be found opposite housing, with 80% of these being found opposite social housing. This is in contrast with traditional housing estates, which are often separated from their surrounding street network and organized into relatively large building blocks, often with blank facades, and with fewer entrances.

When the railways were built, there were concerns amongst commentators such as Charles Booth that they would accentuate problems of poverty in the city by creating 'barriers' between neighbourhoods and reinforcing 'slum tendencies' (Reeder & Hyde, 1984). The idea of railways as barriers and dead-ends has continued to be prevalent in the literature. In South London, the seven wards that the railway viaduct straddles are within the 20% most deprived in the country. The Cross River Partnership (2003) argues that

> The high levels of deprivation on employment, income and education indices in an area located so close to Central London, with its high number of jobs, can in part be explained by the physical separation, and the dissecting impact of the viaduct itself.

However, space syntax analysis shows that the arches in the case study neighbourhoods are in fact relatively accessible as destinations and open to 'through movement', compared with their surrounding urban fabric – perhaps because tunnels through the arches regularly increase connectedness. The Mentmore Terrace arches in Hackney, for example, host six short tunnels over a distance of approximately 400 m (see Figure 3). The extent to which viaducts act as barriers may depend, however, on the width of the railway tracks – the viaducts in south London host particularly long tunnels, with four miles of tunnels in London's south central arc from Vauxhall to Bermondsey. This can be off putting to pedestrians, particularly at night.

Overall, the arches appear to create adaptable commercial and industrial spaces that are interwoven into street networks as opposed to being separated off into industrial estates.

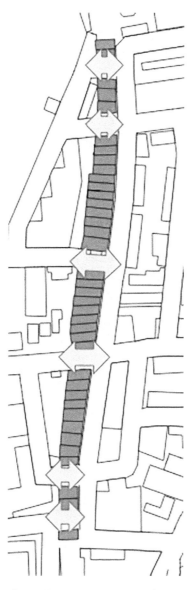

Figure 3. Tunnels through the arches in Mentmore Terrace, Hackney. Source: Author's illustration using an OS VectorMap Local basemap.

When locked up the arches can create 'blank facades' that might discourage pedestrian movement, particularly at night. However, when the arches are well used, they bring industrial and commercial activity into the heart of residential areas.

Railway arches as business sites

To gain a better understanding of the predominant types of business use under the arches, the business uses of the 165 different railway arches were analysed against UK Standard Industry Classification Codes. Six days of fieldwork were carried out at the three sites, observing pedestrian movement, and documenting how the arches were used. In addition, face-to-face interviews were carried out with 47 businesses. The interviews centred on the questions: What is your trade? How long have you been here? Is this your only business? Who do you communicate with in the other arches? and What is it like being based in an arch?

Within the three case study areas, the dominant business categories were found to be vehicle sale and repair, manufacturing and retail (see Figure 4). The predominance of manufacturing firms is perhaps surprising – it was found that 23% of the firms identified in the arches were manufacturing whereas manufacturing firms constituted only 6% of all private-sector businesses in London as a whole at the end of 2013 (Department for Business, Innovation and Skills, 2013). Within the manufacturing sector, industries included metalworking, printing, stonemasonry, carpentry and furniture (see Figure 5). However 45% of the firms were in the food and drink industry, with a particular focus on high-quality specialist products. This tendency towards specialization was also found in the retail sector – out of the arches' retail firms, 95% were found to be specialists. The arches were often found to host smaller individual firms as opposed to chains –

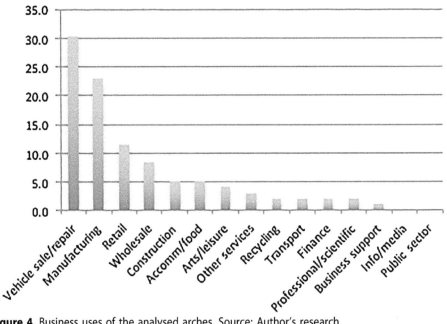

Figure 4. Business uses of the analysed arches. Source: Author's research.

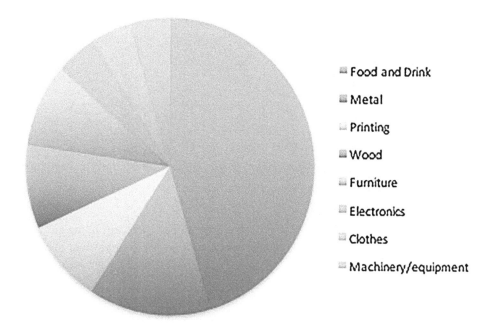

Figure 5. Proportion of different types of manufacturing found in the analysed arches. Source: Author's research.

roughly 50% of the firms interviewed identified that this was their only firm. This reflects a broader pattern of use of the arches by SMEs and micro-enterprises. Network Rail claim that fewer than 20 of their 4000 business units are let to national chains.

The specific business use of the arches may reflect their relative accessibility to patterns of local and city-wide movement – those arches with the highest accessibility to through movement in the case study areas were found to host transport/ logistics and retail firms, suggesting that these businesses may prioritise accessibility when selecting an arch to locate in. The business use of the arches is also affected by local stations. Near Whitechapel, Watney Street passes under the viaduct with the Docklands Light Railway (DLR), close to both the Shadwell DLR station and the Shadwell Overground station. Businesses in nearby arches include several busy convenience stores, attracting customers walking between these two stations and nearby residential areas.

Concentrations of firms in the case study areas

While statistical analysis provided a picture of the overall types of business being hosted in the arches, the neighbourhood case studies uncovered more qualitative information, revealing local concentrations of particular activities in the arches, and the experiences and perceptions of arch users.

The arches in Three Colts Lane and Dunbridge Street in Bethnal Green host a cluster of firms that specialize in servicing taxis. Nineteen firms rent out and repair taxis, or provide specialist parts, insurance and advertising (see Figures 6 and 7). The arches here are surrounded by residential land uses and some retail. Proximity to a major route into the city (Bethnal Green Road) may be one factor in attracting trade, while the concentration of

Figure 6. Business use of the arches in Bethnal Green. Source: Author's research using an OS VectorMap Local basemap.

similar businesses in one place has also provided a multiplier effect, attracting customers through 'critical mass'. One of the taxi repair firms identified, for example, that they never had to advertise but operated through 'word of mouth'. This local cluster seems to have supported longevity amongst local firms – a quarter of the companies in the arches had been there for over 20 years.

One interviewee identified that his cab hire company had been under the arches for 30 years and had been passed on to him by his father. He employed eleven people, operating in three arches which were not side by side (which he found frustrating). Overall he found that although the arches leaked, they were good buildings, more appropriate for manufacturing and servicing than retail due to their large size. While his firm collaborated with other firms under the arches, they did not share staff, in order to avoid sharing 'tricks of the trade'. A neighbouring firm identified that they collaborated in a spirit of 'healthy competition', while another described how 'there is definitely a community here'. Interestingly, while taxi-related companies dominate in Three Colts Lane and Dunbridge Street, the arches further towards the city centre hosted more diverse firms. For example, a printing company mainly uses social media to advertise, while working with local taxi firms and the Bangladeshi community nearby in Brick Lane. They were a relatively new firm, hoping to use the branding brought by the arches to branch into higher value-added markets.

The arches in Mentmore Terrace also host a more diverse set of firms, including bakeries, cafés and restaurants, a brewery, fitness clubs, metal workers, furniture manufacturers, a car wash and a furniture shop. These arches are found between a small industrial estate, and the London Fields park, while also hosting the London Fields railway station. Their location appears to have made the arches attractive to passing trade, although again a multiplier effect has played a role. Following the development of a particularly successful local bakery, the E5 Bakehouse (see Figure 8), the area has started to attract a local 'bohemian' clientele (Huston, Wadley, & Fitzpatrick, 2015; Lloyd, 2004), with several new cafes and restaurants opening up, and pop-up restaurants and bars taking over the yards behind the arches in the summer. Elsewhere in Mentmore Terrace, a very different business specializes in wood-frame production for sofas, working with a firm based in the local industrial estate, who specialize in upholstering. Old and new types of business thus co-exist side by side – although the wood-frame producer expressed concern about potentially being 'priced out' of the viaduct. Local businesses were found to be taking advantage of the 'modular' spaces provided by the arches – for example, the

Figure 7. Taxis outside the local arches in Bethnal Green. Source: Author's photograph.

Figure 8. Interior of E5 bakery, Mentmore Terrace, Hackney. Source: Author's photograph.

London Fields Brewery in Mentmore Terrace owns a number of adjacent arches, each being used for a different type of activity. They host brewing facilities for 13 varieties of local beer, a small bar, a larger beer hall and concert venue and an office (constructed as a mezzanine).

The arches in Bermondsey also show strong diversity of uses, including car and motor-bike companies, a bedding firm, storage facilities and florists. They appear to host greater diversity and a greater industrial presence than the surrounding area, which hosts office accommodation, residential and retail. The food and drink industry is particularly prevalent, as the area has benefitted from spinoffs from the local Borough Market, which specializes in gourmet food products. The many food manufacturers, retailers and wholesalers originally used arches as storage units servicing Borough Market, but the use of those arches has since diversified, partly because the popularity of the Borough Market caused local rents to rise. In addition, an enterprising architectural salvage firm, LASSCOs has taken a long-term lease on the arches in Rope Walk in Bermondsey, using them for storage during the week but renting them out to food market stallholders on Saturdays as the Maltby Street Market. Over the past few years this market has become increasingly successful. One stallholder interviewed sells olive leaf tea, sourced from a grove of 1000 olive trees in Italy. In addition to selling at the market, she also dealt with major London firms such as Harrods, seeing her activities at the market as mainly constituting PR. She commented that the combination of arches, antique furniture and gourmet food creates a three-fold 'branding' that increases attractiveness as a destination. Away from the Maltby Street market, businesses were again found to be exploiting the modular and expandable nature of the arches. Neal's Yard Dairy on Druid Street uses two arches side by side, one for the maturing of cheeses and the other as office accommodation.

Common to the different sites under investigation is a relatively high degree of communication between firms. Within the arches, communication was most frequent with immediate neighbours (cited by 21 businesses), but also between a larger set of firms in the arches (21 businesses) and in the surrounding locality (9 businesses). Only two firms said that they had no communication with the firms around them. Types of cooperation included sharing and using each other's products, and making referrals and helping out in a crisis, while as reported above, some firms appeared more reluctant to share staff. In Maltby Street market, there was a particularly high degree of sharing of ingredients and ideas between the stallholders, leading to a number of new product innovations – for example, a seller of African sauces and condiments had managed to convince the local burger stall to cross-promote their sauces. There was also evidence of the benefits of local networking to support business start-ups. The owner of the E5 Bakehouse in Mentmore Terrace, for example, benefitted from initially being able to set up a kiln to start baking at the neighbouring 'Happy Kitchen', a wholesale-oriented firm that operates from an arch a few doors down. The Happy Kitchen itself initially started up in a business incubator at the Westgate Centre, only a few streets away.

Analysis: the need for a hierarchy of commercial space within the city

Arguably, the leasing of railway arches represents one strategy amongst many in the quest of entrepreneurs to find suitable commercial space, of the right size and at affordable rents, in an increasingly tight property market. They form part of a hierarchy of available kinds of space in their neighbourhoods that helps support a wide variety of business types and sizes, and creates synergies between businesses that might not otherwise exist. In other words, economic diversity may be helped by the spatial diversity that comes partly from the use of informal and ad-hoc spaces, including railway arches.

A study in Dalston (in and near the Ridley Road Market) and in Whitechapel (Davis, 2013), found that businesses were being established in a wide variety of small commercial spaces, which had emerged in an 'ad-hoc' manner (see Box 1). None of these spaces was designed or built for its present specific purpose, but in all cases, they were able to be modified or repurposed. This research highlighted that small or micro-businesses may often need a very small amount of space to set up, ranging from as little as a couple of square meters (e.g. a cellphone shop in the front window of another retail shop) to 30 or 40 square meters (e.g. a clothing shop) to 80 or 100 square meters. These small space needs may not be easily filled on the ordinary commercial market.

Box 1. Use of marginal commercial spaces in Dalston and Whitechapel. Source: Davis (2013).

Marginal commercial spaces in use in and around Ridley Road Market in Dalston and in Whitechapel include:

- Terraced houses – individual rooms or entire floors are converted for commercial use, with the stairhall sometimes remaining a quasi-public space giving access to different business spaces.
- Retail shops converted into 'mini shopping malls – a narrow aisle in the centre of the shop may lead to small retail stalls, around one and a half metres deep/two metres wide. One shop owner characterized such a space as 'the first shopping mall in Whitechapel'.
- A closed supermarket converted into an indoor bazaar – one such space in Dalston was divided with three parallel aisles that served simply constructed wooden shops, each about 2.7 metres by 3.6 in dimension, occupied by seamstresses, tailors, sellers and makers of music, a faith healer, and others; some were rented as storage space for market stalls.
- Jerrybuilt wooden and metal structures used for retail shops (some such structures in Ridley Road were principally used by Ghanaian merchants).
- Prefabricated metal buildings – in Dalston's Gillett Square, ten such units, of about 8 square metres in area, are rented to micro-businesses such as a juice bar, a tailor, a recording studio and a money transfer service.
- Conversions of shop windows as openings hosting tiny businesses, different from the larger shop. These tend to be in places where pedestrian density is high.
- Temporary metal sheds used for storage of goods sold in market stalls.

Further, small businesses often need cheap space. This was an issue raised by Jacobs (1961), when she argued that neighbourhoods need a mix of old and new buildings, with older buildings being more financially accessible. Railway arches are relatively protected from normal commercial price pressures. Because Network Rail and Transport for London own and rent out many of the arches, they form a 'parallel' rental market to other property, less affected by the threat of local competition for land, creating relatively affordable spaces. The rental cost ranges from £8000 up to £70,000 per annum varying with the size, location and condition of the arches. A survey in London Bridge of 11 arches by the Team London Bridge Business Improvement District found that the cost of rent was an important factor leading to people relocating in the arches.

Flexible leases are also important for smaller firms. Typical lease terms in the ordinary real-estate market may be too long, in particular, for a business that is just starting out and cannot guarantee longevity. In addition to setting relatively affordable rents, both Network

Rail and Transport for London also support short-term leases, with Network Rail introducing a flexible leasing scheme with a three-month notice to quit.

Railway arches and other marginal spaces would appear to be useful not only to long-established business types such as car repairs, but also to businesses that are part of the emerging postfordist economy. The fact that the arches can be converted to serve different types of production, office use, wholesale and retail is particularly relevant given the increasing blurring between these activities (Coyle, 2001; Hutton, 2008) – railway arches are street and customer-facing, whilst also incorporating adequate storage and production spaces. One bakery in Bermondsey was serving 'patisserie' to people attending the local market on a Saturday while producing their goods on site and wholesaling to the restaurant and cafés across the city.

Because railway arches bring production right into more central city areas, businesses can also target smaller-scale and high-quality niche city markets. Toner (2011) points out that richer world economies are increasingly focusing on 'diversified quality production' as they can no longer compete on cost. The fact that the retail firms in the arches sell diverse but specialized products in close proximity helps customers to combine purchases in a multipurpose trip (see Penn et al., 2009), thereby generating multiplier effects (Sevtsuk, 2010). The linking of retail with artisanal production under the arches also appears to tap into a growing desire of people to reconnect with how things get made (as also evidenced by the 'maker movement' in the US) – perhaps boosting the attraction of street-based retail despite competition from the internet.

The railway arches are also particularly well-suited to the 'cultural production' (Hutton, 2008) of goods and services imbued with high design values and symbolic content. Rantisi and Leslie (2010) identify how businesses involved in the cultural economy and small-scale makers are attracted to spaces that are unfinished, that are expandable and that can be easily fitted out with a minimum of structural change. As seen in Maltby Street above, the historical and aesthetic characteristics of railway arches also mean that they 'bring their own brand', providing both material and symbolic resources to businesses (Martins, 2015). In fact, the design characteristics of the arches can act as both 'positive and negative' attractors (Hillier, 1999). Because the arches are sometimes dark (particularly when locked up) and can host noisy and relatively dirty types of industry they can be seen as places to avoid, discouraging pedestrian through movement. For example, the Cross River Partnership (2003) identifies that the railway arches in South London conjure up phrases such as 'scary', 'disgusting' and 'pigeon-shit'. Railway arches have long also been associated with criminality, with people taking advantage of lock ups to carry out clandestine activities.

However, railway arches also act as positive attractors, offering relatively unique and exclusive urban spaces that can be appropriated by certain communities. Analysis of pedestrian movement in Mentmore Terrace, for example, found a very different demographic from the neighbouring Mare Street, with pedestrians being more likely to be young and white, while Mare Street hosted a much broader demographic mix. This may reflect the characteristics of users of London Fields station. However, the cafes and restaurants inhabiting the arches have taken advantage of, and accentuated, this pattern to sell niche food and drink products that are strongly invested with the cultural values associated with the 'bohemian' middle class, a group who are also targeted by the arch users in Bermondsey. The arches would seem to offer notions of 'authenticity' and an 'experience of origins'

(Zukin, 2010), which is particularly attractive to London's bohemian movement. Elsewhere, the arches have become appropriated by particular ethnic groups – in Elephant and Castle, a set of arches have been appropriated by the local Latin American business owners, for example, creating a lively local cultural scene.

Cultures of innovation and resilience

Of particular relevance to this special issue, the level of interaction between firms in railway arches could be important in terms of generating a local culture of innovation amongst local SMEs and micro-enterprises. The high number of entrances onto public space, the open facades of railway arches and their frequent direct relationship to the street appears to support business interaction, and to contribute to the 'communicative fabric of space' (Jansson, 2006). The arches would appear to provide a kind of 'natural boundary without enclosure', supporting interaction between businesses while maintaining connection into the broader urban fabric. They therefore naturally support what Lee and Lipuma (2002) refer to as 'cultures of circulation' – the movement of people, ideas and commodities.

It is increasingly recognized that the circulation of ideas and skills in 'creative urban milieux' can be an important source of innovation and growth amongst SMEs (Hall, 1998; Hessler & Zimmerman, 2008). However, there has been a longstanding debate within economics as to the relative importance of intra- and inter- industrial localized knowledge-sharing between local firms – Jacobs (1969) famously pointed to the 'new work' that emerges from collaboration in situations of local economic diversity, while theorists influenced by Marshall (1890) underline the importance of same sector collaboration to growth and business sustainability. Railway arches are interesting in that they host both local economic diversity and clusters of firms from the same sector, and thus may support both cross-sector and same sector collaboration. The analysis of communication between firms for this study highlighted in particular the benefits of same sector collaboration (for example in providing start-up space for a new bakery in Mentmore Terrace, mutual support between taxi firms in Bethnal Green and product exchanges between food retailers in Ropewalk). However there was also evidence of supply chain linkages enabled through local diversity (for example, the printing and advertising firms providing services to their neighbouring firms in the Bethnal Green arches).

In addition to generating innovation, the knowledge-sharing between railway arch users may also promote sustainability, helping to support the longer term resilience of SMEs in the face of competition from larger more integrated firms (Granovetter, 1985). This was particularly evident in Bethnal Green, where the mutual support evident in the taxi repairs industry may well have contributed to the remarkable longevity of this local cluster.

Policy implications

Arguably railway arches and other marginal commercial spaces help enable a particular kind of economic development that is often not taken into account in mainstream planning efforts. The micro business population is booming, with 5 million such businesses in the UK, up from 3.5 m in 2000 (Dellot, 2015), but institutional support for such enterprise is lacking. Business development agencies are often interested in businesses that are larger than those employing just a few people, or that are literally at the very beginning of their business life. And the kinds of physical spaces that such businesses occupy are 'off the radar' of planners, architects and estate agents.

However, railway arches are increasingly becoming a strategic focus for local authorities, particularly in the context of the progressive local retention of business rates in the UK. Southwark Council is, for example, interested in its local arches for the employment that they can promote, and the degree to which they bring life to local neighbourhoods – they see the arches as a potential 'driver for change' in Bermondsey. The council is also working with other South London local authorities on a new project called 'the Lowline' – a pedestrian and cycle focused 'quiet-way' across the different boroughs, with aims for the arches to be 'activated, tenanted and programmed to support small businesses and enliven street frontages' (Team London Bridge, 2016).

The fact that the arches would also seem to encourage the concentration of similar businesses has been picked up by local policy makers who are using them to encourage their own types of 'induced clusters' (2008). In Morning Lane, Hackney, a set of railway arches are an integral part of a new Fashion Village providing retail and design spaces. The scheme was awarded a 2 million pound Greater London Authority regeneration budget, with Hackney council taking a long lease out on the arches. The private sector has also taken the lead in taking long leases from Network Rail to develop and support large-scale business clusters. For example in Bermondsey, the property company Matching Green has partnered with Monmouth Coffee Company and Neal's Yard Dairy to form Spa Terminus Limited[1] to provide sustainably priced accommodation for food manufacturing and wholesale businesses. After negotiations with Network Rail (which took over three years), a long lease was taken on over 300 railway arches and over 12,000 square metres of development land. In these cases, public and private agencies – in a similar way to Lasscos in Maltby Street – are acting as 'stewards' for the arches, taking longer leases in order to incorporate the arches into longer term economic development strategies.

However, despite their value to bottom up economic growth, railway arches in London may be becoming more inaccessible to some businesses as they rise in importance in commercial and public sector strategies. Until recently, the relatively lower rents charged by railway arches meant that they acted as a bulwark against gentrification and permitted businesses such as taxi services and auto body-repair shops to persist in neighbourhoods where other commercial rents were rising. However, despite being a somewhat 'reluctant rentier' in the past (Rosa, 2014), Network Rail is increasingly interested in how to extract value from its arches,[2] and varying rents according to available pedestrian footfall. The refurbishment of the arches, and the development of particular clusters in local regeneration strategies also often means putting up rents, which can have detrimental effects on local businesses if not managed strategically. In addition, valuable production and storage space may be lost in the fight to create 'active frontages' (Davis, 2013; Zukin, 2010).

Public protests against the industrial gentrification of the arches have often been dramatic. In Brixton, there has been public outcry against plans by Network Rail to refurbish arches along Atlantic Road and Brixton Station Road, with accusations that the council has 'voted to kill the backbone of Brixton' (Milanian, 2016). In response to a petition with over

20,000 signatures, Network Rail has ensured that those businesses that want to return to a refurbished arch are able to do so, with stepped rents phased for five years. There have also been protests in Hackney regarding the conversion of the Morning Lane Arches into the new fashion village, which has again been seen as a form of 'council sponsored' gentrification (Adu, 2016).

Conclusions: a model for new industrial development in cities?

The popularity of railway arches in London highlights the fact that cities need a wide variety of kinds of physical spaces for commercial use, ranging from the very small and 'informal' to the large and established. Economic diversity is supported by the spatial diversity that comes from the use of informal and ad-hoc spaces in particular neighbourhoods, including railway arches.

This article has highlighted the importance of railway arches of London to the urban industrial economy of SMEs and micro-businesses, in the following ways:

(a) The railway arches have traditionally provided useful space to a variety of small businesses, and continue to do so for businesses of the postfordist economy. Architecturally, their simplicity is attractive and their size and flexibility useful.
(b) The arches often form 'industrial streets': linear configurations that allow for convenient access from local neighbourhoods as well as easy communication amongst the arch users. They bring commercial activities into residential areas, including social housing estates.
(c) The below-market rates sought by Network Rail and Transport for London have until recently allowed smaller businesses to persist in neighbourhoods where commercial rents are otherwise rising. But growing interest in the arches is now leading to gentrification pressures. While local authorities (and other private and not-for profit actors) can help to sustain and develop the economic uses of the arches through taking long leases and acting as 'stewards', they need to remain aware of the risk of pricing out valuable business and storage uses in the process.
(d) The arches may be a design model for industrial spaces that are small, flexible and spatially connected to the neighbourhoods in which they are located.

An analysis of the business use of the railway arches and other residual spaces in London points to the importance of flexibility – in amount of space, in rental arrangements and in the ability to expand or retract over time. If such spaces are near each other, they may allow a very small business to grow while staying near its customers; they may allow a family business to expand while allowing the family to maintain its social ties. If they can be occupied with a minimum of investment or bureaucratic red tape, they may allow a very small business to more easily get a start.

It seems likely that given the financial pressure felt by entities such as Network Rail as well as local authorities, at least some of the railway arches– perhaps those that are closer to local high streets and have the highest footfall – will move more firmly into the real-estate mainstream, with rents approaching parity with commercial buildings nearby. The arches further away from local high streets will likely continue to provide inexpensive space for many essential start-up and secondary businesses.

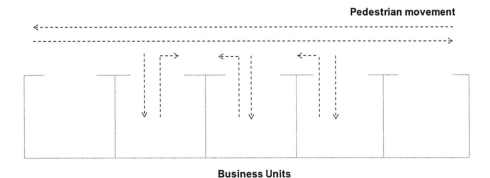

Figure 9. Diagram of an industrial street. Source: Author's illustration.

But the railway arches are not only a current resource but also a model for the future. Collectively they represent a spatial/functional configuration that might be copied in new forms of industrial development. The arches suggest the possibility of a new spatial form – industrial streets rather than industrial estates – that may be lined with spaces that are small and flexible, and that have larger spaces behind them (see Figure 9). The more typical industrial estate, representing a common spatial formation of the twentieth-century economy, is spatially separated from the street network of the larger city – and therefore questionable in its utility for emerging industrial 'mixed-use' formations.

Indeed, the 'pragmatic urbanism' of railway arches, and their close relationship to other commercial and non-commercial uses of urban districts allows us to recognize an alternative to twentieth-century modernist urbanism and its clear separation of uses. Original purposes can be changed, and juxtapositions of use can be helpful. By combining more than one use in the same structure – transportation, commerce and manufacture – the railway arches break down the idea of separation of purpose by their very existence. And by their location in places that host very different kinds of uses, they further the critique of modernist 'zoning' that began with Jane Jacobs.

Notes

1. http://www.spa-terminus.co.uk/map/.
2. http://www.networkrail.co.uk/aspx/1534.aspx.

Acknowledgements

The authors would like to thank Dr Sam Griffiths and Professor Laura Vaughan at the Bartlett School of Architecture for their support and advice while the railway arches in London were being researched in 2013/14 and Matthew Brown, who assisted with the research in Dalston and Whitechapel.

Disclosure statement

No potential conflict of interest was reported by the authors.

References

Adu, A. (2016, March 18). Hackney fashion hub does nothing for Hackney. *Hackney Post.*

Coyle, D. (2001). *Paradoxes of prosperity: Why the new capitalism benefits all.* New York, NY: Texere.

Cross River Partnership. (2003). *Light at the end of the tunnel: Transforming central London's railway viaduct. Volume 1 main findings.* London: Roseveare Projects.

Davis, H. (2013). Making the marginal visible: Microenterpise and urban space in London. In C. Jarrett, K. Kyoung-Hee Kim, & N. Senske (Eds.), *The visibility of research: Proceedings of the ARCC spring research conference* (pp. 104–111). Charlotte, NC: University of North Carolina.

Day, J. D. (2012). *Geographies of movement: Why Bankside's rail viaducts can serve as a model for equitable development.* London: MSc City Design and Social Science, London School of Economics.

Dellot, B. (2015). *The second age of small: Understanding the economic impact of micro businesses.* London: Regional Studies Association.

Dennis, R. (2008). *Cities in modernity: Representations and production of metropolitan space, 1840–1930.* Cambridge: Cambridge University Press.

Department for Business, Innovation and Skills. (2013). *Business population estimates for the UK and regions 2013.* London: UK Government.

Duranton, G., & Puga, D. (2003). *Micro-foundations of urban agglomeration economies* (NBER Working Paper Series). Cambridge, MA.

Dwyer, E. (2009). Underneath the arches: The afterlife of a railway viaduct. In A. Horning & M. Palmer (Eds.), *Crossing paths or sharing tracks? Future directions in the archaeological study of post-1550 Britain and Ireland* (pp. 351–364). Society of Post-Medieval Archaeology, Monograph 5.

Evans, G. (2009). Creative cities, creative spaces and urban policy. *Urban Studies, 46,* 1003–1040. doi:10.1177/0042098009103853

Froy, F. (2013). *Railway arches: A lifeline for manufacturing in London?* (Unpublished report, MSc Spatial Design: Architecture and Cities). London: The Bartlett School of Architecture, University College London.

Granovetter, M. (1985). Economic action and social structure: The problem of embeddeness. *American Journal of Sociology, 91,* 481–510. doi:10.1086/228311

Griffiths, S. (2017/forthcoming). Manufacturing innovation as urban spatial practice: Sheffield's cutlery and metals industries c.1750–1900. In I. V. Damme, B. Blondé, & A. Miles (Eds.), *Unscrewing the creative city: The historical fabrication of cities as agents of economic innovation and creativity (by permission of the author).* Antwerp: University of Antwerp.

Hall, P. (1998). *Cities in civilization: Culture, technology, and urban order.* New York, NY: Pantheon Books.

Hanson, J. (2000). Urban transformations: A history of design ideas. *Urban Design International, 5,* 97–122. doi:10.1057/palgrave.udi.9000011

Harvey, D. (1973). *Social justice and the city.* London: Edward Arnold.

Haywood, R. (2008). Underneath the arches in the East end: An evaluation of the planning and design policy context of the East London Line Extension Project. *Journal of Urban Design, 13,* 361–385. doi:10.1080/13574800802320863

Hessler, M., & Zimmerman, C. (2008). *Creative Urban milieus: Historical perspectives on culture, economy and the city.* Frankfurt: Campus Verlag.

Hillier, B. (1999). *Space is the machine. A configurational theory of architecture.* Cambridge: Cambridge University Press.

Hillier, B., & Hanson, J. (1984). *The social logic of space.* Cambridge: Cambridge University Press.

Huston, S., Wadley, D., & Fitzpatrick, R. (2015). Bohemianism and urban regeneration: A structured literature review and compte rendu. *Space and Culture, 18,* 311–323. doi:10.1177/1206331215579751

Hutton, T. A. (2008). *The new economy of the inner city: Restructuring, regeneration and dislocation in the twenty-first century metropolis.* Abingdon: Routledge.

Jacobs, J. (1961). *The death and life of great American cities.* New York, NY: The Modern Library.

Jacobs, J. (1969). *The economy of cities.* New York, NY: Vintage Books, Random House.

Jansson, A. (2006). *Texture and fixture: Understanding urban communication geographies.* Paper presented at the ESF-LiU conference "Cities and media: Cultural perspectives on Urban Identities in a Mediatized World", Vadstena, Sweden, 25–29 October 2006.

Kellett, J. R. (1969). *The impact of railways on Victorian cities.* London: Routledge.

Knight, C. (1836, January 9). The London and Greenwich viaduct and railway. *Penny Magazine for the Society for the Diffusion of Useful Knowledge (1832–1845).*

Lee, B., & Lipuma, E. (2002). Cultures of circulation: The imaginations of modernity. *Public Culture, 14,* 191–213. doi:10.1215/08992363-14-1-191

Lloyd, R. (2004). The neighbourhood in cultural production: Material and symbolic resources in the New Bohemia. *City & Community, 3,* 343–372. doi:10.1111/j.1535-6841.2004.00092.x

Marshall, A. (1890). *Principles of economics.* London: Macmillan.

Martins, J. (2015). The extended workplace in a creative cluster: Exploring space(s) of digital work in Silicon Roundabout. *Journal of Urban Design, 20,* 125–145. doi:10.1080/13574809.2014.972349

Milanian, K. (2016, August 3). Brixton railway arches protesters glitter-bomb council meeting after decision to approve redevelopment. *The Mirror.*

Penn, A., Perdikogianni, I., & Motram, C. (2009). Generation of diversity. In R. Cooper & C. Boyko (Eds.), *Designing sustainable cities* (pp. 219–237). Chichester: Wiley Blackwell.

Piore, M. J., & Sabel, C. F. (1984). *The second industrial divide: Possibilities for prosperity.* New York, NY: Basic Books.

Rantisi, N. M., & Leslie, D. (2010). Materiality and creative production: The case of the Mile End neighbourhood in Montréal. *Environment and Planning A, 42,* 2824–2841. doi:10.1068/a4310

Reeder, D., & Hyde, R. (1984). *Charles Booth's descriptive map of London poverty, 1889 with introduction by Dr David Reeder, London Topographical Society.* London: London Topographical Society.

Rosa, B. (2014). *Beneath the arches: Re-appropriating the spaces of infrastructure in Manchester* (PhD thesis). Manchester: University of Manchester.

Scott, A. J. (1988). *Metropolis: From the division of labour to urban form.* Berkeley, CA: University of California Press.

Scott, A. J. (2001). Capitalism, cities, and the production of symbolic forms. *Transactions of the Institute of British Geographers, 26,* 11–23. doi:10.1111/1475-5661.00003

Sevtsuk, A. (2010). *Path and place: A study of urban geometry and retail activity in Cambridge and Sommerville* (PhD thesis). Cambridge, MA: Massachusetts Institute of Technology.

Soja, E. W. (2000). *Postmetropolis: Critical studies of cities and regions.* Oxford: Blackwell.

Spittles, D. (2016). 800 new homes planned for Bermondsey as London's network of 10,000 neglected railway arches start to be transformed. *Evening Standard: Homes and Property.*

Team London Bridge. (2016). *London Bridge plan: A collective vision and strategy.* London: Author.

Toner, P. (2011). Workforce skills and innovation: an overview of major themes in the literature (OECD Science, Technology and Industry Working Papers). Paris.

Urban Task Force. (2005). *Towards a strong urban renaissance.* London: Author.

Vaughan, L. (2015). *Suburban urbanities: Suburbs and the life of the high street.* London: UCL Press.

Zukin, S. (2010). *Naked city.* New York, NY: Oxford University Press.

The use of design as a strategic tool for innovation: an analysis for different firms' networking behaviours

Marisa Cesário, Dora Agapito, Helena Almeida and Sílvia Fernandes

ABSTRACT
Current research indicates that the use of design strategy in companies is related to innovation and leads to competitiveness. This research aims empirically to analyse the relationship between firms' networking behaviours and their propensity to engage in design activities. Although much of the literature on networks focuses on the relationship between the development of external linkages and innovation, we argue that small and medium-sized enterprises' (SMEs)' relationships with different agents and intermediaries, on diverse geographic scales, play an important role for how companies use design as an element of innovation. Using the Community Innovation Survey (CIS 2012) database for Portugal, a logistic regression was performed using the 'strategic use of design' as a binary dependent variable. We found that firms' engagement in informal relationships with heterogeneous agents, such as public customers, consultants or conference partners, is positively associated with the strategic use of design. The use of firms' internal assets as information sources also proved to be significant. Regarding market relations, the results indicate that a geographic scaling-up contributes to increasing the odds of a firm recognizing the strategic role of design for competitiveness.

1. Introduction

Current research indicates that the use of design as an integrated element in companies is highly correlated with innovation and economic outcomes. Furthermore, design integration tends to have a positive effect on the success of innovative products and it is found to be significantly related to other innovation activities, both internal and external (Galindo-Rueda & Millot, 2015). Design has developed rapidly in recent years, leading to concepts such as design management and design thinking. Although often associated with aesthetics, the potential of design lies in its broad and multidisciplinary nature, allowing a wide range of considerations in the development of products, services and systems. Its bridging capacity connects technology with the user and engineering with commercial issues, a process leading to transforming creativity into innovation (Brown, 2009).

In fact, research shows that design-driven companies are more innovative than others (Verganti, 2009). Companies that invest in design tend to be more profitable and grow faster. On a macro-economic level, there is a positive correlation between the use of design and national competitiveness, since design-driven innovation builds on existing strengths, heritage, diversity, authenticity and creative potential. Therefore, design-driven innovation is considered as a competitive advantage with potential for the future. Apart from transforming research into commercially viable products and services, design brings creativity closer to user needs and strengthens the communication between the different parts of the innovation process – R&D, production and marketing. Hence, design acts as a bridge between ideas, research and technology, contributing to making products commercially acceptable, user-friendly and appealing (Commission of the European Communities, 2009).

This is a process involving a wide range of interactions along the product value chain. The way firms make use of these interactions to learn and improve their design and innovative capacity may vary. The continuous capacity of firms to learn by interacting with others is seen by many academics as an important response in order for firms to avoid becoming locked into obsolete competitive trajectories (Cesário & Vaz, 2014). Case studies across Europe present empirical and theoretical perspectives on how firms benefit from external linkages with other firms and economic agents (Alvarez, Marin, & Fonfria, 2009; Arndt & Sternberg, 2000; Cantner, Conti, & Meder, 2010).

Hence, considering the role of networking dynamics in innovation (Caloffi, Rossi, & Russo, 2015), one could expect that small and medium-sized enterprises' (SMEs) engagement in relationships with heterogeneous agents and intermediaries, from different geographic scales, plays an important role in how firms use design as an element of innovation. Against this background, this research aims, firstly, to discuss the role of design activities in product and process innovation, and secondly, to understand the relationship between different networking dynamics and the performance of design activities. More precisely, by focusing on a sample of Portuguese firms, the authors' main purpose is to understand to what extent different relational features may effectively be associated with the strategic use of design for the competitiveness of firms' innovation process.

The paper is structured as follows: Section 2 clarifies the relationship between design and innovation, highlighting the different levels of engagement of design in firms; and Section 3 reviews the importance of a firm's networking dynamics, confirming that the development of external linkages on wider geographic scales may be associated with different propensities to innovation and design activities. The remaining sections present the methodological procedures (Section 4), the corresponding results (Section 5) and conclusions (Section 6).

2. Design engagement and innovation in organizations

In the context of assigning meaning and differentiation to businesses, design assumes a decisive role, as a discipline widely linked to industry and services seeking to find solutions for society. Design, focusing on the user, is a key tool for benchmarking solutions in different disciplines and markets (Cockton, 2005). Not limited to the physical appearance of the products, design has extended its reach to consumer experiences, production processes, interaction and enhancements, in order to generate new products and services as well as transform existing ones (Melles, Howard, & Thompson-Whiteside, 2012).

The European Commission is currently addressing efforts to encourage the use of design as a tool for innovation. Design is being approached as the link between technology, creativity and the user, and thus as a crucial tool to increase the scope of innovation, in particular for European SMEs, aiming to enhance firms' and countries' competitiveness (Cunningham, 2008). Indeed, the last version (2010–2012) of the community innovation survey (CIS), which is the main statistical survey on firms' innovation in Europe, attributes to design a more pre-eminent role than the previous versions. In addition to querying firms about their use of design, the recent version assumes that design can be a method (e.g. design registration) that can be used by companies to maintain or increase the competitiveness of product and process innovations.

Hence, design is consolidated as a competitive tool for businesses, ensuring significant returns on institutional image and sales. For example, according to a survey conducted in UK (Design Council, 2004), companies that invest in design experience higher performances then their competitors. Additionally, a study developed by World Economic Forum's Global Competitiveness Index (Raulik, 2006) shows the correlation between the potential competitiveness of a country and the efficient use of design, through comparison between economic development and investments in this area. These findings confirmed that the integration of design tools and techniques in the business sphere can help to deal with complex issues and challenges and lead to competitive advantages (Tschimmel, 2012). Thus, some countries have developed explicit policies of design at the national level (e.g. Finland, Denmark and South Korea), while others primarily at the regional and local levels (e.g. France, Italy and Germany) (Commission of the European Communities, 2009). Some design systems are mainly financed by the government (e.g. Scandinavian countries and South Korea), while others are co-financed by the industry (e.g. the US, Italy, United Kingdom and Germany). Some programmes are conducted primarily by the government (e.g. South Korea) or private actors (e.g. the US) (Commission of the European Communities, 2009). Simultaneously, there are a significant number of detailed reports on design policies by countries (e.g. TrendChart on national and regional policies, design creativity and innovation oriented towards the user).

Considering the role of design within the functional structure of a company, it is possible to find different stages regarding the use of design. The Danish Design Centre developed a ladder model to analyse the level of engagement of design in firms (Danish Design Centre, 2003). This method makes an analogy using a staircase with four steps of increasing complexity: 1 – no design; 2 – design as styling; 3 – design as process and 4 – design as strategy (Galindo-Rueda & Millot, 2015).

Additionally, Kootstra (2009) describes the structure of the Design Management Staircase Model. The researcher states that this model is based on a method comparable with the Design Ladder of the Danish Design Centre. The model aims to enable European businesses to assess and improve their design management capabilities, in order to increase their effective use of design and improve their competitiveness and business success. However, an essential implication of the Design Ladder is that only businesses that reach the highest level will benefit from the full potential of design (Ramlau & Melander, 2004). The Design Management Staircase model describes the characteristic design management behaviour and capability of businesses on four levels: (1) no design management; (2) design management as a project; (3) design management as a function and (4) design management as a culture. The classification ranges from the lowest level (no design management) to design management used strategically as part of the business culture. On this last level, design is an essential part of their differentiation strategy, generating a distinct competitive advantage. For this reason, design is an integral part of the business processes with the involvement of a wide range of different departments. A design-literate top management reinforces the support and significant value of design in the entire business, as part of the business corporate culture.

These theoretical models highlight the ability of design to play a strategic role through innovation within an organization. High stair level companies are open to the vast possibilities of design as the creator of new markets and trends. From this perspective, the design is at the beginning of the process of innovation of a product and service, during its whole life cycle of use, rather than being a mere artefact in the production of purely aesthetic effects (Utterback et al., 2006).

3. Firms' networking dynamics towards design and innovation

The literature confirms that firms which do not co-operate, and which do not formally or informally exchange knowledge, limit their long-term knowledge base and, ultimately, reduce their ability to enter into exchange relationships (Hanna & Walsh, 2002, 2008; Pittaway, Robertson, Munir, Denyer, & Neely, 2004). A diffusion of regional innovation policies supporting networks of innovators has been witnessed in the last 20 years. The goal of these policies is to encourage firms, particularly SMEs, to collaborate with organizations possessing complementary knowledge (Caloffi et al., 2015). More specifically, regarding product and process innovation, positive associations were found in cooperation with customers, suppliers, the public sector and universities (Freel & Harrison, 2006). Although, in some cases, the effects are not as direct because there are sectoral and regional influences in terms of the efficiency with which such networking inputs are translated into innovative outputs (Love & Roper, 2001), it can be emphasized that inter-organizational cooperation is important, corroborating the relevance of the open innovation model at the firm and regional levels (Belussi, Sammarra, & Sedina, 2010; Teirlinck & Spithoven, 2008).

Much of the literature on networks refers to issues such as embeddedness (Granovetter, 1985) and path dependence (Arthur, 1994; Dosi, 1997; Dosi, Freeman, Nelson, Silverberg, & Soete, 1988; Nelson & Winter, 1982), recognizing that geographic agglomerations are embedded in production or innovation networks through linkages which play an important role in supporting innovation and knowledge sharing (Shaowei, MacNeill, & Wang, 2014). These arguments are in line with the idea that, although organizational proximity is important, it does not substitute direct face-to-face communication because some types of knowledge are more mobile than others. While analytical knowledge, which results from the application of scientific laws, has a relatively constant meaning by location, the same is not true for the synthetic or symbolic knowledge,[1] whose meaning is substantially variable (Gertler, 2008).

There is a vast academic literature showing that geographical proximity increases the likelihood that two agents will commit directly to sharing knowledge reciprocally (e.g. Frenkel, Maital, Leck, & Israel, 2015), thus implicitly meaning the efficiency of local linkages. Nonetheless, it can also be argued that the development of external linkages on wider geographic scales may be associated with higher propensities to innovation and design activities as well.

As the drivers of globalization are removing barriers which traditionally segmented the competitive environments of small and large firms, firms of all sizes are joining international networks (Dana, 2001). While some sectors often need to internationalize their activities, especially sales, at a very early stage of their development because of limited domestic markets (Cantwell, 1995; Keeble, Lawson, Smith, Moore, & Wilkinson, 1998), others do this in search of technical advances. Nachum and Keeble (2003) argue that firms need to identify a successful balance between localized sources of interaction and those in wider geographic areas, and to establish linkages on these different geographic scales in order for them to compete successfully.

Accordingly, it can be considered that SMEs' relationships with different agents and intermediaries, on diverse geographic scales, play an important role for how companies use design as an element of innovation (Monteiro-Barata, 2013).

This idea is in line with the work of Hobday, Boddington, and Grantham (2012) which examines the changing role of design in business and policy, from the first-generation technology push to the networking and systemic approaches. From the 1950s to the 1990s, design evolved from an aesthetic or surface activity to a visible and intrinsic innovation function, core to the development of radical new products and novel product categories. More recently, in the post-1990s, the 'fifth generation systems integration and networking models' approach design as a core technical task and a contributor to business differentiation. Strategic design becomes both integral and systemic to new product development. In contrast with the first models, fifth-generation design is originated from a multitude of sources, including customers, designers, engineering departments, design companies and marketing departments, often working in close collaboration with each other. Also, in a fifth-generation approach, the design system would not only be viewed within the boundaries of a single country, as markets are increasingly international and different kinds of design occur within a changing global context. These models emphasize the learning which goes on within and between firms, suggesting that design is fundamentally a distributed networking process and part of an embedded, networked 'open' innovation system (Hobday et al., 2012).

A corroborating line of reasoning is presented by Bertola and Teixeira (2003). The authors examine the relation between design and three domains of knowledge – users', organizational and network knowledge – arguing that the challenge for designers and managers is to be able to apply design strategically to access the knowledge embedded in these three domains in order to promote and support innovation. The authors identify two strategies in which design acts as a knowledge agent: as a 'knowledge integrator' in larger firms, and as a 'knowledge broker' in local smaller companies. In global corporations, internal and external design resources are combined. These firms rely both on knowledge developed internally, and on the network knowledge developed outside their boundaries. Even if there is a propensity to primarily rely on their internal assets to promote innovation, larger firms tend to interact with the knowledge diffused through networks existing outside the organization, in order to bring new experience inside the corporation. In small firms, design is responsible for capturing and representing the knowledge embedded outside the organization in 'users' communities' and 'local networks' In this context, design acts primarily as a 'knowledge broker' promoting knowledge flow from outside to inside the firm. Through design, companies access the knowledge needed to innovation activities. According to the authors, in local companies, network knowledge is a main source for design innovation, as small firms may demand more problem-solving services and consultancy, which are more likely to be available from local institutions from their external environment (Bertola & Teixeira, 2003). The authors acknowledge that design contributes to innovation (in both product and process) by collecting, analysing and synthesizing the knowledge contained in those three domains.

This line of thought confirms the idea that the way firms interact with other agents outside their boundaries impacts on the manner how design is used as an element of innovation.

4. Data and methodology

4.1. The CIS instrument

For this study a secondary data set was used from the CIS 2012 (DGEEC, 2014). The CIS, operation acronym in the Eurostat for Community Innovation Survey, is the main statistical survey (mandatory for EU member states) on innovation in companies. The European Union employs this main statistical instrument to monitor Europe's progress in the area of innovation, which is conducted by national statistical offices. In Portugal, following the methodological recommendations of Eurostat, the CIS aims to directly collect information on innovation (product, process, marketing and organizational) in companies based in Portugal. Data collection, corresponding to the period of 2010–2012, was performed between 3 June and 14 March 2014, through an online electronic platform. The universe contemplates Portuguese companies with 10 or more employees belonging to sections B, C, D, E, F, G, H, J, K, M, Q of the NACE (Statistical Classification of Economic Activities in the European Community) codes. The sample consisted of 9423 companies, based on census combination (for companies with 250 or more persons employed) and random sampling for other companies. Of the 7995 companies of the corrected sample, 6840 valid answers were considered, corresponding to a response rate of 86%.

4.2. Conceptual framework

In this paper, we look for the relationship between firm's networking dynamics and innovation and design. The CIS instrument provides useful information on how firms interrelated with their surrounding external environment in order to acess information considered important for the development of new innovation projects or the completion of existing ones. Firms may use external agents as information sources or engage in more formal cooperation activities, meaning their active participation with other enterprises or institutions on product and process innovation accomplishments.

Regarding these accomplishments, and according to CIS, a firm may be engaged in one or more of the following situations:

(a) Product innovation: that occurs when a firm introduces to the market a new or significantly improved good or service. It does not need to be new to the market;

however, it must be new to the firm and it should not matter if it was originally developed by the firm or by other external partners.

(b) Process innovation: that occurs when a firm implements a new or significantly
improved production process, or new and significantly improved methods of supply-
ing services, or supporting activity. Purely organizational or managerial changes are
excluded. Again, this innovation does not need to be new to market; however, it
must be new to the firm, not mattering if it was originally developed by the firm.

(c) Ongoing or abandoned innovation activities: that include any innovation activities
that did not result in a product or process innovation because the activities were
rather abandoned or suspended before completion, or are still ongoing.

Innovation activities include not only all types of R&D activities, but also the acquisition of machinery, equipment, buildings, software and licenses; engineering and development work, design, training and marketing, when they are specifically undertaken to
develop and/or implement a product or process innovation (DGEEC, 2014).

Another conceptual clarification required regards the firms' propensity for design
activities. Innovative firms were asked about the activities developed aiming product
and/or process innovation. One of the innovation activities considered in CIS 2012 is
the firm commitment in in-house or contracted-out design activities (considered as the
activities to design or alter the shape or appearance of goods or services).

Another important approach to design introduced for the first time in CIS 2012 regards
the efficiency of design registration for the competitiveness of product and process innovations introduced. This information provides an important indicator of what can be
named the level of 'firms' design engagement', following the inspiration provided by the
academic works on the ladder models of design (e.g. Kootstra, 2009; Ramlau & Melander,
2004). These models suggest that there are a possible range of roles of design that are
ordered from no design use to more integrated and sophisticated uses (see Section 2).

In this paper, we use the information provided by the CIS 2012 instrument, which
introduces the issue by asking: 'How effective was the design registration (when existent)
for maintaining or increasing the competitiveness of product and process innovations
introduced during 2010–2012?' Similarly, a four-level' effectiveness degree is possible,
ranging from '0 = Not used, not known, not applicable' to '3 = High effective'. Although
having in mind that only registrations are being considered, this last category offers
close information on the use of 'design as strategy' for the firms' innovation process.

4.3. Methodological framework and research questions

This research assumes the importance of networking aptitudes on firms' innovative
process and design use. The authors start by discussing the role of design activities on
the innovative performance of firms before developing a more extensive analysis on the
relationship between the different ways firms interact with their external environment
and their different levels of design engagement.

The review of the literature suggests the importance of external linkages, recognizing
that small firms are frequently fragments of extended networks with different possible
partners and geographic scales. By accessing other markets, assets and economic agents,
firms not only release themselves from the limits of local and internal competences, but

are also aware of new and more demanding market conditions that constitute a stimulus to innovation, creativity and design.

In the scope of the present paper, a sample of Portuguese firms from CIS 2012 was used. Firms' networking dynamics were assessed by observing their behaviour regarding market interactions and the use of external linkages as sources of information and/or partners of cooperation for the development of innovative activities.

Although we emphasize the social facet of networking (mostly associated with informal linkages), in this paper we also consider market transactions as network activities, based on the idea that, ultimately, all market transactions appear as the outcome of previous social connections along the value chain (horizontally and vertically). According to Staber (2011), 'marketless' conceptions of social networks are overstated and need to be balanced with a stronger concern for the role of competition in the social embeddedness of small firms. Figure 1 summarizes the proposed methodological framework.

According to these considerations, the following research questions were addressed in this paper:

RQ1: What is the role of design on product and process innovation?
RQ2: How different networking dynamics impact on firms' design engagement?

5. Results

5.1. Characteristics of the sample

The Portuguese subsample of CIS 2012 includes a total number of 6840 firms, with the sectoral distribution presented in Table 1. The majority of firms has up to 49 employees (74.8% of the 5776 firms with valid size information) and almost half of the sample firms (48.8%) affirm that performed product, process or have ongoing innovation activities. Within this group, 26.5% engaged in cooperation relationships aiming innovation activities, and 32.5% developed in-house or contracted-out design activities towards product/ process innovation.

5.2. The role of design for innovation and competitiveness

Before concentrating on the relation between networking and performance of design activities, a discussion on the role of design on innovation is previously presented.

The data analysis indicates that the type of innovation, whether related to product or process, is not independent from the development of design activities aiming at product and/or process innovation. The null hypothesis ('innovation is independent from design propensity') for both types of innovations was rejected for the qui-square tests (product innovation: chi-square = 287.462, p-value = .000; process innovation: chi-square = 7.842, p-value = .005), which indicates a relationship between the two variables. From the group of firms that introduced a product or a process innovation, 42% and 34%, respectively, were engaged in in-house or contracted-out design activities.

Among the different possible methods contributing to the competitiveness of product and process innovations presented by CIS 2012, design registration occupies a modest position (0.55 out of 3). Figure 2 provides the mean values of a four-level' effectiveness

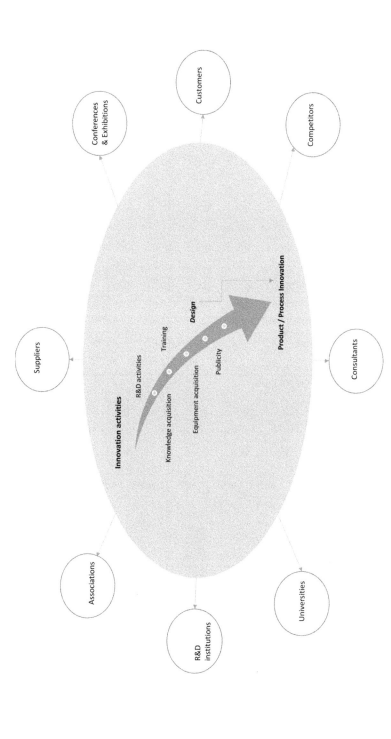

Figure 1. Methodological framework.

Table 1. Characterization of the sample.

Variables	No. of firms	%
NACE code		
Mining and quarrying	73	1.1
Food, beverages, tobacco	323	4.7
Textiles, wearing, leather, wood, paper, printing	889	13.0
Coke, chemicals, non-metal, metal products	1436	21.0
Computer, electrical equip	144	2.1
Machinery, transport equip, furniture	808	11.8
Electricity, gas, water supply, sewerage, waste	284	4.2
Construction	36	0.5
Wholesale, retail trade, transportation, storage	1642	24.0
Information, communication	376	5.5
Financial, insurance, legal, accounting, others	735	10.7
Health	94	1.4
Total	6840	100.0
Number of employees		
10–49	4320	74.8
49–250	1073	18.6
>250	383	6.6
Total	5776	100
Product/process/ongoing innovation activities		
No	3499	51.2
Yes	3341	48.8
Total	6840	100
Cooperation towards innovation activities		
No	2456	73.5
Yes	885	26.5
Firms with Product/Process/Ongoing innovation activities	3341	100
Design developed as an innovation activity		
No development of design activities	2254	67.5
Development of design activities	1087	32.5
Firms with Product/Process/Ongoing innovation activities	3341	100

Source: Own elaboration based on CIS 2012 data.

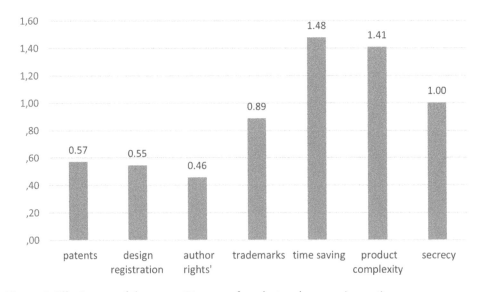

Figure 2. Effectiveness of the competitiveness of product and process innovations.

degree, ranging from '0 = not used' to '3 = high effective' with respect to the effectiveness of different instruments to the competitiveness of product and process innovations.

According to previous studies developed in Portugal, concerning design as a strategic resource to companies (Monteiro-Barata, 2012), this research highlights design as a crucial driver of the innovation dynamics in firms. However, our findings are also in line with the idea that Portuguese companies are still underestimating the potential of design as a strategic resource and that few firms are approaching design management as a culture. Indeed, from the 3341 Portuguese firms developing product, process or ongoing innovations, 985 made use of design registration, of which only 224 (22.7%) considered it highly effective (Figure 3).

Although there is a growing trend in the use of design, this is not an optimized and properly integrated process into organizational internal strategies. About some of the Portuguese SMEs, Branco (2006) refers main factors that may delay the strategic use of design, such as: (1) the lack of sophistication in technology and management instruments in most companies leads to 'lack of sensitivity to the use of design' at various levels and (2) not the appreciation of design as an essential management tool, since the formulations/strategic options for the development of a project /product in particular.

The next section provides a more comprehensive analysis of the relationship between these different levels of 'design engagement', namely the strategic use of design and the ways firms interact with their external environment. The different types of relational features considered in the present paper – information sourcing, cooperation and market interactions – were taken into consideration for the analysis, together with additional information on firms' sector and size.

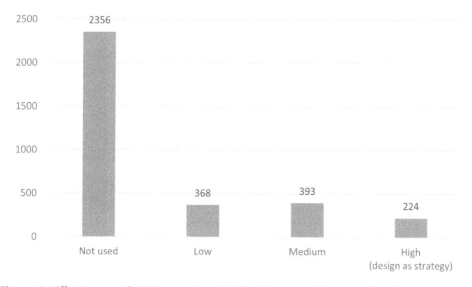

Figure 3. Effectiveness of 'design registration' for the competitiveness of product and process innovations.

5.3. Firms' networking dynamics and design engagement

The main objective of this section is to understand to what extent the different relational features considered may effectively be associated with the strategic use of design for the competitiveness of firms' innovation process, following the inspiration provided by the academic works on the ladder models of design.

The aim is to explore the actual relationship between these different networking dynamics and the presence and role attributed to design activities, as an element of firms' innovation. The authors endeavour to contribute to a more precise understanding of the respective relevance of each of them (or some of them) as they correspond to significantly different modes of external interaction, which can result in different impacts on firm behaviour. Our focus will be on the group of firms that demonstrate greater 'design engagement' and attribute a strategic role to this activity, aiming to understand which relational features may effectively be associated with this behaviour.

5.3.1. The variables

The subgroup of the 3341 companies that developed product, process, or have ongoing innovation activities (48.8%) ($N = 6840$) was selected in order to observe the impact of networking dynamics on higher levels of design engagement.

Among these firms, a group of 224 considered design registration as highly effective to the competitiveness of product and process innovation. This information was used to distinguish between firms using design as strategy from firms that do not. Table 2 presents the data set variables in the analysis.

Regarding cooperation on any innovation activities, firms may cooperate with eight different partners (variable PARTCOOP) at different geographical scales (variables COOP1, COOP2 ... COOP8). Information for new innovation projects may come from eleven different sources (variables INFSOURCE1, INFSOURCE2, INFSOURCE3 ... INFSOURCE11), each one with different possible degrees of importance. Finally, firms may sell their goods and/or services in different geographic markets (variable MARKT).

5.3.2. The binomial logistic regression model

The quantitative contribution of each one of the previous predictors to the dependent variable (DESIGNSTRAT) was compared using a binomial logistic regression model, constructed by iterative maximum likelihood estimation, as given by the following equation:

$$\log it(DESIGNSTRAT_i) = \alpha + \beta_1 PARTCOOP + \beta_2 COOP1 + \beta_3 COOP2$$
$$+ \beta_4 COOP3 + \beta_5 COOP4 + \beta_6 COOP5 + \beta_7 COOP6$$
$$+ \beta_8 COOP7 + \beta_9 COOP8 + \beta_{10} INFSOURCE1 + \beta_{11} INFSOURCE2$$
$$+ \beta_{12} INFSOURCE3 + \beta_{13} INSOURCE4 + \beta_{14} INFSOURCE5$$
$$+ \beta_{15} INFSOURCE6 + \beta_{16} INFSOURCE7$$
$$+ \beta_{17} INSOURCE8 + \beta_{18} INFSOURCE9$$
$$+ \beta_{19} INFSOURCE10 + \beta_{20} INFSOURCE11 + \beta_{21} MARKT.$$

For any binomial logistic regression, the predicted dependent variable is a function of the probability that a particular subject will be in one of two categories. In this case, we mean the probability that sample firms use design as a strategic tool for the

Table 2. Variables in the data set.

Database variables		
Variable	Description	Codification
Dependent variable		
DESIGNSTRAT	Design Registration considered HIGH effective to innovative performance	0 = No; 1 = Yes
Independent variables		
PARTCOOP	Most important partner of Cooperation on innovation activities	0 = No Cooperation; 1 = Other firms from the group; 2 = Suppliers; 3 = Private customers; 4 = Public customers; 5 = Competitors; 6 = Consultants; 7 = Universities; 8 = R&D institutions (nominal)
COOP (1–8)	Cooperation for innovation with: 1. Other firms from the group 2. Suppliers 3. Customers (private sector) 4. Customers (public sector) 5. Competitors 6. Consultants 7. Universities 8. R&D institutions	0 = None; 1 = National firms; 2 = National & European firms; 3 = National & European & ROW firms (ordinal)
INFSOURCE (1–11)	Importance of the following information sources for innovation activities: 1. Inside the firm 2. Suppliers 3. customers (private sector) 4. customers (public sector) 5. competitors 6. consultants 7. university 8. R&D institutions 9. conferences & exhibitions 10. publications 11. associations	1 = Not used; 2 = Low; 3 = Medium; 4 = High (ordinal)
MARKT	Main Market	1 = Local/Regional Market; 2 = National Market; 3 = European Market; 4 = Other Countries (ordinal)

Source: Own elaboration based on CIS 2012 data.

competitiveness of innovation ($DESIGNSTRAT_i = 1$). The logistic regression will predict the logit, that is, the natural log of the odds given by:

$$\log it(DESIGNSTRAT_i) = \ln \{P\ (DESIGNSTRAT_i = 1) / [1 - P(DESIGNSTRAT_i = 1)]\}$$

Section 5.3.3 presents the results for the set of recommended procedures and statistical tests developed to assure the adequacy of the model.

5.3.3. Adequacy of the model and goodness of fit
The assumptions required for statistical tests in logistic regression are far less restrictive than those for ordinary least squares regression. There is no formal requirement for multivariate normality, homoscedasticity or linearity of the independent variables within each category of the dependent variable (Spicer, 2005). However, the problem of multicollinearity, which relates to very high correlations among the independent variables, does apply to logistic regression. High multicollinearity is a problem as it affects the reliability of the

coefficients. In this case, the highest correlation registered among two independent variables was 0.745, which does not represent a problem.

The model's goodness of fit was assessed using the Omnibus test of model coefficients. In this case, the model containing the 21 independent variables was compared with the model containing only the constant. In other words, we are testing whether knowledge of the different relational features considered improves our ability to predict the strategic use of design by firms. The null hypothesis that the coefficients of the variables are all jointly equal to zero was rejected ($p = .000$). Complementarily, the Hosmer and Lemeshow Test was also performed – the null hypothesis that the model adequately fits the data was not rejected ($p = .138$). The overall percentage of correctly predicted cases by the present model is 93%, which is highly reasonable.

5.3.4. Results of the estimation of a logistic regression model

Following these procedures, the logistic regression results are presented. Table 3 lists the logistic coefficients, the Wald statistic, its significance and the odds ratio, for the final independent variables in the model.

Logistic coefficients are unstandardized and therefore not directly comparable with each other. They are interpreted as the expected change in the propensity of a firm to use design as strategy for a unit change in the associated explanatory variable, holding all the other variables constant. Logistic coefficients are easier to interpret when converted to an odds ratio using the exponential function (EXP(B)). The odds ratios are simply measures of effect size and are used to comment on their relative sizes when comparing independent variables effects.

The Wald statistic is used to test the significance of individual logistic regression coefficients for each independent variable (i.e. to test the null hypothesis that a particular coefficient is zero).

Of the list of independents initially considered, the following ones are statistically significant: Main Market (MARKT), Information sources: Inside the Firm (INFSOURCE1); Public customers (INFSOURCE4); Consultants (INFSOURCE6); Conferences and Exhibitions (INFSOURCE9) and Cooperation for innovation with: universities (COOP7). All the others variables are not statistically significant.

As stated earlier, the analysis of the odds ratios allows comparing the effect size of each one of the independents on the odds of the dependent. In other words, among the significant predictors, it is possible to identify which ones produce bigger positive (odds ratios > 1) or negative (odds ratios < 1) effects on the odds of a firm using design as a strategic tool.

Table 3. Results of the estimation of a logistic regression model with the final independent variables.

Predictors	Description	B	Wald	Sig.	EXP(B)
MARKT	Main market	0.173	4315	.038	1.189
INFSOURCE1	Information source: inside the firm	0.379	10,879	.001	1.460
INFSOURCE4	Information source: customers (public sector)	0.153	4898	.027	1.165
INFSOURCE6	Information source: consultants	0.201	6879	.009	1.223
INFSOURCE9	Information source: conferences & exhibitions	0.682	65,207	.000	1.977
COOP7	Cooperation for innovation with: universities	−0.357	5958	.015	0.700
Constant	Constant	−6.908	197,434	.000	0.001

Source: Own elaboration based on statistical package for the social sciences software output.

For instance, for every 1-unit increase in market geographical scale, the odds of a firm using design as a strategy increase 18.9%. Also, for every 1-unit increase in the importance attributed to internal sources, public customers, consultants or conferences as sources of information for innovation activities, the odds of a firm making a strategic use of design increase 46%, 16.5%, 22.3% and 97.7%, respectively. To note that, a 1-unit increase in the geographical scale of academic cooperation for innovation produces a 30% decrease in the odds of a firm attributing an important role to design registration for the effectiveness of product or process innovations. These results confirm that different networking dynamics are associated with different firm behaviours and provide an interesting understating of which aspects of relational features are in fact associated with higher levels of design engagement. More than the commitment in more formal cooperation activities, it is the use of some external agents as information sources that seems to play a higher influence on the role attributed by firms to the use of design as a strategic tool.

Additional information on firms' sector and size was explored in order to complement this information and better characterized the small group of firms that strategically uses design.

Industry differences reveal to be statistically different between the two groups. The null hypothesis – the strategic use of design is independent from firms' sector – was rejected (chi-square = 35.685, p-value = .000) indicating a dependence relationship.

Figure 4 allows to observe that, among firms that use design strategically, there is a higher incidence of firms from health industry; financial, insurance and related activities; wholesale, retail trade, transportation and storage; and the production of coke, chemicals and related products, when compared with the incidence of these sectors on the total sample.

Regarding firm's' size, the null hypothesis of independence was not rejected (chi-square = 2.354, p-value = .308), meaning that the use of design as strategy by firms is

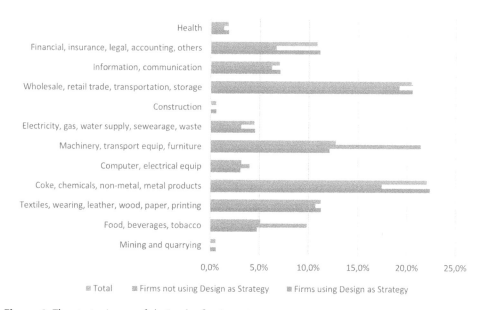

Figure 4. The strategic use of design by firm's sector.

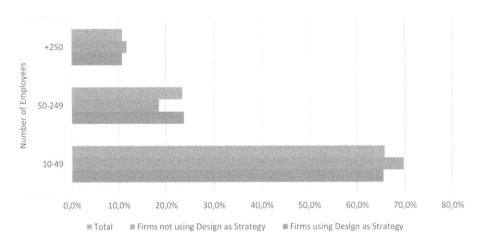

Figure 5. The strategic use of design by firm's' size.

not dependent on firms' dimension in terms of number of employees. In fact, only slight differences (not statistically significant) were found between the two groups, with a prevalence of lower design propensities among smaller firms (Figure 5).

6. Discussion and conclusion

This study performed a binary logistic analysis in order to understand to what extent the development of different external linkages is associated with the strategic use of design for the competitiveness of firms' innovation process. The analysis was based on the CIS 2012 database for Portugal, which provides useful information on how firms interrelate with their external environment in order to access information considered important for the development of new innovation projects. We focused on the group of firms that demonstrate greater 'design engagement' and assign a strategic role to this activity, aiming to understand which external linkages are associated with this behaviour.

Borrowing the ladder models of design use in firms, we concentrate our attention on firms using design strategically, by incorporating design management as a culture amongst the entire business and thus benefitting the full potential of design (Galindo-Rueda & Millot, 2015; Kootstra, 2009). Companies that are in these high stair levels are attuned to the vast possible path of design as creator of new markets and trends. In this perspective, the design is at the beginning of the process of innovation of a product and service, during all its life cycle of use, rather than being a mere artefact in order to produce purely aesthetic effects (Utterback et al., 2006).

In this research, we not only confirm that both product and process types of innovation have a relationship with the development of design activities, which is in line with current literature focusing the role of design in innovation (Bertola & Teixeira, 2003; Commission of the European Communities, 2009; Galindo-Rueda & Millot, 2015), but we also conclude that different relational attitudes are associated with different levels of design engagement.

For instance, we found that firms' engagement in informal relationships with heterogeneous agents such as public customers, consultants or conference mates is positively associated with the strategic use of design as an element of innovation. All these agents, in different ways, revealed to be important sources of information for firms. Moreover, the development of informal contacts with them is associated with better design performances.

Besides the openness to external relationships with these agents, the use of firms' internal assets as information sources also revealed to play a determinant role in this context. As in Cohen and Levinthal (1989), the findings confirm that the firms' capacity to explore the knowledge provided by external linkages depends heavily on the openness towards new opportunities which, in turn, depends on the firm's' knowledge stock and on the qualification of their employees (Pinto, Fernandez-Esquinas, & Uyarra, 2015).

Regarding market relationships, we also found that export propensity is positively associated with higher levels of design engagement, creating a market scaling-up that contributes to increase the odds of a firm recognizing the strategic role of design for competitiveness.

An opposite effect is produced by the geographical scaling-up of more formal academic cooperation towards innovation. This result is not completely surprising as we learn from the work of Hobday et al. (2012) that the public sector in general, including universities, is rarely the main actor in the design–innovation system, as design is primarily the responsibility of firms, no matter their size. Academia is clearly important (e.g. in the supply of graduates) as part of the wider innovation infrastructure, but is rarely responsible for directly generating design ideas or concepts to the industrial sector.

These findings suggest that companies should recognize that design is an important driving force behind competitive innovation. One way they can do this is by becoming co-creators with designers and implementing design strategy as a process of innovation within their own companies. For that, firms need to explore their external environment, and like Cesário and Vaz (2014), and Freel (2003), this research also argues that firms' openness (through markets and competition pressures) is positively associated with design performance.

While the relationship between networking activities (as expressed in CIS data) and innovative performance is an already largely debated and studied theme, the relationship between networking and design is yet a barely explored subject. Although our results are in line with previous research arguing that different modes of external interaction have different impacts on firm performance, mostly innovative performance (Caloffi et al., 2015), the analysis of the impacts specifically on design performance is, however, a new field of study.

As an exploratory research, this study brings a new subject to the academic debate and hopefully contributes to launch the basis to further empirical investigations about the way external environments, with the correspondent policy implications, impact on this important and strategic tool, which is design.

Firms that have characteristics favouring the design integration in their products and services, as well in their own environment, are more likely to make progress in relation to changes or pressures of their environment and have a culture leading to innovation and to competitiveness (Mozota, 2003), a conclusion that can contribute to the debate of public policies and business practices. Hence, the company's culture should integrate design as a method of creating value, rather than a tool for inventing solutions. At this level of understanding, firms' cultural perception mitigates the traditional tendency to expect an immediate and measurable outcome from the application of design processes. Instead, design is now acknowledged to create value for all stakeholders through short-term outputs or long-term outcomes.

Note

1. By synthetic knowledge, Gertler (2008) refers to the application or combination of existing knowledge, mainly through interactive learning with customers and suppliers; symbolic knowledge means creating meaning through highly context-specific learning-by-doing processes.

Acknowledgements

The authors are grateful to the anonymous referees for helpful suggestions and useful insights.

Disclosure statement

No potential conflict of interest was reported by the authors.

Funding

This work was supported by FCT- Portuguese Foundation for Science and Technology [grant number UID/SOC/04020/2013].

References

Alvarez, I., Marin, R., & Fonfria, A. (2009). The role of networking in the competitiveness of firms. *Technological Forecasting and Social Change, 76*(3), 410–421. doi:10.1016/j.techfore.2008.10.002

Arndt, O., & Sternberg, R. (2000). Do manufacturing firms profit from intraregional innovation linkages? An empirical based answer. *European Planning Studies, 8*(4), 465–485. doi:10.1080/713666423

Arthur, W. B. (1994). *Increasing returns and path dependence in the economy.* Ann Arbour: University of Michigan Press.

Belussi, F., Sammarra, A., & Sedina, S. R. (2010). Learning at the boundaries in an open regional innovation system: A focus on firms' innovation strategies in the Emilia Romagna life science industry. *Research Policy, 39*(6), 710–721. doi:10.1016/j.respol.2010.01.014

Bertola, P., & Teixeira, J. C. (2003). Design as a knowledge agent: How design as a knowledge process is embedded into organizations to foster innovation. *Design Studies, 24*(2), 181–194. doi:10.1016/S0142-694X(02)00036-4

Branco, J. (2006). Design: Novos caminhos outros horizontes. *Caleidoscópio: Lusófona Lisbon University of Humanities and Technologies, 7,* 47–53.

Brown, T. (2009). *Change by design: How design thinking transforms organizations and inspires innovation.* New York, NY: Harper Business.

Caloffi, A., Rossi, F., & Russo, M. (2015). What makes SMEs more likely to collaborate? Analysing the role of regional innovation policy. *European Planning Studies, 23*(7), 1245–1264. doi:10.1080/09654313.2014.919250

Cantner, U., Conti, E., & Meder, A. (2010). Networks and innovation: The role of social assets in explaining firms' innovative capacity. *European Planning Studies, 18*(12), 1937–1956. doi:10.1080/09654313.2010.515795

Cantwell, J. (1995). The globalization of technology: What remains of the product cycle model. *Cambridge Journal of Economics, 19*(1), 155–174.

Cesário, M., & Vaz, M. T. (2014). Regional, national and international networks: The suitability of different competitive strategies for different geographic profiles. *International Journal of Entrepreneurship & Small Business, 21*(3), 317–333. doi:10.1504/IJESB.2014.060895

Cockton, G. (2005). A development framework for value-centered design. In G. Veer & C. Gale (Eds.), *CHI '05 extended abstracts on human factors in computing systems* (pp. 1292–1295). New York, NY: ACM Press.

Cohen, W. M., & Levinthal, D. A. (1989). Innovation and learning: The two faces of R&D. *Economic Journal, 99*(397), 569–596. doi:10.2307/2233763

Commission of the European Communities. (2009) *Design as a driver of user-centered innovation: Commission staff working document*, Brussels. Retrieved May 10, 2015 from http://ec.europa.eu/ enterprise/policies/innovation/files/design_swd_sec501_en.pdf

Cunningham, P. N. (2008). *Monitoring and analysis of policies and public financing instruments conducive to higher levels of R&D investments*. The POLICY MIX Project: Thematic Report, European Commission.

Dana, L. P. (2001). Networks, internationalization & policy. *Small Business Economics, 16*(2), 57–62. doi:10.1023/A:1011199116576

Danish Design Centre. (2003). *The economic effects of design*. Copenhagen: NAEH.

Design Council. (2004). *The impact of design on stock market performance: An analysis of UK quoted companies 1994–2003*. London: Author.

DGEEC. (2014). *CIS 2012 – Community innovation survey, general direction of statistics in education and science, Lisbon*. Retrieved March 13, 2015, from http://www.dgeec.mec.pt/np4/207/

Dosi, G. (1997). Opportunities, incentives and the collective patterns of technological change. *The Economic Journal, 107*, 1530–1547. doi:10.1111/j.1468-0297.1997.tb00064.x

Dosi, G., Freeman, C., Nelson, R., Silverberg, G., & Soete, L. (1988). *Technical change and economic theory*. London: Pinter Publishers.

Freel, M. S. (2003). Sectoral patterns of small firm innovation, networking and proximity. *Research Policy, 32*(5), 751–770. doi:10.1016/S0048-7333(02)00084-7

Freel, M. S., & Harrison, R. T. (2006). Innovation and cooperation in the small firm sector: Evidence from Northern Britain. *Regional Studies, 40*(4), 289–305. doi:10.1080/00343400600725095

Frenkel, A., Maital, S., Leck, E., & Israel, E. (2015). Demand-driven innovation: An integrative systems-based review of the literature. *International Journal of Innovation and Technology Management, 12*(2). doi:10.1142/S021987701550008X

Galindo-Rueda, F., & Millot, V. (2015). *Measuring design and its role in innovation*. OECD science, technology and industry working papers. Retrieved April 15, 2015 from http://www.oecd-ilibrary. org/science-and-technology/measuring-design-and-its-role-in-innovation_5js7p6lj6zq6-en

Gertler, M. S. (2008). Buzz without being there? Communities of practice in context. In A. Amin & J. Roberts (Eds.), *Community, economic creativity and organisation* (pp. 203–226). Oxford: Oxford Scholarship Online Monographs.

Granovetter, M. (1985). Economic action and social structure: The problem of embeddedness. *American Journal of Sociology, 91*(3), 481–510. doi:10.1086/228311

Hanna, V., & Walsh, K. (2002). Small firm networks: A successful approach to innovation? *R&D Management, 32*(3), 201–207. doi:10.1111/1467-9310.00253

Hanna, V., & Walsh, K. (2008). Interfirm cooperation among small manufacturing firms. *International Small Business Journal, 26*(3), 299–321. doi:10.1177/0266242608088740

Hobday, M., Boddington, A., & Grantham, A. (2012). Policies for design and policies for innovation: Contrasting perspectives and remaining challenges. *Technovation, 32*, 272–281. doi:10. 1016/j.technovation.2011.12.002

Keeble, D., Lawson, C., Smith, H. L., Moore, B., & Wilkinson, F. (1998). Internationalisation processes, networking and local embeddedness in technology-intensive small firms. *Small Business Economics, 11*(4), 327–342. doi:10.1023/A:1007942612220

Kootstra, G. L. (2009). *The incorporation of design management in today's business practices, an analysis of design management practices in Europe*. Rotterdam: Centre for Brand, Reputation and Design Management, Holland University of Applied Sciences.

Love, J. H., & Roper, S. (2001). Location and network effects on innovation success: Evidence for UK, German and Irish manufacturing plants. *Research Policy, 30*(4), 643–661. doi:10.1016/S0048-7333(00)00098-6

Melles, G., Howard, Z., & Thompson-Whiteside, S. (2012). Teaching design thinking: Expanding horizons in design education. *Procedia-Social and Behavioral Sciences, 31*, 162–166. doi:10.1016/j.sbspro.2011.12.035

Monteiro-Barata, J. M. (2012). Design as a strategic resource: Results from a Portuguese online questionnaire. In C. Vivas & F. Lucas (Eds.), *Proceedings of the 7th European conference on innovation and entrepreneurship 2*, (pp. 492–501). Sonning Common: Academic Publishing International.

Monteiro-Barata, J. M. (2013). Innovation, design and competitiveness: Results from a Portuguese online questionnaire. In P. Teirlinck, S. Kelchtermans, & F. Beule (Eds.), *Proceedings of the 8th European conference on innovation and entrepreneurship* (pp. 442–453). Sonning Common: Academic Publishing International.

Mozota, B. (2003). *Design management.* New York: Allworth Press.

Nachum, L., & Keeble, D. (2003). Neo-marshallian clusters and global networks: The linkages of media firms in central London. *Long Range Planning, 36*(5), 459–480. doi:10.1016/S0024-6301(03)00114-6

Nelson, R., & Winter, G. (1982). *An evolutionary theory of economic change.* Cambridge, MA: Harvard University Press.

Pinto, H., Fernandez-Esquinas, M., & Uyarra, E. (2015). Universities and knowledge-intensive business services (KIBS) as sources of knowledge for innovative firms in peripheral regions. *Regional Studies, 49*(11), 1873–1891. doi:10.1080/00343404.2013.857396

Pittaway, L., Robertson, M., Munir, K., Denyer, D., & Neely, A. (2004). Networking and innovation: A systematic review of the evidence. *International Journal of Management Reviews, 5–6*(3–4), 137–168. doi:10.1111/j.1460-8545.2004.00101.x

Ramlau, U. H., & Melander, C. (2004). In Denmark, design tops the agenda. *Design Management Review, 15*(4), 48–54. doi:10.1111/j.1948-7169.2004.tb00182.x

Raulik, G. (2006). *International scene of policies for promotion and incentive of design, report commissioned by the Brasilian ministry of development.* Brasília: Industry and Foreign Commerce.

Shaowei, H., MacNeill, S., & Wang, J. (2014). Assessing overall network structure in regional innovation policies: A case study of cluster policy in the West Midland in the UK. *European Planning Studies, 22*(9), 1940–1959. doi:10.1080/09654313.2013.812066

Spicer, J. (2005) *Making sense of multivariate data analysis: An intuitive approach.* London: Sage.

Staber, U. (2011). Partners forever? An empirical study of relational ties in two small-firm clusters. *Urban Studies, 48*(2), 235–252. doi:10.1177/0042098009360679

Teirlinck, P., & Spithoven, A. (2008). The spatial organisation of innovation: Open innovation, external knowledge relations and urban structure. *Regional Studies, 42*(5), 689–704. doi:10.1080/00343400701543694

Tschimmel, K. (2012, June 17–20). *Design thinking as an effective Toolkit for innovation.* Proceedings of the XXIII ISPIM Conference – Action for innovation: Innovation from Experience, Barcelona.

Utterback, J. M., Vedin, B.-A., Alvarez, E., Ekman, S., Sanderson, S. W., Tether, B., & Verganti, R. (2006). *Design inspired innovations.* Danvers: World Scientific.

Verganti, R. (2009). *Design driven innovation: Changing the rules of competition by radically innovating what things mean.* Boston, MA: Harvard Business Press.

Index

Notes: Page numbers in *italics* refer to figures
Page numbers in **bold** refer to tables
Page numbers with 'n' refer to notes